Paul

AND FIRST-CENTURY LETTER WRITING

Secretaries, Composition and Collection

E. RANDOLPH RICHARDS

InterVarsity Press
P.O. Box 1400, Downers Grove, IL 60515-1426
World Wide Web: www.ivpress.com
E-mail: mail@ivpress.com

Design: Cindy Kiple

Images: Alinari/Art Resource, NY

ISBN 0-8308-2788-9

Printed in the United States of America ∞

Library of Congress Cataloging-in-Publication Data

Richards, Randolph (Ernest Randolph)
    Paul and first-century letter writing: secretaries, composition,
    and collection/E. Randolph Richards.
        p.
    Includes bibliographical references and indexes.
    ISBN 0-8308-2788-9 (pbk.: alk. paper)
    1. Bible. N.T. Epistles of Paul—Criticism, interpretation, etc. 2.
    Classical letters—History and criticism. 3. Letter writing,
    Classical.
    BS2650.52.R53
    227'.067—dc22
                                                    2004017267

| P | 21 | 20 | 19 | 18 | 17 | 16 | 15 | 14 | 13 | 12 | 11 | 10 | 9 | 8 | 7 | 6 | 5 | 4 | 3 | 2 | 1 |
| Y | 21 | 20 | 19 | 18 | 17 | 16 | 15 | 14 | 13 | 12 | 11 | 10 | 09 | 08 | 07 | 06 | 05 | 04 |

This book is dedicated to my parents,

Rick and Susie Richards,

who encouraged me to go boldly into the world

and also gave me a safe place to return to.

Contents

PREFACE

*P*aul has always been my hero. He told us to imitate him (1 Cor 4:16). Aside from Christ himself, perhaps no one else has impacted the world like Paul. I fear that many of us place Paul on such a high pedestal (just a few inches below Jesus) that we believe it impossible to imitate him. This motivates me to study the details of Paul's life, particularly those details that provide a more realistic picture of the flesh-and-blood Paul. My hope and prayer is that, after reading this book, you will see Paul more clearly and thus be encouraged to imitate him.

When we read Paul's letters without any thought as to how they came to be, we are at risk of reading our culture, customs, values and ideas back onto Paul. Once, as I stood in the ruins of a workshop on a dusty side street in Pompeii, I wondered if such things had any relevance for Paul. Then I noticed that the windows were fairly small and I thought, "Those wouldn't give enough light to write a letter." In much the same way this book is designed to help us see Paul in the real world and in his world. I have not written this for my fellow scholars, although I think they will find some of the ideas interesting. Rather, I have written to the serious reader of the New Testament. I have tried to avoid technical jargon—as much as is possible when talking about Greco-Roman letter writing.

This project has consumed much of my free time for the last three years, and I was not the only one who sacrificed. I want to thank my wife, Stacia, and our two sons, Josh and Jacob, who in times past have followed me around the United States, through the jungles of Indonesia, and now to rural Arkansas. They are my greatest treasures and my biggest fans. While in Italy recently, they wanted to see the Vatican but instead followed behind me as I rummaged through the ruins of some apartments in Ostia. That's true love. I am also privileged to teach with some outstanding colleagues and scholars; "iron sharpens iron," and they have motivated me by their words and by setting the standards high. Several must be singled out for a special word of thanks: Scott Duvall, Danny Hays, Preben Vang and Marvin Pate. The university's administration encourages us to publish by providing resources, and yet it never pressures us. I remain thankful to those who were my teachers on Paul almost twenty years ago: Earle Ellis, W. D. Davies, Bruce Corley and Robert Sloan. My students over the years also have shaped my thinking on Paul in the crucible of the classroom. My student assistant, Brandon O'Brien, a man whose mind and wit are equally sharp, prepared the indexes, caught mistakes, and brought humor and perspective on many a long afternoon. I am indebted to him. Dan Reid at InterVarsity has been a gentleman-scholar. His kind encouragement and keen insights have made this a better manuscript. With so many helpful friends, there should be no mistakes left in the book, but I managed to sneak in a few.

Randy Richards
Lent 2004

ABBREVIATIONS

AB	Anchor Bible
Ant.	Josephus, *Antiquitates Judaicae* [*Antiquities of the Jews*]
Ap.	Josephus, *Contra Apionem* [*Against Apion*]
Arr. Epict. Diss.	Arrian, *Dissertations of Epictetus*
BA	*Biblical Archaeologist*
BBR	*Bulletin for Biblical Research*
BGU	*Aegyptische Urkunden aus den Königlichen (Staatlichen) Museen zu Berlin, Griechische Urkunden, Berlin*
BI	*Biblical Illustrator*
BJ	Josephus, *Bellum Judaicum* [Jewish War]
BNTC	Black's New Testament Commentaries
BR	*Bible Review*
CBQ	*Catholic Biblical Quarterly*
Cic. *Att.*	Cicero, *Atticus* [*Letters to Atticus*]
Cic. *Br.*	Cicero, *Brutus* [*Letters to Brutus*]
Cic. *Fam.*	Cicero, *Familiares* [*Letters to Friends*]
Cic. *QFr.*	Cicero, *Quintum fratrem* [*Letters to his brother, Quintus*]
CIG	*Corpus Inscriptionum Graecarum*
CIL	*Corpus Inscriptionum Latinarum*
EDNT	*Exegetical Dictionary of the New Testament*
ExpT	*Expository Times*
Euse. *Chronica*	Eusebius, *Chronicon* [Chronicles]
Euse. *H.E.*	Eusebius, *Historia Ecclesiastica* [Ecclesiastical History]
HTR	*Harvard Theological Review*
ICC	International Critical Commentary
Ign. *Polycarp*	Ignatius, *Letter to Polycarp*
JBL	*Journal of Biblical Literature*
JETS	*Journal of the Evangelical Theological Society*
JJS	*Journal of Jewish Studies*
JSNTS	*Journal for the Study of the New Testament Supplement*
JSOT	*Journal for the Study of the Old Testament*
JTS	*Journal of Theological Studies*
LCL	Loeb Classical Library
LSJ	Liddell, Scott, Jones, *Greek-English Lexicon* (1996)
Mani. *Ast.*	Manilius, *Astronomicon*
Mart. *Epig.*	Martial, *Epigrammata*
NA^{27}	Nestle-Aland, *Novum Testamentum Graece* (27th ed.)
NIBC	New International Bible Commentary
NICNT	New International Commentary on the New Testament
NIGTC	New International Greek Testament Commentary
NIV	New International Version
NRSV	New Revised Standard Version

NTAbh	Neutestamentliche Abhandlungen
NTS	*New Testament Studies*
NTTS	*New Testament Tools and Studies*
NovT	*Novum Testamentum*
PCol.	Columbia Papyri. Edited by W. L. Westermann et al.
PFay.	Fayûm Towns and Their Papyri. Edited by B. P. Grenfell et al. (1900)
PGeiss.	Also commonly cited as PGiss. Griechische Papyri im Museum des oberhessichen Geschichtsvereins zu Giessen. Edited by O. Eger et al. (1910-1912)
PLond.	Greek Papyri in the British Museum. Edited by F. Kenyon et al.
PMich.	*Michigan Papyri*, Youtie and Winter (1951)
PMur.	*Les grottes de Murabba'at*. Edited by P. Benoit et al. (1961)
POxy.	*Papyri Oxyrhynchus*. Edited by B. P. Grenfell et al.
PSel.	*Select Non-Literary Papyri*. Edited by Hunt and Edgar (1932-1934)
PZen.	Zenon Papyri. Edited by W. L. Westermann et al. (1934-1940)
PTebt.	Tebtunis Papyri. Edited by B. P. Grenfell et al. (1902-1938)
Pliny *Ep.*	Pliny, *Epistulae*
Pliny *N.H.*	Pliny (the Elder), *Naturalis Historia*
Plut. *Alex.*	Plutarch, *Alexander*
Plut. *Caes.*	Plutarch, *Caesar*
Plut. *Cato Min.*	Plutarch, *Cato Minor*
Plut. *Cic.*	Plutarch, *Cicero*
Plut. *Demos.*	Plutarch, *Demosthenes*
Plut. *Eum.*	Plutarch, *Eumenes*
Ps-Soc. *Ep.*	Pseudo-Socrates, *Epistle*
Quint. *Inst.*	Quintilian, *Institutio Oratoria*
RB	*Revue Biblique*
RevQ	*Revue de Qumran*
SBL	Society of Biblical Literature
SBLDS	Society of Biblical Literature Dissertation Series
SBLSBS	Society of Biblical Literature Sources for Biblical Study
SNTSMS	Society for New Testament Studies Monograph Series
Sen. *Apolo.*	Seneca, *Apolocyntosis*
Sen. *Ep.*	Seneca, *Epistulae Morales*
Suet. *Aug.*	Suetonius, *Augustus*
Suet. *Tit.*	Suetonius, *Titus*
Suet. *Vesp.*	Suetonius, *Vespatian*
TAPA	*Transaction of the American Philological Association*
UBS	United Bible Society
Vit.	Josephus, *Vita [Life]*
WBC	Word Biblical Commentary
WUNT	Wissenschaftliche Untersuchungen zum Neuen Testament
ZNW	*Zeitschrift für die neutestamentliche Wissenschaft*
ZPE	*Zeitschrift für Papyrologie und Epigraphik*

INTRODUCTION

*A*s Christians we are quite used to reading someone else's mail. In our New Testament we find letters *from* people, such as Paul, Peter and James, written *to* other people, such as the Romans, the Galatians and the folks in Bithynia. (Odd, isn't it, that we put so much stock in old letters?) We claim to know quite a bit about these letters, but most of us have never read any ancient letters apart from those in the New Testament. Our knowledge of how such letters were written is limited to what we, as alert readers, are able to glean from the letters themselves. To gain broader perspective, we need to filch some letters from other ancient Mediterranean mailboxes, to see what insights they offer us into Paul's world.

My generation grew up with telephones. My students grew up with e-mail and Instant Messenger. We struggle to understand how much a handwritten letter, which was already weeks old, meant to the reader. Although usually battered from the journey, such letters did more than just bring news; one could almost feel the warmth of the hand that wrote it and the sound of the voice that spoke it. I spent eight years on a remote island near Borneo, where the people still are a letter writing society. Even today these gracious people often begin with sentences like, "I give thanks that we can meet together even though only through a letter." I often saw them eagerly pounce upon a visitor, in the hope that he or she might be carrying a letter for them from a loved one.

Across a gap of two thousand years, yet in a strikingly similar way, Paul's society also longed for letters. An Egyptian from a generation after Paul received a letter from his brother and replied, "I rejoiced exceedingly as if you had come."[1] Archeologists have uncovered thousands of personal letters written from the general time and place of Paul. Many of these letters had been thrown into trash heaps or found in the debris of destroyed homes. They give us a random yet real glimpse into the everyday world of Paul.

ANCIENTS AND THEIR LETTERS

One surprising discovery was just how much ancients loved to send and receive letters. A slave girl wrote to her master, "We die if we do not see you daily" and then begged him

---

[1]PMich. 8.482.

to send a letter.[2] Even though it is impossible for us to know precisely what was going on in the life of this slave and her master, we can draw general conclusions without knowing the details of their lives. For example, we can see that even slaves sent letters, even letters to their masters. Letters were in some way a substitute for being there in person. Thus, we find a letter from a sailor longing for news from home.[3] Another ancient letter tells a man that his brother is alive and well—welcome news in a world of short lifespans.[4] A soldier writes home to his wife, "I received your letter . . . and was greatly delighted about the health of the children."[5] Another man writes, "I beg you, brother, to write me about your being all well, as I heard at Antinoopolis that there has been a plague in your neighborhood. So do not neglect to write, that I may feel more cheerful about you."[6] Letters brought assurance in a world filled with disease and calamity.

SOURCES OF INFORMATION

Christian monks painstakingly copied and thereby preserved the letters of prestigious, ancient, non-Christian letter writers. We are indebted to these unnamed copyists who preserved for us literary works that would likely have been lost. It was long thought that wooden tablets or papyrus could not survive for millennia because climate quickly destroys them; wooden tablets need to stay waterlogged; papyrus needs continuous desiccation. There are few places in the world that have stayed continuously waterlogged or bone dry for the last 2,000 years. To make matters more difficult, people don't usually live in places like that, so we do not stumble across old Roman tablets or papyrus sheets every time we dig a hole in a yard in Europe or the Middle East. However, in the few inhabited places that have stayed "just right" for two millennia, either waterlogged or desiccated, such as the bogs of England or the deserts of Egypt, we find the remains of letters. From the time of Emperor Trajan we have found the wooden tablets of a soldier in Britain, private letters of soldiers in the Judean desert, and others in the trash piles of Egypt. In all three places we have found everyday letters. Even in the fringes of the empire we have consistent evidence that ancient people wrote, sent and retained letters.

Archaeologists and other adventurers also have uncovered for us thousands of other private letters from rank and file members of the empire. Unlike the literary letters of philosophers, poets, playwrights and politicians, these other letters recovered from ancient city dumps and destroyed homes reveal the normal, messy side of everyday life: news of marriages, divorces, births and death; expressions of pride, shame, anger and approval; feelings of estrangement and reconciliation, depression and joy.

---

[2]PGeiss. 17, cited in Eldon Epp, "New Testament Papyrus Manuscripts and Letter Carrying in Greco-Roman Times," in *The Future of Early Christianity,* ed. Birger A. Pearson et al. (Minneapolis: Fortress, 1991), p. 41.
[3]*BGU* 423.
[4]PMich. 8.482.
[5]PMich. 8.495.
[6]POxy. 1666.

Although they rarely discussed the mechanics of letter writing, such letters still help us see how ancients wrote theirs. Most ancient letters were so brief that the writers never remarked about how the letter was written, so the most common way that we learn about letter writing is from their incidental comments. For this reason, one of the best ancient sources is Cicero.

However, it is a fair to ask how the practices of an ultra-wealthy Roman aristocrat such as Cicero have any points of comparison to Paul. Our information does not depend upon Cicero as much as a casual perusal of later footnotes might imply, because (a) although the reference may read Cicero (Cic. *Fam.*), sometimes the letter cited was a letter to Cicero and not by him; and (b) usually there is evidence of a particular practice in other writers and even in the papyri, but often Cicero is cited because he is the clearest example. David Trobisch, in a fine little book on Paul's letters, comments how he "investigated about two hundred different authors, covering more than three thousand letters."[7] Yet when he cites an example of an ancient custom, he usually cites Cicero.[8]

Additionally, when you read Cicero's letters you immediately notice how often he commented upon the most mundane of matters, including how he was using his secretary, where he was sitting when he wrote the letter, even the attitude of the carrier that brought the letter. This might seem odd to us: why write if there was nothing more important to write about? Cicero, however, was maintaining a steady rotation of letter carriers with several colleagues and would of necessity write merely to have something to place in the hand of the returning carrier. For the ultra-wealthy such as Cicero, the expense of writing was trivial. He maintained a full-time secretary slave. Cicero once commented to his friend Atticus, "When you have nothing to write, write and say so."[9] For these writers, "how something was stated" (i.e., the rhetoric) was paramount; the actual content was much less important. Their letters often expounded upon routine matters; something not usually found in the brief and highly stereotyped papyri (common letters) from Egypt, although there is still some evidence for these letter-writing practices among the papyri as well.

In this book I will not argue that the letters of Cicero, Seneca and their peers are analogous to Paul's. Rather I will show that the basic mechanics of letter writing were a part of the culture, for we find evidence for various customs across the literary spectrum, in Cicero (and his friends) as well as in the papyri.[10] For example, we find evidence of copying another person's letter at the bottom of one's own letter in Cicero (*Att.* 3.9), among his

---

[7]David Trobisch, *Paul's Letter Collection* (Minneapolis: Fortress, 1994), p. 50.

[8]Ibid., e.g., p. 53. See also Jerome Murphy-O'Connor, *Paul the Letter-Writer: His World, His Options, His Skills* (Collegeville, Minn.: Liturgical Press, 1995).

[9]Cic. *Att.* 4.8a.

[10]This is not to conclude that Cicero's content is completely irrelevant. For example, Darryl Palmer argues that Cicero provides the likeliest parallel for the book of Acts; see Palmer, "Acts and the Ancient Historical Monograph," in *The Book of Acts in Its Ancient Literary Setting*, ed. Bruce Winter and Andrew Clark, The Book of Acts in Its First Century Setting Series (Grand Rapids: Eerdmans, 1993), pp. 1-29.

friends (Cic. *Att.* 1.17), and in the papyri (PZen. 10). I therefore feel confident to conclude that this was a common enough practice.

PAUL LOVED TO WRITE LETTERS

Paul did not just write the typical, single-page letter. We have massive letters from him preserved in our New Testament. Why did Paul so obviously love to write letters? We used to think he wrote letters only as a substitute for when he could not visit a church personally.[11] In fact, it was thought that Paul's first choice was to visit personally, failing that he sent a representative, such as Timothy, and only as a last resort did he send a letter.[12]

While such a scenario makes sense, Margaret Mitchell has argued from Paul's own comments that on occasion Paul actually *preferred* a letter to a visit.[13] While Paul may have initially turned to letters to meet the practical needs of his situation, the extensive length and development of themes indicate that Paul saw enormous benefit in sending letters.[14] For example, a personal visit to Corinth ended in disaster (2 Cor 12:20-21); Paul's use of an envoy, Titus (7:5-16), and a "painful letter" (2:4) proved more effective. Mitchell is led to conclude that

> the letter (and envoy, in some cases) was not an inadequate substitute for the more desirable Pauline physical presence, but was in fact deemed by him a superior way to deal with a given situation.[15]

Thus, there was no clear hierarchy (personal visit, then envoy, lastly letter). Rather, Paul chose in each situation which option would be most effective.

OTHER BOOKS ON PAUL AND LETTER WRITING

An ancient scribe once quipped: "Of the writing of books there appears no end." This seems especially true about modern books on Paul. Ancient letter writing, however, has received only a small fraction of that attention. Nonetheless, that still means several books on letter writing. Let me describe a few of these that I have found most helpful.[16] On the general topic of ancient Greco-Roman letter writing, Stanley Stowers's work on letter writing describes the historical context and provides a helpful survey of the various types of ancient letters. Narrowing the topic to the letters of Paul, the older work by Calvin Roetzel

---

[11]Robert Funk, "The Apostolic *Parousia*: Form and Significance," in *Christian History and Interpretation: Studies Presented to John Knox,* ed. W. R. Farmer, C. F. D. Moule and R. R. Niebuhr (Cambridge: Cambridge University Press, 1967), pp. 249-69.

[12]Ibid., p. 258.

[13]Margaret Mitchell, "New Testament Envoys in the Context of Greco-Roman Diplomatic and Epistolary Conventions: the Example of Timothy and Titus," *JBL* 111 (1992): 641-62.

[14]Ibid., p. 642 n. 6. Mitchell also argues that envoys "could perform special functions that he himself could not perform *even if present*" (p. 643, emphasis hers).

[15]Ibid., p. 642.

[16]The bibliographic data on these works can be found in the back of this book.

continues to be useful. He reminded us that Paul's letters were "half of a conversation," and that we have to know some of Paul's situation to understand his letters. Other works have a more specific focus, such as the similarity of Paul's letters to official letters (Stirewalt), theological themes in Paul (Charles Cousar), or "what Paul fought for" (Leander Keck). The little book by Jerome Murphy-O'Connor on Paul as a letter writer comes closest to what I plan to do in this book.[17]

Other books discuss in greater detail a particular aspect of letter writing. In a previous book I describe the ways secretaries were used to write letters in the time of Paul. Jeffrey Weima has given us a wonderful analysis of the way Paul used the closing sections of his letter. Several recent works have discussed the question of literacy in Paul's day. Catherine Hezser looks at the Jewish community. Alan Millard analyzes quite nicely the specific situation of Jesus. Alan Bowman provides a delightful look at the letters of Roman soldiers serving on the frontiers of the empire. There are also detailed discussions of more technical aspects of letter writing, such as a style analysis by Anthony Kennedy and another by Kenneth Neumann, or theories about the collection of Paul's letters by David Trobisch, or an examination of Jewish exegetical techniques by Earle Ellis. I will note these and other works in the footnotes when we come to these topics. Harry Gamble and Richard Bauckham have given us works that discuss the New Testament in much broader terms, and yet their far-reaching studies have implications that sift down all the way to my discussion of the practicalities of letter writing. I will also mention these.

WHY READ THIS BOOK?

Although these related books are outstanding, none of them addresses the writing of Paul's letters from a very practical point of view. As much as Paul's letters have been read and re-read and examined under an exegetical microscope, it is surprising how little has been done on the nuts and bolts of Paul's letter writing. Timothy Johnson, in his Anchor Bible commentary on 1-2 Timothy, complains:

> It is startling to find . . . how carelessly formulated and executed many of the arguments are
> . . . The most fundamental category, that of authorship, remains largely unexamined. The
> model of Pauline authorship therefore remains anachronistic . . . the image of Paul as an "author," . . . or even as a solitary letter writer, is inaccurate.[18]

I hope to help bridge this gap. Archaeologists and sociologists such as Meeks, Malherbe, Neyrey and Malina have given us much more accurate descriptions of the world in which Paul lived and worked. It is time to bring these insights to the question of how Paul wrote his letters, and to ask very pragmatic questions. How (and where) did letter writers usually work? How long did it take? Did they write rough drafts? What were the logistics of using a secretary? Did writers keep copies? How much did it cost to write and send a letter?

---

[17]His book deserves more thoughtful consideration than it has received to date.

[18]L. Timothy Johnson, *The First and Second Letters to Timothy*, AB 35A (New York: Doubleday, 2001), p. 58.

This work will try to peek over Paul's shoulder, looking at how he likely wrote his letters, with the hope of seeing more accurately how our New Testament letters came into being. A more careful consideration of Paul as a letter writer should affect how we view the authorship of Paul's letters (coauthors and pseudonymity), how we recreate the original text (text criticism, interpolations), and perhaps even how we interpret some passages in his letters. We will see the extraordinary amount of work that went into his letters. We also will see more clearly how letters were sent and how we likely came to have a collection of Paul's letters. With those goals in mind, let us begin the journey back into the first-century world of letter writing.

I

A MODERN, WESTERN PAUL

*I*n this chapter we are going to question how appropriate is our current understanding of "author." We will then look at authorship in the time of Paul.

When scholars discuss how Paul wrote his letters, they usually talk about how he shaped his words and sentences or how he painted his arguments or how he cleverly answered the objections raised by his opponents.[1] However, these works rarely discuss the actual mechanics of the letter-writing process. About the only places to find a description of how letters were actually written down are introductions in technical books[2] or in textbooks on textual criticism. Although most of us do not spend much time reflecting on exactly how Paul wrote his letters, we all have some model in mind of how Paul's letters came to be.

Commentary writers often broach this topic in the introductions to their commentaries. Older models often had Paul with "pen in hand," cloistered in pensive solitude, scribbling away to his churches. Archaeological and sociological studies have since shown how this image of Paul looks more like how we write than how an ancient Mediterranean Jew wrote. Realizing that our modern and Western presuppositions are inappropriate, scholars have begun to describe him writing in a manner at least possible if not probable in the ancient world. However, after introducing Paul in this way, they often write the remaining commentary as if Paul wrote his letters with "pen in hand."

Scholars, like most readers, describe Paul as a letter writer using their own writing experiences and preferences as the pattern.[3] The writing utensils are changed into some sort of first-century equivalent, but the paradigm remains that of the way a 1950s Westerner wrote. After a cursory description of letter-writing customs, many scholars plunge passionately into the topic of their research, such as analyses of Paul's rhetoric, his argumen-

---

[1]As early as Bultmann's dissertation, rhetorical analyses have been applied to Paul. Since the monumental commentary by H. D. Betz, *Galatians: A Commentary on Paul's Letter to the Churches in Galatia*, Hermeneia (Minneapolis: Fortress, 1979), rhetorical analyses have been producing fruitful results in exegetical studies of Paul.

[2]One of the best recent examples is Ben Witherington, *The Paul Quest: The Renewed Search for the Jew of Tarsus* (Downers Grove, Ill.: InterVarsity Press, 1998).

[3]Obviously scholars have no desire to describe Paul in their own image, yet Bruce Malina and Jerome Neyrey recently complained of scholars who wish merely to collect data on writers like Paul and then "describe them as though they lived in our own society and were motivated by the same concerns as we are"; see Bruce Malina and Jerome Neyrey, *Portraits of Paul: An Archaeology of Ancient Personality* (Louisville, Ky.: Westminster John Knox, 1996), p. xii.

tation and use of asyndeton,[4] skipping over the mundane mechanics of how such matters were actually put onto papyrus. Yet some ethereal analyses quickly fall to earth under the weight of the practical realities of scratching letters onto a sheet of papyrus.[5] We should not describe Paul writing in ways that were not realistic for his time.

MODERN MODELS OF PAUL THE LETTER WRITER

Many Christians have simply given little or no thought as to how Paul's letters were actually written down. Most of us today can still envision the old "paper, pen and desk" model enough to project this paradigm back onto Paul and the first century. We are not alone. The artist of the painting on the front cover of this book did the same thing. If we imagine Paul writing in a 1950s paradigm, does it affect how we interpret Paul? In writings on Paul as a letter writer, two general models emerge.

The optimistic model. Gene Edwards, a popular Christian writer, is currently influencing the church about Paul's letter-writing habits. A prolific writer, Edwards has written a bestselling series called "First-Century Diaries," historical fiction that recounts the life of Paul as told by some of his colleagues: Silas, Titus, Timothy, Priscilla and Gaius.

Edwards is well informed on the typical reconstruction of Paul's ministry, taking very few creative liberties in his reconstruction of Paul's life. With our postmodern love for storytelling, it is not surprising his books are so popular. In Edwards's first book, *The Silas Diary,* he describes (through the eyes of Silas) how Paul wrote Galatians:

> Paul finally felt sure his anger was under control. He then asked me to spend the day with him. When I entered his room, I saw that an amanuensis was also present. He was one of the brothers of the Antioch ecclesia. Why an amanuensis? Why did Paul not pen his letter in his own hand?
>
> There is a saying among those who cannot read:
>
> Why learn to read?
>
> By the time you are thirty-five your eyes cannot see what is written on the paper.
>
> Why learn to write?
>
> By the time you are forty you cannot see the paper!
>
> Paul was past forty-four, hence the amanuensis.
>
> I sat down, and Paul began to talk softly. We must have talked for hours. It was his way, at least that day, of preparing to write a letter. Paul and I also talked to the amanuensis so he might have some idea what was about to be written and why. . . .
>
> Paul took a deep breath and then began dictating the incredible letter . . . I never moved or spoke during the whole time Paul dictated the letter; rather, I sat transfixed. He never stopped or corrected or changed. He knew every word he wanted to say. He had struggled

---

[4]E.g., the fine piece by Eberhard W. Güting and David L. Mealand, *Asyndeton in Paul: A Text-Critical and Statistical Enquiry into Pauline Style*, Studies in the Bible and Early Christianity 39 (Lewiston, N.Y.: Mellen Press, 1998).

[5]See Richard L. Rohrbaugh, "Introduction," in *The Social Sciences and New Testament Interpretation,* ed. Richard L. Rohrbaugh (Peabody, Mass.: Hendrickson, 1996), p. 5.

with an earlier draft, but this time the man was inspired!

As Paul neared the end of the letter, he took the pen from the amanuensis, squinted his eyes, and wrote a sentence of his own in large letters, so large that even a man over fifty could read it. . . .

The letter, four copies in all, left Antioch the next day. The brothers had hired a horseman to deliver it to Derbe. The brothers in Derbe were to see that it was sent on to the other churches as fast as their means could afford.[6]

Gene Edwards is a delightful storyteller. He weaves in details of everyday life in the first-century world with politics of the Jerusalem church and problems caused by those of the "circumcision party." Readers are drawn in, wanting to see what happened next. It is the power of story.

Edwards reiterates this model of Paul the writer in his later books with few modifications.[7] In his second book, *The Titus Diary*, Paul no longer uses a professional secretary, conscripting Timothy instead to write 1 Thessalonians because, again, most people over forty no longer had eyesight adequate for reading and writing letters.[8] Edwards alters the letter-writing process slightly in this second book: Paul stops on occasion in the writing to ponder a matter before resuming and Silas is permitted to give input.[9] As Paul dictates 1 Thessalonians 3 his eyes fill with tears. He tells Silas "Truthfully, this is a little personal, so pay no attention to what I say next."[10] It is implied that the use of an amanuensis prevented Paul from having the privacy he wanted. The letter was then dispatched the very next day.[11]

In his third book, *The Timothy Diary*, Edwards describes 1 Corinthians as having been written in much the same way, with two additional elements. First, Sosthenes is included in the letter address because, according to Edwards, Paul asked him to attend and to be a witness to the letter, and thus able to vouch for it being authentically Pauline. Sosthenes provides no input whatsoever into the letter.[12] This is a common assumption in scholarly commentaries as well.[13] Second, Titus is permitted to make sug-

---

[6]Gene Edwards, *The Silas Diary*, First-Century Diaries 1 (Wheaton, Ill.: Tyndale House, 1998), pp. 204-11.

[7]Gene Edwards, *The Titus Diary*, First-Century Diaries 2 (Wheaton, Ill.: Tyndale House, 1999). In later books (after 2001), Edwards makes a few shifts. Evidently, he continues to benefit from contemporary scholarship. It is unclear if Edwards would maintain these changes in Paul's letter-writing habits only for Paul's later ministry or project them back into the earlier volumes.

[8]Edwards, *Silas Diary*, p. 189.

[9]Ibid., p. 191.

[10]Ibid., p. 193. We are later told how Paul wrote 2 Thessalonians. The process remains the same with one exception. According to Edwards (p. 228), Paul intended to end the letter after 2 Thessalonians 2. However, the next morning Paul decides to add another section (2 Thess 3).

[11]Ibid., p. 230.

[12]Gene Edwards, *The Timothy Diary*, First-Century Diaries 3 (Wheaton, Ill.: Tyndale House, 2000), p. 163.

[13]See, e.g., C. K. Barrett, *A Commentary on the First Epistle to the Corinthians*, BNTC (Peabody, Mass.: Hendrickson, 1993), who notes "Paul and Sosthenes write to the Church," but in the very next point speaks of "Paul's letter" and so throughout (pp. 31-32). Leon Morris in his Tyndale commentary on 1 Corinthians notes, "With him Paul associates Sosthenes" (*The First Epistle of Paul to the Corinthians: An Introduction and Commentary*, TNTC 7, rev. ed. [Grand Rapids: Eerdmans, 1988], p. 34), but Sosthenes does not appear elsewhere. Anthony

gestions that include content. Paul even quotes what Titus suggests. Nevertheless, the entire scenario casts Paul as the wise, old teacher who gently guides his student to draw the right conclusions. Edwards even has Titus objecting, "You know I learned everything I know from you!" Thus, even this input from Titus is not truly independent input, but merely masterful discipleship by Paul as he brings along the next generation of leaders.

Why spend so much time describing a series of popular historical fiction? Edwards's reconstruction of Paul's dialogues with Silas is amusing, perhaps even helpful to laypeople and probably harmless, although some may feel uncomfortable with putting words in Paul's mouth, even if labeled fiction. However, is Edwards's scenario for how Paul wrote his letters all that different from most New Testament scholarship?

Edwards is well-versed in Pauline studies. His historical reconstructions demonstrate familiarity with many technical issues in Paul and are rather consistent with contemporary scholarship,[14] albeit fleshed out. He suggests what would be an accurate unpacking of the implications of many academic reconstructions. If scholars were to write this type of fiction, would their reconstructions be so different?

The pessimistic model. Others take a more pessimistic approach, claiming we can know nothing of how Paul wrote his letters.[15] Actually, there is too much evidence merely to write off the subject as "unknowable" and hence able to be ignored. Complete pessimism is unwarranted. We can know some of how Paul the letter writer worked. William Doty outlines some general options for how Paul wrote, but he hesitates to be more specific.[16] Cautiousness is a sign of careful research; however, we should examine more closely the actual mechanics of how Paul wrote his letters. This may complicate some exegetical discussions and even require some revision of related topics, such as discussions of authorship, Paul's use of rhetoric/argumentation, the presence of interpolations. Nev-

---

Thiselton, *1 Corinthians*, NIGTC (Grand Rapids: Eerdmans, 2000), debates the possible literary role of Sosthenes (pp. 69-72). Ben Witherington, *Conflict and Community in Corinth* (Grand Rapids: Eerdmans, 1995), finally rejects a literary role for Sosthenes, but only after a considered argument and not presuppositionally. Jerome Murphy-O'Connor argues Sosthenes' hand may be seen in 1 Cor 1:18-31 and 2:6-16; "Co-Authorship in the Corinthian Correspondence," *RB* 100 (1993): 562-79.

[14]This is not to preclude minor problems. With this type of work, it is often hard to distinguish if he is making a point or merely filling in details, such as his claim that Galatians was written with a professional secretary (*Silas*, p. 204), and if a statement might be merely a slip of the mind, such as his claim that Titus was less familiar with the Greek mind than Timothy (*The Timothy Diary*, p. 166).

[15]To the assertion that Paul used a secretary, A. Q. Morton replied: "The rejoinder to this assertion is that it is something which we do not know" (A. Morton and J. McLeman, *Paul, the Man and the Myth: A Study in the Authorship of Greek Prose* [London: Hodder & Stoughton, 1966], pp. 94-95). Yet, I respond, we do know that Paul used a secretary. Morton further argued: "Homer was blind and must have used one but no Homeric scholar has felt obliged to defend the purity of the text against the amanuensis." I respond, if Homer were blind, then he always used a secretary and there would be no texts from the hand of Homer alone. Josephus does use a secretary in various roles and Josephus scholars do appeal to the secretary to explain some differences.

[16]William Doty, *Letters in Primitive Christianity*, Guides to Biblical Scholarship, New Testament Series (Philadelphia: Fortress, 1973), p. 41.

ertheless, whether considered or unconscious, the image we hold of Paul as a letter writer carries with it certain assumptions which do affect how we interpret Paul's letters.

UNDERLYING ASSUMPTIONS IN BOTH MODERN MODELS

We begin by looking at some of the assumptions common to most reconstructions of Paul as a letter writer. My contention is that both fanciful reconstructions, such as Edwards's, and most scholarly reconstructions share common assumptions in three key areas: where the author wrote, who helped the author, and the actual mechanics of writing.

The letter writer's study. In typical reconstructions we see three assumptions about Paul's study.

1. Paul wrote in a room away from the public.

2. Only those whom Paul personally desired to be with him were present when he wrote.

3. Only a day or two of uninterrupted privacy were required to write a letter.

The letter writer's "helpers." The common perception assumes several ideas about those who "helped" Paul write his letters: his coauthors and his secretaries.

Coauthors. Paul mentions colleagues such as Timothy or Sosthenes in the opening verses of a letter (the letter address).

1. Most scholars assume these colleagues are mentioned for some reason other than co-authorship.

2. Scholars assume that these named colleagues might remind Paul of topics, perhaps even broach topics, but Paul was the sole author of the letter. It is customary to speak of *Paul's* letters.

Secretaries. Paul's letters clearly indicate that he used a secretary to write at least some (and probably all) of his letters.

1. Paul often used a secretary—only as a necessary second choice—because he was unable to write himself. Edwards blames poor eyesight, such as was common for older people in the first-century world.[17] Deissmann blamed arthritis.[18] Whatever the cause, the clear implication is that Paul would have written the letter himself were he able. In

---

[17]Paleopathologists tell us that eyesight was commonly poor; see Rohrbaugh, "Introduction," p. 5. This view (as is oft cited for Gal 6:11) has not faired well among biblical scholars. C. K. Barrett brushed it off as Pauline sarcasm, "don't pretend you can't see this" (Barrett, *Freedom and Obligation: A Study of the Epistle to the Galatians* [Philadelphia: Westminster Press, 1985], p. 84). Ben Witherington correctly notes arguments are weak for the large letters as some sort of "bold print" (*Grace in Galatia: A Commentary on Paul's Letter to the Galatians* [Grand Rapids: Eerdmans, 1998], p. 441 n. 10). Witherington argues that it is indeed due to eye problems, though Paul specifically mentions it because the problem was not chronic, but temporary and known to the Galatians (4:11).

[18]See A. Deissmann's oft-quoted description of an aged Paul whose hands twisted by years of tent making were not able to grasp the pen well; *Light from the Ancient East*, trans. L. R. M. Strachan (Grand Rapids: Baker, 1978), pp. 174, 246.

other words, it is assumed a secretary brought no advantages or additional skills to the equation. He was merely a poor substitute for what Paul would have preferred to do himself.

2. Although Paul used a secretary,[19] he alone generated every word. No one else, not even the secretary, contributed to the written text except Paul.

3. Some insist Paul dictated the letter from beginning to end without stopping.[20] Others allow Paul to pause, contemplate and even discuss. Most, though, have no place for Paul to correct or alter what was already written. In other words, Paul's first draft was his final draft.

4. The secretary is assumed capable of accurately recording every word Paul said, presumably as long as Paul spoke slowly and allowed appropriate pauses. This is based upon a prior assumption that someone who was literate could also take dictation.

5. Hiring a secretary, or amanuensis, is assumed to be the most expensive aspect of sending a letter; hence Paul used a colleague as a secretary to save money. Materials and dispatching are assumed to have been minor expenses.

6. Timothy was literate.[21]

The writing process. Many people today have not thought about how Paul actually went about composing and writing his letters. Most realize he wove in material that he was quoting (at the least Old Testament passages); many have not considered whether he had rough drafts, etc.

The inclusion of traditional material. Scholars have long recognized that Paul included material quoted from the Old Testament or early Christian hymns or sayings in his letters.

1. When Paul incorporated Old Testament material, it is usually assumed he was merely quoting from memory or reading from a scroll. In either case, the material was entered into the letter directly by Paul weaving it into his dictation.

2. Christian hymns and other preformed traditions were woven into the letter in the same manner as Old Testament quotations, by Paul dictating the material.

---

[19]When Galatians 6:11 reads: "See what large letters I make when I am writing in my own hand," it is an indication that Paul has now personally begun writing. The previous section was written by the secretary.
[20]Such as Edwards, in his first book, *The Silas Diary,* p. 209.
[21]While this is possible and perhaps even likely, it cannot be assumed. Recent research evolving from orality studies has led many scholars to agree with William Harris: "We must suppose the majority of people were always illiterate." William V. Harris, *Ancient Literacy* (Cambridge, Mass.: Harvard University Press, 1989), p. 13. While I believe Timothy was probably literate, this is a far cry from saying he was able to take dictation. Orality research crashed into NT studies with the work of Werner Kelber, *The Oral and the Written Gospel: The Hermeneutics of Speaking and Writing in the Synoptic Tradition, Mark, Paul, and Q* (Philadelphia: Fortress, 1983). Recent scholars have underlined this orality, arguing that the NT writings are "oral to the core" (Paul Achtemeier, *"Omne verbum sonat:* The New Testament and the Oral Environment of Late Western Antiquity," *JBL* 109 [1990]: 19).

3. Paul made use of certain types of seemingly preformed material, such as midrash on an Old Testament passage,[22] extended chiastic material,[23] *topoi*,[24] tribulation lists,[25] virtue/vice lists, etc. These also presumably entered Paul's letter through the dictation of Paul.

There is no difficulty in arguing that Paul dictated extemporaneously a memorized, stereotyped piece, especially when talking of standard epistolary formulae (set phrases).[26] Extemporaneous dictation is even plausible for things like the vice lists in Colossians.[27] However, the elaborate rhetorical structure of many of Paul's letters, particularly Galatians, does not seem likely to have been dictated extemporaneously.[28] At least some of the letters seem more carefully composed than extemporaneous dictation.

Editing. Most Christians do not consider the possibility that Paul might have edited or revised his letters before sending them.

1. It is usually assumed that the first draft was the only draft. Paul did not correct, edit or polish the text before dispatching it. When he finished the last sentence, the letter was finished.

2. It is often assumed that the first draft was written on the papyrus that was sent. Thus the draft was written in penmanship suitable for dispatching. It must be assumed, therefore, that the secretary could not only take dictation but could do so in handwriting suitable for sending to a church for public reading.

Copying. Modern readers correctly assume that ancient letter writers made copies of letters.

---

[22]See, e.g., E. Earle Ellis's dissertation, *Paul's Use of the Old Testament* (1957; reprint, Grand Rapids: Baker, 1981) and his "Midrash *Pesher* in Pauline Hermeneutics," in *Prophecy and Hermeneutic in Early Christianity: New Testament Essays*, WUNT 18 (Tübingen: Mohr, 1978), pp. 173-81.

[23]See, e.g., J. Jeremias, "Chiasmus in den Paulusbriefen," *ZNW* 49 (1958): 139-56, or J. W. Welch, "Chiasmus in the New Testament," in *Chiasmus in Antiquity: Structure, Analyses, and Exegesis* (Hildesheim: Gerstenberg, 1981), 211-49.

[24]See David Bradley, "The *Topos* as a Form in the Pauline Paraenesis," *JBL* 72 (1953): 238-46, or T. Y. Mullins, "*Topos* as a NT Form," *JBL* 99 (1980): 541-47. According to Doty, *Letters*, p. 39, *topoi* (plural) were "miniature essays of stereotyped good advice," a type of stock response frequently used by street preachers as an answer to a common question.

[25]Ancient speakers often listed difficulties (tribulations) they faced in carrying out their tasks. Paul also did this (e.g., Rom 8:35; 2 Cor 6:4-5; 11:23-29; 12:10). See Robert Hodgson, "Paul the Apostle and First Century Tribulation Lists," *ZNW* 74 (1983): 59-80.

[26]E.g., the stereotyped formulae for disclosure, petition, astonishment, ironic rebuke, thanksgiving, greeting, expression of joy, or statement of compliance. For a concise list with descriptions, see E. R. Richards, *The Secretary in the Letters of Paul*, WUNT 2/42 (Tübingen: Mohr/Siebeck, 1991), appendixes B-D.

[27]These three lists with the repetition of five vices/virtues (with the fifth summarizing each list) are clearly structured. Lists of five, or pentaschema, were used among Iranian philosophers. Paul however is certainly not alluding to their complex theory of two cosmic men with five members each. He is merely using a common rhetorical technique. His selection of which virtues and vices also differ. See E. R. Richards, "Stop Lying," *BI* (Spring 1999): 77-80. For more detail, see E. Lohse, *Colossians and Philemon*, Hermeneia series (Philadelphia: Fortress, 1971), p. 137.

[28]So argues, e.g., Witherington, *Galatia*, p. 442, and Betz, *Galatians*, p. 312.

1. It is usually assumed that copies were made quickly and easily.[29]

2. It is also assumed that Paul did not keep a copy for himself.

Dispatching the letter. Haste seems always in the background of Paul's literary activities. Paul is rarely portrayed as having written leisurely. Dispatch was always immediate. Only modern Americans seem to rival Paul's pace of life. Ever since Deissmann, Paul is usually pictured dashing off his letters amidst a flurry of other mission activities, in order to quell a burgeoning problem recently brought to his attention.[30]

PROBLEMS WITH MODERN MODELS

Some scholars snicker at historical fiction, perhaps prematurely.[31] Many scholars share in common at least some of these popular assumptions. These largely unspoken assumptions are typical because many popular writers—and some scholars—are recreating Paul as a letter writer in a twentieth-century image. Some modern western misconceptions have been projected back onto Paul.

Misconceptions about the letter writer's study. We are all aware that Paul's culture was neither modern nor Western. Nevertheless, many reconstructions of Paul as a letter writer are built upon a modern and Western framework. We shall examine several areas where the modern picture is at odds with the probable sociological realities of Paul's world.

Modern Western concepts of privacy. Recent sociological studies suggest that modern Western values such as privacy and individualism not only color our reconstructions but also have no real equivalent in Paul's world. Paul's world was group-oriented; they thought in group terms and not as independent individuals,[32] and Paul presented himself in this way.[33] Paul saw himself as articulating the values and views of his group.[34] As modern Western writers we articulate our individualistic values and views when we write, and

---

[29]Edwards (*The Silas Diary,* p. 211) mentions copies because he assumes they were made for each of the multiple destinations for Galatians, rather than circulating one letter around. Most would agree that Galatians 6:11 strongly implies only one copy was dispatched. Galatians 6:11 becomes meaningless if Paul planned originally to send multiple copies, unless we argue Paul personally autographed all copies. See the persuasive argument for only one dispatched copy of Galatians by J. A. Ziesler, *The Epistle to the Galatians* (London: Epworth, 1992), p. 98. Incidentally, positing multiple originals raises interesting questions about which would be the "original text."

[30]A. Deissmann, *St. Paul: A Study in Social and Religious History,* trans. L. R. M. Strachan (London: Hodder & Stoughton, 1912), pp. 13-14.

[31]Recently, we have seen scholars capitalizing upon the power of historical fiction; see, e.g., Bruce Longenecker, *The Lost Letters of Pergamum: A Story from the New Testament World* (Grand Rapids: Baker, 2002); or Marvin Pate and Daniel Hays, *The Apocalypse* (Grand Rapids: Zondervan, 2004).

[32]See among others, Malina and Neyrey, *Portraits of Paul,* pp. 16-18 and 227-29.

[33]Malina and Neyrey, *Portraits of Paul,* p. 51.

[34]See the insightful comments by Thiselton, *1 Corinthians,* p. 70 (and bibliography, p. 59). Meeks demonstrates well how Paul's mission work was collaborative, working with a "staff" [Meeks's term]; see Wayne Meeks, *First Urban Christians: The Social World of the Apostle Paul* (New Haven, Conn.: Yale University Press, 1983), p. 133, and G. Theissen, *Social Setting of Pauline Christianity* (Philadelphia: Fortress, 1982), pp. 87-96; and R. Banks, *Paul's Idea of Community,* rev. ed. (Peabody, Mass.: Hendrickson, 1994), pp. 134-69.

for this reason we need privacy. Why would Paul want to separate himself from his group in order to write? He was writing their values.[35]

I personally cannot do serious writing in a busy room with people coming and going, stopping by to toss in ideas or to critique what I am doing. It is assumed Paul shared our view on this matter. We need quiet and solitude to write, but would a desire for quiet and solitude even have occurred to Paul? Most Westerners who have lived in the East are well aware of this difference. Not only is there no privacy in most of the East; they cannot imagine why one would want it.[36] Westerners emphasize individual ideas. For Paul the group's comments were neither interruptions nor extraneous thoughts.[37] Their input only further defined the group's thought. Paul's letter was the expression of the group's consensus reached by dialogue.[38]

Modern conveniences. Typically, Paul is portrayed at a desk, scribbling away by candle-light, the necessary books and sources lying open in front of him. In reality, ancient writers lacked the basic conveniences we now consider essential. Lamps were smoky and dim. Writers placed the paper on their laps because there were no desks. As for Paul, he neither quoted everything from memory, nor had a well-equipped study where he could spend quiet evenings writing in solitude.

Misconceptions about the letter writer's "helpers." Modern writers are usually solitary writers. Even on joint projects with two or more authors, we rarely sit and write together. For us, authorship is an intensely individualistic activity. A modern writer may have helpers, but those helpers do not usually look over the author's shoulder and make comments as he writes.

Modern Western concepts of individualism. The a priori assumption today is toward an individual author rather than a team. The implied argument of many scholars is that an individual author is assumed unless there is strong indication otherwise. There are two objections to this assumption. First, this assumption is based upon a modern Western preference for individuality,[39] a trait shared by a minority of the world.[40]

---

[35]Malina and Neyrey, *Portraits of Paul*, p. 199.

[36]My editor Dan Reid shared with me how his wife, living in the Philippines, retreated to a quiet room to write in order to escape the noise of household workers. Her Filipino workers followed her to "keep her company." Indonesian has no word for "privacy," the closest equivalent is *kesepian* meaning "loneliness." For an Indonesian, to have privacy is to feel lonely. *Menemani*, "to befriend," is used to describe "accompanying someone so they do not have to do the task alone," because that is what friends do.

[37]Quintilian (*Inst.* 10.3.22) noted the need for silence and privacy to do serious writing. Yet his argument for this practice suggests that the custom was the opposite. Also Quintilian would have considered comments by those around him as beneath his standard. His helpers were never "colleagues." See also Sen. *Ep.* 56.1.

[38]As in Luke's example in Acts 15.

[39]For a contrast between the first-century Mediterranean culture and modern American culture on "individualism," see Jerome Neyrey, "Dyadism," *Biblical Social Values and Their Meanings: A Handbook,* ed. John Pilch and Bruce Malina (Peabody, Mass.: Hendrickson, 1993), p. 52.

[40]According to Harry Triandis, 70% of the world is group-oriented; "Cross-Cultural Studies of Individualism and Collectivism," in *Nebraska Symposium on Motivation 1989,* ed. J. J. Berman (Lincoln: University of Nebraska Press, 1990), p. 48. See Malina and Neyrey, *Portraits of Paul*, p. 155.

Second, even if we allow that an individual author should be assumed without some strong indication otherwise, there is strong evidence otherwise for the letters of Paul. To argue for Paul as a solitary writer requires actually ignoring the evidence, particularly that of explicitly named coauthors and secretaries.

Misconceptions about coauthors. To some extent, in a group-oriented society like Paul's, "No one really has his or her 'own' opinion, nor is anyone expected to."[41] There is an inherent "we" to all New Testament writers. An ancient writer cited tradition, not to garner support for his argument (as we do), but to show he was part of a collective. Paul was not less group-oriented than his culture.[42] Yet it is sometimes subconsciously assumed Paul did not need or want a coauthor: a colleague could broach a topic, but surely Paul alone determined the written expression. In most popular descriptions of Paul as a letter writer, only Paul selected the words that were put to papyrus.

Misconceptions about secretaries. Most scholars now acknowledge Paul's use of a secretary.[43] Yet three misconceptions about Paul's secretary are common.

It is assumed a colleague of Paul could easily be conscripted to serve as an amateur secretary. Werner Kelber is perhaps overly pessimistic in seeing literacy in the hands of only a few.[44] Alan Millard's assessment is probably accurate:

> Throughout the Hellenistic and Roman world the distinction prevailed in that there were educated people who were proficient readers and writers, less educated ones who could read but hardly write, some who were readers alone, some of them able to read only slowly or with difficulty and some who were illiterate.[45]

It is probable that Paul had colleagues who were literate. Nonetheless, it is a mistake to assume that any literate person could also write. Scholars in that field maintain that ancient literacy was primarily determined by the ability to read not write.[46] A literate person was someone who could read. Our only biblical reference that defines literacy is Isaiah 29:11-12, which describes it as the ability to read.[47] Ancient literacy cannot automatically be equated with all the characteristics of modern literacy. It is often difficult for people today to separate reading and writing. For example, even though I can read, I would struggle to write with my left hand. Why? I am right-handed. I have had little practice writing with my left hand. So also the literate man in antiquity often wrote only with

---

[41]Malina and Neyrey, *Portraits of Paul,* p. 73.

[42]Malina and Neyrey argue throughout that Paul was a typical if not quintessential group-oriented person (e.g., *Portraits of Paul,* p. 217).

[43]I am perhaps being overly optimistic. Many concede the secretary but only in the sense of a stenographer; e.g., I. Howard Marshall, *The Pastoral Epistles,* ICC (Edinburgh: T & T Clark, 1999), p. 65.

[44]Kelber, *Oral and Written,* p. 17.

[45]Alan Millard, *Reading and Writing in the Time of Jesus* (Sheffield: Sheffield Academic Press, 2000), p. 154.

[46]So Eric Havelock, *The Literate Revolution in Greece and Its Cultural Consequences* (Princeton, N.J.: Princeton University Press, 1982), pp. 38-59.

[47]I am indebted to L. B. Yaghjian for this insight ("Ancient Reading," in *The Social Sciences and New Testament Interpretation,* ed. R. L. Rohrbaugh [Peabody, Mass.: Hendrickson, 1996], p. 213).

difficulty for the same reason: he had little practice writing. If I imagine writing with my left hand, I can better understand Paul's comment "See what large letters I make when I am writing in my own hand." Experts on papyri often describe a secretary's handwriting as "a practiced hand." Thus, it is an error to assume any literate person could also write fluently. Concerning Paul's letters, the error is often compounded. It assumed that Paul's colleagues who could read could also write fluently enough to follow dictation.

A second common misperception is that a secretary offered no additional skills other than those held by anyone who could write. Since Timothy is listed in a letter address, it is assumed he was literate; thus he could write and was qualified as a secretary. Scholars incorrectly assume Paul could easily conscript a member of his own band to serve as a secretary. Yet, secretaries required skills with the writing materials beyond what the ordinary individual possessed. Papyrus was sold by the individual sheet or by the standard roll. Paul's letters did not fit either size. Additional sheets needed to be glued on to lengthen a roll (or trimmed off to shorten it). A secretary needed to mix his own ink and to cut his own pens. A secretary also needed to draw lines on the paper. Small holes were often pricked down each side and then a straight edge and a lead disk were used to lightly draw evenly-spaced lines across the sheet. A secretary also needed a sharpening stone to keep his pen sharp and a knife to cut new tips as necessary.[48] Less mechanical but more significantly, Ben Witherington adds, "A good secretary would have to know the mind of his employer, how to write, the proper form for a letter, and also rhetoric and its conventions."[49]

A third common misconception may be termed the "Stenographer vs. Cowriter Fallacy." Many readers permit Paul to have had a secretary, but only a secretary who took Paul's exact dictation, that is, a stenographer. Since allowing any secretarial role beyond a stenographer opens the door for notes, drafts and editing, quite a few assume that allowing a secretary to exert any influence on the text means taking control of the text away from Paul and giving it to another (the secretary). This is the reason I. H. Marshall, in his ICC commentary, rejects my theory that the secretary had input in the Pastoral Epistles:

> There is the possibility that the details of composition are due to a colleague or "secretary" who was given a rather free hand by Paul. Here again the effect is to "rescue" the PE [Pastoral Epistles] for Paul at the cost of denying that he himself was responsible for their contents.[50]

This may not be a required conclusion. We are not required to accept the secretary as a cowriter, who barges in and takes over the Pastorals obscuring Paul's hand and over whom Paul had no oversight. We are not limited to only two options: either Paul's secretary was a stenographer or we must take the letter from Paul's hand and give it to an unsupervised secretary. Rather, these are extreme opposite ends of a continuum, when the actual process no

---

[48]Witherington, *Paul Quest*, p. 99.
[49]Ibid., pp. 100-101.
[50]Marshall, *Pastoral Epistles*, p. 64. He is responding to my suggestion for secretarial mediation in the pastoral letters.

doubt rested more in the middle. Furthermore, this argument ignores that

> irrespective of any secretarial influence, the author assumed complete responsibility for the content, including the subtle nuances. Because of his accountability, he checked the final draft.[51]

When Cicero and others wished to disclaim problems in earlier letters, such as omitted items or poorly phrased sentences, they never blamed their secretary for misrecording it, even though they used secretaries.[52] Such excuses were untenable. The author was assumed responsible for every phrase and nuance, no matter the secretarial process.

Misconceptions about the writing process. Many assume dictation was the common method of writing letters. In actuality there was a range of methods for writing a letter (discussed in chapter four). Many assume Paul dictated his letters, imagining a situation like this: Timothy struggled to keep up when Paul was speaking passionately; yet somehow Timothy managed.[53]

This unsubstantiated optimism, that the secretary managed somehow to record Paul's rapid dictation verbatim, is not warranted. Otto Roller demonstrated convincingly that to dictate a letter word for word usually required the writer to speak so slowly it was actually more like syllable by syllable.[54] If the secretary were writing directly onto a papyrus sheet with the typical reed pen, and he intended the letter to be legible, this required writing even more slowly. Yet most scholars would rule out such a possibility for Paul's letters. His letters do not read like Paul dictated them syllable by painful syllable. Nevertheless, these problems are often just glossed over. Somehow the secretary still managed to take Paul's dictation, as is argued by I. H. Marshall:

> there is a homogeneity about [Paul's] authentic letters which shows that he dictated them himself and added his signature at the end.[55]

In an earlier work, I demonstrated that Greek shorthand existed in the first century.[56] Many scholars have found this to be the solution they needed to this sticky dictation problem. I am cited as demonstrating Greek shorthand, but without noting that I argued it was

---

[51]Richards, *Secretary,* p. 127; see also pp. 54-55. The summary subscriptions served a similar purpose for the marginally illiterate; see Gordon Bahr, "The Subscriptions in the Pauline Letters," *JBL* 87 (1968): 29.

[52]They sought other excuses, such as disclaiming the entire letter; for examples, see Richards, *Secretary,* pp. 54-55.

[53]See Edwards, *Timothy,* p. 174: "I found it difficult to keep up."

[54]Otto Roller, *Das Formular der paulinischen Briefe: Ein Beitrag zur Lehre vom antiken Briefe* (Stuttgart: W. Kohlhammer, 1933), p. 333. Many make a token nod to Roller, citing him in an early footnote, but do not take seriously his conclusions.

[55]Marshall, *Pastoral Epistles,* pp. 64-65. Since this comment comes in a section where he is critiquing my secretary hypothesis, I shall respond. With due respect, Marshall does indeed find a homogeneity in Paul's "authentic letters" because whatever letters were not homogenous have been eliminated as non-Pauline. This appears to me to be a circular argument. See E. E. Ellis, "Pastoral Letters," in *Dictionary of Paul and His Letters,* ed. Gerald F. Hawthorne, Ralph P. Martin and Daniel G. Reid (Downers Grove, Ill.: InterVarsity Press, 1993), pp. 660-61.

[56]Richards, *Secretary,* pp. 26-43.

not readily available to Paul. It is incorrect to assume Paul regularly had the services of a *notarius,* a shorthand writer.[57] If it is unlikely Paul dictated his letters verbatim, then we must allow for a process that includes editing; that is, Paul had notes and rough drafts.

A second misconception about the writing process is the assumption that the first draft was the dispatched letter; that is, there was no editing and rewriting. Yet, if the limitations of ancient pen and paper made dictating directly to a final draft highly unlikely, we must allow for a process that included rough drafts. Many seem hesitant to allow room for editing, wanting only one draft though willing to permit some minor final editing, as we might check a final draft for minor changes.

Is an appeal to rough drafts yet another instance of reading modern conventions back into the first century? Modern writers take notes and make rough drafts, but is there any evidence that ancient writers did this? Yes. In chapter three we will point out the prevalent use of wax tablets and washable parchment notebooks whose purpose was to record notes to be fleshed out into a rough draft.[58]

CONCLUSIONS FOR PAUL AS A LETTER WRITER

The topics broached in this chapter will be expanded later in the book, but a summary is appropriate at this juncture.

1. Several misconceptions are common about Paul, such as assuming that (a) he wrote in privacy with only a secretary at hand who recorded his dictation; (b) he dictated to the secretary all quoted material, either reciting it from memory or reading it aloud; and (c) when he finished dictating, the letter was sealed and sent.

2. Paul's writings show clear evidence of careful composition. They were not dashed off one evening in the flurry of mission activity. For example, Witherington and Betz both allow Paul to have worked through at least one draft of Galatians before sending it. Betz argues:

   > the very employment of an amanuensis [secretary] rules out a haphazard writing of the letter and suggests the existence of Paul's draft and the copy by an amanuensis, *or a sequence of draft, composition, and copy.*[59]

3. Since Paul named coauthors in some of his letters, our understanding of *author* must be expanded beyond meaning "Paul alone."

---

[57]*Pace* Witherington, *Paul Quest,* p. 101. I do think Tertius may have been a *notarius.*

[58]Among the Vindolanda Tablets (Roman Britain) are what appear to be sketchy drafts of the "meat" of a letter from a military commander. Obviously he or a secretary planned to flesh it out into a full letter. We have other examples as well; PZen. 57, also perhaps PZen. 111 and PTebt. 13. The best accessible discussion of tablets and parchment notebooks is Harry Gamble, *Books and Readers in the Early Church: a History of Early Christian Texts* (New Haven, Conn.: Yale University Press, 1995), pp. 50ff.

[59]Betz, *Galatians,* p. 312 (emphasis added); also cited by Witherington, *Galatia,* p. 442.

2

PAUL AS A FIRST-CENTURY
LETTER WRITER

*I*f the typical modern image of Paul as a letter writer is built on multiple faulty assumptions—if we have portrayed Paul writing like a modern American—how then should we describe Paul? Using archaeological and sociological data from the first century, as well as comments from Paul's letters themselves, I shall attempt to cast a more accurate picture of Paul, a first-century, Mediterranean letter writer.

PAUL AS THE LEADER OF A MISSION TEAM

Paul did not work alone. As a first-century Mediterranean Jew it would not even have occurred to him to do so. Neither his letters nor Acts describe Paul working alone. "Paul does not perceive himself as commissioned to lead or to minister as an isolated individual, without collaboration with co-workers."[1] When Paul lost his partner, Barnabas, he sought another before beginning the next journey (Acts 15:36-41). When trouble in Athens caused Paul to leave early, leaving behind his team (Silas and Timothy), Acts implies that he traveled alone to Corinth.[2] We cannot be entirely sure he was alone since team members suddenly show up elsewhere without any indication when they had joined the team, such as Demas and Aristarchus (Philem 24). Nevertheless, assuming Paul was alone entering Corinth, we see him gaining team members, Priscilla and Aquila, before he is described as debating in the synagogue. When Paul was shipped away to Rome as a prisoner, he had team members accompany him. Even under Roman arrest he still had team members with him. Whether Paul was actually ever alone at some particular moment is immaterial. The point is that our modern Western love for individuality has no equivalent in Paul's world. He was the leader of a team. "From the beginning the Pauline mission was a collective enterprise, with something that can loosely be called a staff."[3]

---

[1]Thiselton, *1 Corinthians*, p. 69.

[2]Luke tells us Paul traveled by foot on one occasion rather than sailing with the team by ship. The very mentioning of such an occurrence, since nothing else is said about it, speaks of how unusual it was (Acts 20:13-14). Luke mentions Paul sending two team members to Macedonia while he remained in Ephesus (Acts 19:22). He was not without team members in Ephesus (Acts 19:29).

[3]Meeks, *First Urban Christians*, p. 133; so also Theissen, *Social Setting*, pp. 87-96; E. E. Ellis, *Prophecy and Hermeneutic*, pp. 3-22; and Thiselton, *1 Corinthians*, p. 70.

We should not, however, envision a team of equal collaborators. Paul was clearly in charge. He had disciples, such as Timothy and Titus. He also had peers, such as Barnabas and Luke. Yet these peers were not described as permanent members of the mission team. We see them moving in and out of the Pauline itinerary. They were associates, not understudies. Perhaps it was easier to work as an equal with Paul in small doses. The glimpse Luke gives us of Paul's relationship with Barnabas may be Luke's veiled defense of why he was not ever-present at Paul's side. In Luke's picture, when Paul decided a course of action, the final decision was cast. If a team member disagreed, he could accompany Paul anyway (as did Luke in Acts 21:12-14) or he could leave (as did John Mark in Acts 13:13 and Barnabas in Acts 15:39). Luke shows us that Paul could be difficult to work with as an equal.[4] He had a team, but he was the leader.

I make this distinction between associates and understudies for a reason. Associates are never named as cosenders in Paul's letters; only understudies are. We are arguing that Paul's letters were a team project, but not a team of near-equals. Paul was the leader and the dominant voice; the others were his disciples.

If Paul was the stand-apart leader, one might ask why he bothered to name cosenders? Isn't that lowering oneself? Cicero, Josephus and other ancient writers clearly had "helpers;" yet they did not name them and most certainly did not list them in the letter address as cosenders. Actually, listing cosenders at all was a rare phenomenon. Cicero and Josephus, for instance, claimed the credit of the letter all for themselves.[5] We must also note, however, that Cicero and Josephus never called themselves a "slave" (*doulos*) in the letter address. This is a Christian phenomenon, and one of the many ways Paul differed from the epistolary elite of society. Unlike their letters, Paul's were not intended as examples of the author's skill. As a "slave" of Jesus Christ, Paul was willing to work with his fellow "slaves" to send letters.

PAUL AND HIS COAUTHORS

Are the named cosenders in the letter address coauthors of the letter? Was coauthorship even practiced in antiquity? We find several examples of letters in antiquity with named cosenders. These letters fall into two general types.

1. A letter could be sent in the name of a group, such as the priests of Philae or the Jews of Alexandria, usually to a government figure asking for a redress of wrongs.

2. We also find an "occasional" letter from a husband and wife.

---

[4]It is interesting to note that Luke uses examples where readers would know Paul was mistaken: the readers knew John Mark was a trusted worker (Col 4:10; 2 Tim 4:11; Philem 24; 1 Pet 5:13), vindicating Barnabas, and Paul's hopes that his famine offering (as a glorious bridge joining Jewish and Gentile believers) was the plan of the Spirit (Acts 20:22) were not realistic and collapse in the Acts narrative, implicitly vindicating Luke (Acts 21:4, 11).

[5]This is not entirely correct, of course, or we would never know of their "helpers." Cicero concedes the help of Tiro, his secretary, in several private letters (see, e.g., Cic. *Fam.* 16.4.3). So also Josephus; see *Ap.* 1.50 (and also Thackeray, introduction to *The Life, Against Apion, and the Jewish War [Bellum Judaicum]*, 3 vols., LCL [Cambridge, Mass.: Harvard University Press, 1976], p. xv).

It is quite legitimate to question how much the named cosenders in either of these examples actually contributed to the letter.

Other than these two scenarios, the practice of named cosenders seems quite rare. Atticus wrote one letter together with others.[6] Among the extant ancient letter collections, Cicero, Seneca and Pliny wrote none. Among the 645 private letters from Oxyrhynchus, Tebtunis and Zenon listed by Kim,[7] I found six.[8] Yet none of these letters is even remotely analogous to Paul's letters.[9]

First Thessalonians 1:1 reads: "Paul and Silvanus and Timothy to the church of the Thessalonians." Assuming that Paul is an author, what reasons do commentators offer for arguing that the other two individuals are not? Often no reason is given or only arguments from within the letter itself are given. Paul is assumed to be the sole author, and explanations are given later as to why Paul included these two non-authors in the address. Leon Morris's comments are typical: it was "largely a matter of courtesy."[10] He argues "the practical difficulty of seeing how three people could combine to write such homogenous letters" and the fact the style matches that of Paul's other letters, rule out any true coauthorship. Silvanus and Timothy, Morris concludes, merely consulted and endorsed the letter.[11]

There are at least two difficulties with this common view. One relates to letter writing in general and the other relates specifically to Paul's letters. First, there is no evidence that it was a practice of courtesy to include non-authors in the letter address. If it were a common courtesy to include colleagues in the letter address, why is the custom so rare? It is not that courtesy was rare, but that true coauthorship was rare. As we just argued, this entire practice seems largely to be a Christian phenomenon. Second, Paul's letters themselves make a "courtesy argument" difficult. Philemon provides the best example. The letter address lists Paul and Timothy, but Timothy is not the only colleague with Paul at the time. The letter ends with greetings from Epaphras, Mark, Aristarchus, Demas and Luke. Why are they not in the letter address? Why was Paul courteous to Timothy but not to Luke? We must conclude Timothy was being distinguished in some way from the others, even if it is argued Timothy played only the smallest role in the composition of Philemon. It cannot be considered mere courtesy.

---

[6]According to Cic. *Att.* 11.5.1. Gordon Bahr, "Paul and Letter Writing in the First Century," *CBQ* 28 (1966): 476, is mistaken in calling this the solitary reference to the practice.

[7]C.-H. Kim, "Index of Greek Papyrus Letters," *Semeia* 22 (1981): 107-12.

[8]POxy. 118, 1158, 3064, 3094, 3313 (all third century) and 1167 (n.b. A.D. 37-41). PZen. 35 may be from two persons but the text is too fragmentary to be certain.

[9]The example from Atticus might have been analogous but we do not have his letter, only Cicero's comment: "For my part I have gathered from your letters—both that which you wrote in conjunction with others and the one you wrote in your own name" (*Att.* 11.5.1). In fact, Cicero's comment suggests Atticus's letter may fall in the more common category of "group letter to request an authority to redress a wrong."

[10]Leon Morris, *The First and Second Epistles to the Thessalonians*, NICNT (Grand Rapids: Eerdmans, 1959), p. 46. Interestingly, his subsequent exegesis leads him to concede that for 1 Thessalonians, Silvanus and Timothy had a "somewhat larger share in the letter."

[11]Morris, *Thessalonians*, p. 47.

Jerome Murphy-O'Connor states it plainly: the "we" in Paul's letters should be "taken at face value as referring to the senders."[12] When Paul lists a cosender, there is no evidence to claim this is anything other than a coauthor.[13] Yet modern commentators often presume a *we* in the text carries little or no force; they are "editorial *we*'s." While it is necessary to allow room for an editorial *we* in Paul, all *we*'s are not merely editorial.[14] As Murphy-O'Connor correctly complains, scholars usually make no distinctions between those letters Paul wrote with co-senders and those letters he wrote without them.[15] For example, Paul uses a plural thanks-giving formula only in the letters that he coauthored with Timothy.[16] The first person singular is the most common Greco-Roman thanksgiving formula and is also typical for Paul.[17] It may be coincidental, but he does not use a *we* thanksgiving in a letter without Timothy.[18] In another example, Paul cites Timothy as a coauthor of 1 Thessalonians. Most commentators agree that Timothy is joining his voice with Paul in the thanksgiving, yet further into the commentary Timothy is dropped from most of the discussion. Many commentators push Timothy's voice to the background, explaining passages as though Paul alone framed the words.[19]

To critique the "courtesy argument" from another direction we may ask why Timothy is not listed as a cosender in Paul's letter to the Romans? He sends greetings in Romans 16:21. We must conclude that Timothy's role is somehow different in Romans than in 2 Corinthians, where he is named in the letter address. We may quibble over how large a role Timothy played in 2 Corinthians, but we must still acknowledge that the role was differ-

---

[12]Murphy-O'Connor, *Paul the Letter-Writer*, p. 19. So also Witherington, *Paul Quest*, pp. 101-2; and Roller, *Formular*, p. 170.

[13]Otto Roller argued rather convincingly that the naming of another person in the letter address was not a meaningless convention (*Formular*, p. 153). So also Murphy-O'Connor, *Paul the Letter-Writer*, pp. 16-19; and Gamble, *Books and Readers*, p. 99.

[14]Paul may use *we* to refer to himself and his audience (so Witherington, *Conflict and Community in Corinth*, p. 79), but at least sometimes the *we* refers to the coauthor.

[15]Murphy-O'Connor, *Paul the Letter-Writer*, p. 16.

[16]1 Thess 1:3; 2 Thess 1:3 and Col 1:3. Second Corinthians has no thanksgiving formula, using instead a plural disclosure formula (2 Cor 1:8).

[17]See Rom 1:8; 1 Cor 1:4; Eph 1:16; Phil 1:3; 1 Tim 1:12 ; 2 Tim 1:3. I am aware of no published study comparing singular to plural thanksgiving formulae.

[18]Only Philippians and Philemon are coauthored with Timothy and use a singular formula. Yet Philemon has no *we* at all in the letter beyond the letter address. The only first-person plural (*ours* in v. 6) is universal. Paul is the "friend of the slave-owner" (*amicus domini*), interceding for Onesimus. A *we* would have been inappropriate in this legal matter between peers. Since the Philippian gift was for Paul, a singular thanksgiving is not inappropriate.

[19]E.g., Wannamaker, NIGTC (1990), p. 68; and Holmes, NIV Application (1998), p. 36. Both of these claim (without citing evidence) that listing Timothy in the address indicated he was the letter carrier. Letter carriers were not indicated in this manner; see my article, "Silvanus was not Peter's Secretary: Theological Bias in Reading 1 Pet 5:12," *JETS* 43/3 (2000): 417-32. Pushing out Timothy's voice is by no means universal. In fact, commentators have long seemed more likely to grant Timothy a collaborative voice in 1-2 Thessalonians than in any other letters (as in 1 Thess 2:18-20). See, e.g., the commentaries by Weiss, ICC (1910), p. 2; Frame, (1912), p. 68; Bruce, WBC, (1982), p. xi; Fee, NIBC (1987), p. 30. See also M. Prior, *Paul the Letter-Writer and the Second Letter to Timothy*, JSNTS 23 (Sheffield: JSOT, 1989), p. 40; and Witherington, *Conflict and Community in Corinth*, p. 79.

ent. Our modern understanding of *author* must expand beyond just "Paul alone."[20]

THE LETTER WRITER'S OFFICE

Archaeologists have provided much information not only about first-century letter writing but also about the homes and businesses of Paul's world. Where did Paul and his team write, for example, the letter to the Romans? The usual answer is Corinth, but is it possible to be more specific, since that city covered over two square miles and was encircled by a six-mile wall? Obviously, we cannot say the fourth shop on the left side of Lechaion Street, two blocks past the Temple of Apollo, but can we determine in what type of place ancients liked to do their letter writing?

The workshop. It is often suggested that Paul wrote at least some of his letters during down time in the tentmaker's shop. For example, in Corinth Paul is sometimes described as discussing the issues with his partners Aquila and Priscilla as they labored together over tents (Acts 18:1-3), but neither Aquila nor Priscilla was ever listed as the cosender of a letter. The point remains, though, that perhaps Paul wrote in a workshop.

Archaeologists have uncovered numerous ancient shops. A typical shop, such as those preserved in several cities in Asia Minor and Europe, was usually among a row of

Figure 2.1. A typical street in Pompeii

---

[20]Michael Gorman recently voiced the same concern: *authorship* must be expanded beyond a single writer to include cosenders. See Gorman, *Apostle of the Crucified Lord: A Theological Introduction to Paul and His Letters* (Grand Rapids: Eerdmans, 2004), pp. 87-89.

shops, lining both sides of a street (see figure 2.1). These shops ranged from taverns and brothels to bakeries and laundries. Some shops sold pots, others sold idols (Acts 19) and some evidently sold tents (Acts 18:3). Most shops were a fairly standard size, somewhat determined by how long a span a wooden beam could support between walls or columns. In a shop in the market of Corinth, the back wall of the shop still shows the holes where the beams were placed. In smaller towns or on side streets, buildings often had three or four floors. The bottom floor usually contained the shops, the upper floors were for apartments. In Ostia one can see the shop entrances and the stairs next door that led up to apartments (see figure 2.2). On larger, more decorative streets, the shops were spaced between the columns that ran in rows down both sides of the street. In Hierapolis, a sister-city near Laodicea and Colossae, visitors can still see the holes in the columns where wooden beams were placed to make the walls between the shops.

A standard shop seemed to be about ten feet wide. A few larger shops used two sections, as can be seen in a shop lining the colonnaded road in Pergamum, which connects the center of town with the Asklepion (a temple for the god of healing). Shop-lined streets were the major component of most towns. Modern attention often focuses on the Forum or the few large temples, but the majority of a town consisted of narrow streets lined with shops (see figure 2.3). Pompeii, a town of about 200,000, was preserved largely intact when buried suddenly in the volcanic eruption of Vesuvius in A.D. 79. Pompeii had a typical city structure. This town had forty bakeries and thirty brothels, with dozens of streets lined with shops and apartments. Occasionally, a wealthier home can be found among the shops. Most towns, particularly further east in the empire where Paul usually served, were poorer than Pompeii.

Most shops consisted of a front and back room on the first floor. The front room had a counter open to the street from which business was conducted (see figure 2.4). This room was, of course, noisy and busy, and therefore probably inappropriate for letter writing even for an ancient. The back room, usually about ten feet wide by ten feet deep, was more private, since a wall separated it from the front room and street and the windows were small and high (larger windows provided opportunities for thieves). Lighting came from these small windows and through the front room's open door (see figure 2.5). Besides being cramped, filled with supplies and likely the place where work went on (baking, sewing, cooking, etc.), this room was poorly lit. It is unlikely that Paul wrote his letters in a workshop downtown. In fact, in the case of Aquila and Priscilla, the emphasis was always on their *house* (Rom 16:3-5; 1 Cor 16:19) rather than on their workshop.

The home. Could Paul have written his letters in a home? Typically, homes did not have a study, except perhaps the estates of ultra-wealthy lawyers and rhetoricians. In most cities these wealthy estates are all archaeologists have to study. Generally, only the palatial stone and marble homes of the wealthiest survive through the ages, which explains why modern tourists see temples and theaters when they tour ancient ruins. Mud-brick, the building material of the poor, quickly erodes. For example, we know that ancient people lived in houses scattered across the countryside, but these mud-brick homes of the poor farmer have washed away.

Figure 2.2. Shops and apartments in Ostia

Figure 2.3. Shops along street in Pompeii

Figure 2.4. Shop counter at Pompeii

Figure 2.5. Pompeii shop and back room

The mud-brick homes of remote, rural regions like Galilee, however, were not the urban world of Paul. In the cities, the poor lived in *insulae,* crowded high-rise buildings (2-5 floors) of small apartments. In the Roman Empire of Paul's day, 90 percent of the free population and more than 90 percent of the slaves lived in these high-rise apartments. In Rome the percentage was closer to 97 percent of the population.[21] No examples of the lowest-class apartments have been discovered, but they are occasionally mentioned in ancient writings.[22] Vitruvius may be describing these high-rise apartments of the very poor when he argues that staircases need to be lit because there is heavy traffic in them, sometimes with those carrying burdens on their shoulders (6.6.7). Yet Paul probably did not regularly live in the apartments of the very poor.

Both Ostia (the ancient port city of Rome) and Pompeii have preserved numerous homes of the urban middle class.[23] These were also apartments. In Ostia there remain eight of the larger, more comfortable apartments of the upper-middle class. These are insightful for our understanding of Paul. We would not suggest Paul fell into this class—although he may well have—but certainly most of those who hosted him and his team fell into this class.

The oldest apartments in Ostia date to the end of the first century.[24] The most common type of apartment had a locking outside door. As we saw in figure 2.2, the stairway went up from the street. From the stairway, you enter a wide, shallow room rather like a large hallway, about twenty feet wide and five feet deep, with windows on the front side. Because this *medianum,* or middle room, gave access to all the other rooms, such apartment styles are called today the *medianum* apartment. This hallway, though, was not just the access corridor for the rooms. It also served as the kitchen and dining area. As we can see from the photo, the hallway had multiple windows, often with balconies, looking out over the street to help clear the smoke.[25] The bedrooms (*cubiculum*) were small, about nine feet by nine feet, and usually lit by one back window. The largest room, the living room (*exedra*), was about fifteen by twenty feet. The term *exedra* was often used to refer to a spacious, partially covered room, or peristyle, which was the main living room of a large Roman home (see figure 2.6). In an apartment, the living room was not open air but did have multiple windows, and hence (perhaps euphemistically) was termed a living room by apartment dwellers.

---

[21]See, e.g., John McRay, *Paul, His Life and Teaching* (Grand Rapids: Baker, 2003), p. 393.

[22]Vitruvius admits the existence of these *insulae* (2.8.17), but his interest is in the wealthier homes. The best description of these Roman apartments is found in Gustav Hermansen, *Ostia: Aspects of Roman City Life* (Edmonton: University of Alberta Press, 1981), esp. chap. 1, "The Roman Apartment." I am indebted entirely to him.

[23]It is somewhat anachronistic to refer to these as "middle class," for antiquity had little or no true middle class with spacious private homes; see Murphy-O'Connor, *Paul the Letter-Writer,* p. 149. These were the homes of the less wealthy, compared to the palatial estates of the landed aristocracy.

[24]The Casette-tipo apartments (Region III xiii 2); see Hermansen, *Ostia,* p. 25.

[25]Hermansen, *Ostia,* p. 22.

Figure 2.6. The Exedra or "living room" of the house of the tragic poet at Pompeii

Some apartments in Ostia were smaller, having one main room, serving as both the living room and the dining room/kitchen. These rooms were about 8 feet deep by 11 feet wide, with small balconies overlooking the street. Those who hosted Paul and his team probably owned apartments larger than these; however, when Paul was under house arrest in Rome, he likely rented this type of apartment.

On occasion Paul's patron probably provided a more spacious house. In Pompeii, there is an excellent example of a moderately wealthy home, the "home of the tragic poet." Wealthier Roman houses were built in a rectangular format. All the outer walls were solid, without windows, for security reasons. The rooms encircled a large open-air atrium, as we saw in the "house of the tragic poet" in Pompeii (figure 2.6). The atrium, with its adjacent dining room (the triclinium), was the public area of a villa. In the case of a larger villa, these two rooms together could accommodate up to fifty people.[26] It is quite reasonable to assume that a successful merchant like Lydia owned a home of comparable size and layout. The open-air atrium, with its adjoining room, made a very pleasant place. Luke mentions Lydia and others as "of high standing" (Acts 16:14; 17:12). Luke probably noted these because they are above the norm for the team's benefactors. If Paul stayed in a villa, he would have found the courtyard in such

---

[26]For this reason, many scholars estimate that the early churches of Paul probably each consisted of about 40-50 members.

homes inviting. This may explain why Paul seemed to prefer Philippi to Troas (Acts 20:4-5). It may have been a choice between the villa of Lydia (Acts 16:15) and an apartment in Troas (Acts 20:6-8).

How does this brief depiction of ancient architecture relate to letter writing? We should observe several characteristics about these homes. Vitruvius (6.5.1) mentions bedrooms as the room where privacy was respected, while rooms like the living room were public.[27] It is unlikely that Paul retreated to a bedroom to write, since they were smaller and poorly lit. The living room was the largest and best-lit space in an apartment. This room was the main area for all occupants of the apartment. If there was a dinner with guests, the meal was eaten here. Whether Paul wrote in an urban apartment or a larger villa, this living room is the natural choice. It was well suited for writing, with good lighting and ventilation as well as places to sit. There was, however, no privacy, since it was a public room.

While traveling. Paul's letters most likely were written in a home where he and the other team members were staying. We should not, though, restrict Paul only to writing while settled in a home. When reconstructing the life of Paul, scholars usually posit as a location for writing only those places where Paul was settled for at least a few months. For example, Paul wrote Romans on his third missionary journey, and it is usually suggested he wrote the letter while in Corinth because he was there for three months.[28]

We have, however, stories of writers composing while traveling.[29] Plutarch mentions that Julius Caesar wrote while being carried about in a carriage or litter.[30] Obviously, this is merely boasting of the skills of Caesar; even the wealthy appeared to consider letters composed in a litter to be less serious works.[31] On one occasion, Cicero was traveling and needed to compose a serious letter to his brother, so he arose before dawn to write it, rather than do so in a litter.[32] In any event, this luxury extended only to the wealthy who were carried about,[33] an option certainly not available to Paul.

Cicero also wrote while aboard ship, including one instance when he had no secre-

---

[27]Hermansen, *Ostia*, pp. 19-22. The poor of old Rome, the *humiliores*, had to share such apartments. They were unable to light a brazier and cook in their private quarters (the bedroom) because they would be choked with smoke. All cooked and dined in the *medianum*. Hence, several old Latin translations of Mk 14:15 describe Jesus sending his disciples to find a *medianum* where they can eat Passover.

[28]Second Corinthians is usually the only letter suggested as composed while traveling (from Ephesus to Corinth); yet we usually suggest he wrote it during an extended stay in Philippi or Thessalonica.

[29]Pliny *Epp.* 9.36; 3.5 (speaking of the Elder's literary habits); Cic. *Att.* 5.17.1.

[30]Plut. *Caes.* 17.4-5.

[31]Pliny *Ep.* 9.10. Pliny calls one such letter a "few trifles . . . written with the same negligence and inattention that one usually chats upon the road." This actual letter is more than a "trifle," but Pliny's rhetorical "excuse" demonstrates the point.

[32]Cic. *QFr.* 2.5.5.

[33]Like his nephew, Pliny the Elder similarly composed while traveling in his chariot, with a reader and a "shorthand writer" by his side; Pliny *Ep.* 3.5.

tarial help and had to write the letter personally.[34] The letter had no critical information; it could have waited until landfall. Apparently Cicero used the leisure time aboard ship to write.[35] We should not exclude such a possibility for Paul. Writing aboard ship or during a brief stay on a journey are not as unlikely as sometimes implied.

Since we have examples of Pliny the Younger dictating notes while out hunting, in a litter traveling on the road, aboard ship[36] and dining with friends, should we open the matter and say letters were commonly written "on the fly"? No. The stories of Pliny (and others) writing in these locations were told to amaze listeners at the exceptional skill of the writer. They do not indicate a standard practice among writers, but are meant to make us marvel at how diligent he was in his studies that he even studied while out hunting.[37] Cicero composed a letter at the dinner table[38] to display his rhetorical skills in front of his dinner guests. We should not conclude these demonstrate a preferred custom.

Nonetheless, it would be an error to eliminate any opportunity for writing during a journey. Cicero wrote a brief letter during an overnight stop on a journey. Since Paul's financial means were considerably less than Cicero's, it is unlikely that Paul rented spacious lodging for brief stops.[39] Since modest roadside inns were cramped (and of questionable reputation), it is unlikely Paul wrote a letter during a one-night stop on the road. We will still maintain that some writing occurred while Paul traveled; opportunities like a stop of a few days provided time to continue working on a draft of a letter or sermon.

Outside. Most of us assume Paul wrote indoors. I have never seen suggestions otherwise. However, let us observe Hippocrates paying Democritus a visit:

> Democritus himself was sitting alone on a stone seat under a low spreading plane tree, wearing a coarse tunic, barefoot, very pale and thin, and with his beard untrimmed. . . . He was holding a book very carefully on his knees, with others lying around on both sides of him. There was also a large pile of animal bodies, completely dissected.[40]

---

[34]Cic. *Att.* 5.12. He excuses the less polished nature of the letter by concluding "I will write a longer letter when I am on dry land. At present I am far out at sea." We can deduce that Cicero had no secretarial help because he mentioned in this letter that he had been forced to leave his secretary, Tiro, behind in Athens because Tiro was ill. Inclement weather had insured Tiro's continued absence.

[35]Pliny also cited the leisure time provided by travel as giving opportunity to write; Pliny *Ep.* 3.5.

[36]Cicero wrote at sea (Cic. *Fam.* 14.7.2; *Att.* 5.12).

[37]Pliny *Ep.* 1.6: "However, I indulged at the same time my beloved inactivity, and whilst I sat at my nets, you would have found me, not with spear and dart, but pen and tablet by my side. I mused and wrote, being resolved if I returned with my hands empty, at least to come home with my pocket-book full." Pliny is, of course, emulating his much admired uncle who wrote in the midst of other activities. His uncle even wrote while in the "bath," stopping only during the time he was actually in the water! Pliny *Ep.* 3.5: "for all the while he was rubbed and wiped, he was employed either in hearing some book read to him, or in dictating himself."

[38]E.g., Cic. *QFr.* 3.1.9; *Att.* 14.21.4; 15.13.5; 27.3.

[39]Ben Witherington maintains that Paul stayed in government inns (*New Testament History: A Narrative Account* [Grand Rapids: Baker, 2001], pp. 314-26).

[40]Hippocrates to Damagetus 17.2.

Democritus is described as writing outside.[41] He was dissecting animals to discover their balance of bile as an explanation of madness. Perhaps he was writing outside because he was dissecting animals as part of his research. Yet we have other ancient examples of writing outdoors. Pliny the Younger wrote while sitting "at the nets" on a hunt (*Ep.* 1.6). Pliny the Elder wrote while sunning himself (*Ep.* 3.5). While temporarily held captive by pirates, Julius Caesar wrote poems and sundry speeches as he sat on the deck of a ship (Plut. *Caes.* 1.2).

Why do we neglect the outdoors as a good place to write? Because writing outdoors is not our custom. With modern conveniences such as lighting and temperature controls, writing indoors is much to be preferred. In antiquity, if the weather were pleasant, outdoors was actually more conducive to writing: the lighting was vastly superior and the room was not smoky. At least it is clear that ancient writers felt less restricted to an indoor "study" than do modern writers.

It is also common to imagine Paul writing in the evenings, "after a full day's toil"; yet for an ancient, evenings were the worst time to write because of the particularly poor lighting. Furthermore, Paul's letters were not his leisure activity after work, but were part of his work, perhaps his primary work. Pliny the Elder commonly wrote during repose after lunch. Democritus is pictured as writing under a shade tree. Taking afternoon time to write was a luxury unavailable to the poor, but it was available to Paul. We should not preclude the possibility that Paul paused after lunch to rest in the shade or on a courtyard bench in order to write. Writing materials were compact, light and easy to carry (a writer's palette was about the size of a student's pencil box today), as was a roll of papyrus. For these reasons writers kept their supplies with them.

Though the writing habits of Pliny and other wealthy Romans are helpful as we discuss where Paul may have written, perhaps a better parallel is the experience of Ignatius, a church leader around A.D. 120. On his journey to Rome for certain martyrdom, Ignatius wrote letters to various churches.[42] It was a leisurely journey—Rome was not pressing the aged bishop—but the stops along the way were never extended, probably no more than a few days or weeks. In the midst of these travels, Ignatius was able to write multiple letters with a length and complexity similar to Paul's. We must, therefore, allow the possibility of Paul writing during stops on a journey and not limit the options to those times when he stayed for months in one location. Even during rest stops on a journey, we should not exclude the possibility that Paul found a cool seat under a shady tree and worked on a draft of a letter.

---

[41]This is, of course, a fictional letter, a philosophic letter, dating before or in the first century. These letters reflect the customs at the time of their actual writing and not those of the "supposed" time of writing. Thus, these letters tell us about first-century writing practices and *not* those at the time of Hippocrates. These have recently been made more accessible in both Greek and English translation (on opposing pages) in a helpful little book: C. D. N. Costa, *Greek Fictional Letters: A Selection with Introduction, Translation and Commentary* (Oxford: Oxford University Press, 2001).

[42]According to Eusebius *Historia ecclesiastica* 3.36.3-10.

Conclusions for Paul as a Letter Writer

For the most part, Paul was the guest of a host. On some occasions, that host was wealthy and probably provided Paul and his team room in a villa. I suspect this of Lydia. The option to spend Passover as a guest in a more spacious villa may have been a factor in Paul's decision to remain in Philippi (at Lydia's home) when the remainder of his team pressed on to Troas (Acts 20:4-5). Aside from the occasional villa, I assume Paul stayed in apartments and that these apartments were larger, since someone volunteering to host Paul was likely to have been wealthier.[43] I picture Paul sitting in the living room of an apartment (or occasionally in the spacious atrium of a Roman villa), the noise of the street below filtering through the many windows of the room. With Paul may be a team member who joins in the writing of the letter. A secretary is nearby.

We have seen that ancient letter writers wrote in places we might not have considered. Paul and his team most likely wrote in the living room of the home in which he was staying, but he may have done some writing at the synagogue (when he was welcome there), aboard ship and even outdoors in afternoon rest breaks. They were constantly preparing notes and polishing drafts of material. Preaching and debating in the synagogues and marketplaces provided Paul and his team constant opportunity and motivation to rework material. Many of his basic arguments took shape in the crucible of this mission work. Sometimes a messenger arrived with problems and questions from another church, and these specific questions and issues caused new insights as he and his team sought to provide answers.

Friends stopped by and heard the material, making comments and suggestions. Sometimes their comments and suggestions precipitated changes. Small discourses on topics and other snippets of material were written in the notebooks for future use.[44] There were other opportunities to try the material. In the culture of Paul's day, philosophers commonly traveled from town to town sharing their particular views. A wealthier member of the town commonly invited the traveling teacher to stay in his or her home. In Greco-Roman culture, dinner parties were also very important. As part of the evening meals, dinner guests wanted to hear any material that the host had written or received. In fact, if the host was providing hospitality to a traveling teacher, it was somewhat assumed that the teacher would share material with his host's dinner guests; the guest teacher was providing "entertainment" during the meal by reciting or reading something he had written. Paul no doubt used evening meals as opportunities to teach those present, probably using materials from his notes. The resulting discussion would prompt revision and clarification of what had been written.

Paul's letters to the Thessalonians, Corinthians and Romans were likely written in the

---

[43]See, e.g., Acts 16:14-15; 17:5-9; 18:7-8; Rom 16:23; 1 Cor 16:19.

[44]Memorized fixed little discourses on certain topics (*topoi*) were common in Greco-Roman philosophical preaching and Christian examples have been identified in the letters of Paul; see Bradley, "*Topos*," p. 240.

living room of his host's larger apartment or villa. Several of Paul's letters were written "from prison," the so-called Prison Epistles of Ephesians, Colossians, Philemon and Philippians. Luke tells us those two years of prison in Rome were at his own expense (Acts 28:30), which most likely means Paul rented a smaller middle-class apartment. First Timothy and Titus appear to have been written while Paul was under greater haste to travel, perhaps even running from the authorities. These two letters are better candidates for composition on the road and during short stays. We should expect some variations in these letters from those written at greater leisure, but of this we cannot be sure. According to tradition, 2 Timothy was written from an actual prison, such as the Mamertine Prison in Rome: a slimy, circular cell carved in rock with a low ceiling. Prisoners were dropped in through a hole in the ceiling. It would not have been possible to write in this dark, dank hole in the ground. Paul's secretary must have remained outside, up one level and more than twenty feet away. This does not require that the writing style be different or that Paul grant the secretary greater freedom; Paul and his secretary could have talked in loud voices. Nonetheless, the logistics of the situation were considerably different from previous letters.

I conclude that, when Paul was a guest in someone's home, he had access to a comfortable workspace and probably a good secretary. I assume the same for the Prison Epistles. The two pastoral letters written while traveling hastily, 1 Timothy and Titus, probably were written under less comfortable work conditions, although the larger problem would have been finding a competent secretary. For those letters we might expect Paul to incorporate more preformed (pre-written) material (discussed in chapters six and seven) and less spontaneous composition. Paul's final letter, 2 Timothy, was written in miserable conditions, but most likely with a good secretary. I suspect a good secretary in a poor situation was better than a poor secretary in a good situation.

3

THE TOOLS OF A LETTER WRITER

Since Paul probably carried his supplies with him, it is appropriate to describe briefly what ancients used to write their letters. Although the quality of materials has improved, it is remarkable that letter writing had changed very little over two thousand years. Until the recent advent of typewriters and computers, letters remained for millennia the work of pen and paper.

WRITING MATERIALS

Pen and ink. In the first century, ink was somewhat standardized. There were two types: red ink and black ink. Red ink was prepared by mixing ochre with gelatin, gum and bee wax. Black ink was prepared from lamp black or ground charcoal mixed with gum arabic, which produced a fairly serviceable, fade-resistant ink. Most writers used black ink because it was cheap and easy to make. Its one major weakness, however, was that it was not waterproof. While this did make it possible to wash a document off and reuse it, writing could also be lost accidentally. Cicero bemoaned the loss of some letters because the carrier had carelessly allowed the letters to become soaked with water. The paper survived, but the letters were "lost" because the ink had washed off.[1] For this reason valuable scrolls were kept in waxed leather cases.

Ancient writers also had a cheap source of pens. The pen most often used was a small reed (from the Juncus Maritimus plant that grows on the banks of the Nile), cut about 8-10 inches long. One end of the reed was cut to make a point. The point was cut with a small split (see figure 3.1). The result was like the quill pen of yesteryear or the metal nib (fountain) pen of today. The technology is the same, only the quality of material has improved. Each improvement allowed the writer to draw a finer line.[2]

Tablets. Ancients wrote on a variety of materials. For sending a quick note, they often wrote on shards of broken pots. Such notes were called *ostraca*. For quick notes or receipts to be given to another, it was also common to write on the back of an old document. For a temporary note there was also another method. Clay tablets of an older age had been

---

[1] Cic. *QFr.* 2.12.4.
[2] Many artists today will dispute the idea of improvement. The reed pen remains popular with some artists because it has attributes that are lost when a quill or metal nib is used.

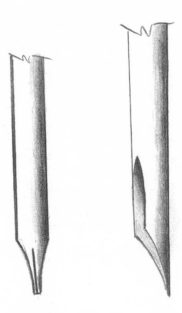

Figure 3.1. Drawing of a reed pen (Larry Thompson)

replaced with wooden tablets. Thin sheets of wood were incised to create a recessed middle with a thin border rim. The recessed middle could be written on directly with ink or, more commonly, was filled with a thin layer of wax (see figure 3.2). The raised rim protected the wax when the tablets were stacked. These wax tablets were commonly used for temporary notes since the wax was easily smoothed and reused.

Parchment. For dispatched letters during the time of Paul, there were two major options for "paper": parchment and papyrus. Parchment sheets were made of leather, usually the hide of a calf, goat or sheep. The hide was soaked in lime then the outside of the hide was scraped to remove the hair, etc. and the inside was scraped to remove the flesh. Next, the skin was stretched on a frame to dry. The dried skin was smoothed and thinned by rubbing it with a stone, such as pumice, and whitened by rubbing it with chalk. Finally, it was trimmed into sheets. These sheets, if properly done, were tough but light and flexible.

The two sides of the sheet were not the same. The original hair side was darker and rougher. Ancients considered it not as good for writing, although it did absorb the ink better. The inner side was smoother and lighter in color and was the preferred side for writing. Technically, this side is called the "recto" (Latin, *rectus*), because you are writing "on the proper" side. The other side is appropriately called the "verso" (Latin, *versus*) because you have "turned over" the sheet.[3]

---

[3]Many papyrologists (experts on papyri) now prefer "hairside" and "fleshside" when discussing parchment.

Figure 3.2. Drawing of wax tablets (Larry Thompson)

The sheets were sewn together with vegetable or animal fibers to make a longer strip that was rolled up, what is today commonly called a scroll.[4] These seams were strong but not smooth, so one did not write across a seam. Parchment endured rough handling and lasted longer than papyrus, its competitor; however, it was probably more expensive[5] and more difficult to write upon. Often modern writers will regale the superiority of parchment over papyrus; yet the greatest advantage of parchment was its ability to survive for hundreds, even thousands, of years. This was not a major consideration for the typical first-century letter writer. Letter writers in Paul's day probably preferred papyrus.[6]

Papyrus. Papyrus reeds grew in abundance along the banks of the Nile. Reeds grow five to fifteen feet tall. The reed is about as thick as a man's wrist. A cross-section would be tri-

---

[4]Technically, the noun is *roll* and the verb is *scroll*. Thus, one would scroll up a roll. However, in modern vernacular the terms are often reversed. The rolled up strip is commonly termed a scroll, so we now roll a scroll, much to the dismay of the English purists among us. In practice, the terms are often interchanged (as they are in this book), but context always keeps the meaning clear.

[5]This is actually only conjecture. Theoretically papyrus should be considerably cheaper; yet Egypt did have the market monopolized. There is not enough ancient data to be certain that parchment truly was more expensive. See the extended discussion in R. R. Johnson, "The Role of Parchment in Graeco-Roman Antiquity" (unpublished dissertation, University of California, 1968), pp. 113-18. Since parchment also came in various qualities and the price of papyrus fluctuated, we cannot be sure; so also the conclusion of Gamble, *Books and Readers,* p. 46.

[6]So Gamble, *Books and Readers,* 45.

angular in shape and fill a man's palm. To make papyrus paper, the reeds were cut into sections about as long as a man's forearm. The husk was removed and the inner pith sliced lengthwise in thin, tape-like strips about two to three fingers wide.[7] These strips were laid side by side on a pattern board. Another layer of strips was placed on top of these at a right angle. These mushy, pithy strips were then pressed or beaten until the juice ran out. This removed most of the temptation for bugs to eat the paper. It also broke down the cellular structure of the reed. The remaining cellulose effectively glued the strips together into a sheet.[8] The dried sheet was then smoothed in a similar manner as parchment (with pumice) and polished with shell. The sheet was trimmed to a standard size (see figure 3.3). Although different "factories" made different size sheets, the somewhat standard size was roughly 8 by 10 inches, a little smaller than a modern sheet of paper. On one side of the sheet the strips ran horizontally (the recto), on the other side the strips ran vertically (the verso).

Papyrus was more easily damaged, especially by water. We have a wonderful contrast provided by an archaeological find at Wadi Murabba'at in the Judean wilderness that

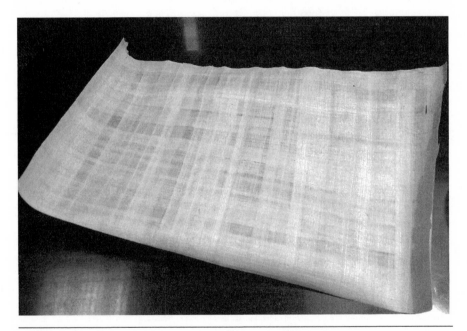

Figure 3.3. A sheet of papyrus

---

[7]Gamble, *Books and Readers*, p. 44, notes recent experiments may suggest an alternative procedure, but the process described above is still the more likely.

[8]The elder Pliny (*Nat. Hist.* 13.77) mistakenly claimed it was the Nile water that glued the strips into sheets. The best discussion of how papyrus was made remains Naphtali Lewis, *Papyrus in Classical Antiquity* (Oxford: Clarendon, 1974). An excellent brief description is found in Gamble, *Books and Readers*, pp. 44-45.

dates to about the time of Paul.[9] Letters, which were often individual sheets of papyrus, were commonly carried in a pouch. A soldier had taken a discarded parchment letter, cut it in half and sewed the two halves together to form a crude parchment pouch in which he stored his more fragile papyrus letters.[10]

Rolls. Papyrus was not normally sold in individual sheets. Like parchment, sheets were pasted together to make a scroll. The sheets were turned so the recto faced up, taller than wider. The sheets were glued one after another by overlapping the sheets by a finger or two. The joints were also thinned and polished. The result was that, unlike parchment, you could write across the seams. The edge of the next sheet was placed under the edge of the previous sheet so that, when writing, your pen would slide "downhill" onto the next sheet. The strip was then rolled up. The horizontal fibers were inside and the vertical fibers were on the outside, making the rolling process easier.

Rolls of either parchment or papyrus could be made any length, but a roll of twenty sheets (about twelve feet) seems to have been the standard at the time of Paul. This standard roll, or *chartes*, was the usual unit of sale. The *chartes* was not, however, the standard length for a published book. (During Paul's day, published books were always in scroll form.) The Isaiah Scroll, a copy of the book of Isaiah found among the Dead Sea Scrolls, dating to roughly the time of Paul, is 10 inches by 24 feet, about double the length of a *chartes*. Theoretically, scrolls could be continuously lengthened, but ancients had discovered that scrolls over 30 feet became too cumbersome to handle. For example, Luke-Acts was probably two volumes because each book filled a long scroll.

It is difficult to estimate the cost of papyrus. Egypt had a monopoly on the market and the price did fluctuate. Our best evidence sets the price of a *chartes*, purchased in Egypt at the time of Paul, at about four drachma. Often scholars note that "the purchase of papyrus is not likely to have been regarded as an expenditure of any consequence."[11] We must consider two factors:

1. Presumably the cost of papyrus was higher outside Egypt.

2. An unskilled laborer at the time of Paul typically made about a half drachma per day. A skilled laborer made twice that.[12]

---

[9] PMur. 164.

[10] So the editors conclude; P. Benoit et al., *Les grottes de Murabba'at,* DJD 2 (Oxford: Oxford University Press, 1961), pp. 275-79.

[11] So Lewis, *Papyrus in Classical Antiquity,* p. 134.

[12] See Harris, *Ancient Literacy,* p. 195; and Alan Millard, *Reading and Writing in the Time of Jesus* (Sheffield: Sheffield Academic Press, 2000), p. 165. At the time of Paul, the exchange rate was about four drachma to three denars. It is not clear, however, how this affected wages between the two halves of the empire. Jesus gave a rate of one denar per day (Mt 20:2). Although it is common, we should not use Jesus' figure to set routine wages in Palestine for several reasons: (a) Jesus' parables often used unrealistic amounts (e.g., Mt 18:24); (b) Jesus may have intended, by suggesting a generous salary, to insure the owner was seen as "fair" by all his hearers; and (c) it is quite likely that day laborers during the crush of harvest season commanded a higher wage than normal, since they were in short supply (as the parable implies).

The question becomes what to do with this data. Converting currencies is largely a useless endeavor because, for example, ten dollars in Indonesia has a vastly different buying power than ten dollars in Texas. However, using a worker's wage for one full day can be a helpful comparison because this also varies by country and reflects buying power. If a *chartes* cost four drachma, then it cost about eight days' wages (for an unskilled worker). Although it is indeed a rough estimate, in 2004 an unskilled laborer in a rural area (like Arkansas, where I live) makes about $8 per hour or about $60 for a full (ancient) day's (7-8 hours) work. A *chartes* would cost today, then, about $500. Whether this constitutes "an expenditure of any consequence" is still relative. Although it can be questioned how helpful such a comparison is, it does provide us with at least an emotional sense of the cost of papyrus. (The estimated cost of each of Paul's letters will be discussed in chapter ten.)

However, estimating the cost of a letter also has to include the cost of the labor as well. One of the few pieces of evidence from the time of Paul tells of a man paying two drachma (in Egypt) for a copy of a letter. Alan Millard insists this price was too high and implies there must have been additional reasons why it was so expensive.[13] It is not clear this was an exorbitant cost; the letter writer did not mention the cost as particularly high. Using our "worker's conversion rate," this copy cost about $250. Even if this was an unusually high price, we can safely conclude that letter writing was not the trivial expense it is today. Millard estimated a copy of Isaiah to cost in Paul's day as little as ten denars. He then concludes that, "While this is not cheap, it would not put books out of the reach of the reasonably well-to-do."[14] This estimate is probably too low; nevertheless, even at ten denars, the copy still cost about $1200 in today's currency. We must be careful not to imply that ancient letter writing was a negligible expense.

Most ancient letters were very brief and were written on a single sheet of papyrus. A customer bought a sheet from a papyrus vendor in the market, who cut a sheet off of a roll. One could also purchase an entire roll and cut sheets as needed. A longer letter was written on the roll, not on a series of individual sheets. If you were writing a long letter or a book and ran out of room, you could have a few more sheets glued onto the end. If you finished a letter and had extra room at the end, the extra sheets were cut off and used elsewhere. The typical papyrus letter consisted of one or two sheets. Paul's letters were not typical length. We think of Philemon as a very short letter, but in actuality, it was a fairly typical letter in length, perhaps even a trifle long. Imagine the church's surprise when Paul's letter to the Romans arrived!

---

[13]Millard, *Reading and Writing*, pp. 164-65. He suggests perhaps it was an official communication or was difficult to acquire.
[14]Ibid., p. 165.

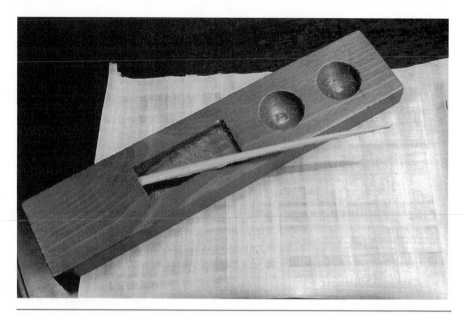

Figure 3.4. A writer's palette with recesses for black and red ink

DESKS

Once our first-century letter writer gathered paper and pen in the spot where he was choosing to write, what did he use for a desk?[15] To return to the account of Hippocrates, he interrupted Democritus who was in the process of writing, with his scroll perched upon his knees.[16] This might seem odd, since tables were already in use in Paul's day for eating and other purposes. "Did not the ancient scribe instinctively recognize from the very beginning the convenience of writing on a table?"[17] Oddly enough, the evidence is to the contrary. Art, archaeological finds and literary references all indicate that ancient scribes wrote without desks.[18]

When a scribe was making a brief note on a wax tablet or a sheet of papyrus or parch-

---

[15]The use of the masculine pronoun is intended to be gender-inclusive; however, all known ancient professional scribes were men. The ruins of Pompeii revealed a wall painting, now known as "Stapho," showing a young woman holding a tablet and stylus. The portrait was no doubt to indicate her literacy and not to imply she was a professional scribe.

[16]Hippocrates to Damagetus 17.2: "He was holding a book very carefully on his knees."

[17]Bruce Metzger begins his still classic discussion of ancient desks by positing this rhetorical question as the place where most of us begin. His article still remains the best discussion of this topic; "When Did Scribes Begin to Use Writing Desks?" in *Historical and Literary Studies: Pagan, Jewish, and Christian* (Grand Rapids: Eerdmans, 1968), p. 123.

[18]A possible lap desk from Egypt in the Chicago Museum of Antiquities appears to be one of the many innovations of Akhenaton that did not catch on.

ment, he merely stood and wrote, holding the "paper" and his palette in his left hand. To correct a mistake while the ink was still wet, a scribe kept a wet rag tied with a string to his waist (or often just a little spit on the end of his finger). A mistake or change was thus "wiped out" with water. This is probably the idea behind Genesis 6:7, where God "wipes out" humanity from the earth using the flood (water). Again, in Exodus 32:32-33, God "wipes out" from his book those who sin against him.[19]

For writing more than a short note the scribe would sit, occasionally on the ground but more commonly on a bench or stool. He then stretched his tunic between his knees to form a semi-firm writing surface[20] and placed the scroll (or tablet or notebook) upon his knees, which were sometimes raised by placing his feet on a footstool. His writer's palette (see figure 3.4) was placed nearby or held in his left hand.

The earliest clear evidence for the use of a writing desk is a fourth-century engraving from Ostia, where Jesus(?) is shown speaking, while the four Evangelists are listening, and two seated scribes are recording what was spoken by Jesus on tablets placed upon low desks.[21] There are other pieces of evidence which indicate the use of desks by scribes in the fourth century and later.[22] The one piece of evidence used to argue that first-century writers used desks is the table discovered in 1953 in one of the rooms of the Dead Sea Scroll Community at Qumran. This table likely dates around the time of Paul. It was initially identified as a writing table because it was in a room archaeologists had labeled the Scriptorium (a room for copying manuscripts) because two portable inkwells had been found scattered among the debris. This is significant for it would place writing desks back into the time and culture of Paul.

Very quickly, however, the identification of the table as a writing desk was disputed. The table is oddly shaped: 16 feet long, a little over a foot wide and a foot and a half tall. Within five years, experts were saying this table was too strangely shaped to be a writing desk. It was too low and the attached bench was too low and too far a reach from the table. Metzger initially suggested the "table" was actually a bench where scribes sat and the "bench" was actually the footrest.[23] He later modified that position arguing the "table" was not even appropriate for that use.[24] This table or bench is still being discussed. At most we could conclude that some professional scriptoria (book copying factories) might have used desks.[25] This still would not be

---

[19]The Hebrew verb *machah* is used consistently for scribal corrections. See Menahem Haran, "Book-Scrolls in Israel in Pre-Exilic Times," *JJS* 33 (1982): 163.

[20]For archaeological evidence indicating these conclusions, see Metzger, "Desks," pp. 123-25.

[21]The identity of the characters in this famous engraving is naturally disputed, but not the use of desks by the scribes.

[22]Metzger, "Desks," pp. 133-34.

[23]Metzger, "The Furniture of the Scriptorium at Qumran," *RQ* 1 (1958-1959): 509-15.

[24]Metzger, "Desks," p. 136.

[25]Charlesworth concludes that Qumran became "a center of religious activity that included making leather for scrolls and copying scrolls." James Charlesworth, *The Pesharim and Qumran History: Chaos or Consensus?* (Grand Rapids: Eerdmans, 2002), p. 61. See his photos of the Scriptorium (p. 69) and "plastered benches" in the Scriptorium (p. 71).

relevant to Paul.[26] For an ancient letter writer the actual writing upon a sheet was done while seated, with the sheet on one's lap. As one scribe quipped, good writing involved the cooperation of right hand, pen *and knee*.[27]

Once Paul was seated in a (somewhat public) place of his choosing, with team members around him, pen and paper at hand, how did an actual letter result? Many modern letter writers often just pick up the pen and begin writing. For ancient letter writers, we must also address the issue of notes and rough drafts.

NOTES AND NOTEBOOKS

In Greco-Roman times, notes were traditionally taken on tablets (*codicilli*) of wood, but sometimes ivory. The notes were scraped in the wax by a stylus.[28] Writers also wrote directly on the tablets with ink, which could be washed off when finished. Tablets were also called *tabellae* or *pugillares* ("hand notebooks"), and came in various sizes of two, three, five, or more tablets[29] tied into a codex form. (A codex is the technical name for a form like our modern book; that is, a stack of pages sewn on one edge.) In addition to using tablets to dash off a quick note,[30] they were also used for recording notes to be used later and for preparing a rough draft of a letter to be rewritten later on papyrus or parchment.

Each of these uses has implications for letter writing. First, tablets were used for keeping notes. Evidently ancient writers used these "notebooks" to keep notes for two similar purposes:

1. to record notes from another speaker, much as students today make notes during lectures; and

2. to keep personal notes and extracts from other works they are reading.

Thus, Xenophon writes to the Friends of Socrates that he has notes from his time with

---

[26]If ancients did not think to use desks in Paul's day, then why did they later begin to use them? Metzger ("Desks," pp. 132-33) suggests two reasons. First, the vocation of scribe became more honorable after the legalization of Christianity. Originally, scribes were usually slaves. The comfort and convenience of slaves were not normally considered. Second, with the legalization of Christianity, deluxe copies of Scripture became more common. These were larger and perhaps too cumbersome for the lap.

[27]A scribal colophon in a copy of the *Iliad*, dated third century (emphasis mine). For this colophon, see T. C. Skeat, "The Use of Dictation in Ancient Book-Production," *Proceedings of the British Academy* 42 (1956): 138.

[28]Hence, Latin used the verb *exarare* ("to plough") for writing on a tablet.

[29]Duplices (*diptycha*), tripices, quinquiplices, or multiplices; see Cic. *Att.* 13.8, and Tyrrell and Purser, *Cicero*, 1:55.

[30]Retina sent by *codicilli* (a tablet) a note to Pliny the Elder that Vesuvius had just erupted (Pliny *Ep.* 6.16.8). The note was written and dispatched fast enough for Pliny to receive the message and to travel close enough to die in the ash fall. Acidinus informs Servius Sulpicius by *codicilli* that Marcellus was dead (Cic. *Fam.* 4.12.2). Cicero (*Fam.* 6.18.2) sent Balbus *codicilli* when he requested some quick information about a law. When Atticus requested a reply as soon as possible, Cicero dashed it on a tablet (Cic. *Att.* 12.7). When Cicero's brother dashed off a note in passion, Cicero chides him for not pausing to consider his language (Cic. *QFr.* 2.11.1).

Socrates.[31] The discourses of Epictetus come to us from the notes of his disciple, Arrian.[32] Ancients took notes more often than is commonly thought and they usually did so on tablets (or notebooks).[33]

When an ancient writer read an interesting passage in a work, he often copied that passage into a notebook for later use. In discussing the writings of Plutarch, W. W. Tarn remarks, "Greeks compiled endless *hypomnemata,* collections of snippets on any and every subject."[34] The Elder Pliny kept notebooks of extracts to use in other works. The younger Pliny describes his uncle at work, with a slave by his side to hold a book from which to read and tablets (*pugillares*) on which to take down anything the Elder wished to be extracted or noted.[35] Probably early Christian preachers, including Paul, kept notebooks with relevant Old Testament passages for use in their preaching and teaching.

Tablets were used for keeping notes. They were also commonly used for preparing a rough draft of a letter.[36] Cicero began a letter by noting, "[I] am jotting down a copy of this letter in my note-book." He then had a secretary (*librarius*) make a copy on *chartae* for dispatching.[37] Other ancient writers give us examples as well of first composing on a tablet, with the finished letter being written later on papyrus.[38] This was certainly more likely for a letter intended for public reading, such as the letters of Paul (Col 4:16).

Our literary evidence, like the comments by ancient letter writers, is unfortunately limited to the extreme upper class. Is there any evidence that letter writers other than the aristocratic elite used tablets for rough drafts? We would not expect to find any actual tablets. They rot too quickly, and the wax disappears. However, archaeologists have once again helped in our quest. Sets of tablets from the Roman era were uncovered near the English-Scottish border.[39] The moist climate of Britain—the bane of papyrus—has preserved these

---

[31]Ps-Socr. *Ep.* 18. This is of course a forgery, and more contemporaneous to Paul. For the forger to describe himself as writing down memoirs (*apomnemoneumata*) of Socrates indicates such practices were not unknown.

[32]How accurate the notes are may be disputed, but nonetheless ancients did not dispute the idea of Arrian taking notes of his teacher's lectures. See Epictetus, *The Discourses as Reported by Arrian [Epicteti Dissertationes], the Manual, and Fragments,* ed. and trans. W. A. Oldfather, 2 vols., LCL (Cambridge, Mass.: Harvard University Press, 1925-1928).

[33]During the political intrigues of Rome, Cicero in a quip about Pompey comments, "But if it is true that our friend has in his notebook as many pages of names of future consuls as of past"; Cic. *Att.* 4.8a (Autumn 56 B.C.).

[34]W. W. Tarn, *Alexander the Great. II: Sources and Studies* (Cambridge: Cambridge University Press, 1948), p. 307.

[35]Pliny *Ep.* 3.5.15-16.

[36]So, e.g., R. Tyrrell and L. Purser, *The Correspondence of M. Tullius Cicero,* 7 vols., 3rd ed. (London: Longmans, Green & Co., 1901-1933), 2:124 n. 1.

[37]Ibid. 4:419.

[38]Pliny *Ep.* 1.6: ". . . whilst I sat at my nets, you would have found me, not with spear and dart, but with pen and tablet by my side," and Plut. *Caes.* 1.2.

[39]Paul Berry, *Roman Handwriting at the Time of Christ,* Studies in Classics 15 (Lewiston, N.Y.: Edwin Mellen Press, 2001), pp. 18-21. The tablets are now available in Alan Bowman and David Thomas, *The Vindolanda Writing Tablets* (London: British Museum Publication, 1995).

tablets. These are Latin notes belonging to a Roman centurion. None of the tablets is a complete letter.[40] The contents suggest these notes were the bare bones of a letter, taken down by a secretary.[41] The secretary then presumably fleshed out the letter by adding the epistolary structure, greetings and other stereotypical features of a standard Greco-Roman letter. The finished letter presumably was written on papyrus and sent, and the centurion kept the tablet as his record of the letter. Therefore these particular tablets seem to represent an earlier stage of the letter-writing process, something we have not had previously.

By the time of Paul, notebooks made of parchment (very similar to our modern book) were beginning to replace the traditional wooden tablet. Parchment, when prepared appropriately, was easily washed off and reused. Parchment notebooks also were lighter, easier to handle and could hold more "pages" than sets of wooden tablets. Colin Roberts and T. C. Skeat demonstrate conclusively the existence in Paul's time of parchment notebooks, *membranae,* used for much the same purposes as the wooden tablets.[42] Thus a writer could own scrolls and *membranae,* books and notebooks. The notebooks usually contained unpublished notes.[43] Thus, writers used the term *notebooks* to refer to unpublished material, which was kept in notebooks. Properly published material was written on scrolls.

Paul also referred to *membranae.* He told Timothy, "Bring . . . the books, and above all the parchments [*membranae*]" (2 Tim 4:13). Paul was telling him to bring the books (or scrolls), probably Old Testament scrolls. These were valuable, and Paul did not wish to lose them. Yet he also wanted the parchments (notebooks). These would be notebooks of material Paul carried with him.[44] He emphasized bring the notebooks ("above all") because they were the kind of thing that Timothy might not have bothered to bring; they were just notebooks, after all. Paul particularly wanted those with him in Rome.

---

[40]Berry, *Roman Handwriting,* p. 19.

[41]Berry (*Roman Handwriting*) does note that the handwriting on the tablets is of "a quicker, less structured hand" (p. 20) that is quite distinct (p. 21) from that customary of Roman officers, who were trained to write letters with precision (pp. 8-9), producing a script with "simplicity of form and plainness of execution" (p. 10). Berry draws no implications from the fragmentary nature of the contents. He does not seem to be an epistolographist, judging from his misunderstanding of letter addresses (pp. 69, 71) and his confusion of codex and scroll in a discussion of Mart. *Epig.* 1.117 (p. 32). This is not to detract from his excellent study of Roman handwriting.

[42]C. H. Roberts and T. C. Skeat, *The Birth of the Codex,* 2d ed., (London: Oxford University Press, 1983), pp. 15-23. See also Mart. Epig. 14.7 and *CIL* 10.6. Sherwin-White defined *pugillares* as meaning "either the usual wax tablets or the recently introduced 'pugillares membranei'"; *Letters of Pliny: a Historical and Social Commentary* (Oxford: Oxford University Press, 1985), p. 100; so also Tyrrell and Purser, *Cicero,* 1:55.

[43]Roberts and Skeat base their argument primarily on the classical jurists. Roman lawyers, as lawyers today, were plagued by problems with precision in language. In legal writing, how did one distinguish between books and unpublished notes or manuscripts? *Membranae* were used to designate the latter. A work of the jurist Neratius Priscus, a generation after Paul, was entitled *Liber sextus membranarum.* Roberts and Skeat propose that using *membranae* in the title was equivalent to calling it "Jottings from a Lawyer's Notebook." See Roberts and Skeat, *Codex,* pp. 21-22, 30.

[44]See T. C. Skeat, "Especially the Parchments: a Note on 2 Timothy IV.13," *JTS* n.s. 30 (1979): 172-77; Roberts and Skeat, *Codex,* p. 22; and Roller, *Formular,* p. 342.

CONCLUSIONS FOR PAUL AS A LETTER WRITER

It seems likely that Paul kept materials such as Old Testament excerpts, traditions and rough drafts in notebooks that he carried with him as he traveled. In addition, the evidence we have indicates that Paul and his team probably were constantly preparing notes and polishing drafts of material.

I have suggested that, for a letter such as 1 Corinthians, we imagine Paul sitting in the living room of an apartment, with the noise of the Ephesian street below filtering in through the window. With Paul is Sosthenes, who is joining in writing the letter. A secretary is seated nearby, a tablet on his lap. Other team members drop by to visit, listen and comment on occasion. Paul is seated on a chair with a few scrolls in a bag beside him and notebooks scattered about him which contain the material they had been honing for weeks. Paul is also referring to a few tablets full of new notes specific to the problems they are going to address with their letter.

4

SECRETARIES IN THE
FIRST-CENTURY WORLD

*S*ince most of us have never read any ancient letters apart from those in the New Testament, our knowledge of ancient secretaries is limited to what we picked up from reading Paul's letters. How were Paul's contemporaries using secretaries? Do they mention them in their letters? Was there an annual Secretary's Day in Rome? Were the secretaries merely invisible hands behind the letters, leaving no impact on either the process or the resulting letter, or can we discern their influence?

Most private letters from the Greco-Roman world can be described as we would our personal letters today: correspondence between individuals, typically not intended for public viewing. Most of these letters were painfully brief, highly stereotyped, and written in the *koine,* or "common," Greek of the marketplace. Adolf Deissmann termed these "letters" (*Briefe*), and brought to scholars' attention that the language of the New Testament was strikingly similar to that of these private letters. However, there are also Greco-Roman letters that seem private and are written in a much more educated, rhetorically-structured Greek, like a treatise in letter form. These Deissmann termed "epistles" (*Episteln*) to distinguish them from the others. These epistles were addressed to individuals but seem to have been intended for publication, to propagate ideas. We have no modern equivalent now, although perhaps our "letter to the editor" is similar.

Another method sometimes used is to speak of literary versus non-literary private letters.[1] Yet this is not a helpful solution. Stanley K. Stowers criticizes this as an overlaying of a modern category upon an ancient system.[2] The public and private realms were not so well differentiated. Witherington terms the entire public versus private distinction a modern invention.[3] Many public matters were administered through private channels. Many private letters handled an item or two of business. Moreover many letters, especially

---

[1] In his dissertation on Greco-Roman letters, William Doty opted for a less finely distinguished scale, using a public vs. private polarity within the common category of letter; Doty, "The Epistle in Late Hellenism and Early Christianity: Developments, Influences, and Literary form" (Ph.D. diss., Drew University, 1966).
[2] Stanley Stowers, *Letter Writing in Greco-Roman Antiquity* (Philadelphia: Westminster Press, 1986), p. 19.
[3] Ben Witherington, *The Acts of the Apostles: A Socio-Rhetorical Commentary* (Grand Rapids: Eerdmans, 1998), pp. 335, 338.

the letters of Paul, cannot be easily classified. Paul's letters would be considered private and yet they were addressed to a community and were encouraged to be read to other communities. In a sense Paul's letters were no less public than Cicero's were originally intended to be.

Furthermore, even with the variations between the more literary and the less literary private letters, there is no evidence that one type of secretary was used for one and another type for the other. Certainly a more literary letter (since its author was usually wealthier) probably was written by a better-trained, more professional secretary. Nonetheless, such a secretary was better skilled and not of a different type than other secretaries. The same tasks and skills were required across the letter spectrum. A secretary for a wealthy writer such as Pliny the Younger was no doubt much more qualified, but he was not a different creature than the secretary hired in the marketplace to scratch a brief wedding invitation. Since we are examining secretaries in this chapter and not the letters per se, we shall examine both the more official/business letters as well as the more private letters.

HOW COMMON WERE SECRETARIES?

Official and business letters. Evidently, secretaries were used up and down the spectrum of public life, from royal secretaries to the marketplace secretaries. They were a vital part of the administrative structure of the Greco-Roman world, as can be seen by the bureaucracy in Roman Egypt. From the "central office" in Alexandria, with its hordes of secretaries who kept the main accounting and recordkeeping, there was a hierarchical structure of secretaries that reached all the way down to the local village secretary. Secretaries were critical to the functioning of the Roman government. They were the record keepers for the massive bureaucracy.[4]

Even a cursory examination of the papyri reveals a widespread use of secretaries in the business sector as well. Many of these business letters contain the "illiteracy formula"; that is, a concluding sentence that reads, for example, "Eumelus, son of Herma, has written for him because he does not know letters."[5] This formula served to authenticate the letter, since no part of the letter was actually written by the author. A change in handwriting at the end of a letter as well as the pervasive use of illiteracy formulae in the predominant number of papyrus business letters indicate the widespread use of secretaries in the business sector.[6]

Private letters. In the Greco-Roman world, the private sector consisted of two definite

---

[4]The system probably even predates the satrap, Ptolemy I. See Roger S. Bagnall and Peter Derow, eds., *Greek Historical Documents: The Hellenistic Period [GHD]*, SBLSBS, no. 16 (Chico, Calif.: Scholars, 1981), Appendix 1, pp. 253-54.

[5]See Francis Exler, *The Form of the Ancient Greek Letter: A Study in Greek Epistolography* (Washington, D.C.: Catholic University of America, 1922), pp. 126-27, for examples.

[6]Many papyri can be cited to indicate the widespread use of secretaries in the business sector, but this point is not disputed.

socioeconomic divisions: the upper class and the lower class. The use of secretaries by these two classes, because of their concurrent economic variables, is considered separately.

The upper classes. Clearly the upper classes could afford to use secretaries. The questions are only whether they preferred to use one and how pervasive was the practice. In a pseudonymous letter dated to the early second century, "Speusippus" reports that his health is poor but that he is still able to "write" because "my tongue and the faculties of my head are intact."[7] Thus to "write" a letter, Speusippus needed his voice and not his hand.

The author of a fourth-century letter, requesting someone to help him during his recovery from a serious accident,[8] evidently used a secretary. The letter appears to end with the customary greetings. Then a postscript is appended, still in the original hand. The indication of a secretary comes, however, with the inclusion of a closing health-wish in a second hand, no doubt the author's.

This particular letter was from a member of the upper class, as seen from his discussion of the finances for a trip as well as from the fact that the author was injured while riding a horse. The author could have chosen to employ a secretary because of his accident, but because he did not comment upon his use of a secretary in that letter, it probably was not unusual for him.

When Clodius became tribune (ca. 58 B.C.), he wanted Cato the Younger out of Rome and removed as an influence so that he, Clodius, might further the plans of Caesar, his ally and Cato's opponent. Concerning this plan Plutarch states:

> When Cato set out, Clodius gave him neither ship, soldier, nor assistant, except two clerks, of whom one was a thief and a rascal, and the other a client of Clodius.[9]

The obvious tone is that Clodius was doing all he could to hinder the effectiveness of Cato. Evidently by sending unreliable secretaries, Clodius was hobbling the work of Cato, not because Cato was illiterate or even unfamiliar with letter writing,[10] but because he customarily made extensive use of his secretaries.

A comment by Cicero (106-43 B.C.), who boasted that he was writing to his friends in his own hand,[11] has been used to argue that the upper classes did not prefer to use a secretary.[12] Yet Cicero's comment was clearly made as a point of pride; it could hardly have been usual custom among their peers. Many other examples can be cited to demonstrate

---

[7]Pseudo-Socrates and the Socratics *Epistle* 31 (hereafter Ps-Socr. *Ep.*). The texts and translations of all the Cynic letters are from *The Cynic Epistles: A Study Edition*, ed. A. Malherbe, SBLSBS, no. 12 (Missoula, Mont.: Scholars, 1977). The letter is pseudonomous and hence of little relevance for the time of Socrates, but it was forged during the time period under consideration (ca. A.D. 200 [see Malherbe, "Introduction," *The Cynic Epistles*, pp. 28-29]), and thus is appropriate for our study.

[8]POxy. 3314 (fourth century).

[9]Plut. *Cato Minor* 34.3.

[10]See, e.g., Plut. *Cat. Min.* 24.1-2.

[11]Cic. *Att.* 2.23.1.

[12]Bahr, "Letter Writing," p. 468.

that the use of secretaries among the upper classes was pervasive.[13] Quintilian even denounces the fashionable use of a secretary.[14]

The lower classes. The situation among the lower classes is more complex. It is often assumed that members of the lower classes were illiterate, yet literacy was more common than has been supposed.[15] John Winter discusses a papyrus letter evidently written by a son to his mother.[16] The son knew his mother could not read and also anticipated that his brother would be reading the letter to her, because he appends at the bottom of his letter to his mother a confidential note to his brother, offering filial advice concerning his mother.

Another example of literacy among the lower classes is a papyrus of the second century in the Michigan collection.[17] It has been labeled the most illiterate letter in the collection for its poor spelling and grammar. Doubtlessly, it was written by the sender herself, for a professional scribe would not have had such an awkward hand, to say nothing of the marginal literacy.

Even if we allow that the poor were more literate than was previously thought, the preponderance of evidence still indicates that most members of the lower classes were functionally illiterate. For example, a second-century letter from Oxyrhynchus (Egypt) discusses the inability of the senders to fill a friend's request for roses for a wedding.[18] In the modern editor's judgment, the style of this letter is rather high and contains several phrases either rare or unknown in the papyri. The papyrus concludes with a customary health-wish, written in the plural and by a second hand, indicating that a secretary wrote the letter proper.

In addition to the longer, more elaborate, or more important letters, evidently the lower classes on occasion used secretaries to write even minor letters.[19] Several papyri from Oxyrhynchus are small letters of invitation.[20] Having only the barest epistolary framework and containing only the scantest stereotyped text on a shred of papyrus, one

---

[13]The works of both Plinys, Cicero, Atticus, Seneca, Cato et al., indicate the widespread use of secretaries. It was not, however, unheard for a member of the upper classes to write personally, especially if the letter was quite personal; see Plut. *Demosthenes* 29.3-4.

[14]Quintilian *Institutio oratoria* 10.3.19.

[15]Exler, *Form*, p. 126, cautions "The papyri discovered in Egypt have shown that the art of writing was more widely, and more popularly, known in the past, than some scholars have been inclined to think." See, e.g., PZen. 6, 66, POxy. 113, 294, 394, 528, 530, 531, and esp. 3057.

[16]John G. Winter, *Life and Letters in the Papyri* (Ann Arbor: University of Michigan Press, 1933), pp. 48-49. The papyrus was published in H. I. Bell, "Some Private Letters of the Roman Period from the London Collection," *Revue Egyptologique*, n.s., 1 (1919): 203-6.

[17]PMich. 188. See also Winter, *Life and Letters*, p. 90.

[18]POxy. 3313. Other aspects of this papyrus are discussed in E. A. Judge, *Rank and Status in the World of the Caesars and St. Paul* (Christchurch, New Zealand: University of Cantebury Press, 1982), p. 25.

[19]*Pace* J. A. Eschlimann, "La rédaction des epîtres pauliniennes: d'après une comparison avec les lettres profanes de son temps," *RB* 53 (1946): 186, who argues that often ancients wrote in their own hand because they were too poor to pay a scribe. Although a reasonable conjecture, the evidence does not support his claim.

[20]POxy. 1484-87.

might expect such notes to be written personally by the sender if he were able to write at all. Yet even some of these letters were written by a secretary.[21]

In an opisthograph (an ancient document containing writing on both sides) found among the Oxyrhynchus papyri, the recto (the front side) contains a government record. After this record was trashed, the sheet was salvaged and reused. The verso (the back side) contains a letter to a brother.[22] Oddly, the health-wish, written in a second hand, is a verbatim repetition of the last line of the letter:

> [Original handwriting]: I wish you farewell, sister.
> [Second hand]: I wish you farewell, sister.

While it could be pure coincidence that the secretary and the author both chose the same formula, it was unusual for a secretary to include a closing wish if the author himself intends to do so. A reconstruction suggests itself: the author was functionally illiterate and requested a secretary to write the letter. The secretary, knowing his employer was basically illiterate, included a customary closing. The sender, for whatever reason (perhaps authentication?), wished to add something in his own handwriting but was too unsure of his skill. Therefore he copied verbatim the closing provided by the secretary's formula.

It is clear that the use of a secretary was prevalent among both the upper and lower classes, although perhaps for different reasons. Of course, both classes made widespread—almost exclusive—use of a secretary in the composition of business and official letters. Yet, both class members still used a secretary in the writing of private letters, although at times they would send private letters in their own hand as well.[23]

There is one noticeable difference in the practice of the illiterate. It has already been demonstrated that the illiterate made equal use of a secretary in business and official correspondence; yet this was probably required or unavoidable correspondence. What is striking is the rarity, at least among our current papyri, of private letters from a completely illiterate person; that is, a letter written strictly for private, nonbusiness reasons by a secretary for someone who had no ability to write at all.

There are two possible explanations. The first explanation is that it is false impression. Perhaps there actually are private letters from illiterates, but because they could not write at all, there was no change in handwriting to evidence a secretary.[24] Since illiteracy formulae were usually reserved for legal documents, the secretary did not need to indicate his presence. A second explanation is that an illiterate person did not send purely private letters. When they needed to send such a message, they sent it orally. Several factors suggest

---

[21] POxy. 1487.

[22] POxy. 1491.

[23] For literates who used a secretary see, e.g., Cicero, also PZen. 88 and POxy. 2985, and possibly PZen. 74 and POxy. 118. For literates who did not use a secretary, see, e.g., the well literate POxy. 3057, the fairly literate POxy. 113, 394, 530, 531, PZen. 6, and the marginally literate PZen. 66, POxy. 294, 526, 528.

[24] A simple EPP "farewell," however, was quite sufficient, and evidently easily within the grasp of many illiterates. See, e.g., POxy. 2983; also 2860, 3063 and 3066.

to me that illiterate persons preferred to send simple personal letters orally. First, the cost of hiring a secretary plus the materials was a significant sum for a member of the lower classes. Second, the expense of a scribe (or the time needed to visit an obliging friend) might have seemed frivolous when the letter was not required for business. Third, even in modern times those who cannot read or write often prefer oral messages, trusting less the medium they cannot understand (or control). Lastly, the types of philophronetic (personal, relationship-building) messages common to a private letter could as easily be given and conveyed orally and, due to the use of carriers, was perhaps just as likely to arrive. Consequently, when an illiterate sent a simple personal message, he easily might have preferred an oral message since it was considerably less expensive, much more convenient, and probably as reliable as one in writing.

How Did Secretaries Work?

The use of a secretary is complicated further by the flexibility available to the sender. The author could grant to the secretary complete, much, little or no control over the content, style and even the form of the letter. The examination of ancient letters below reveals that the role of the secretary may be described as a spectrum. At one extreme the secretary was a transcriber who had no input in the letter, taking strict dictation from the author. At the other extreme the secretary composed the letter for the author. Most letters fell somewhere in between.

The secretary's role:	Transcriber . . . . . Contributor . . . . . . Composer		
Who had the most control:	Author . . . . Secretary		
The quality of the notes:	More Detailed . . . . More Sketchy		
The influence of the secretary:	More Unintentional . . . . More Intentional		

Figure 4.1. The secretary in letter writing

On this spectrum we can mark the two clear extremes; the middle area is less clearly defined.[25] In the case of a transcriber, the author dictated the letter that was then recorded verbatim by the secretary. If a final polished copy was prepared later, the contents remained unchanged.[26] In this role the secretary was merely a transcriber. On the other extreme the secretary was the true composer of the letter. In this role the author instructed

---

[25]John McKenzie, *Light on the Epistles: A Reader's Guide* (Chicago: Thomas More, 1975), pp. 14-15, rejects the existence of shorthand and divides the other two categories into three. Roller, *Formular*, p. 5, lists three uses roughly parallel to transcribing, editing and contributing.

[26]See, e.g., Cic. *Att.* 5.12; 7.13a; 8.15; 12.32.1; 13.32; *Fam.* 11.32.2; and *QFr.* 2.2.1; 2.15b.1; 2.16; 3.1.

his secretary to send a letter to someone for some general purpose without specifying the exact contents.[27] For example, an author could tell the secretary to write a letter to an associate in a particular town to tell him that he had been providentially delayed in coming and that when he was able, he would visit. It was possible to compose a personal letter from such general guidelines because of the highly stereotyped nature of most Greco-Roman letters, including even personal letters.

The gray area in between these two extreme roles needs further elaboration. In this middle area, the secretary contributed in some way to the content of the letter. Perhaps the secretary, who usually had more training in letter writing than the author, edited the author's content to conform better to epistolary standards. For example, the writer recited his letter while the secretary made extensive notes, or perhaps he even gave a rough draft to the secretary.[28] In this role the secretary was more an editor, because he was responsible for minor decisions about syntax, vocabulary and style. He remained, however, within the strict guidelines of the writer's oral or written draft. The secretary could also be permitted more latitude, working from notes that were far less extensive.[29] In this broader role, the form, syntax, vocabulary and style as well as specific pieces of content were contributed by the secretary, who usually was more experienced in matters of epistolary expression, while the general content and perhaps argumentation remained the author's. Thus, a secretary's role ranged from transcriber to contributor to composer. Each of these roles needs further elaboration.

The secretary as transcriber. In the third century, Isadora clearly dictated a letter to a professional secretary.[30] Near the end of the letter the secretary began to decrease the size of his letters and compress his writing as if he was worried about having enough space. However, the letter ended with two inches of empty space at the bottom of the page. Obviously, the secretary had no idea how much longer Isadora intended to dictate. There are numerous other examples, but the composition[31] of letters in antiquity by dictation is not disputed.[32] McKenzie plainly states:

> Dictation . . . was the normal means of producing letters. Many of the ancient letters which have been preserved were letters of the poor, so dictation was not the luxury which it is in modern times.[33]

---

[27] See, e.g., Cic. *Att.* 3.15; 11.3.
[28] See, e.g., PZen. 111 and PTebt. 13, or some of the tablets from Vindolanda.
[29] See, e.g., PZen. 57; also see Cic. *Att.* 11.5.
[30] PMich. 8.514.
[31] Around the turn of the twentieth century, E. I. Robson drew a distinction between composition and dictation. By "dictation," Robson meant the author drafted the letter by speaking extemporaneously, and by "composition" he meant the author wrote personally the drafts. Robson's distinction in terms is not used here. E. Iliff Robson, "Composition and Dictation in New Testament Books," *JTS*, o.s., 18 (1917): 288-301.
[32] There are many references to dictation, particularly in the letters of Cicero. E.g., Cic. *Att.* 5.12; 7.13a; 8.15; 12.32.1; 13.32; *Fam.* 11.32.2; *QFr.* 2.2.1; 2.15b.1; 2.16; 3.1. See also Pliny *Ep.* 3.5 [concerning the elder Pliny] and Plut. *Caesar* 17.3-4.
[33] McKenzie, *Light*, pp. 13-14.

The question concerning dictation is not its existence but its nature. Was the text dictated at the speed of normal handwriting (that is, slowly), or was the text dictated at the speed of normal speech (that is, faster than anyone could write normally)? Obviously there is a considerable difference. We will see that most secretaries could take dictation slowly, but a secretary trained in a special technique was needed to take dictation at the speed of speech.

Slow dictation. In a passing description of curriculum requirements in ancient Athens, C. E. Robinson comments:

> Schooling began when a boy was six, and its elementary stage lasted until he was fourteen. In the grammar-school he would learn to write with a metal instrument on a tablet of soft wax. *Lessons in dictation followed.*[34]

Robinson was referring to a drill in which a teacher slowly read a text while the students wrote. Thus, most educated people in antiquity had at least some training in taking dictation recited "syllable by syllable." However, most also had little or no practice doing this after finishing school. Therefore, while in theory most could take dictation, in practice, most were not proficient enough to take down a letter of any length.

Cicero explained to Atticus that when he composed a particular letter to Varro, "I dictated it to Spintharus [a secretary] syllable by syllable."[35] Such a procedure was naturally slow. Consequently, Seneca must be referring to slow dictation, when he advised Lucilius about proper speech. Seneca's comment shows that dictation could be painfully slow.[36]

SENECA

Although someone without taste may come along, like the person who said when he [Vinicius, the stammerer] was pulling out individual words, as if he were dictating, not speaking, "Tell me, you do not actually have anything to say, do you?"

In his description of the amazing abilities of Julius Caesar (102?-44 B.C.), Pliny the Elder (A.D. 23/24-79) notes that Julius often dictated to his secretaries (*librariis*) four letters at once, if the matters were serious, and seven letters at once if he was at leisure.[37] Gordon Bahr correctly argues that this refers to slow dictation, for Caesar "could not have been dictating fluently as we are accustomed to doing it, but if he did it word for word, or syllable by syllable, then a man of Caesar's ability would be able to dictate several letters at

---

[34] C. E. Robinson, *Everyday Life in Ancient Greece* (Oxford: Clarendon, 1933), p. 139 (emphasis mine). Ronald Hock likewise places writing (especially letters) in the secondary level (ages 11-15); "Writing in the Greco-Roman World," *SBL Forum,* May 10, 2004 <www.sbl-site.org/Article.aspx?ArticleID=264>.
[35] Cic. *Att.* 13.25.3.
[36] Sen. *Ep.* 40.10. So also argues Bahr, "Letter Writing," p. 470.
[37] Pliny *H.N.* 7.25.91

once."[38] While the truth of Pliny's boasts about Caesar might rightly be questioned, we may still conclude that Pliny must be stating something that others would have viewed as amazing but not inconceivable.[39]

This slow dictation is what we usually imagine for Paul. Deissmann's description of Paul at work is still often quoted:

> The amanuensis [secretary], whose swift pen was scarcely able to record the eloquent flow of Paul's dictation upon the course papyrus leaves, had a minute commonplace handwriting.[40]

While Deissmann describes the secretary as "swift," it is still true that to record—transcribe as Deissmann means—Paul's dictation required Paul to speak slower than normal speech.

Rapid dictation. Dictating at the speed of writing is not commonly doubted. It is the art of taking diction at the speed of normal speech that is usually debated. To take dictation at the speed of speech required a secretarial system capable of recording text at that speed or, to use modern terms, the existence of a practical system of Greek shorthand.

Scholars are confident that, by the time of Paul, there existed a working system of Latin shorthand capable of recording dictation at the speed of normal speech. In a letter discussing the marvelous things invented by slaves, Seneca speaks of such a system: "What about signs for words, with which a speech is taken down, however rapid, and the hand follows the speed of the tongue?"[41] The same idea is clearly implied by Seneca's remark that when Janus addressed the Senate the speech was so eloquent that "the secretary is not able to follow him."[42] Since Seneca's purpose is to impress the reader with Janus' oratorical skill, it must be presumed that a secretary could have followed a normal speech without difficulty. By Paul's time there was a working system of Latin shorthand that was so efficient a secretary could even record a speech in the Roman Senate.[43] This task was considerably more difficult than merely recording a dictated letter, since (1) a speech usually had a faster cadence, (2) a speech usually had more complex diction and style, and (3) a secretary could not interrupt an orator to ask for something to be repeated.

Yet the existence of Latin shorthand can be pushed back to the century before Paul.

---

[38]Bahr, "Letter Writing," pp. 40-71.

[39]Pliny is known for preferring facts that are extraordinary if not hyperbolic (e.g., *H.N.* 7.21). It must be remembered, however, that the pivotal issue is not Caesar's ability but Pliny's statements.

[40]Adolf Deissmann, *Bible Studies* (Edinburgh: T & T Clark, 1909), p. 348.

[41]Sen. *Ep.* 40.25 (ca. A.D. 63/64).

[42]Sen. *ApoloCol* 9.2, written shortly after the death of Claudius in A.D. 54. For the use of the term *notarius* for a shorthand writer, see also Sen. *Ep.* 90.25; Suet. *Tit.* 3; Paulus *Digesta* 29.1.40 (ca. A.D. 210); Ausonius *Epigrammata* 146 (†ca. A.D. 395).

[43]So Arthur Mentz, *Die tironischen Noten: eine Geschichte der römischen Kurzschrift* (Berlin: de Gruyter, 1944), p. 66 and Arthur Stein, "Die Stenographie im romischen Senat," *Archiv für Stenographie* 56 (1905): 182. Other references, which alone are questionable, may be cited for additional support: Manilius *Astronomicon* 4.197-99; Martial *Epigrammata* 14.208 (ca. A.D. 84/85); and Quint. *Inst.* 10.3.19.

The earliest important reference is found in Plutarch's discussion of the speech of Cato the Younger, which was delivered on December 5, 63 B.C.[44] Plutarch's use of the term "shorthand writers" (*sēmeiographos*) indicates that he was familiar with the practice of shorthand.[45]

PLUTARCH ON CATO

This is the only speech of Cato which has been preserved, we are told, and its preservation was due to Cicero the consul, who had previously given to those clerks who excelled in rapid writing instruction in the use of signs, which, in small and short figures, comprised the force of many letters; these clerks he had then distributed in various parts of the senate-house. For up to that time the Romans did not employ or even possess what are called shorthand writers, but then for the first time, we are told, the first steps toward the practice were taken.

Cicero was an avid user of Latin shorthand; he commonly dictated his letters to others.[46] His connection to the rise of Latin shorthand is further strengthened by the strong tradition that his freedman and personal secretary, Tiro, introduced shorthand to the Romans.[47] Tiro's name has since become synonymous with a system of Latin shorthand, Tironian Notes.[48]

How does the existence of a system of Latin shorthand relate to Paul, who wrote in Greek? When did Greek shorthand develop? Although Plutarch claimed that Cicero introduced Latin shorthand at Rome, he did not speak of it as an innovation but only as something new to Romans: "For up to that time the Romans did not employ or even possess what are called shorthand writers, but then for the first time, we are told, the first steps toward the practice were taken."[49] Moreover, Plutarch used Greek terms to describe

---

[44] Plut. *Cat. Min.* 23.3-5. See also Arthur Stein, "Die Stenographie im römischen Senat," *Archiv für Stenographie* 56 (1905): 186.

[45] So argues also Mentz, *Noten*, p. 83. Although Plutarch does define the term here, it is probably only another example of his tendency to explain offices and functions. The historicity of Plutarch's account is not disputed. See Hermann W. G. Peter, *Die Quellen Plutarchs in den Biographien der Römer* (Halle: Waisenhaus, 1865), pp. 65-68. This text is dated ca. A.D. 100 but his sources may be much earlier. The recording of Cicero's speech in defense of Milo, eleven years later, is widely accepted as an instance of functional shorthand; see Bahr, "Letter Writing," p. 472.

[46] See, e.g., Cic. *Att.* 10.8 which has every appearance of being the very words of Cicero and yet was written by a secretary. In a letter to Atticus, he mentioned that he was dictating the letter rather than writing it with his own hand, but he then included the observation that he usually wrote personally to Atticus, thereby indicating it was not his usual custom with others.

[47] Eusebius *Chronica* 156 and Isidor (ca. 602-36) *Etymologiae* 1.22.1; Isidor notes that the system employed in his day had undergone revision since its invention by Tiro.

[48] Arthur Mentz, *Die Geschichte der Kurzschrift* (Wolfenbüttel: Heckners, 1949), pp. 18-19, in his discussion of the Tironian notes indicates that Jacques Gohory, a French scholar, first coined this term in 1550.

[49] Plut. *Cat. Min.* 23.3-5.

this practice: *sēmeiographos* ("shorthand writer") and *sēmeion* ("shorthand signs")[50] implying that the Romans borrowed the art from the Greeks.[51] One may contend that the Greek terms were a necessary anachronism for Plutarch since he wrote in Greek. However, Cicero also used a Greek description for shorthand in a Latin letter to Atticus.[52] Why would a Latin invention be described by Greek names? Furthermore, Cicero employs these terms as technical words, strongly suggesting the existence of an established form of Greek shorthand at least as early as a hundred years before Paul's letters.[53]

It is not surprising that Cicero was the one to modify a Greek system for Roman use. He was well versed in Greek as well as Latin. We can see this in several ways.

1. Plutarch, in his life of Cicero, mentions an interesting interchange on one of Cicero's tours of Greece between Cicero and Apollonius, a Greek rhetorician:

> Apollonius, we are told, not understanding the Roman language, requested Cicero to declaim in Greek, with which request Cicero readily complied.[54]

Apollonius then commended Cicero, regretting only that it was not a native Greek who had spoken so eloquently.

2. To illustrate Cicero's wit, Plutarch mentions several of Cicero's Latin puns that actually required a play on the Greek equivalents.

3. Plutarch also speaks of Cicero as being the man who supplied the Romans with appropriate Latin terms for Greek philosophical thoughts.[55]

4. Cicero occasionally himself writes sections of his letters in Greek, particularly when writing to his Greek friend, Atticus.

5. Tiro, his trusted secretary, apparently wrote frequently in Greek, and may have been a Greek himself. For example, after Tiro returned from visiting Atticus, Cicero writes to Atticus and notes, "Tiro had said you looked to him rather flushed."[56] Yet in this Latin sentence, the term *flushed* is Greek. It is reasonable to infer that Cicero was giving the exact term Tiro himself had used.

---

[50]This is the earliest known occurrence of *sēmeiographos*. LSJ define these terms as "shorthand writer" and "a shorthand symbol," respectively.

[51]H. J. M. Milne plainly evaluates the Cato incident in this way: "And who more fit than he [Cicero], *utriusque linguae peritus*, to sponsor the transfer of a Greek invention to the Roman use?" (Milne, *Greek Shorthand Manuals: Syllabary and Commentary* [London: Oxford University Press, 1934], p. 1). He further notes five points of similarity between the two systems of shorthand to support his contention that the Latin system was borrowed from the Greeks (ibid., p. 2).

[52]"*dia sēmeiōn.*" Cic. *Att.* 13.32.

[53]So also argue Bahr, "Letter Writing," p. 474; Milne, *Greek Shorthand Manuals*, pp. 4-5; and V. Gardthausen, "Zur Tachygraphie der Griechen," *Hermes* 2 (1876): 444-45.

[54]Plut. *Cic.* 4.4-5.

[55]Plut. *Cic.* 25.4 and 40.1-2, respectively.

[56]Cic. *Att.* 12.4.

It is likely that Tiro's claim to fame with regard to shorthand ought to be the adaptation of an established Greek system of tachygraphy into Latin instead of the creation of a Latin system *de novo*.

Shorthand is not to be connected only with Rome and the wealthy aristocracy. Arrian (ca. A.D. 96-180), the disciple of Epictetus (ca. A.D. 50-120), preserved his teacher's lectures, *The Discourses of Epictetus*. Scholars of this material argue that Arrian was able to reproduce the truth, freshness and color-fidelity of Epictetus' teachings, as well as retain accurately the details, because Arrian was able to take rapid dictation.[57]

But was shorthand only used by the wealthy? Did the average person have access to a shorthand writer? Evidence from the Egyptian sands indicates "yes." A papyrus contract from Oxyrhynchus, dated A.D. 155, records that a former official apprenticed his slave, Chaerammon, to Apollonius, a writer of shorthand (*sēmeiographos*).

POxy. 724

Panechotes also called Panares, ex-cosmetes of Oxyrhynchus, through his friend Gemelles, to Apollonius, writer of shorthand, greeting. I have placed with you my slave Chaerammon to be taught the signs which your son Dionysius knows, for a period of two years dating from the present month Phamenoth of the 18th year of Antonius Caesar the lord at the salary agreed upon between us, 120 drachmae, not including feastdays; of which sum you have received the first installment amounting to 40 drachmae, and you will receive the second installment consisting of 40 drachmae when the boy has learned the whole system, and the third you will receive at the end of the period when the boy writes fluently in every respect and reads faultlessly, viz. the remaining 40 drachmae. If you make him perfect within the period, I will not wait for the aforesaid limit; but it is not lawful for me to take the boy away before the end of the period, and he shall remain with you after the expiration of it for as many days or months as he may have done no work. The 18th year of the Emperor Caesar Titus Aelius Hadrianus Antonius Augustus Pius, Phamenoth 5.

Fortunately for us the owner of the slave was careful to state his expectations and payment schedule. Payment was to begin as soon as Chaerammon started learning the signs.

---

[57]Karl Hartmann, "Arrian und Epiktet," *Neue Jahrbücher für das klassische Altertum, Geschichte und deutsche Literatur und für Pädogogik* 8 (1905): 257. W. A. Oldfather, the Loeb translator of Epictetus, concludes, "that Arrian's report is a stenographic record of the *ipissima verba* of the master there can be no doubt." See also Whitney J. Oates, ed. and trans., *The Stoic and Epicurean Philosophers: the Complete Extant Writings of Epicurus, Epictetus, Lucretius, Marcus Aurelis* (New York: Random House, 1940), p. xxii: "an apparently almost stenographic record."

The last payment would not be made until "the boy writes fluently in every respect and reads faultlessly." We should also note that even though this legal contract carefully explains many details, it does not define the term *sēmeiographos* nor *sēmeiōn* (signs). Apparently those were common enough terms not to need explanation. If we allow a reasonable period of time for an established apprenticeship system to develop and spread to provincial Egypt, this text indicates a flourishing practice of Greek shorthand at the time of Paul. Various wax tablets from the second and third centuries undergird the evidence of this papyrus.[58] There is also other supporting evidence for Greek shorthand by at least A.D. 100 from a gravestone inscription (dated ca. A.D. 120) marking the grave of a shorthand writer.[59]

Evidence from Rome, Greece and Egypt allows us to conclude that the practice was widespread in the empire. Archaeologists have provided even more evidence. Various letters dating to the second Jewish revolt have been discovered in the Judean wilderness at a place called Wadi Murabba'at Among these letters is a parchment containing Greek shorthand symbols.[60] In its present state, the parchment is in two pieces; it is not certain whether it was originally one piece. The two pieces apparently had been commandeered, probably from the scrap pile, and sewn together on three sides to form a mail pouch to hold other letters, which was a fairly common practice.

Without a translation and analysis of the text, any conclusions remain tenuous. Nonetheless, two points may be made with reasonable certainty. First, the parchment dates most probably with the other papyrus letters found in the wadi (i.e., the second Jewish revolt in the early second century[61]). We can be confident about the date because Wadi Murabba'at was a barren place of refuge for Jews fleeing from the Romans. The vast bulk of the Judeo-Greco-Roman material discovered there dates to the period surrounding the revolt. Second, while the content of the text is yet unascertained, we are certain it is shorthand.[62] It would not be wise to argue these sheets are some of the earliest examples of Greek shorthand, imported directly from Greece or Rome to be dis-

---

[58]E.g., POxy. 42 (A.D. 323) has three lines of shorthand at the end of this (apparent) rough draft of a letter. The editors do not translate them (p. 89 n. 10).

[59]A. Mentz, "Die Grabschrift eines griechischen Tachygraphen," *Archiv für Stenographie* 54 (1902): 49-53. The inscription can also be found in *CIG* 3902d. See Richards, *Secretary,* pp. 26-43, for a more extensive argument.

[60]PMur. 164. The parchment (with a drawing of the text) is described in Benoit et al., *Murabba'at,* pp. 275-79. (Since this parchment was uncovered after Mentz wrote, it cannot be the lost piece to which he referred.) The editors had noted its stenographic nature but did not make any further textual analysis, deferring the topic to scholars in that field; however, as far as I know, no further work has been done on the parchment. There are few if any living scholars who can read Greek shorthand. Nonetheless, this text needs further study. Line 11 contains a *Chi-Rho,* which could possibly be a Christian sign.

[61]Benoit et al., *Murabba'at,* p. 277.

[62]A comparison of the symbols of the text to Milne (*Greek Shorthand Manuals*) reveals numerous symbols in common, as well as a similarity in general appearance to known Greek shorthand texts. The editors agree (*Murabba'at,* pp. 276-77).

carded in the Judean wilderness.[63] When a piece of shorthand is found in the remote Judean wilderness, a generation after Paul, we should conclude there was a widespread use of Greek shorthand by the late first century. Alan Millard argues that this parchment is too fragmentary to be useful, since we are not even able to decipher the text.[64] It is not unusable, however, because it is like "Friday's Footprint." In Daniel Defoe's classic story, Robinson Crusoe finds a solitary footprint in the sand. While a single footprint is indeed too little to determine much, the footprint is still all Crusoe needed in order to know that there was another human on the island. We don't know what the text says, but we do know that it is shorthand.

We have uncovered many clues that point to the fairly widespread use of shorthand.[65] Let's summarize our pieces of evidence.

1. Quintilian, a contemporary of Paul, wrote against the fashionable practice of dicta-tion.[66]

2. The numerous references to dictation in the writings of Cicero a generation before Paul indicate his preference for using a secretary capable of recording rapid speech.[67] Sen-eca, Pliny the Younger and others also mentioned the use of dictation, particularly in private letters.

3. The desert sands have given up two important clues: the discovery in Oxyrhynchus of a teacher of shorthand and a shorthand text in the remote Judean desert.

4. In a Socratic letter (*Ep.* 14) dated about A.D. 200,[68] Aeschines supposedly is recounting to Xenophon the events surrounding Socrates' death, particularly the trial. He de-scribes how the prosecutor gave a very poor speech, a speech he says was recorded.[69] These letters are well-known forgeries; however, the forger of this letter implies that

---

[63]The Roman soldiers that captured and later garrisoned the wadi were from the X Fretensis Legion that had been stationed in Jerusalem since its fall in A.D. 70.

[64]Millard (*Reading*, p. 176) concludes, based upon the research of H. Boge, *Griechische Tachygraphie und Tironische Noten: ein Handbuch der antiken und mittelalterlichen Schnellschrift* (Berlin: Akademie Verlag, 1973), that the Greek system arose from the Latin and dates after the time of Paul. I must respectfully disagree for the reasons cited above.

[65]*Pace* scholars such a McKenzie, *Light*, p. 14, who asserts boldly "no generally used method of shorthand is attested for ancient times." Of those who recognize the existence of shorthand, not all share the view that shorthand was fairly common, notably Roller, *Formular*, p. 333 and F. R. M. Hitchcock, "The Use of *graphein*," *JTS*, o.s., 31 (1930): 273-74. They *both* maintain that dictation was uncommon. By dictation, however, they mean dictation syllable by syllable, not rapid dictation. Certainly slow dictation was un-common, being too impractical.

[66]Quint. *Inst.* 10.3.19.

[67]He notes *once* (*Att.* 13.25.3) that he chose specially to dictate syllable by syllable, indicating that usually he does not, preferring to dictate to Tiro who recorded "whole sentences." See also *Att.* 2.23.1; 4.16.1; 5.17.1; 7.13a.3; 8.12.1; 8.13.1; 10.3a.1; 13.25.3; 14.21.4; 16.15.1; *QFr.* 2.2.1; 3.1.19; 3.3.1. Note also *Att.* 6.6.4, where Cicero mentions a letter from Atticus that was dictated.

[68]So dated by Malherbe, "Introduction," pp. 28-29.

[69]Ps-Socr. *Ep.* 14.4.

Socrates' speech was recorded verbatim.[70] Obviously such a comment has no value for the time of Socrates, being anachronistic. Nonetheless, for the forger to make such a careless mistake, it is unlikely that Greek shorthand was a recent innovation known only in elite Roman circles; it implies the art of taking rapid dictation was well established and pervasive by the forger's time.

5. We should note all these references are widespread geographically and across the spectrum of social prominence, from the elite upper class in the heart of the empire down to minor officials in provincial Egypt.

We now summarize the arguments for the use of Greek shorthand at the time of Paul. Undisputedly Latin shorthand existed by the first century and was capable of recording speech. That Latin system most probably was derived from a similar earlier Greek system. There are ancient references that strongly imply the use of Greek shorthand before the Christian era; several extant fragmentary texts of Greek shorthand may be dated to the early second century. Finally, the early evidence has a wide geographical distribution: Rome, Greece, Asia Minor, the Judean desert and provincial Egypt.

Should we assume then that all our ancient speeches and letters are verbatim recordings, captured for us by shorthand writers? No, the very nature of shorthand presents several problems. Ancient shorthand probably used one sign for several syllables or words. Similarly, difficult words could be recorded by a simpler synonym. Stock phrases, articles and other common words frequently were noted by a short stroke or sign.[71] In other words, the conversion of a shorthand text into longhand required, as it does today, some recall on the part of the stenographer. A shorthand text of one writer was not always convertible by another writer, as perhaps illustrated by Cicero:

> What I said about the ten legates, you did not fully understand. I suppose because I wrote it in shorthand.[72]

Nevertheless, we may assume a competent stenographer in antiquity was able to convert his own text accurately, especially if converted immediately.[73]

---

[70]This may be reading too much into the text. However, in the responding letter, *Ep.* 15.2, "Xenophon" commends these "Friends of Socrates": "You do well to have Aeschines among you so that he can write to me. I think that we certainly need to record what that man said . . ." What does "Xenophon" mean? Surely Aeschines was not the only one there capable of writing a letter. Rather perhaps he means that they were fortunate to have someone like Aeschines who could record what Socrates said, *viz.*, a tachygraphist.

[71]E.g., the first letter of a word can be used to represent an entire word with appended dots to indicate the declensional ending, or the first and last letter can represent an entire phrase. Milne, *Greek Shorthand Manuals*, pp. 5-6.

[72]Cic. *Att.* 13.32. Cicero probably tried to disguise the meaning of the text from interceptors by using "signs" that he thought Atticus (or Alexis?) would understand. There is no other discernable reason why Cicero (or Tiro?) would have left this part of the text in shorthand.

[73]According to the expectations of POxy. 724 (p. 70).

Should we assume Paul's letters are verbatim recordings of his dictation? Although we have demonstrated the likely existence of Greek shorthand across the empire of Paul's day, it is unwise to conclude a typical secretary in the marketplace took shorthand. The evidence does not support a claim that most secretaries took shorthand, only that some did. It is stretching the evidence too much to assume Paul had ready access to secretaries who took shorthand.

The secretary as contributor. In theory, the ways to use a secretary can range from transcriber to composer. In between these extremes is the role of contributor. "Contributing" has its own range, from making minor editorial changes to significant contributions. Sizeable contributions include: selecting the proper genre for the letter, the proper way to broach the topic (introductory formulae), the appropriate stereotyped phrases, and even the names and titles of the appropriate people to greet. In the last case, the author determined the basic content of the letter but the secretary offered much of the phraseology.

Is there evidence that an ancient secretary modified an author's work in much the same way as an executive secretary might today? How and why a letter writer might utilize a rough draft is discussed later. At this point, the task at hand is to investigate whether ancient secretaries had a contributing hand in the author's work.

If an author preferred the text exactly as he stated it, he could dictate it syllable by syllable or write it himself, since most writers did not have ready access to a shorthand writer. If he was not extremely picky about having every little jot and tittle exactly as he dictated—likely only the rhetoricians were so demanding—then a skilled secretary could satisfy this demand by taking dictation at the speed of slow speech. However, most writers probably did not have access even to skilled secretaries. If the secretary could not follow the author's every word, then what the secretary was really doing was taking notes as extensively as possible, to recreate the text later. The observation of John McKenzie mentioned earlier: "Dictation . . . was the normal means of producing letters"[74] probably describes this process rather than strict transcribing. Obviously in a letter of any length, inevitably the secretary introduced minor changes in vocabulary, syntax and style, but not in content. In light of this we must note two aspects of Greco-Roman antiquity that might surprise the modern reader.

First, formal education included training in the art of paraphrase. Theon, a teacher of rhetoric from roughly the time of Paul, described a school exercise where a student "who has read a passage reflects upon the sense and then seeks to reproduce the passage, in so far as possible keeping the words of the original in the original order."[75] It was not a verbatim reproduction but a paraphrase, and was valued as a sign of rhetorical skill.

Second, most typical letter writers from Paul's day did not have the educational

---

[74]McKenzie, *Light*, pp. 13-14.
[75]Aelius Theon *Exercises* 109 as translated in George Kennedy, *Progymnasmata: Greek Textbooks of Prose Composition and Rhetoric,* Writings from the Greco-Roman World series (Atlanta: Society of Biblical Literature, 2003), p. 70.

training to compose a pleasing letter. These less literate writers likely wanted the secretary to improve the grammar, etc. Such improvements were perhaps one of the perks of hiring a secretary.

Consequently, editorial changes by a secretary theoretically could occur intentionally, at the author's request or the secretary's initiative, or unintentionally, due to the limitations of the secretary. Obviously, since shorthand was not so pervasive that all secretaries knew it, and since many letters were not worth the time and labor of either dictating slowly or writing oneself, cases of unintentional changes must have occurred. Yet it would be virtually impossible to find examples of unintentional changes because we would need proof that a letter was changed from its oral original (or from a temporary draft). In the case of intentional changes, however, the situation is different. In this scenario the author desired the secretary to correct a faux pas if he found one. There is ample evidence for such a practice as indicated in the following examples. As might be expected, these examples come from those writers who were prone to comment on what others viewed as mundane.

In a letter that Cicero wrote to his secretary, Tiro, who was elsewhere convalescing, he laments:

> Your services to me are past all reckoning—at home, in the forum, in the City, in my province, in private as in public affairs, in my literary pursuits and performances.[76]

What skill did Tiro possess that made him so valuable? Certainly it is not just Tiro's ability to take shorthand. (Plutarch has already indicated that Cicero had several shorthand writers available for his use.[77]) Cicero had come to rely upon the editorial skill of Tiro. Certainly this was Cicero's meaning in his unexpected use of the Greek term "rule" (*kanōn*) in a Latin letter to Tiro. Tiro, being sick, wrote to assure Cicero that he would care "faithfully" for his health. Cicero wrote back chiding Tiro good-naturedly for his improper use of "faithfully" (*fideliter*):

> But look you here, sir, you who love to be the "rule" of *my writings*, where did you get such a solecism as *"faithfully ministering to your health"*?[78]

Tiro's role as Cicero's "rule" was that of a correcting editor, particularly since Cicero offers it as ironic justification for his correction of Tiro.

As another example, Cicero in an earlier letter to Tiro declares:

> My poor little studies (or if you like *ours*) have simply pined away from longing for you . . .

---

[76]Cic. *Fam.* 16.4.3. See also 16.3.2.

[77]Plut. *Cat. Min.* 23.3-5. It is unlikely that Tiro's "skill" lay outside the usual secretarial repertoire. Slave duties were strictly defined. There were lectors, nomenclators (slaves who walked with their masters and supplied the names of other men who approached them), etc., and their duties were not commonly combined; see Sherwin-White, *Letters of Pliny*, p. 225 n. 15.

[78]Cic. *Fam.* 16.17.1 (July 29, 45). Italics in text and translation are the editor's.

Pompey is staying with me as I write these words; . . . When he expresses a desire to hear something of mine, I tell him that, without you, I am altogether dumb. Please be ready to render due service to our Muses.[79]

It was customary for a work recently finished to be read as after-dinner entertainment. It is not that Cicero, the great orator, was unable to write but that he evidently had nothing recently written that was in a form suitable to present to a peer like Pompey. Thus, Cicero was "altogether dumb." It is less likely that Cicero was experiencing a brief period of un-productiveness than that the absence of Tiro prevented any recent works from being checked and ready for presentation. Cicero's phrases "or if you like *ours*" and "our Muses" are a further indication of Tiro's role.[80]

Tiro and other secretaries made minor editorial changes to letters. We would scarcely expect more than minor changes to any writing composed by premier rhetoricians like Cicero. However, the papyri also are filled with examples of well-formed letters, with all the appropriate language and phraseology, being sent by an illiterate writer who could scarcely scratch a closing farewell. Obviously, the secretary took quite a bit of license in shaping those letters, well beyond merely correcting grammar or phraseology. Since the ancient letter had such a rigid structure, often with a predetermined arrangement of the contents, and stereotyped formulae, a secretary's expertise was quite welcome, if not es-sential, for the marginally literate.[81]

This practice was not limited to the less literate. In many cases, even the more edu-cated left the mundane aspects of a letter to the secretary. Perhaps the best example is the standard Greco-Roman "Recommendation Letter."[82] These letters of recommendation were written by a person of note and carried by the recommended person to serve as a letter of introduction, a guarantee of character, and often a request for assistance. Cicero, as may be expected of a person of his fame, wrote many letters of recommendation. In fact, one entire book of his collected letters consists entirely of recommendation letters.[83] Cicero was well aware of the danger of monotony when he sent yet another recommen-dation letter (*Fam.* 13.27.1) to a colleague to whom he had already sent a number of such letters for others.

---

[79]Cic. *Fam.* 16.10.2; Apr. 17, 54/53.

[80]Several scholars also argue this editorial role for Tiro; see, e.g., Bahr, "Letter Writing," p. 470 and Roller, *Formular*, pp. 307-8. It is possible that Cicero's relationship to Tiro was unique; however, Cicero on oc-casion compared his relation to Tiro with Atticus' relation to his secretary, Alexis (Cic. *Att.* 5.20) Plutarch gave a similarly large role to Eumenes, the secretary of Alexander the Great (Plut. *Eum.* 12.1-2). Although the evidence is scant, every example that comments upon this role grants it to the secretary.

[81]An examination of the papyrus letters demonstrates their stereotypical nature. See also Doty, *Letters*; Stowers, *Letter Writing*, pp. 17-26; and John White, "The Ancient Epistolography Group in Retrospect," *Semeia* 22 (1981): 10.

[82]John White, "The Greek Documentary Letter Tradition, Third Century B.C.E. to Third Century C.E.," *Se-meia* 22 (1981): 95-97, offers a convenient summary of the structure, essential elements and distinctive of this type of letter.

[83]Cic. *Fam.* 13, with the singular exception of *Ep.* 68.

CICERO ON RECOMMENDATION LETTERS

It is inexcusable to use exactly the same terms over and over again in sending you letters of this kind, thanking you for so punctiliously attending to my recommendations; I have done so in other cases, and shall do so, I foresee, ever so often; but for all that I shall make every effort to do in my letters what you lawyers habitually do in your formulae, and that is, "to put the same case in a different way."

Clearly Cicero was trying to vary his letters, because such letters were usually the same. Since the phrases were so stereotyped, they had already lost their impact. In one letter Cicero apparently truly meant what he was saying, and therefore had to emphasize it (*Fam.* 13.69.1).

What does this have to do with Paul? The first verses in the final chapter of Romans are clearly a recommendation for Phoebe. It follows closely the pattern for Greco-Roman recommendation letters (allowing for a Christian flavor). It is possible that Paul asked Tertius, the secretary for this letter, (Rom 16:22) to add a recommendation for Phoebe, who was to carry the letter. Tertius, likely a professional secretary,[84] composed a standard recommendation, noting the commendable things about Phoebe that Paul had mentioned. This may also explain why the list of greetings in Romans 16 is so long.[85] Paul never troubled to list long greetings. Also, his lists were always in the section before Paul began the postscript in his final hand. We will see in chapter nine that secretaries often added details like these.

The secretary as composer. Because of the highly standardized nature of most ancient letters, letter writers had the option of asking the secretary to compose the letter, without detailing its contents. This procedure was possible only because ancient Greco-Roman letters, especially official and business letters, had a set form, vocabulary and style. For example, an author could request that a letter be written to a local official assuring him of compliance with all the latest ordinances. The secretary would then compose a suitable letter. In this role the secretary was actually the author of the letter, although the stated author assumed full responsibility for it.

Private letters were in many ways no less stereotyped than official and business letters. Although written to keep a relationship warm,[86] private letters usually employed stereo-

---

[84]See Richards, *Secretary,* pp. 170-72.

[85]See Jeffrey Weima, *Neglected Endings: the Significance of the Pauline Letter Closings,* JSNTS 101 (Sheffield: JSOT, 1994), pp. 215-30, for an alternative explanation for the long list of greetings in Romans.

[86]Heikki Koskenniemi uses *philophronēsis* to denote the desire of the sender to establish, strengthen or restore his personal relationship with his recipient; Koskenniemi, *Studien zur Idee und Phraseologie des griechischen Briefes bis 400 n. Chr.* (Helsinki: Suomalainen Tiedeakatemia, 1956), pp. 115-27. E.g., Cicero, *Fam.* 4.9 and 4.10 were apparently written purely for philophronetic reasons.

typed health-wishes, affirmations of prayers and offerings to the gods on the recipient's behalf, and assurances of the well being and concern/love of the sender. We can see this stereotyped repetition in a couple of private letters from Egypt written a few decades after Paul. Terentian begs his father to come to visit him in Alexandria because he is too sick even to feed himself (PMich. 8.477). In a later letter (PMich. 8.478), his father has already visited his son and returned home. The illness has passed, and Terentian now writes other news. Although a private letter, we are struck by how nearly verbatim the initial greetings are.

PMICH. 8.477:

Claudius Terentianus to Claudius Tiberianus, his father and lord, very many greetings. Before all else I pray for your health and success, which are my wish, and I make obeisance for you daily in the presence of our lord Sarapis and the gods who share his temple. I received your letter . . .

PMICH. 8.478:

Claudius Terentianus to Claudius Tiberianus, his father and lord, very many greetings. Before all else I pray for your health, which is my wish. I myself am in good health and make obeisance for you daily in the presence of our lord Sarapis and the gods who share his temple. I want you to know that . . .

Literate people used a secretary on occasion to draft letters. Naturally, references to this practice within the letters themselves are rare. Presumably one did not wish his recipient to know that a secretary, not he, wrote the letter. Nonetheless, instances of and allusions to this practice are not unknown. Three examples, from writers we know were very literate, will suffice.

1. During one period in his life, Cicero repeatedly asked Atticus to write to their various friends in Cicero's name.

   I should like you to write in my name to Basilius and to anyone else you like, even to Servilius, and say whatever you think fit.[87]

   Any confusion about Cicero's meaning is removed by the additional instructions he gives to Atticus, "If they look for [my missing] signature or handwriting, say that I have avoided them because of the guards."[88] Clearly Cicero intended for Atticus to write letters for him that the recipients would believe were from Cicero.

---

[87]Cic. *Att.* 11.5. See also *Att.* 3.15; 11.2; 11.7.
[88]Cic. *Att.* 11.2.4.

2. Cicero himself may have performed the same task for Valerius, an intimate friend. Evidently Valerius, who was currently in Cilicia, asked Cicero to write on his behalf to Lentulus, the proconsul. This phrase, "writing on his behalf," need not mean that Cicero composed a letter for him as his secretary. Cicero's reply, however, implies that he did that very thing: "I have heartily thanked our friend Lentulus by letter in your name."[89]

3. Cicero's brother, Quintus, apparently employed his secretary in this way, although it may have been limited to more official correspondence.[90] Cicero sent a lengthy letter of advice to his brother (Cic. QFr. 1.2.8) who was on his first Roman appointment. Cicero discussed Quintus' customary methods of using his trusted secretary, Statius.

CICERO TO HIS BROTHER, QUINTUS

Statius told me that they were often brought to your house ready written, and that he read them and informed you if they contained anything inequitable, but that before he entered your service there had never been any sifting of letters, with the result that there were volumes of dispatches picked out which lent themselves to adverse criticism.

The implication is that Quintus had various secretaries compose letters for him. He then had Statius, probably in a role as chief secretary, read the letters to check for inconsistencies and advise him. What is notable here is that Cicero did not criticize him for using secretaries to compose letters, but rather for not having the letters checked, since he was responsible for them.

I must note that in all the instances I found of using a secretary to compose, the author *intended* to deceive his recipients into thinking he wrote the letter. Ancients had scruples regarding literary property and pseudonymity.[91] In examples where the author was not attempting to deceive, he invariably took a more active hand. This shifted the secretarial role away from pure composer.

CONCLUSIONS FOR PAUL AS A LETTER WRITER

There is ample evidence that ancient secretaries were employed in the three ways described by the spectrum below.

---

[89]Cic. *Fam.* 1.10 (so LCL).

[90]This limitation is not indicated in the texts and may be inappropriate, for as a Roman official all correspondence, no matter how philophronetic, may have carried official connotations. See Stowers, *Letter Writing*, p. 19.

[91]See the persuasive arguments of Terry Wilder in his Aberdeen dissertation, recently published as *Pseudonymity, the New Testament, and Deception: An Inquiry into Intention and Reception* (Lanham, Md.: University Press of America, 2004), esp. pp. 41-63.

Secretarial Roles

◀ – ▶

Transcriber . . . . .Contributor . . . . Composer

Some blending of these roles should be allowed. Since the distinctions between these roles are artificial, the uses were frequently separated more by gray areas than by hard and fast lines. The role played by the secretary depended on how much control the author exercised at that particular moment in that particular letter, even shifting roles within the same letter.[92]

---

[92]E.g., Cic. *QFr.* 3.1 contains sections from his own hand as well as parts he dictated.

5

PAUL'S USE OF A SECRETARY

*C*ertainly Paul used a secretary. Six of his letters explicitly mention it, either by stating when he wrote the postscript in his own hand (1 Cor 16:21; Gal 6:11; Col 4:18; 2 Thess 3:17; Philem 19) or by having a word of greeting from the secretary (Rom 16:22). There are other indicators in Paul's other letters.[1] However, using a secretary was standard procedure in antiquity and does not require explicit evidence in each letter. The question is not whether Paul used a secretary but how Paul used a secretary.

We have looked at how secretaries in general were used in the Greco-Roman world. We now want to bring this information to focus on Paul and his various secretaries. Where on the spectrum of secretarial roles did Paul's secretary likely fall? Did his secretary merely transcribe from Paul's dictation? Was Paul's secretary the true composer of Paul's letters?

DESCRIBING PAUL'S SECRETARY

In order to describe his secretary more clearly, we need to also discuss three items related to the work of a secretary: (1) who was responsible for the content of the letter, (2) what training a professional secretary customarily received and (3) what practical issues were involved in using a secretary to write a letter.

Responsibility. Even though a secretary was the one actually writing down the letter, the ancient author spoke as the writer, not just the author. For example, Cicero says in a letter, "When I was writing this, Drusus was . . . ,"[2] yet a secretary actually was the one doing the writing. The author assumed full responsibility for the purpose, content, style and even the form of every letter, whether actually from his pen or not. When responding to a recent letter from Appius Claudius, Cicero stated:

> At last, after all, I have read a letter worthy of Appius Claudius . . . For the letters you sent me en route . . . I have read with much pain.[3]

Apparently Claudius had sent several letters that implied some unfriendliness toward

---

[1]See E. R. Richards, *The Secretary in the Letters of Paul*, WUNT 2/42 (Tübingen: Mohr/Siebeck, 1991), pp. 189-94.
[2]Cic. *QFr.* 2.16.3.
[3]Cic. *Fam.* 3.9.1.

Cicero. Claudius was held responsible for the unfriendly language. Cicero was willing to allow that a return to the intellectual atmosphere and leisure of Rome had restored Claudius to his senses. Yet, Cicero never suggested the secretary as a possible excuse for his friend to use. Rather, he lamely suggested that the rigors of provincial life had affected his friend's perception.

Again, in reply to a private letter from Pompey, Cicero wrote that he felt snubbed because Pompey's letter contained "but a slight expression of your regard for me." To offer an excuse for Pompey, he commented, "I can only suppose that you omitted any such reference because you were afraid of wounding anybody's feelings."[4] Once again, he never suggested that the secretary failed to include those remarks. The contents of a letter, even to the point of omissions, were considered to be exactly what the author intended.[5]

When Cicero wished to disclaim the phrasing of several remarks in a particular letter, he was forced to disclaim the entire letter.

CICERO DISCLAIMS HIS LETTER (CIC. FAM. 3.11.5.)

What letter of mine it is you describe as unduly choleric I cannot make out. I wrote to you twice, clearing myself carefully, and mildly rebuking you for having too readily believed what was said of me; . . . But if, as you write, the letter was badly expressed, you may be sure I never wrote it.[6]

Of course this is mere rhetoric and not true confusion on Cicero's part.[7] He was using the opportunity to re-express the intention of his previous statements. Nevertheless it is notable that he did not blame the choleric phrases on the secretary, because this was not an acceptable excuse. I have found no ancient examples of poor wording being blamed on a secretary (or fine wording attributed to one). Apparently it was assumed that the author was responsible for every phrase and nuance contained in his letter no matter how much the secretary actually formulated. The author could correct even a final draft ready for dispatch. Minor corrections were written directly on the sheet; larger corrections required rewriting the offending part. For a single sheet, the secretary could recopy the entire letter. For longer letters on a short roll, a secretary could cut the papyrus before and after the offending column. The column was rewritten correctly and then glued before and after as sheets were regularly done in rolls.

---

[4]Cic. *Fam.* 5.7. Of course, these remarks like the previous were steeped in rhetoric with political overtones and subtle innuendos; nevertheless, the basic point is still pertinent.

[5]Thus in *QFr.* 2.15b.2, Cicero feels justified in expressing his indignation over the form and content of a letter from his brother, for whom he knew Statius often wrote.

[6]Cic. *Fam.* 3.11.5.

[7]He admits this later in the letter, chiding an earlier writer Aristarchus for the same thing (Aristarchus tries to argue that a poor line from Homer was not Homer's).

An error in a letter was not excused by blaming the secretary. The author was expected to check the final draft. That this was the practice of official correspondence has already been demonstrated by Quintus' use of his secretary[8] and by the imperial routine of Vespasian.[9] In another example, a costly one, evidently Cicero and Quintus were to inherit a portion of the estate of a man named Felix.[10] The filed copy of the will did not include them:

> About Felix's will, you would complain still more bitterly, if you only knew the facts. The document he thought he was sealing, in which we most certainly have a place as heirs to a twelfth of his estate (his slip was due to a mistake on his own part as much as on that of his slave Sicurra), he did not seal; the document he didn't want to seal, he sealed! But let him go hang, so long as we keep our health.[11]

Carelessly Felix had sealed (and thereby authenticated) an incorrect copy. Although apparently his slave (secretary?) was to blame, Felix was responsible, and thus the older will stood uncontested.[12]

We have seen that official letters were proofread; is the same true for private letters? Responsibility was more casual for private letters, and the evidence less abundant. Among some wedding invitations discovered at Oxyrhynchus, one had the date corrected by a second hand,[13] indicating that the text had been checked after the invitation was prepared. This text, though, typifies the problem of differentiating authorial corrections from mere changes. Wedding dates did—and do—change. The correction may have precipitated from a change of wedding plans and not from the author's correction of the final draft.

An analogy may be drawn from two examples. The first involves a problem with the letter carrier, mentioned in a reply of Cicero to a question of his brother.

CICERO TO HIS BROTHER

I come now to your letters, which I received in several packets when I was at Arpinum . . .
the first thing you noticed was that my letter to you bore an earlier date than that to Caesar.
That is what Oppius occasionally cannot help doing—I mean that, when he has decided to
send letter carriers and has received a letter from me, something unexpected hinders him,

---

[8]Cic. *QFr.* 1.2.8.
[9]Suet. *Vesp.* 21.
[10]One source of revenue for prominent Romans was wills. Evidently obscure "millionaires" enjoyed giving a portion of their estates to famous men they did not even know. It honored the giver (although it perhaps cheated the rightful heirs).
[11]Cic. *QFr.* 3.9.8.
[12]Whether Cicero's reconstruction is accurate, only wishful thinking or clever rhetoric (to avoid the insult of being excluded from the will) is immaterial for the point here.
[13]POxy. 1487.

and he is unavoidably later than he intended in sending the carriers; while I, when once the
letter has been handed to him, do not trouble about having the date altered.[14]

Cicero's effort to explain his custom implies perhaps that usually one corrected the date of the letter, presumably because, like the other parts of the letter, the author is responsible even though such peripheral details were handled customarily by the secretary.

In the second example Cicero, at the end of his term as a provincial governor, turned in the official books, accounting for all the financial dealings during his term. A controversy arose concerning some alterations; that is, Cicero was accused of "fixing the books." Cicero defended himself in a letter,[15] and it became apparent that some persons—quite probably those friendly to him and wishing to acquit him of a crime that they believed he probably committed—had suggested that the alterations were actually done by his secretary and were unknown to him. Such a defense did not absolve him from responsibility but, at least, did not impugn his character as severely; it was better to be thought careless than a thief. Cicero indignantly replied that he had, *according to custom*, checked all the work his secretary had done.[16] Authors checked the final draft because they were held responsible for it.

Training. The average secretary probably learned the necessary basic literacy skills within the established educational system. Special skills like shorthand were acquired by apprenticeship.[17] A brief look at basic Greco-Roman education is helpful.[18] Then we shall examine the question of ancient textbooks for secretaries.

John White, discussing the highly standardized character of certain parts of the ancient

---

[14]Cic. *QFr.* 3.1.8. The LCL translator, W. Glynn Williams, renders the last line with a singular; yet it is plural *we*. While Cicero frequently employs an editorial *we* he has been speaking here in the singular, and further one would not expect a plural in such a statement. Is he saying that neither he nor his secretary cared to make such a correction?

[15]Cic. *Fam.* 5.20.

[16]Cic. *Fam.* 5.20. He defended the changes, which he asserted that he himself had made, and also defended fervently the unimpeachable character of Tiro, his secretary. The hush-hush nature of the entire affair is clear from Cicero's reply near the end of the letter: "There is no reason why I should wish this letter to be torn up."

There are instances where a *dead* official's secretary was procured by devious individuals to alter the dead man's records to their advantage, since the handwriting of these later corrections would be the same as that of any original corrections. E.g., Cic. *Att.* 14.18: "he [Dolabella] has freed himself from enormous debts by the handwriting of Faberius." E. O. Winstedt, the LCL translator, explains that Faberius was Caesar's secretary, and was used by Dolabella to alter some of Caesar's records about the public treasury. See also Cic. *Att.* 7.3.

[17]POxy. 724.

[18]This has been explored in-depth elsewhere; see esp. Abraham Malherbe, "Ancient Epistolary Theorists," *Ohio Journal of Religious Studies* 5 (1977): 7-14, who presents the more traditional view; also John White, "Retrospect," pp. 9-10, idem, "Greek Documentary Letter Tradition," p. 90, and many others. But cf. Stanley Stowers, *Letter Writing*, 32-34, who disagrees slightly with the traditional understanding. The most recent treatment is Ronald Hock, "Writing in the Greco-Roman World," *SBL Forum*, May 10, 2004 <www.sbl-site.org/Article.aspx?ArticleID=264>.

letter, asserted that this conformity most likely was caused by widespread elementary training in letter writing.[19] In much the same way, our high school typing courses today account for the standardized format of our modern business letters. Abraham Malherbe argues that the essential continuity found in the basic form and style of the Greek private letter across *several centuries* indicates that education included rudimentary instruction in letter writing.[20]

Usually Greek and Roman education is described as progressing through three stages: elementary school, secondary school under a grammar teacher (*grammaticus*), and finally, rhetorical training. Stan Stowers, however, argued that such a picture is seriously misleading.[21] First, it is very unlikely that all three levels of education were available throughout the empire, since it was driven by local needs and resources. Likely smaller cities offered only elementary and secondary levels and often only elementary education plus whatever additional skills the local teacher had.[22]

Second, these supposed levels were generally not successive stages but socially differentiated tracks. Thus elementary school, taught by a "teacher of letters," was more universal (at least in the cities) and was usually all the education the lower classes received.[23] Boys from the upper classes may well have received their elementary instruction in their homes from a tutor or from the *grammaticus* himself before progressing to the secondary level. These boys might then advance to the teacher of rhetoric. According to Stowers, there usually was no advancement from a teacher of letters to a *grammaticus*; that is, boys from the lower classes usually did not advance from the elementary level to secondary education.[24]

Many of the advanced grammatical handbooks used in the secondary stage, for example those of Dionysius of Alexandria (first century) and Apollonius Dyscolus (second century),[25] clearly presupposed that the student already knew the basic forms for letter writing. This presupposition prompts Malherbe to conclude that "a knowledge of basic forms . . . must therefore have been learned very early in secondary education."[26] He adds that

---

[19]White, "Retrospect," p. 10.

[20]Malherbe, "Theorists," pp. 4-5.

[21]Stowers, *Letter Writing*, p. 32.

[22]Ronald Hock also noted that for someone to advance to a higher level of education, the student often needed to relocate to a larger town. For this reason, most unmarried (aristocratic) girls had to stop when they reached the limits of the local teacher (which often coincided with puberty and marriage); "Writing in the Greco-Roman World."

[23]At the primary stage, students learned only the most basic skills: "to recognize and write the letters of the alphabet; to write their own names; to read individual words and short sentences, usually maxims; to copy these maxims as beautifully as possible; to read brief poetic selections; and to do some simple arithmetic"; Hock, "Writing in the Greco-Roman World."

[24]Ibid.

[25]See G. A. Gerhard, "Untersuchungen zur Geschichte des griechischen Briefes, 1. Die Anfangsformel," *Philologus* 64 (1905): 27-65. See also the classic H. I. Marrou, *A History of Education in Antiquity*, trans. George Lamb (New York: Sheed & Ward, 1956), pp. 235-37, 369-71; and more recently Raffaella Cribiore, *Gymnastics of the Mind: Greek Education in Hellenistic and Roman Egypt* (Princeton, N.J.: Princeton University Press, 2001).

[26]Malherbe, "Theorists," p. 12.

the majority of papyrus letters also point to rudimentary instruction in letter writing early in secondary education.

From the sands of Egypt have come notebooks of model letters, which ancient students copied, in order to learn basic letter writing.[27] One papyrus appears to be a student's actual exercises in writing various letters, no doubt following a handbook.[28] In this student's notebook, each letter was copied in Greek and Latin. The student had only modest linguistic skills. Such methods were probably the general practice all over the Greek world. This was general training in rudimentary letter writing for those in the secondary level of education.

Advanced training in letter writing was of little interest to most rhetoricians. Nicholaus the Sophist comments upon the importance of using the proper style of letter writing, considering the character of both the sender and the recipients; yet he then adds, it "is not something to be considered at this time."[29] Letter writing skills were omitted from consideration in the rhetorical handbooks of Cicero and Quintilian.[30] Although they must have known of the handbooks of rudimentary letters, they did not speak of them. They were dealing with more advanced material. Training in letter writing occurred before the stage of refined rhetorical education.[31] Since we have seen exercises from the early stage of secondary education and since it was assumed already learned by the third stage, we can safely conclude that those who had a secondary level of education were given training in letter writing.[32] The majority of people, those with only an elementary level of education, had perhaps a little exposure to letter writing, enough probably to handle the rudimentary forms. Our question then becomes, Where did secretaries, who probably had only an elementary education, learn the additional skills of letter writing?

Handbooks were composed for the purpose of advanced instruction in letter writing. The prologue of one manual, credited to Demetrius of Phaleron and dating probably around 100 B.C.,[33] indicated that the work was written to serve as an instructional guide in letter writing. As Malherbe notes, the manual in its present form is not merely a collec-

---

[27]Model letters discovered in the Egyptian desert have been dated as early as 164-63 B.C.; see A. Erman, *Die Literatur der Aegypter* (Leipzig: Teubner, 1923), pp. 252, 257, and 260; see also *PParis* 63, which contains four model letters.

[28]The widespread use of these collections, or handbooks, of elementary model letters may be seen in the bilingual Bologna Papyrus; *PBononiensis* 5, probably from the third or fourth century. The text is translated by Benjamin Fiore in Malherbe, "Theorists," p. 43.

[29]See Kennedy, *Progymnasmata*, p. 166.

[30]Nonetheless, Hermann Peter asserts that Cicero knew a well-rounded Greek system of letter writing (*Der Brief in der römischen Literatur* [Leipzig: Teubner, 1901], pp. 22-24). Indeed, Cicero wrote of his frustration over the lack of an appropriate letter type for one situation; *Fam.* 4.13. Theoretical discussions of letter writing are found in other writings of Cicero as well as such rhetorically cultured writers as Philostratus and Gregory of Nazianzus.

[31]Koskenniemi, *Studien*, pp. 62-63, correctly points out that the rhetorical handbooks presuppose some rhetorical skill and deal mainly with the subtleties.

[32]So also Hock, "Writing in the Greco-Roman World."

[33]Demetrius, *On Style*, and so dated by Malherbe, "Theorists," p. 8, and Stowers, *Letter Writing*, p. 34.

tion of sample letters, but addresses more often the selection of the proper style and tone for a particular epistolary situation. "It is aimed at meeting the practical needs of its readers, who are assumed to be accomplished stylists, and not to be in need of instruction in basic rhetorical technique."[34] The prologue contains Demetrius' critical observation that many professional secretaries lacked the awareness to select the appropriate letter style and tone, and thus needed the training he provided. His handbook, in contrast to the collections of model letters used at the more rudimentary level, was (1) to provide instruction in the proper selection of the style appropriate to various epistolary occasions, (2) to serve as a guide for the correct tone in which the letter should be written, and (3) not to teach basic letter types. His apparent audience for the handbook was the professional secretary.[35] We may safely assume secretaries were trained through apprenticeship with some additional guidance from training manuals.

Practical considerations. In his discussion of the events leading to the death of Julius Caesar, Plutarch related the following:

> On the day before [the Ides of March], when Marcus Lepidus was entertaining him at supper, Caesar chanced to be signing letters, as his custom was, while reclining at table, and the discourse turned suddenly upon the question what sort of death was the best.[36]

In this passage Plutarch indicated that Caesar often used mealtimes as an opportunity to check the final drafts prepared by his secretaries.

Writers often combined letter writing with other activities. Pliny the Younger described the writing preferences of his famous uncle and namesake, Pliny the Elder, revealing that Pliny the Elder wrote even during other activities.

PLINY DESCRIBES HIS UNCLE (PLINY EP. 3.5)

Before daybreak he used to wait upon Vespasian, who likewise chose that season to transact business. When he had finished . . . he returned home again to his studies. After a short and light repast at noon . . . he would frequently in the summer . . . repose himself in the sun; during which time some author was read to him from whence he made extracts and observations, as indeed this was his constant method whatever book he read. . . . Then, as if it had been a new day, he immediately resumed his studies till dinnertime, when a book was again read to him, upon which he would make some running notes.

In his journeys, as though released from all other cares, he found leisure for this sole pursuit. A shorthand writer, with book and tablets, constantly attended him in his chariot, who, in the winter, wore a particular sort of warm gloves, that the sharpness of the weather

---

[34]Malherbe, "Theorists," pp. 8-9.
[35]See White, "Greek Documentary Letter Tradition," p. 90.
[36]Plut. *Caes.* 63.4.

might not occasion any interruption to his studies; and for the same reason my uncle al-
ways used a sedan chair in Rome.

The Elder Pliny was assisted by a *notarius* ("shorthand writer") as well as the *lector* ("reader"), when reading a book. The *notarius* was used to take down the Elder's reflections, resulting in immense collections of notes and excerpts of selected passages.[37] These anthologies were often used later in the composition of major works.

Like Caesar, the Elder apparently liked to use mealtimes for literary endeavors, enjoying the recitation of books during his meals,[38] presumably also, as was his custom elsewhere, having a secretary at hand to record his notes and extracts. This use of a secretary, however, was not the unavoidable and undesirable result of the cramped schedule of a busy man, for the Younger also discussed the daily routine of his uncle while at leisure in his country home. There also the Elder spent the majority of his time in literary pursuits, including, to the exasperation of his nephew, his time at bath. Pliny exclaimed that while his uncle did not work during his bath, he meant only that time he was actually in the water, "for all the while he was rubbed and wiped, he was employed either in hearing some book read to him, or in dictating himself."[39]

The home was not the only place where secretaries were used. We can see this again in textbox 5-3, in Pliny's description of his uncle writing while on journeys. Obviously Pliny intended us to view his uncle as the quintessential scholar who studied all the time. Nevertheless, this passage affords several observations. First, the Loeb translator renders *notarius* as "shorthand writer," a choice well justified by the context. Second, the remark about the cold of winter implies that anything that hindered the notarius was an interruption of the Elder's studies; the notarius was an indispensable part of his work. Third, Sherwin-White observes that the use of only a notarius indicates that there must not have been room in the litter for a lector as well. The notarius was forced to perform both duties.[40] Fourth, the mention of the codex notebook (*pugillaribus*) in addition to the scroll implies they had different functions. Finally, using a secretary to write while in the litter must have been a convenient process, since the Elder chose to use one also in Rome, where not only was it unnecessary but may have been viewed contemptuously.

Others also preferred the convenience of having a secretary in the litter. While discussing the routine of Julius Caesar, Plutarch observed that Caesar frequently sought ways to improve the use of his time. For example, he often slept in a litter, thus using his rest time for transportation as well.

---

[37]Sherwin-White, *Letters of Pliny*, pp. 224-25 n. For the use of a *notarius* to record notes from readings, see also Pliny *Epp.* 9.29.2; 36.2. Evidently Pliny adopted this practice from the Elder, *Ep.* 6.20.5.
[38]Pliny *Ep.* 9.36.4.
[39]Pliny *Ep.* 3.5.
[40]Sherwin-White, *Letters of Pliny*, p. 225.

PLUTARCH ON CAESAR

And in the Gallic campaigns he practiced dictating letters on horseback and keeping two scribes at once busy, or, as Oppius says, even more. We are told, moreover, that Caesar was the first to devise intercourse with his friends by letter, since he could not wait for personal interviews on urgent matters owing to the multitude of his occupations and the great size of the city.

. . . and in the day-time he would have himself conveyed to garrisons, cities, or camps, one slave who was accustomed to write from dictation as he traveled sitting by his side, and one soldier standing behind him with a sword. (Plut. Caes. 17.3-4)

His preference for the efficient use of secretaries, according to Plutarch, was not limited to the litter. Since the context is the excellence of Caesar's horsemanship, it is quite plausible that what Plutarch considered incredible were Caesar's ability to dictate on horseback *and* to more than one secretary at a time. Thus, for our purposes, these citations allow us to conclude that dictating to one's secretary while strolling about, reclining at meal or sitting by the roadside was hardly worthy of praise but rather routine.

To summarize our discussion thus far, (1) a secretary was used for letter writing in several ways and in a host of situations, whether he was an amateur or professional, and (2) regardless of when, where or through whom a letter was written, the sender was held completely responsible for the content and form of the letter.

IDENTIFYING PAUL'S SECRETARY

As was typical for Greco-Roman letters, Paul did not identify his secretary by name. In Romans, Paul's secretary sent a greeting, and thus we learn that his name was Tertius. Other than having a Latin name, this information does little to help us identify him. When we say we are seeking to identify Paul's secretary, we do not mean this type of personal information, but rather we are seeking to identify him professionally.

Team member, private slave or contracted secretary? Was Paul's secretary (or secretaries) a member of his team? Although those having secondary level education had some basic training in letter writing, taking down a letter required skills beyond that of the typical literate member of society. Being literate did not qualify someone to be a secretary. There are no indications in Paul's letters or in Acts that any member of Paul's team had specialized training as a secretary. Therefore, it is unwise to presume that Timothy or some other member of the team could take dictation and prepare a proper letter.

There is also no indication that all wealthy members of society retained personal secretaries (usually slaves). Certainly, those who were so inclined kept personal secretaries, as all the ultra-wealthy of Rome probably did. However, we cannot presume that a wealthy member of an early church automatically had a personal secretary who could be loaned to Paul.

Paul most likely found his secretaries in the same place as almost everyone else, in the market. Like other craftsmen, secretaries could be contracted in the marketplace. We cannot be certain there was a guild (a "Secretaries Union") that maintained a stall in the main market; however, most other trades did. When a person wished to send a letter, he or she sought a secretary in the market. This was more likely the procedure for short letters and business contracts. In the case of longer letters, a secretary likely went to the author. We need not imagine Paul standing in front of a counter at a secretary's shop dictating Romans. Likely he hired a secretary to come to him to prepare the letter. Whether Paul and his team personally paid the expense or a patron paid for the secretary is uncertain. Nonetheless, as we will see in chapter ten, letter writing was not an insignificant expense that was taken on lightly.

Training. While a particular letter (e.g., Romans) may have used a better trained secretary, there is no evidence to suggest Paul's secretaries in general were better or less well trained than what is seen in most papyrus letters. There are ample instances from the papyri to show that most secretaries had good penmanship and could prepare a neat letter. There are also plenty of examples of letters with adequate grammar and spelling, written by a secretary for someone who was illiterate or barely literate.

However, two common mistakes should be avoided here. We can illustrate these mistakes from Ephesians 6:12. First, we should not assume the typical secretary was capable of fine nuances of rhetoric. While there were secretaries like Tiro and Eumenes, who apparently were well versed in advanced rhetoric, neither of these men was a typical secretary. They were the elite. We should not credit such skills to all secretaries, for the evidence from the papyri does not demonstrate a pervasive rhetorical sophistication among secretaries. In describing the Christian's struggle against evil, Paul laid out four prepositional phrases without conjunctions (Eph 6:12), a "powerful rhetorical device."[41] When such elements are present in Paul's letters, we should first assume they came from Paul or a team member and not immediately credit the secretary. Since a fairly consistent, medium-level rhetorical sophistication is found in all of Paul's letters,[42] it is more reasonable to conclude that Paul was the common thread rather than his various secretaries or occa-

---

[41]Peter O'Brien, *Ephesians,* Pillar Series (Grand Rapids: Eerdmans, 1999), p. 466 n. 112.

[42]Bultmann is probably correct when he maintains that Paul's use of the diatribe (and other rhetorical elements) was an unconscious, unintentional imitation (see the discussion in Stan Stowers, *The Diatribe and Paul's Letter to the Romans,* SBLDS 57 [Chico, Calif.: Scholars, 1981], pp. 18-19). Furthermore, Paul's frequent use of certain stereotyped formulae and conventions, as well as his lack of a large repertoire of rhetorical elements, support the consensus that Paul was not trained in a rhetorical school but rather picked up elements in his preaching style from the (Diaspora) synagogue; so Nigel Turner, *Style,* vol. 4 in *A Grammar of New Testament Greek,* ed. J. H. Moulton (Edinburgh: T & T Clark, 1976), p. 87, and Doty, *Letters,* p. 45. Paul's use of rhetoric was forged in the crucible of his mission work rather than in a classroom.

sional coauthors. Luke likewise paints a picture of Paul as a rhetorician.

Second, while secretaries often corrected grammar, this did not necessarily include fine points of grammar. Paul stated our struggle was against "blood and flesh" rather than the more customary "flesh and blood."[43] This was a minor stylistic faux pas,[44] and probably too fine a grammatical distinction to be a concern for any but the pickiest of grammarians. Issues such as unconventional word order evidently did not concern Paul or his secretary.

Place of work. As we saw in the life of Pliny the Elder, writers composed material in the midst of daily life. Certainly Pliny was being held up as a premier example of the dedicated scholar by his admiring nephew, and we would not want to describe Paul as "dictating material to a secretary while being scrubbed after a bath." Allowing for Pliny as an extreme, we can feel comfortable saying that Paul did take opportunities afforded by a few days' stopover in a town to compose material. Paul preached in synagogues and in the market; he no doubt spoke to guests after dinner in the homes where he was hosted. He debated and discussed material with his team as they walked along the road or rode aboard ship. All of these occasions produced opportunities for Paul to take notes and hone material. It is reasonable that Paul, like other ancient writers, was always in the process of composing, editing and polishing material as he traveled and ministered.[45]

This material under construction might best be termed "pre-letter" bits of writing. Composing a major letter, moving from notes to a complete letter, was a significant undertaking. This process required more time than a few nights' stopover afforded. First, Paul and his team needed to locate an available secretary and reach an agreement about when the work would be done and how much it would cost. Presumably, the secretary did not begin that moment. When available, the secretary came to Paul with the proper materials ready. The secretary had to write down the first draft of notes, leave and prepare a written first draft. After returning with a first draft, he would jot down the corrections, additions, etc. noted by Paul and his team, then leave and prepare another draft.[46] This process would continue until the draft was approved. Then a polished copy was prepared. This entire process (described in more detail later) required more time than a few days. Cicero told his friend Atticus that to write longer letters he needed a more extended stay in one place.[47] We are probably wise to locate the writing out of the actual letters in places where Paul had longer stays, such as Corinth or Ephesus or Rome.

---

[43]See also Rom 14:9; Col 3:11.

[44]See Turner, *Style*, p. 86.

[45]Paul Barnett, *Jesus and the Rise of Early Christianity: A History of New Testament Times* (Downers Grove, Ill.: InterVarsity Press, 2002), p. 339, suggests this for Romans.

[46]See Betz, *Galatians*, p. 312; and Witherington, *Galatia*, p. 442.

[47]Cic. *Att.* 5.14.

CONCLUSIONS FOR PAUL AS A LETTER WRITER

Once the secretary arrived with his supplies, he was ready to take down Paul's letter. Although there is no way to be certain exactly how Paul employed his secretary, we can lay out some probable parameters, especially by eliminating the less likely options.

It is unlikely that Paul dictated slowly to the secretary, thus using him as a transcriber of his letters. Philippians and 1 Thessalonians could have been dictated in about two and a half hours, but 1 Corinthians would have required over ten hours of continuous dictation and Romans would have needed over eleven.[48] It is not just an issue of time. Paul's letters do not read like a letter dictated slowly, as required by a transcriber. We are reminded of Seneca's criticism of someone who stammered badly, saying that he spoke like someone who was dictating,[49] or Cicero's description of dictating syllable by syllable.[50]

It is also unwise to assume Paul had routine access to a secretary trained in shorthand. It is possible Tertius was trained in shorthand and the initial draft of Romans was taken down in this way;[51] the book of Romans demonstrates more oratorical features than Paul's other letters. Nevertheless it would be an error to assume this for all of Paul's letters. Shorthand writers were probably too uncommon as well as too expensive for Paul's general use.

It is also unlikely that Paul used his secretary as a composer of letters in his name. Here are several reasons why:

1. It was not a common practice.

2. The author used the method when he did not care about the letter's content; Paul and his team were writing *because* they had something particular they wished to say.

3. The method was used, according to the few examples we have, to deceive the recipients (except for the example where a government official, Quintus, had secretaries compose official letters).

4. The secretary was actually a peer of the writer and not a typical secretary. This would not by definition preclude Timothy, for instance, from composing in Paul's name, but it does argue against a secretary doing so. Yet, we must then argue that Timothy or another colleague was deliberately deceiving his readers.[52]

---

[48]According to the conservative estimates of Eduard Strange, "Diktierpausen in den Paulusbriefen," *ZNW* 18 (1918): 109-17.

[49]Sen. *Ep.* 40.10.

[50]Cic. *Att.* 13.25.3.

[51]See Richards, *Secretary,* pp. 170-73, 195. Philippians also shows less noticeable influences from a secretary.

[52]The fact that the writer intended to deceive (not to honor) must be taken into account in any argument for apostolic pseudepigrapha. See the conclusions of Wilder, *Pseudonymity,* p. 123: "First, a concept of intellectual property which could be violated existed in Greco-Roman antiquity. Second, many writers in Greco-Roman antiquity had scruples regarding literary property. In many cases these authors did not regard plagiarism, tampering, and the fictive use of another person's name with indifference. Third, similar hesitations were operative within Christian circles."

Most likely Paul's secretary fell in that middle area between the extremes of transcriber and composer. Paul (and his team) dictated the letter, compromising between a painfully slow, syllable-by-syllable rate of speech and the rapid rate of normal speech. The secretary, unable to take shorthand, also compromised. Unable to maintain the complete precision of verbatim transcription, the secretary took notes as complete and detailed as he could. He then prepared a rough draft, probably on washable papyrus sheets or stacks of wax tablets. Paul and his team heard the letter read and made corrections and additions. (The way these changes were inserted will be discussed in the next chapter.) The process of editing and revising continued until Paul and his team were completely satisfied, since they, and especially Paul, had ultimate responsibility for every word of the letter.[53]

---

[53]Cicero could argue over the use of a preposition; Cic. *Att.* 7.3.

6

IDENTIFYING INSERTED MATERIAL

*S*cholars have long recognized that Paul's letters contain material he himself did not compose, such as Old Testament passages. New Testament scholars also recognize that Paul on occasion quoted traditions of the early church. For example, in 1 Corinthians 15:3-5 Paul noted that he passed on to the Corinthian church material that had been passed on to him:

> For I handed on to you as of first importance what I in turn had received: that Christ died for our sins in accordance with the scriptures, and that he was buried, and that he was raised on the third day in accordance with the scriptures.

More than this Paul quotes sections from early Christian hymns, confessional statements and other material known to his church members. Such material is often now termed "preformed" because it was composed some time prior to the composition of the letter itself. Preformed material is evident in Paul, not only in well-known passages like the Philippian hymn (Phil 2:6-11),[1] but also in lesser-known passages.[2] While scholars may want to debate over a particular passage, whether it was composed by Paul or quoted by Paul, they all agree that Paul's letters contain preformed material.

MODERN CONCEPTS OF PLAGIARISM AND COPYRIGHT

In modern Western society, to use another person's material, a writer must give credit— and often pay for it. Plagiarism is commonly defined as using material without indicating that the material originated with someone else. Writers today copyright their material to insure their ideas are not "borrowed" without giving due credit (and often compensation).

Obviously modern copyright and plagiarism laws did not exist in Paul's time. Yet more than this, the idea of restricting the use of someone else's material did not occur to an-

---

[1]The exact structure of this hymn is still debated. The classic treatment remains Ralph Martin, *Carmen Christi: Philippians 2:5-11 in Recent Interpretation and in the Setting of Early Christian Worship*, SNTSMS 4, rev. ed. (Grand Rapids: Eerdmans, 1983). For a more recent discussion see Gordon Fee, *Philippians*, NICNT (Grand Rapids: Eerdmans, 1995).

[2]E. E. Ellis recently argued (*The Making of the New Testament Documents* [Leiden: Brill, 2002], p. 116) that large portions of Paul's letters are quoted or reworked pieces of preformed tradition: Rom 27%, 1 Cor 17%, 2 Cor 11%, Gal 32%, Eph 54%, Phil 7%, Col 42%, 1 Thess 37%, 2 Thess 24%, 1 Tim 43%, 2 Tim 16%, Tit 46%, Philem 0%.

cients. They considered a new writing merely to be the latest row of bricks laid atop the previous layer in the wall of knowledge. Knowledge was not "owned" by anyone but everyone. All ideas came from building upon what was previously discovered by another.

Ancients had no compunctions against using another's words. First Corinthians 15:33 reads, "bad company ruins good morals." Paul was quoting Menander, a Greek poet, without "proper documentation." We know Paul was plagiarizing only because we have the Greek comedy *Thais,* where this line originated. Paul pulled this line from the play, but neither Paul nor any other ancient writer would have considered himself "caught" at anything. They freely borrowed material. Pliny the Younger told how, when his uncle found a passage he liked in someone else's work, he had his secretary copy it into his notebooks for him to use later.[3] W. W. Tarn demonstrated that ancient writers kept "endless collections" of snippets they pulled from other sources.[4] We must not unfairly apply our modern concepts and standards back on Paul.

Since there are clearly demonstrated places where Paul used material from another without specifically indicating it, we must assume there are other instances of borrowed material we have not "caught" because we do not have the other sources. Actually, we don't even have to assume this; often the borrowed material still shows signs of its foreign birth, since it was originally created for another time and context.

Preformed Material

Preformed material is a broad category which incorporates all forms of material imported into Paul's letters; that is, anything that wasn't composed on the spot. This can mean Old Testament quotations, other quotations, early church hymns and confessions, etc. Paul had composed some of these; others had been composed by someone else. In either case, the piece was formed sometime prior to the composition of the letter, hence, preformed.

Criteria for detecting preformed material. Paul and his coauthors did not always say when they were quoting material. Then, like now, they knew their readers would recognize it. If in a personal testimony, I tell a group of senior adults at a church: "I can never thank Jesus enough for what he did for me on a hill far away," the group would recognize the phrase "on a hill far away" as part of a much-loved hymn. More importantly, they would be able to complete the phrase with ". . . stood an old, rugged cross." In fact, for my testimony to make full sense, I *need* them to be able mentally to complete the phrase. In my testimony I was thanking Jesus for his work on the cross. Quoting preformed tradition was—and is—a very powerful tool for building bridges with an audience. In my example my allusion to this hymn also brought into my testimony all the positive images the congregation held for that hymn. Since it is a hymn much loved by that population of the church, I benefit from the allusion. I have tried this same allusion

---

[3]Pliny *Ep.* 3.5.15-16.
[4]Tarn, *Alexander the Great,* 2:307.

with college freshman with very mixed results. However, when I describe Paul visiting Ephesus and then deciding he will return as soon as he can, I can say "I'll be back" in my best Arnold Schwarzenegger voice and they immediately recognize the quote from *The Terminator* movies.

Quoting preformed material is most successful when the hearers also know and recognize the quotation. As modern readers we often do not recognize when Paul is using preformed material. When the quoted material is very short, like "on a hill far away," it is difficult for a foreigner to recognize it as quoted material. So, as foreigners in Paul's world, we sometimes struggle to detect this material. Scholars suspect several short phrases in Paul's letters were actually quoted snippets familiar to the readers. For instance, the traditional confession, "Jesus is Lord," was taken over by Paul and his team. While these phrases are preformed, it is difficult to decide if they should be considered "quoted." A phrase like "Jesus is Lord" is so short that it probably became part of their own thought, so integrated with their theology that it was no longer a borrowed piece. There are other bits that also may have begun as preformed traditions, but these are too brief, or perhaps too assimilated into the team's thought, to be labeled as quoted material every place they occur (e.g., "Christ died for,"[5] "one God,"[6] the clothing metaphors about doffing vices[7] and donning Christ, "image of God," and deliverance formulae[8]). W. D. Davies called these "fragments of kerygma."[9]

Sometimes Paul told when he was quoting some material, such as "for it is written" (Gal 3:10) or "I handed on to you what I in turn had received" (1 Cor 15:3) or "the saying is sure" (1 Tim 3:1). Paul evidently did not choose to indicate always when he was citing preformed pieces. We are left with the task of distilling them from his letters.

So Paul's use of preformed material falls on a spectrum. On one extreme there are snippets of quoted material that are too elusive to be certain the material was quoted or already integrated into the team's theology. On the other extreme there are places where the quoted material was introduced by a phrase that clearly identified it as preformed. The challenge is identifying the material between these extremes.[10] Criteria can be helpful to

---

[5]Rom 5:6, 8; 14:15; 1 Cor 8:11; 2 Cor 5:14-15.

[6]Rom 3:30; 1 Cor 8:4, 6; Gal 3:20; Eph 4:6; 1 Tim 2:5; cf. Mt 19:17 and elsewhere; Mk 12:29; Jn 8:41; Jas 2:19.

[7]Rom 1:29-31; 13:13; 1 Cor 6:9-11; 2 Cor 12:20-21; Gal 5:19-22; Eph 5:3-5; Col 3:5-8.

[8]Rom 2:16; Gal 1:3-4; 1 Thess 1:10. Other "bits" may include words of the Lord (1 Cor 7:10; 9:14; 13:2; Rom 12:14; 13:9; 16:19; 1 Thess 4:2, 15), liturgical elements, such as "amen" (1 Cor 14:16; 2 Cor 1:20), *abba* (Rom 8:15; Gal 4:6), and the triad "faith, hope, and love" (1 Thess 1:3; 5:8; Col 1:4-5; Eph 4:2-5; Gal 5:5-6; Rom 5:1-5; and esp. 1 Cor 13:13; cf. Heb 6:10-12; 10:22-24; and 1 Pet 1:3-8, 21-22). See also A. M. Hunter, *Paul and His Predecessors*, 2nd ed. (London: SCM Press, 1961), pp. 33-34.

[9]W. D. Davies, *Paul and Rabbinic Judaism*, 4th ed. (Philadelphia: Fortress, 1980), pp. 136-41.

[10]E.g., Eph 1:3-14 is quite likely a christological hymn, but it is often not identified as such; see, e.g., J. T. Sanders, *The New Testament Christological Hymns*, SNTSMS 15 (Cambridge: Cambridge University Press, 1971). It is, however, strongly asserted to be a tradition by Felice Montagnini, "Christological Features in Eph 1:3-14," in *Paul de Tarse: Apôtre du notre temps*, ed. L. De Lorenzi (Rome: Abbey of St. Paul, 1979), esp. pp. 538-39.

detect preformed material in the letters of Paul.

Establishing criteria can be a difficult task. The best approach is to examine passages that are already widely accepted as traditional and distill some characteristic criteria from them; that is, indicators in the text that can then be taken to other texts.[11] The following helpful criteria are divided into two general categories based on whether they identify a passage as preformed because of its content or its form.[12]

Criteria related to content. These criteria use the content of a passage as an indication the passage was preformed.

1. A formula may introduce material as a tradition. Often technical terms like "receiving" (*paralambanō*) and "handing over" (*paradidōmi*), or less technical formulae, like "this saying is sure," are employed. In the case of confessional traditions, more specialized vocabulary may be used, such as "confess" (*homologein*) followed by "that" (*hoti*), a double accusative, or an infinitive.[13]

2. Often preformed material begins with "who"; that is, the material deliberately omits the name of the one being praised and instead begins with a relative pronoun.[14] The best-known example is the Philippian hymn (Phil 2:6-11), which begins: "who, though he was in the form of God, did not . . .""

3. Multiple attestations[15] (when the material is cited in more than one letter) can indicate a preformed tradition, especially if there is little probability of direct literary dependence.[16]

---

[11]This is not a circular method; it is a common procedure in such diverse disciplines as sociology, chemistry and geometry. Such criteria must be evaluated in terms of their reliability (the ability of a criterion to produce consistent results) and their validity (the ability of a criterion to measure what it claims to measure).

[12]My initial search for criteria was aided considerably by gathering suggestions from the casual observations of a host of writers. Three works, though, were especially helpful: R. Jewett, "The Redaction and Use of an Early Christian Confession in Romans 1:3-4," in *The Living Text*, ed. D. E. Groh (Lanham, Md.: University Press of America, 1985), pp. 100-102; C. L. Palmer, "The Use of Traditional Materials in Hebrews, James, and 1 Peter," (Ph.D. diss., Southwestern Baptist Theological Seminary, 1985), pp. 6-8; and Markus Barth, "Traditions in Ephesians," *New Testament Series* 30 (1984): 9-10.

[13]See V. H. Neufeld, *The Earliest Christian Confessions*, NTTS 5 (Grand Rapids: Eerdmans, 1963), p. 20.

[14]See M. Barth, "Traditions in Ephesians," p. 10. He also notes that "whether hymns sung in praise of God actually are older than obvious Christ-hymns (W. Bousset; R. Deichgräber) does not affect the fact that both types stem from traditions."

[15]To adapt a criterion from source criticism in the gospels, D. R. Catchpole, "Tradition History," in *New Testament Interpretation: Essays on Principles and Methods*, ed. I. H. Marshall (Grand Rapids: Eerdmans, 1972), pp. 174-76, may be justified in his rejection of this for gospel studies, but for the present application, "multiple attestation" may be valid. The criterion of "coherence" (p. 177) may be useful for determining traditional *concepts*; e.g., Paul's teaching on divorce (1 Cor 7:10) is likely traditional, being coherent with Jesus' (Mk 10:2-9; Lk 16:18; Mt 8:22 [=Lk 9:60]), especially since this particular teaching may be disconsonant with the establishment. Coherence, though, is insufficient to indicate more than a traditional *concept*.

[16]See, e.g., Ellis's use of this for determining the traditional nature of (1) certain Old Testament expositions. (2) the virtue/vice lists, and (3) the *Haustafeln*. E. E. Ellis, "Traditions in 1 Corinthians," *New Testament Series* 32 (1986): 482-83.

4. When a brief passage has multiple peculiar idioms or infrequent words or concepts, it may be an indicator of quoted material. When attempting to isolate non-Pauline traditions, this criterion becomes more important. It can be used, however, for any type of preformed material, since the genre of the literature affects diction and idiom. A piece composed originally as a different type of literature, such as a hymn, may still bear some marks of its original genre. This criterion must be applied with caution.[17]

5. Traditional material may be indicated by the presence of extraneous details; that is, details that are an integral part of the tradition but extraneous to its present context. A tradition piece was usually cited because one element of the tradition called it to mind. Yet the entire piece was quoted and later parts of the material may not fit as well. In fact, the tradition may drift off in a different direction. For example, to return to the Philippian hymn, Paul was arguing that the readers needed to have the same humble spirit that was in Christ, who was willing to put aside his heavenly glory and take on the lowly form of a servant. The hymn goes on to speak of Christ subsequently being highly exalted. It seems that this second part was not germane to Paul's argument. He was not wanting to emphasize that his readers will be highly exalted. The hymn perhaps came to Paul's mind because of the initial point, that Christ humbled himself.

6. Occasionally the actual content of the piece may indicate that it was a preformed tradition. Markus Barth suggests two situations: (1) when a passage summarizes the substance of the gospel, without concern for historical details or witnesses, or (2) when a passage suddenly comments on the cosmic reign of Christ, such as his preexistence or the parousia, coupling it with remarks about Christ's specific care for the church.[18] These may well be indicators the letter was quoting a preformed tradition.

Criteria related to form. These criteria use the format of the passage as an indication the passage is a preformed tradition.

7. The insertion of traditional material may interrupt the syntax or thought flow of the author; that is, the larger passage may read more smoothly when the material is removed.

8. Traditional material in Paul's letters often took a rhythmic form. Of course this can only be seen well in the original Greek. The material can often be arranged in parallel sense-lines or stanzas. Sometimes the lines begin or end with matching syllables (*homoiarcha* or *homoiteleuta*).[19] This parallelism, including chiasm, is a strong indicator of ancient preformed material.[20]

---

[17]The role of the secretary can easily account for many of these differences.
[18]M. Barth, "Traditions in Ephesians," p. 10.
[19]E.g., see Rom 14:7-9. Also see M. Barth, "Traditions in Ephesians," p. 10.
[20]E.g., see the chiasm in Rom 10:9-10. Also see M. Barth, "Traditions in Ephesians," p. 10.

9. Certain syntactical features (noticeable in Greek) appear to be common in the traditional material of the New Testament: the use of appositives, predicate nominatives, participial[21] and relative clauses (frequently in parallel), changes in person and number, and anarthrous nouns (nouns without an article) where usually the article was used.[22]

No criterion is decisive by itself. However, material that meets several criteria, especially if in both content and form, may well be preformed.

INTERPOLATIONS

Preformed material is the first of two types of material that have been inserted into Paul's letters. The second type is an interpolation. Many New Testament scholars talk about interpolations—a phrase, sentence or even a paragraph that has been inserted by someone else into Paul's letter. These scholars often discuss the telltale "signs" that indicate a particular passage is an interpolation. Yet most—if not all—of the "signs" of an interpolation are actually "signs" of any type of inserted material, including preformed material. It is necessary to distinguish interpolations from all other types of material woven into a letter. We need to isolate what exactly makes something an interpolation and not merely a preformed piece.

Defining an interpolation. William Walker provides a simple definition: "an interpolation is foreign material inserted deliberately and directly into the text of a document."[23] Since we do not have any of Paul's original letters, the problem of interpolations has long been a part of textual criticism. (Textual critics are scholars who compare the hundreds and even thousands of manuscript copies of a New Testament passage in order to determine what was the reading of the original text.) To cite a common example, Paul writes in Romans 8:1, "There is therefore now no condemnation for those who are in Christ Jesus." Some later Christian copyist felt this was perhaps too broad a statement, implying that someone could live however he or she wanted since there was no condemnation for those who are in Christ. Since Paul later mentioned (in v. 4) that the "just requirement of the law might be fulfilled in us, who walk not according to the flesh but according to the Spirit," this scribe interpolated his phrase "who walk not according to the flesh but according to the Spirit" back into verse 1. How can we be sure this phrase was interpolated? The addition does not appear in verse 1 until the fifth century. Earlier copies of Romans do not

---

[21]See Jewett, "Confession," p. 100. Participles at the beginning of subordinate clauses may be a strong indicator, esp. third-person singular aorists, so M. Barth, "Traditions in Ephesians," p. 10.

[22]Jewett, "Confession," p. 101. Barth generalizes this into a criterion of "brevity achieved by the use of anarthrous abstract nouns—sometimes coupled with repetitions and pleonasms in the form of synonyms or genitive appositives"; "Traditions in Ephesians," p. 10.

[23]William Walker, *Interpolations in the Pauline Letters*, JSNTS 213 (New York: Sheffield Academic Press, 2001), p. 23. Although I shall disagree with Walker, his work is a carefully argued and well-researched thesis. I am indebted to him. He has done much to bring the entire interpolation issue to the forefront.

have this addition.[24] Someone other than Paul inserted it. It is a clear interpolation.[25]

Ever since the late 1800s, when the presence of these interpolations became well known, some scholars have insisted that Paul's letters are filled with interpolations.[26] Broad scholarly agreement quickly developed for two conclusions:

1. Whenever there is manuscript evidence to indicate that material was later interpolated into the text, the added material is recognized as a later interpolation and removed from the text.

2. Theories arguing for extensive interpolations in Paul's letters—for which there is no manuscript evidence—are ungrounded. Scholars have consistently rejected the idea that Paul's letters were heavily interpolated soon after they were written.[27]

These two conclusions leave some middle ground. While most scholars reject the notion that there are many interpolations in Paul's letters, they do argue for some, even when there is no manuscript evidence to support this view. Their basic thesis is this: since our oldest copies of Paul's letters date no earlier than A.D. 200, there was still over a hundred years for material to be interpolated into Paul's letters with no manuscript evidence to reveal it. This requires, though, that all copies of that particular letter before the material was interpolated perished and that only the interpolated copies survived.

To argue for an interpolation without manuscript evidence requires us to recognize "inserted foreign material" when we read a letter of Paul. An interpolation is defined as foreign material inserted deliberately and directly into the text of a document. Yet, an Old Testament quotation is foreign material inserted deliberately and directly into the text. A writer often inserted foreign material into his text; we have seen many of these as preformed traditions. What exactly makes one a preformed tradition and another an inter-

---

[24]See Bruce Metzger, *A Textual Commentary on the Greek New Testament,* corr. ed. (New York: United Bible Societies, 1975), p. 515. The "c" corrector of Codex Sinaiticus dates to the seventh century; see Metzger, *Manuscripts of the Greek Bible: An Introduction to Paleography* (Oxford: Oxford University Press, 1981), p. 77.

[25]Walker (*Interpolations,* pp. 22-23) distinguishes between *gloss* and *interpolation*. A gloss is an explanatory note written in the margin of a manuscript (a copy of a book of the Bible) by a copyist to explain a passage. Copyists commonly wrote glosses in the margins. However, if a copyist also noticed he or some previous copyist had accidentally omitted a word or phrase when the manuscript was copied, what could he do? He could write the omitted phrase in the margin. So glosses and corrections are both in the margins of manuscripts. Occasionally a later copyist would think a gloss was actually a correction and would insert it into the text (like a correction) when he made his new copy. In such an instance the gloss became an interpolation. Walker suggests this is what likely happened in Romans 8:1. Most scholars, though, use the terms *gloss* and *interpolation* interchangeably.

[26]E.g., Carl Clemen (1894), P.-L. Couchoud (1923), A. F. Loisy (1935), and more recently, J. C. O'Neill (1972). Winsome Munro argued for extensive interpolations in Paul's letters (see *Authority in Paul and Peter: The Identification of a Pastoral Stratum in the Pauline Corpus and 1 Peter,* SNTSMS 45 [Cambridge: Cambridge University Press, 1983]). See also Walker, *Interpolations,* pp. 15-16.

[27]See, e.g., Victor Furnish's stringent critique of O'Neill; Furnish, "Pauline Studies," in *The New Testament and Its Modern Interpreters,* ed. E. J. Epp and George MacRae, pp. 321-50 (Philadelphia: Fortress, 1989), p. 324.

polation? Walker compiles the characteristics of interpolations noted by scholars and concludes that interpolations have the following characteristics: they disrupt the flow of thought or add specific details, they can be removed because of an identifiable literary structure, and they may contain terms, symbols, or ideas foreign—or even antithetical—to the context.[28]

Yet these characteristics apply to any non-Pauline preformed piece. Walker then concludes his introduction by adding that an interpolation is "material that was neither composed by Paul nor included by Paul in the letter in which it now appears." He specifically excludes material composed by Paul for some other occasion and then inserted also in its present location and also any material composed by someone other than Paul but inserted in the letter by Paul himself.[29] At this point Walker has rightly eliminated from discussion the other forms of preformed material. Here we have found the true characteristics of an interpolation. An interpolation is not merely preformed material. It must have two defining characteristics to be an interpolation: it must be non-Pauline (not from the mind and pen of Paul) and it must be post-Pauline (Paul did not insert the material). Conservative scholars—myself included—become uncomfortable in even discussing the possibility of an interpolation that escaped detection in the manuscript tradition. However, Walker is correct that we cannot and should not rule out this possibility a priori.

Criteria for detecting interpolations. Although many works on interpolations list criteria, most of the criteria merely detect preformed material. While these are a good first step, they cannot be deemed evidence of an interpolation. To be criteria for detecting an interpolation, they must be able to determine the material was non-Pauline *and* post-Pauline.

Determining material is non-Pauline. In actuality, being non-Pauline is only a characteristic of an early but still detectable interpolation. Let us return to our example of an interpolation in Romans 8:1. All scholars agree this is an interpolation. Yet the material is clearly Pauline (drawn from verse 4). Without the manuscript evidence it would never have been labeled an interpolation.

Obviously the passage does not have to be non-Pauline to be an interpolation. It only must be non-Pauline to be detectable without manuscript evidence. Since all scholars agree on removing interpolations detectable in the manuscript tradition, the only dispute is over detecting interpolations where there is no manuscript evidence. To find these the material must be non-Pauline.

We must be careful not to be overly confident in our ability to determine that material is non-Pauline; secretarial influences dilute our ability to do style analyses. Nevertheless, there are still useful criteria to suggest a passage may be non-Pauline. I discussed them earlier under the category of "criteria for detecting preformed material." These criteria can

---

[28]Walker, *Interpolations*, pp. 23-24.
[29]Ibid., p. 24.

identify passages that may well be non-Pauline. They cannot, however, differentiate between a non-Pauline preformed tradition and a non-Pauline interpolation. They indicate only that a passage may be non-Pauline.

Determining material is post-Pauline. The passage does not have to be post-Pauline to be an interpolation. There were three opportunities to add non-Pauline material to a letter.

1. Paul himself could choose to incorporate some material by another in his letter. This is a standard preformed piece. Paul used this material to support and enhance the argument he was making. This "foreign material" was redacted into what he was doing. The Philippian hymn is a good example of where we can still detect the insertion. Sometimes, though, the insertion was woven so smoothly into the letter that it becomes difficult to detect. Walker quotes an agricultural metaphor from Eugene Lovering to illustrate the difference:

   > interpolation is like pushing a shovel in the ground, separating two portions of soil, inserting something, and removing the shovel; evidence is left, but the breaks are reasonably clean and contained. Redaction, on the other hand, much more closely resembles a plant which has grown in the ground; in pulling it up, the roots come too, and it is unclear where the redaction ends.[30]

   In such cases, we sometimes are unsure about which verses actually begin or end the imported material because the material has been woven in so well.

2. During the writing of the letter, another team member could insist on adding some material that he thought was relevant. It was not the direction Paul was headed. It interrupts his argumentation and probably cannot be redacted seamlessly into what he is doing. It sticks out. This means it was not part of the logical flow for the letter Paul had working in his mind. It likely also reflects a viewpoint distinct from the one Paul was developing in the letter. It was "foreign."

3. After the letter was finished and dispatched, someone else could later interpolate material into the letter, as we saw in Romans 8:1.

Of the three opportunities to interpolate that we just described, the first opportunity is not truly an interpolation at all; it is merely Paul incorporating someone else's material into his letter. We have already seen multiple examples of his use of preformed material. This category should not be labeled an interpolation. The other two options must be explored. The third option is that of the traditional interpolation. The second option is what is less commonly considered. Is this really an interpolation? Traditionally, scholars have limited discussions of interpolations to material added after the letter was written and dispatched; that is, after the letter left the control of Paul. The definition of interpolation, however, must be broadened since the criteria for detecting an

---

[30]Walker, *Interpolations,* p. 23. Lovering attributes the metaphor to James H. Charlesworth, but there is no written record of Charlesworth using this metaphor.

interpolation cannot differentiate between these two options.

We saw earlier that it is unwise to view Paul as a solitary author who wrote the letter with pen in hand and without the presence of others. It is describing Paul in our own modern Western image. Paul had coauthors, a secretary, and usually colleagues, all of whom felt varying degrees of freedom to contribute to the letter's formation and content. When any of them added material that was not at the initiative of Paul, how would it differ from the traditional interpolation?

Identifying possible interpolators. I have already discussed that Paul had coauthors. While coauthorship was rare, Witherington rightly concludes "it was equally rare for the opening line of a letter to formally mention the name of someone who had nothing to do with the document."[31] The listing of a cosender was not a meaningless convention.[32] As we demonstrated in chapter two, the "we" in Paul's letters must be taken seriously. Witherington argues:

> Neither was it pro forma to say "we" even if one meant "I" in a letter. This means that in Pauline letters where more than one person is mentioned in the address *and* the first-person plural "we" is used to refer to the senders of the letter, we should probably assume that collaborators were involved in composing the letter.[33]

It may be helpful to review who were the coauthors and team members for each of Paul's letters (see table 6.1). The letter address identifies the coauthor(s) while the closing greetings tell who else was working with Paul at that time and place. Listing these in chronological order[34] suggests some interesting observations.

The early letters (Galatians, 1-2 Thessalonians) list all the known companions in the address and have no one left to send greetings. Had Paul not yet learned to distinguish between those who coauthored and those who were his coworkers who contributed more informally? Or did all coworkers engage as they were able in the writing of the letter? Whatever the situation in Galatians, Paul did not continue this custom.

I must note some intriguing observations related to Timothy. By most chronological reconstructions, the letters where Timothy is mentioned are placed in this order: Early Letters, 2 Corinthians, Romans and then the Prison Letters. Some status issues seem to suggest themselves. In the early letters, Paul and Timothy are co-equals in the address. This is likely another sign that Paul was still developing his epistolary practice. Later, Paul stands apart in the address, with Timothy (or Sosthenes) taking a distant second, as in 1-2 Corinthians. In Romans, Timothy is only a sender of greetings. Much later, near the end of his first Roman imprisonment (Philippians), Timothy is again raised to equal status in the address.

---

[31]Witherington, *Paul Quest*, p. 101.

[32]So Murphy-O'Connor, *Paul the Letter Writer*, p. 18.

[33]Witherington, *Paul Quest*, pp. 101-2.

[34]I am following a standard Pauline chronology with an early South Galatian scenario. I find the best current articulation of this view to be Witherington, *Acts*, pp. 81-97.

Table 6.1. Coauthors and Team Members in Paul's Letters

Letter	Address (ordered according to the Greek)	The Letter sends greetings from
Galatians	Paul, an apostle . . . and all the brothers with me to the churches	None
1 Thessalonians	Paul and Silas and Timothy to the church	None
2 Thessalonians	Paul and Silas and Timothy to the church	None
1 Corinthians	Paul, called an apostle . . . and Sosthenes, the brother	The churches of Asia; Aquila and Priscilla, and the church in their home; and all the brothers. [Note: Timothy was not with Paul at the time (1 Cor 4:17; 16:10; Acts 19:22). Apollos was there but sent no personal greeting (1 Cor 16:12.)]
2 Corinthians	Paul, an apostle . . . and Timothy, the brother	All the saints
Romans	Paul, a servant . . . to God's beloved (in Rome?)	Timothy, Lucius, Jason, Sosipater, Tertius, Gaius, Erastus, Quartus and all the churches of Christ
Colossians	Paul, apostle . . . and Timothy, the brother	Aristarchus, Mark, Jesus, Epaphras, Luke and Demas.
Philemon	Paul, a prisoner, and Timothy, the brother	Epaphras, Mark, Aristarchus, Demas and Luke
Ephesians	Paul, an apostle	None [Note: Tychicus is the carrier]
Philippians	Paul and Timothy, servants	The brothers who are with me and all the saints
1 Timothy	Paul, an apostle	None
Titus	Paul, a servant and apostle	Everyone with Paul
2 Timothy	Paul, an apostle	Eubulus, Linus, Claudia and all the brothers

Paul seems so aware of Timothy's presence that he cannot use "I" in a Thanksgiving Formula when he cowrites with him. Timothy is a coauthor for 2 Corinthians; he is not present for 1 Corinthians. Yet Timothy is not always a coauthor. He is not listed as a coauthor for Romans, although he is obviously there for he sends greetings, and then he is a coauthor again for Colossians and Philemon.

There may be indications of status in how the letter address was shaped. After the early letters, Paul was clearly the leader and was described more elaborately with titles like "apostle," while the coauthor was termed "the brother" (e.g., 1-2 Cor; Col). Even though Timothy was merely termed "the brother," he was still a coauthor. The named cosenders were not merely coworkers because in letters with named coauthors, there are also named coworkers in the closing greetings. Something has differentiated them.

One might argue that if a team member was present when the letter was drafted, then he was included in the letter address; otherwise, he merely sent greetings later. But this is probably too simplistic. Writing took multiple stages and arguing that a team member was absent during the entire drafting process except the ending (on multiple letter writing occasions) seems unlikely. It is more likely that the team member had to contribute to be listed as a cosender. If he was part of the ministry team, he sent greetings.

One might argue that a team member had to be connected to the letter to be placed in the address; otherwise, he was listed in the closing greetings. Epaphras, though, was integrally involved in the Colossian letter. He was "a beloved fellow servant" and "a faithful minister on their behalf." He was likely the one who brought the news that prompted the letter (Col 1:7-8). Paul took pains to indicate his support of Epaphras, including him as part of the "thanksgiving" of the letter. Nonetheless, despite this key role, Epaphras was not listed in the letter address.

One might argue that as someone became closer to Paul, they were promoted from being merely a sender of greetings at the close of a letter to being a named colleague in the letter address, but the problem with Timothy in Romans prevents this. Timothy was a named coauthor in 2 Corinthians. Was he subsequently demoted for the letter to the Romans and then promoted again for Colossians? Being in the letter address does not appear to be merely an indicator of favored status with Paul.

Whatever the role of the named cosender, it went beyond courtesy, presence, connection or favored status. I must conclude that a named cosender, at least after the early letters, had a different—presumably larger—role than the other team members. Otherwise, I see no explanation for some team members being in the letter address while others are in the concluding greetings, especially when Timothy appears first in the address, then in the greetings, then back again in the address.[35] It cannot merely represent status or personal closeness.

A coauthor was also distinguished from a secretary. Secretaries were not named as coauthors in letters. (Secretaries could perhaps have as much influence as a coauthor, but social roles kept secretaries out of the letter addresses.) What of the occasional suggestion that Luke served as a "secretary" for the Pastorals and hence coauthored them? Luke is

---

[35]It has been argued that Timothy was deliberately omitted from Roman's address because Paul was seeking to keep the focus on him and his authority. Yet, this argument still implies that placing Timothy's name in the address afforded him a larger role than listing him in the closing greetings. Also, I suggest that listing Timothy in the address did not dilute Paul's authority, since Timothy was known by all as a subordinate member. If anything, it would increase Paul's authority by showing consensus.

not named as a coauthor in the Pastorals. While he could have played a major secretarial role in 2 Timothy, he chose (or Paul chose for Luke) not to be a named coauthor.[36]

Pre- vs. post-dispatch interpolations. Paul had coauthors. However, the question may be raised whether Paul allowed his coauthors to interpolate (i.e., did he allow them to add material that was "foreign" to what he was doing)? An initial reaction might be to say "no." Yet to maintain this we must argue that any input from a colleague had to be completely consistent with Paul's theology and completely in line with his argumentation. One must argue Paul did not allow a colleague to express a tangential or complementary thought, and certainly not a contrasting thought. Thus, we must be willing to assert that Paul's ultimate interest was in expressing his individual viewpoint. While this might describe a modern Western writer, it does not fit a first-century Mediterranean writer. We should not reduce the contribution of his team members to mere thoughts and ideas that Paul would have had anyway. We reduce coauthorship to a meaningless term if what the coauthor adds is not non-Pauline. One might still object that Paul would not allow another to "tamper" with his letter. We might not allow it, but we have already seen that Paul shared his letter address with others. He lists coauthors. His secretary had editorial license. Paul was the leader, but the leader of a team. We must not automatically exclude a contributing coauthor.

It is fair to ask why such material is called an interpolation. If the material was put into the text at the time of composition, why is this insertion not merely another non-Pauline preformed piece, like the Philippian hymn? What makes it an interpolation? This material was put into the text at the wishes of someone other than Paul, and that is the classic definition of an interpolation. To be an interpolation, the material did not have to be post-Pauline, but it did have to be foreign to what Paul was doing. As such the material was not initiated by Paul or perhaps even desired by Paul, but merely permitted by Paul.

It would be impossible to find every time a colleague interjected an idea into the letter. Indeed most of the time their input would be indistinguishable from Paul's. But we could perhaps see their input when they introduced ideas quite distinct from Paul's. This material could be added at two different times in the process of letter writing: either when the letter was first being woven into a draft or when a draft was read, edited and modified.

If the material was interjected during the early drafting of that section, then it would be woven rather seamlessly into the passage. The theology or idea or method of argumentation might distinguish it, but there would be little signs of the seams. Lovering's plant metaphor describes it well.

If the material was interjected during a reading of that section (that is, during later editing), then it would perhaps interrupt more the flow of the passage. There is less chance Paul would make extensive modifications to weave the passage better into the text. It will look much like the typical later interpolation.

---

[36]Since Luke appeared to prefer an identity distinct from the Pauline team, I suspect it was Luke's preference not to be listed as a coauthor of the letter. Luke doesn't show any particular fondness for Paul's letters.

In either scenario a coauthor has interjected his thoughts and material into the letter, either early in the process or in a later draft. In both scenarios the interpolation occurred before it was dispatched; that is, in the original letter before it was sent off. For lack of a better term, I call this a pre-dispatch interpolation.

I also noted, as in the example from Romans 8:1, that someone centuries later, could interpolate something into a letter of Paul; that is, into some copy of the letter. It was after the original letter was dispatched and out of the hands of Paul and his team. It was a post-dispatch interpolation. This is what scholars typically mean by an interpolation. As such it is truly post-Pauline.

I suggest that there are two opportunities for someone besides Paul to interpolate material into his letter: pre- and post-dispatch. How do we distinguish between them? Is there any evidence that allows scholars to distinguish between pre- and post-dispatch interpolations? The only reliable method is manuscript evidence, however scant. All internal indicators would be unable to distinguish between material added before and after dispatch.

The issue of authorization. Since it is difficult to distinguish between pre- and post-dispatch interpolations, we must now ask why we should be concerned to distinguish between them. The answer is the issue of authorization. We commonly assume that all non-Pauline interpolations were post-dispatch. This may be a faulty assumption. Thus, when Gordon Fee concluded that 1 Corinthians 14:33b-35 was non-Pauline, he immediately described it as a post-dispatch interpolation, for which there was no evidence. By arguing it was post-dispatch, it can be labeled "unauthorized" by Paul and hence able to be ignored. Fee assumed "non-Pauline" equaled "post-Pauline."[37] If, however, material was interpolated into the letter before it was dispatched, then ultimately it had Paul's blessing as the leader of the team, whether or not he personally was thrilled with the addition. It may be too hasty to assume all interpolations were unauthorized additions. Perhaps there were pre-dispatch interpolations.

While we might consider coauthors only meddlers to be endured if not avoided, Paul might have viewed them as team members with whom to work toward consensus. Paul saw teamwork as the key to his mission. Witherington correctly notes:

> We cannot assume that Paul was much like a modern individualist. . . . In his letters he reflects the collectivist mentality again and again. His social networks are crucial to him personally but also in carrying out the shared task of spreading the good news.[38]

This does not suggest that Paul sacrificed his theology on the altar of teamwork. There were issues that superceded teamwork, as seen in Paul's break with Barnabas (Acts 15:39) or his refusal to heed Luke (Acts 21:14). Therefore, if Paul allowed the material into his

---

[37]Gordon Fee, *The First Epistle to the Corinthians*, NICNT (Grand Rapids: Eerdmans, 1987), pp. 699-708. Fee is a premier text-critic, a careful exegete and an exceptional scholar, but I must disagree with his conclusions here.

[38]Witherington, *Paul Quest*, p. 114.

letter, it must have carried his blessing. Witherington concludes that genuine letters of Paul could contain non-Pauline material with Paul's blessing.[39] Paul's letters were "group communications, and as such are often closer to official pronouncements than private correspondence."[40]

CONCLUSIONS FOR PAUL AS A LETTER WRITER

Paul's letters included preformed material such as Old Testament quotations, sections from early Christian hymns and snippets of early Christian traditions. Some of Paul's letters included material inserted by a coauthor into the letter during composition. This material was not part of Paul's original plan; the material sometimes interrupted his particular train of thought. Even though this material was non-Pauline, it was not un-Pauline or post-Pauline. The material was inserted during the letter's composition and thus had Paul's ultimate authorization. Some material was inserted into the letter during the early drafting of the letter. This material was usually woven rather seamlessly into the letter. Some material was added during the final editing of the letter and was not as neatly integrated.

---

[39]Witherington rightly distinguishes between *non*-Pauline material and *un*-Pauline material. The former, Paul would permit; the latter he would not. Ibid., p. 112.
[40]Ibid., p. 107.

7

WEAVING TOGETHER A LETTER

We saw in the last chapter that Paul inserted preformed materials into his letters. This was likely done in light of the procedures and limitations of ancient letter writing. To illustrate we will then look at several famous (or infamous) passages in Paul and consider if and how these might have been preformed passages inserted into his letters.

WEAVING INSERTED MATERIAL INTO A LETTER

When Paul wanted to insert preformed material, like quotations and previously composed sections, into his letters during composition, how did he do it? If a coauthor inserted material into a letter (a pre-dispatch interpolation) how was this done? The logistics of letter writing can help us understand this process better. As always, any suggestions should be consistent with letter-writing practices of the first century.

Weaving in preformed material. When composing his letters, Paul had preformed material he wished to insert. Often the material was brief and he incorporated it directly into what he was saying. Sometimes the inserted material was longer and therefore not as likely to have been dictated to the secretary. There was not any reason to dictate it. The material was just handed in written form to the secretary to be incorporated into the next draft.

In the first instance, the spontaneously dictated pieces of preformed material could be woven in so smoothly that they would be difficult to discern now. However, material that was pre-written might not be so smoothly incorporated. The secretary probably would not compose additional material to help seamlessly integrate the preformed material.

We believe Paul used both types of inserted material. Five examples will suffice.

1. Paul often quoted brief pieces, such as single sentences from the Old Testament (Gal 3:10-12, 16; 1 Cor 6:16) or short Jesus traditions (1 Cor 15:3), hymn fragments (1 Tim 3:16) or common sayings in the church (1 Tim 2:11-13). Paul did not look these up in a notebook; he had them memorized and incorporated them into his speech. Thus, visualizing how this type of oral material was inserted into a letter is not difficult. It is the prewritten material that needs further illustration.

2. In the Philippian hymn, Paul is exhorting his readers to have the same humble spirit that was in Christ, who willingly set aside his place of honor and took on the form of a servant. Though the hymn continued on to speak of Christ being highly exalted, that does

not seem to be Paul's point here. So it appears the hymn initially came to mind because it emphasized Christ humbling himself. When dictating the material directly, performed material was probably incorporated more smoothly into the context. For example, in the case of the Philippian hymn, the second section might have been truncated.

I suggest that, when drafting the letter, Paul made his point, "Let the same mind be in you that was in Christ Jesus," and then he (or a team member) remembered the hymn and instructed the secretary to insert it there. It is unlikely the hymn was dictated to the secretary, especially if it was recorded somewhere in a notebook. The secretary probably made a note to insert the material. Doing it this way freed the authors from having to recall the entire passage and also from having to edit it to prevent the material from going in another direction. If it was preformed and handed to a secretary, the entire piece would be inserted. During later editing the hymn was left intact since deleting existing material takes more initiative than shortening a quotation while dictating. I argue that if the extended material was contradictory or otherwise unacceptable, Paul would have edited the material. Since the extra material was tangential, it was left alone. Regardless of one's view of the Philippian hymn, the point is that a preformed piece inserted later by a secretary may contain subsequent parts of the material that drift from the letter's context and be superfluous or tangential to the main argument.[1]

3. It was stated earlier that the insertion of traditional material often interrupted the author's syntax or thought flow. The larger passage reads more smoothly without the material. This would be more likely when the inserted material was not dictated to the secretary. For example, Paul may have begun his letter to the Romans, paused to instruct his secretary to insert a preformed piece (Rom 1:3-4) in the next draft, and then continued speaking.[2] The passage thus reads more smoothly without the material because it was not "there" in the original presentation of the material. In this example, the Pauline introduction reads smoothly without the material, perhaps following more closely the typical Pauline form: ". . . the gospel concerning his son, [preformed material] Jesus Christ our Lord, through whom we have received grace and apostleship."

4. As another example, in 1 Corinthians 8:6, idols are nothing, Paul argues, because there is only one God and the food offered to idols is clean because Christ created all things. A tradition piece is then cited because it speaks of God as one and Christ as creator ("through whom all things"). Yet the piece goes on to speak of Christ as savior, a point unnecessary—even irrelevant—to the argument in 1 Corinthians 8.[3]

---

[1]Although Barth ("Traditions in Ephesians," p. 10) notes its subjective nature, he nonetheless considers this a valid indicator: an "interruption of the context, perhaps even contradiction to it which, however, is toned down by interpolations."

[2]This piece also meets criteria #2, 4, 8 and 9 (see pp. 97-99).

[3]Incidentally, this passage also meets other criteria (#4, 7, 8 and possibly 9). On the traditional character of 1 Cor 8:6, see also Ellis, "Traditions in 1 Corinthians," pp. 494-95.

5. Romans 14:7-9 is not usually considered traditional material,[4] yet at least six criteria are evident in this passage. (a) There are details, such as lording over the living and the dead, which are an integral part of the piece (note the consistent contrast of living and dying throughout) but are extraneous to the argument in Romans 14. (b) The flow of Paul's argument reads well with this piece removed, although these verses do provide the theological foundation for his argument. (c) There is the use of "Christ" alone. (d) as well as an abrupt change in person and number. (e) The parallelism, rhythm and similar endings (*homoiteleuta*) are striking.[5] And (f) although based on a common Pauline idiom, the language does deviate from his preferred expressions. For example, Paul prefers "Christ died and was raised" (1 Thess 4:14; 1 Cor 15:3-4; Rom 8:34),[6] but here the idiom is different: "Christ died and came to life." These six factors indicate this was likely a preformed piece, inserted here to give a theological basis for his argument. Paul inserted the piece, probably familiar to his readers, to help draw the readers to his argument.

Most readers recognize that there are preformed pieces of material in Paul's letters. I have only suggested ways in which these pieces might have been placed into the text. I have also suggested that the logistics of how material was woven in does have minor implications for interpreting the text.

Weaving in interpolations. If Paul's coauthors interpolated materials into his letters as they were being composed, how could these have been woven in? Even if we discount those scholars who find (post-dispatch) interpolations under every rock, there are still particular passages in various letters of Paul that have been declared interpolations by multiple scholars and at least suspect or difficult by many others.[7]

Let us look at 1 Corinthians 14:33b-35 ("women should keep silent") as a possible non-Pauline interpolation.[8] What valid reasons are offered to argue that this piece is an

---

[4]It is not cited as preformed in the commentaries (see, e.g., the commentaries by U. Wilckens, Thomas Schreiner, and Douglas Moo) or apparently by the UBS editors.

[5]It can be seen most clearly in the Greek:

1. *oudeis gar hēmōn heautō zē*
2. *kai oudeis heautō apothnēskei*
3. *ean te gar zōmen, tō kyriō zōmen,*
4. *ean te apothnēskōmen, tō kyriō apothnēskomen.*
5. *ean te oun zōmen*
6. *ean te apothnēskōmen*

[6]So, e.g., Doug Moo, *The Epistle to the Romans*, NICNT (Grand Rapids: Eerdmans, 1996), p. 845.

[7]Walker, *Interpolations*, p. 20. Nonetheless, no single passage in any letter of Paul has even general scholarly agreement as an interpolation. Scholars seem more willing to consider an entire letter pseudonymous than to consider only parts of the letter to be from someone other than Paul.

[8]It is considered such by many, among them: H. Conzelmann, *1 Corinthians*, trans. J. W. Leitch, Hermeneia (Philadelphia: Fortress, 1975), p. 246; Barrett, *1 Corinthians*, pp. 330-33; Fee, *First Epistle to the Corinthians*, p. 700; R. Hays, *First Corinthians*, Interpretation (Louisville: Westminster John Knox, 1997), p. 244. For the best discussion, see Thiselton, *1 Corinthians*, pp. 1146-62.

interpolation? (Whether someone likes or dislikes this passage is immaterial.) The manuscript evidence cannot support this as a post-dispatch interpolation.[9] There are five common arguments raised for this as an interpolation.[10]

1. These verses, 33b-35, seem tangential to the main theme or themes of chapters 12-14.

2. These verses also seem to interrupt the flow of instructions about the prophets. However, these first two arguments only identify it as a preformed piece. The next two factors suggest these verses are non-Pauline.

3. The appeal to "the Law" as a basis for church discipline seems non-Pauline.

4. The expression "all the churches of the saints" is not characteristic of Paul.

These first four arguments, at best, only demonstrate that these verses are a non-Pauline, preformed piece. The fifth argument is necessary to say that these verses are an interpolation.

5. Some have suggested these verses contradict Paul's position elsewhere on the role of women in the church (e.g., 1 Cor 11:5). These verses, they argue, are somewhat inconsistent with Paul's usual stance on women. This has led some scholars to see these words as an interpolation by a copyist.[11]

Taking a different approach to this difficult passage, some scholars have argued that Paul was quoting here a Corinthian slogan.[12] Paul has already used such an approach (e.g., 1 Cor 6:12; 7:1; 10:23). He quoted their slogan, seemed to agree, and then gently added elements to steer them away from their position and toward a correct theology. So in 1 Corinthians 6, Paul agreed with them, "All things are lawful," but then added, "Not all things are beneficial," to steer them to see Christians should strive to do only what is beneficial to the Kingdom. In 1 Corinthians 7 he agreed with them, "It is well for a man not to touch a woman," but then he gently steered them toward a view that permitted marriage. This is clearly a Pauline pattern; yet, there are problems with seeing our verses in 1 Corinthians 14 as a slogan. Where does the slogan end? Are all the verses (33b-35) a part of the slogan? Verse 36 seems to rebuff the Corinthians, but not necessarily the theology of the slogan. In the other places in 1 Corinthians, the slogans were short and immediately followed by the phrases Paul used to modify the slogans. Not so here. It is not

---

[9]A painstakingly careful and detailed analysis of the manuscripts by A. C. Wire reveals the few variants almost certainly come from "a common archetype"; Wire, *The Corinthian Woman Prophets* (Minneapolis: Fortress, 1990), pp. 149-52. See the excellent summary in Thiselton, *1 Corinthians*, pp. 1148-50.

[10]Nicely summarized in Thiselton, *1 Corinthians*, p. 1150.

[11]Walker (*Interpolations*, pp. 63-90) uses this passage as the common illustration to describe his criteria for detecting interpolations. Fee, *1 Corinthians*, p. 699, argues these verses are "a very early marginal gloss." He bases this upon the common criterion of "which reading best explains the origin of the others." But one must question if theology was not an impetus in Fee's decision to read against P^{46} and B.

[12]D. W. Odell-Scott is best known for arguing this position. See the excellent summary in Thiselton, *1 Corinthians*, pp. 1151-52.

at all clear that 1 Corinthians 14:33b-35 was a Corinthian slogan.

More recently discussion has centered on the meaning of certain keywords in this passage. Earle Ellis and Ben Witherington have demonstrated that these verses, 33b-35, pick up and use again four key terms: "speak" (14:14-32), "silent" (14:28, 30, 34), "in the church" (14:28, 35) and "submit" (14:32, 34). On the basis of detailed exegesis they have concluded that Paul was not forbidding speech but the abuses of speech.[13] They argue correctly that this passage is not un-Pauline. It does not contain ideas that contradict Paul's teachings elsewhere.

While the passage is not un-Pauline, it does have a non-Pauline flavor to it. Others also see a tension between what Paul says elsewhere and these verses.[14] Earle Ellis himself argues it is a pre-Pauline piece that Paul himself wrote in the margin of his letter.[15] Thiselton finds Ellis's argument appealing because it "would account for supposedly non-Pauline phrases without regarding them as post-Pauline."[16] Thiselton has hit the nail squarely on the head in seeing the need for a means to have a non-Pauline insertion that was not post-Pauline. Ellis's suggestion of a marginal note is possible;[17] yet, there may be a more probable solution. Paul is not eschatologically schizophrenic. Perhaps there is a tension here, not within Paul himself but within his team. These verses may represent the input of Sosthenes, Paul's coauthor. Thus, Christianity has an eschatological tension, but it is seen in the community rather than in the individual.

Scholars are drawn toward the conclusion that the Sosthenes named by Paul in 1 Corinthians is the same Sosthenes described as a ruler of the synagogue in Corinth (Acts 18). This connection has a long history in church tradition and has much to commend it, although it cannot be conclusively demonstrated. Thiselton argues that Paul included Sosthenes as a "poignant reminder of the power of the gospel."[18]

While certainly true, there may be an additional reason Paul wanted to include Sosthenes as a cosender. Problems had arisen in the church since Paul left Corinth. Several of the problems relate directly to cultural issues in Corinth. Allow me a personal illustration. As a missionary in Asia I often included coworkers from that region. I did this because of cultural factors. When applying a Christian principle in a foreign culture it was helpful to have a "cultural insider," someone who was intimately informed on the subtle

---

[13]See the discussion in Witherington, *Women in the Earliest Churches*, SNTSMS 59 (Cambridge: Cambridge University Press, 1988), pp. 90-104, and also Thiselton, *1 Corinthians*, pp. 1152-56.

[14]After a careful exegesis of this passage, Marvin Pate concludes: "Here is genuine tension, but no real contradiction." He sees Paul holding concurrently both an egalitarian and a complementarian view of women in ministry—to use the modern terms—in an eschatological tension within Paul himself. See Pate, *The End of the Ages Has Come: The Theology of Paul* (Grand Rapids: Zondervan, 1995), pp. 211-15.

[15]E. E. Ellis, "The Silenced Wives of Corinth (1 Cor 14:34-35)," in *New Testament Textual Criticism and Its Significance for Exegesis* (*Festschrift*, Metzger), ed. E. J. Epp and G. D. Fee (Oxford: Clarendon, 1981), pp. 213-20.

[16]Thiselton, *1 Corinthians*, p. 1156.

[17]So Barton, Eriksson, and Thiselton, *1 Corinthians*, pp. 1156-57.

[18]See Thiselton, *1 Corinthians*, p. 70.

cultural issues of that region. Many of the problems in 1 Corinthians dealt with such cultural issues: "Now, concerning food sacrificed to idols . . ." (1 Cor 8:1).

Yet, why had Paul failed to deal with those problems during his previous eighteen months of ministry in Corinth? Why was it now suddenly an issue?[19] Bruce Winter argues that these issues arose after Paul left Corinth.[20] Social changes in Corinth raised new issues. Some Corinthian church members were responding to the issues with "accepted" Corinthian ways of doing things, ways Paul and his team (and some other Corinthian Christians) were finding objectionable. Paul realized he was dealing with sticky, cultural problems. I suggest Paul invited Sosthenes to join him because Sosthenes knew the church (as did Paul) but also knew well the Corinthian culture (of which Paul was a novice). Sosthenes' insider knowledge of Corinthian culture was a strength Paul needed. This is the reason, I argue, that Sosthenes appears here in 1 Corinthians as a coauthor and nowhere else.

This is, of course, a hypothetical historical reconstruction, as are all reconstructions. The question is, Which reconstruction best explains the data? Obviously, this is not the place to begin a detailed argument over the structure and content of 1 Corinthians. I am only suggesting that we consider the presence of predispatch interpolations as a possible option when we are exegeting Paul's letters. By way of illustration, I ask, Is it coincidence that scholars find interpolations more often in 1 Corinthians than in Paul's other letters? Non-Pauline elements seem more common in 1 Corinthians, in the eyes of some scholars. Perhaps this is because Sosthenes was the coauthor least integrated into the Pauline band, least influenced by Paul's theology, and thus least likely to sound Pauline. Unlike Timothy, Sosthenes was not trained under the tutelage of Paul. Sosthenes was also a man of status. He was a ruler of the synagogue. He was less likely to be cowed by Paul, more likely to freely interject. As a ruler of the synagogue, it is not surprising to hear appeals to Torah, midrash, and other indicators of Jewish exegetical training, although perhaps from a different slant than Paul.

Nonetheless, my purpose here is not to defend a particular passage as a pre-dispatch interpolation by Sosthenes, but rather to suggest that we should consider the possibility. In that light let us consider two possible passages where a coauthor's influence might be seen (Sosthenes in 1 Corinthians and Timothy in 2 Corinthians) in order to illustrate

---

[19]This is by no means a new question. Scholars blamed Gnosticism (so Hans Jonas, later W. Schmithals). The failure of scholarship to demonstrate the existence of first-century Gnosticism, or even the more palatable "incipient Gnosticism," has led others to seek alternative explanations. An over-realized eschatology (so W. Schrage, later Fee) or even an over-zealous Paul has been blamed (so J. C. Hurd Jr.). Stoicism (so Herbert Braun) or more recently (and creatively) Jesus himself has been blamed for the problems at Corinth. David Wenham has argued the Corinthians were familiar with Jesus tradition and Paul strongly objected to how these traditions were being applied by the Corinthians to new situations not encountered in Palestine.

[20]Bruce Winter, *After Paul Left Corinth: The Influence of Secular Ethics and Social Change* (Grand Rapids: Eerdmans, 2001), p. 4.

how this approach might better explain the data.

A possible interpolation during the early drafts. After Paul left Corinth on his second missionary journey, the government probably closed the Jewish meat market in Corinth.[21] Christians were struggling with the ethical problem of buying meat in the regular market, meat that probably had been sacrificed in a temple earlier that day. The Isthmian Games were being reinstated in Corinth. As part of the pomp and ceremony, major banquets were being held for those who were citizens of the city. It was a significant civic honor (and responsibility) to be invited to a banquet commemorating the games. Yet these banquets also included sacrifices to idols, drunkenness, and "dinner escorts" (prostitutes). What were Corinthian Christians to do? Some (the wealthy who would have been invited?) argued "all things are lawful" (1 Cor 6:12). Others (those not invited?) argued it was participating with idols to join in these feasts (1 Cor 6:13-20).

Paul addressed the issue of eating "food sacrificed to idols" in 1 Corinthians 8:1. Paul seems to argue that the matter was neutral, "No idol in the world really exists" (8:4) so "we are no worse off if we do not eat, and no better off if we do" (8:8), and that Corinthian Christians should avoid eating the meat only if it offends a "weaker brother" (8:9). A problem arises, however, in the minds of many commentators because in 1 Corinthians 10:1-22 the letter takes a stronger stance against eating the meat, arguing, "Are not those who eat the sacrifices partners in the altar?" (10:18) and that they become "partners with demons" (10:20). Then in 1 Corinthians 10:23—11:1, the text seems to return to a more neutral stance on the subject, "Eat whatever is set before you" (10:27), arguing to restrict oneself only for the sake of the other's conscience (10:29).

Some have suggested that 1 Corinthians 10:1-22 is a non-Pauline interpolation that was added years later to Paul's letter, even though there is no manuscript evidence to support this.[22] Several scholars (while arguing for the passage as post-Pauline) do make a fair case for the passage as non-Pauline. (They assume these are the same things.) Indicators that the passage may be non-Pauline include:

1. The vocabulary is unusual for Paul or is used differently than Paul customarily does.[23]

2. The midrash is more elaborate than customary for Paul and "has wandered far more technically into the arena of midrashic exegesis than at any other point in [Paul's] letters."[24]

3. Idols are connected with demons. Richard Horsley notes there were two common positions in Judaism toward idols. One view (seen in Deutero-Isaiah) argued idols are nothing and their worship is foolishness. The other view agreed idols were nothing but

---

[21] As suggested by Winter, *After Paul Left Corinth*, pp. 293-301.
[22] E.g., Walker, *Interpolations*, pp. 232-36.
[23] See ibid., pp. 233-34.
[24] Lamar Cope, *First Corinthians 8-10: Continuity or Contradiction*, ATRSup. 11 (Evanston, Ill.: Anglican Theological Review, 1990), p. 119.

"saw in idolatry the service or the influence of demons (Jub. 11.4-6; 22.16-22; 1 Enoch 19; 99.6-10; Test. Naph. 3.3-4)."[25] Cope argues that Paul takes the former position in 1 Cor 8 and 10:23—11:1 but the latter position in 1 Cor 10:1-22.[26]

In light of this let me continue my suggested scenario. Because the Corinthian Christians were confused about what to do, Paul advised them in 1 Corinthians 8 that it was "permissible" as long as it did not damage another's faith. Paul was probably influenced by Deutero-Isaiah's view of idols. Since Paul was raised in Jerusalem,[27] idols posed no real temptation for him, nor had he seen childhood friends destroyed by idolatry. Sosthenes, having lived as a Jew in Corinth—moreover having lived as a leader in the synagogue in Corinth—felt Paul's position was too neutral, and would perhaps open the door to permissiveness. Sosthenes had his own opinion on the matter that, while not contradicting Paul's, did take a firmer stance. He had grown up with the dangers of God-fearers, perhaps even Jews, slipping into Corinthian customs. He viewed the temptation to join the banquets in the same light as Israel being tempted in the wilderness to worship in the same manner as their Egyptian masters had done. He had worked out his argument, including a midrash on the Exodus story.[28] Perhaps it was a message Sosthenes had already used in the synagogue to persuade others to stay away from the pagan banquets.

I suggest that Paul had just concluded his argument that he had rights as an apostle by saying, "those who serve at the altar share in what is sacrificed on the altar" (9:13). This struck a cord with Sosthenes, who had used the same idea to argue against the pagan feasts. Sosthenes had a strong opinion on that subject and felt that Paul was not saying all that should be said.[29] He picked up Paul's argument and said "sharing at the pagan altar" was the same as "serving at the altar" (10:18-20). In the team, Paul was the Patriarchal Voice, the final authority, but even the Patriarchal Voice had to make room for the team, as James did in Acts 15. Paul permitted the material because it was not a direct contradiction to what he said in 1 Corinthians 8. After Sosthenes' contribution in 1 Corinthians 10:1-22, Paul then continued (10:23—11:1) with a subtle argument that at least clarified

---

[25]Richard A. Horsley, "Gnosis in Corinth: 1 Corinthians 8.1-6," NTS 27 (1980): 38-39.

[26]Cope, First Corinthians 8-10, pp. 121-22. Horsley ("Gnosis," p. 39) also sees 1 Cor 10:1-22 as reflecting the latter position, but he does not differentiate between the passages.

[27]Following the arguments of W. C. van Unnik, Tarsus or Jerusalem: The City of Paul's Youth, trans. G. Ogg (London: Epworth, 1962).

[28]See also C. Marvin Pate, The Reverse of the Curse: Paul, Wisdom and the Law, WUNT 2/114 (Tübingen: Mohr/Siebeck, 2000), pp. 303-4. This passage actually gives Pate's thesis a touch of trouble because it connects Jesus with Wisdom (10:4) but does not directly undermine the kashrut system, as Paul does in 1 Cor 8 and 10:23-11:1. The passage does not contradict what Pate sees Paul doing elsewhere (connecting Jesus with Wisdom apart from Torah), but it fails to make the point clearly as Paul usually does. This is perhaps because the passage is Sosthenes'.

[29]Inspiration is a theological discussion independent of this historical inquiry. However, I would argue that the Spirit also wanted this added; this insertion by Sosthenes was inspired as well and added a counterbalance to tolerance.

the point and probably moderated it. Because this was done early in the letter, Paul was able to weave all the material in rather smoothly.

This is merely a suggested reconstruction and is not attempting to demonstrate conclusively that 1 Corinthians 10:1-22 was written in this way. Rather, it is offered as an alternative explanation building upon this model of coauthorship.[30] Furthermore, I argue it is at the very least just as plausible as assuming a post-dispatch interpolation, for which there is no manuscript evidence.

A possible interpolation during the later editing. Second Corinthians 6:14—7:1 has often been considered a non-Pauline interpolation that was added decades later.[31] Even to the casual reader this passage seems abrupt and harsh. It seems different from Paul in several ways: [32]

1. The vocabulary is unusual. There are at least six words Paul uses nowhere else (*hapax legomena,* "having-been-said-once-things").

2. Fitzmyer points out the strong parallels with Qumran, especially the use of the term *Beliar* (6:15).[33]

3. The strong dualistic language seems unlike Paul.

More than that, the larger passage seems to read smoother without these verses. William Walker argues that there was an original chiasm (see below), which was lost when the passage was inserted.

A[1] *Assurance of Affection* (6:11): "Our mouth is open to you, Corinthians, our heart is wide."

   B[1] *Disclaimer of Responsibility for Alienation* (6:12): "You are not restricted by us, but you are restricted in your own affections."

      C[1] *Appeal for Affection* (6:13): "And in return—I speak as to children—widen your hearts also."

      C[2] *Appeal for Affection* (7:2a): "Make room for us."

   B[2] *Disclaimer of Responsibility for Alienation* (7:2b-3a): "We wronged no one, we corrupted no one, we took advantage of no one."

A[2] *Assurance of Affection* (7:3b): "I do not say this to condemn you, for I said before that you are in our hearts, to die together and to live together."[34]

---

[30]I find it interesting that in Seyoon Kim's recent thesis on how Paul deals with idol food, he is able to trace a consistent theme through 1 Cor 8-10; however, the theme is *not* demonstrable in 10:1-22. Again, I think the theme is absent because this section arose from Sosthenes. See Kim, "Imitatio Christi (1 Cor 11:1): How Paul Imitates Jesus Christ in Dealing with Idol Food," *BBR* 13 (2003): 193-226.

[31]So, e.g., Bultmann, Bornkamm, Koester and Gnilka; see Walker, *Interpolations,* pp. 199-200.

[32]These differences are well summarized by P. Barnett, *The Second Epistle to the Corinthians,* NICNT (Grand Rapids: Eerdmans, 1997), pp. 338-39.

[33]J. Fitzmyer, "Qumrân and the Interpolated Paragraph in 2 Cor 6,14—7,1," *CBQ* 23 (1961): 271-80.

[34]Walker, *Interpolations,* p. 202.

Against Walker's thesis that this is a post-dispatch interpolation, we must note that there is no manuscript evidence to support a later interpolation, and the passage is not un-Pauline; that is, it does not contradict Paul.[35] In his commentary, Paul Barnett offers persuasive rebuttals to the arguments of Walker. He also adds that this passage cannot be an interpolation for two reasons: (1) "why would anyone insert a non-Pauline passage into a Pauline writing?" and (2) no one has explained in a "practical" way how material would be interpolated.[36]

Barnett's objections do rightly argue against this passage being a post-Pauline interpolation. However, the observations of Fitzmyer and Walker still suggest that it may have been inserted.[37] We do not have to argue that Paul inserted it; perhaps it is a predispatch interpolation by a coauthor. In this scenario, the letter was drafted without this material. Although perhaps unconsciously planned, Paul's original argument had a casual chiastic structure. The passage flowed well. At a later reading, when the letter was being edited, someone on the team took umbrage at the term "open wide your hearts" (6:13). It perhaps encouraged too much tolerance for others, opening the way for relationships. This team member, perhaps Timothy, the named coauthor,[38] wanted to insert a mini-homily showing tolerance had boundaries. In this way, the material was interpolated into Paul's letter but with his permission. The letter was far enough along in draft that Paul was not interested in adding more material to weave the insertion in more smoothly. He left it alone.

Now the possibility of a coauthor, or even a team member, inserting material does not rise or fall on 2 Corinthians 6 or any other passage. The point here is not to argue which specific passages are interpolations, but rather to show that there can be non-Pauline material in the letters, and to illustrate how such material could be inserted into the letters with Paul's approval and before final dispatching.

THE "AUTHOR" AND INSERTED MATERIAL

Scholars rarely contest the presence of preformed material in Paul, and they use internal criteria to detect these pieces. Conservative scholars, however, have been hesitant to allow any internal criteria for interpolations because they assume that to acknowledge an interpolation is to allow post-Pauline, unauthorized interpolations. This is not the case. There

---

[35]H. D. Betz argues it is indeed an anti-Pauline interpolation, originating in Jewish Christianity; Betz, "2 Cor 6:14—7:1: An Anti-Pauline Fragment?" *JBL* 92 (1973): 88-108; however, his arguments have not been universally persuasive.

[36]Barnett, *2 Corinthians*, pp. 339-41.

[37]Fitzmyer argues 6:14—7:1 "has a self-contained, independent character, forming a unit intelligible in itself, like a short homily . . . [the passage] is devoid of any concrete details which would suggest it was dealing with a specifically Corinthian problem"; "Interpolated Paragraph," pp. 271-72.

[38]Timothy is the named coauthor of 2 Corinthians. Acts 16:1 tells us Timothy grew up in the Diaspora in Lystra. His mother, a Jew, had been unequally yoked with a Greek husband, and as a result her son remained uncircumcised, though obviously raised in the faith. Does this passage represent a mother's (heavy-handed) warning to her unmarried son?

can be *authorized* non-Pauline insertions. For example, previously when a passage (such as 2 Cor 6:14—7:1 or 1 Thess 2:13-16 or 1 Cor 10:1-22) seemed very non-Pauline, there were only two options: call it a post-Pauline, unauthorized interpolation or somehow make the passage Pauline.

To return to the example of 1 Corinthians 10:1-22, this passage seems to contrast with what Paul says about eating meat in 1 Corinthians 10:23—11:1. What have scholars traditionally done with 1 Corinthians 10:1-22?

1. Some have argued (without manuscript support) that this passage is a later, unauthorized interpolation and should be removed from the text of 1 Corinthians.

2. Some have argued 1 Corinthians 10:1-22 actually is Pauline. Gordon Fee contends Paul did not contradict himself; he was discussing two different scenarios. In 1 Corinthians 10:1-22 Paul was discussing meat eaten during a meal at a Temple (a public matter) and concluded it was not okay to eat this meat. In 1 Corinthians 10:23—11:1 Paul was discussing meat bought in the marketplace and eaten in the home (a private matter) and concluded it is okay to eat this meat. It is not our purpose here to provide a detailed response to Fee's argument; yet even Fee recognizes the disjointedness, calling 1 Corinthians 10:14-22 "an aside" in Paul's argument.[39]

Yet a third option is possible. We should not approach the text with a pre-determined need for it to be Pauline because we do not wish the other option (i.e., it is an unauthorized interpolation that must be amputated from the text). Whenever we approach a text with a pre-determined need we are at risk of reading our desire into the text. If, before we approach the text, we realize there is a third option, that of a non-Pauline yet still authorized interpolation from a colleague, then we might reach different conclusions about passages such as 1 Corinthians 10:1-22, 2 Corinthians 6:14—7:1 and even 1 Corinthians 14:33b-26.

Paul as "we." When exegeting passages in 1 Corinthians, scholars commonly write, "Paul exhorted them to . . ." Yet the "Paul" who authored 1 Corinthians was not the solitary, modern, Western writer we often envision. He was the leader of a team, not the sole mouthpiece or contributor. The authorial voice of "Paul" was a "we."

This is not to return to the old "Pauline school" arguments of the last century. Such arguments had a school of disciples later producing material in the name of their "master,"

---

[39]Fee, *1 Corinthians*, p. 359. It is probably an error to read a modern public vs. private dichotomy back into Paul's time. Furthermore, Paul had argued against eating the meat both in chapter 8 and 10:23—11:1 because it might offend the conscience of a weaker brother. Yet chapter 8 is clearly public (see 8:10) and refers to the same problem as 10:1-22 (so also Fee, *1 Corinthians*, p. 359). The passages cannot be reconciled, in my opinion, merely by distinguishing between "temple meat" (chs. 8 & 10) and "marketplace meat" (10:23—11:1). The argument in 10:1-22 differs: eating meat was eating with demons. It seems Paul argued in 10:27-29 (as in ch. 8) that meat was inherently neutral; it was only the other person's perception. Yet, in 10:1-22, it does not seem a matter of perception but of spiritual realities. While the passages do not contradict, they seem to approach the matter from different directions.

Paul. In the newer model I am suggesting, Paul was the major, predominant, often overwhelming voice on the team. His imprimatur was not only unmistakable but often overbearing. The arguments went where he intended them to go; the conclusions were what Paul intended to reach. Nevertheless, the smaller, quieter voices of others can still be heard in his letters, not only in the discussions before the letters were written, not just in the discussions as the letters were being written, but sometimes in the letter itself.

There is a risk of labeling every tension in the Pauline letters a sign of a coauthor or other team member. Sometimes more careful exegesis or background study demonstrates that a perceived tension was truly no tension at all. Nevertheless, sometimes careful exegesis is taken to the point of exegetical gymnastics in an attempt to twist a passage into conformity with Paul's teachings elsewhere. To speak with one voice does not require only one voice.

The mistaken quest for the "pure Paul." As individualistic Westerners we often operate under the presupposition that "Paul alone" is better than "Paul + others." It is assumed that "pure Paul" was more inspired than anything written in collaboration, and certainly more than a passage written by another. The underlying presupposition is that anything not solely from Paul somehow dilutes Paul. It is assumed Paul was the "Inspired One" or the "More Inspired One," and therefore anything added to Paul detracts from this "pure Paul." However, we need to let 1 Corinthians remind us: the 1 Corinthians we consider inspired is not the 1 Corinthians written by Paul alone but Paul and Sosthenes (1:1), through a secretary (16:21).

CONCLUSIONS FOR PAUL AS A LETTER WRITER

Preformed material was woven into the letter. Sometimes the material was quoted as part of the dictation of the letter, sometimes it was already written and simply handed to the secretary. These different ways to incorporate preformed material produced different effects in the letter.

Since it is not usually discussed how preformed traditional material was incorporated into Paul's letters, the old presumption was that it was dictated directly into the text by Paul (even if he read it from a notebook), not copied into the text later by a secretary and certainly not merely handed to the secretary. Thus, in the old model, all preformed material passed through Paul's mental filter and was thoroughly "Paulinized." In such a model there could be no non-Pauline interpolations in the original letter.

Yet William Walker and others may be correct that there appear to be non-Pauline interpolations in his letters; that is, verses or sections that contain vocabulary, style and even theology that are not typically Pauline. Walker maintained these must be post-Pauline; that is, added by someone other than Paul (likely a disciple of Paul) after the original letter was dispatched, and thus without Paul's permission. It is a faulty assumption that any non-Pauline interpolation must necessarily be a post-Pauline interpolation. In many of these instances Walker may be correct in arguing certain verses are interpolations added by someone other than Paul, and likely a disciple of Paul. I think he is incorrect in assuming that these had to be added to later copies of Paul's letters, if there is no manuscript evidence.[40]

We do have evidence for disciples of Paul who could add material; they are called co-authors and even colleagues and secretaries. During the writing process they could add (non-Pauline) material into the draft. How would these non-Pauline interpolations differ from later non-Pauline interpolations? These were added during the editorial process and thus under Paul's control. The normal assumption is that a non-Pauline interpolation is post-Pauline and unauthorized. This is not a necessary conclusion. A non-Pauline verse could be the voice of Timothy or Sosthenes expressing a different but complementary theology, with Paul's ultimate approval.

---

[40]Walker contends a lack of manuscript support for an interpolation is not significant; see Walker, "The Burden of Proof in Identifying Interpolations in the Pauline Letters," *NTS* 33 (1987): 610-18; see also Walker, *Interpolations*, esp. pp. 57-62. I argue manuscript evidence is essential to assert the material was added after the letter was dispatched.

8

CLASSIFYING PAUL'S LETTERS

*A*s we briefly noted in chapter four, Greco-Roman letters were often divided into two groups: private (occasioned) letters and public (literary) epistles. Where do Paul's letters fit in this picture? Late nineteenth-century scholars of Hellenistic literature attempted to classify Paul's letters with the literary epistles. After all, Paul's letters were long and complex like these letters were. While some scholars argued that Paul should be ranked with these great letter writers of antiquity,[1] most considered Paul to be unworthy of this category.[2] His letters did not have the lofty prose and complex rhetoric so characteristic of these letters. They took quite literally Paul's statement in 2 Corinthians 11:6, "I may be untrained in speech."

Literary epistles, judging from the remains, comprise only a small percentage of the letters written by ancients. Thousands upon thousands of personal and business letters have been found written on papyrus (and even pottery fragments). These letters were more occasional, dealing with a particular situation, and were not intended necessarily to be preserved. They were found in the remains of trash heaps, ruined homes, old libraries and official record depositories. These letters provided us a glimpse of Greek life not previously available, including examples of business contracts and arrangements, family problems and letters between friends. As these letters were published, New Testament scholars began to note how similar they were to Paul, particularly in terms of diction, style, use of stereotyped expressions and a concern for matters of everyday life. Scholars began to debate whether Paul should be compared to the literary writers of his day. His place, they contended, was among the writers of these papyrus letters. This leaves us with the sticky question of where Paul's letters fit. Determining where and how they fit can help us to establish a framework for understanding his letters.

PUBLIC OR PRIVATE: CLASSIFYING GRECO-ROMAN LETTERS

Public letters were essays in letter form. They were artificial and were intended to be dis-

---

[1]E.g., Ulrich von Wilamowitz-Moellendorff, *Antigonos von Karystos* (Berlin: Weidmann, 1881); and Martin Dibelius, *An Philemon* (Tübingen: Mohr, 1953).

[2]E.g., P. Wendland, *Die hellenistische-römische Kultur in ihren Beziehungen zu Judentum und Christentum,* 2nd ed. (Tübingen: Mohr, 1912); and esp. Eduard Norden, *Die antike Kunstprosa,* 2 vols. (Leipzig: Weidmann, 1898; reprint, 1958), p. 1:499 (Paul's style is totally "unhellenic").

seminated widely. Their style was high, with complex grammar and rhetoric.[3] We might be expected to say the typical private letter was warm and personal with simple language and structure. However, this is not the case at all.

The typical private letter, even though written to beloved family members, was still usually very brief and used the same stock expressions over and over. Like public epistles, these private letters were also written with a secretary. Modern writers might be hesitant to use a secretary to write down a private letter, since our private letters are often, well, private. This was not the case in Paul's day. These personal letters to family were stereotypical, using the same set structure and repeating the same stock phrases, sometimes to the extreme of merely selecting and stacking one stereotyped formulae after another. A papyrus from Karanis (Egypt) actually contained two short letters on the same sheet. What is most striking is that both letters begin the same way verbatim, even though the recipient was able to read the other letter and know it had the identical prayer for the recipient's health, etc.

We have little in common with such stereotyped writing, so it is difficult to imagine. Perhaps the closest American parallel is the use of "Dear" to open a letter and "Sincerely" to close it. These phrases have little true meaning; they merely indicate the opening and closing of a letter. A college woman, intending to callously end her romantic relationship with Mike, writes a harsh letter that nevertheless begins "Dear Mike." A student of mine, Daniel, can write me an excuse for missing class, filling it with the flimsiest excuses and outright lies, and still sign it "Sincerely, Daniel." Neither Mike nor I actually believe our letters were sincerely written; the opening "dear" and the closing "sincerely" are merely stereotyped ways of opening and closing personal letters in America.

In antiquity, private letters were far more stereotyped than ours. Reading just a few dozen ancient letters is enough to realize how typical these two examples from Karanis are.

A THIRD-CENTURY PAPYRUS FROM KARANIS (PMICH. 8.513)

Chairemon to Serapion, greeting. Before all else I pray that you will be well, and I make your obeisance before the lord Serapis daily. I want you to know that you have sent me no word from the day that I came to Alexandria. If then you love me, do not neglect to write to me. I salute Sarapias and her children. Pasoxis the carpenter salutes you and your children.

---

[3] The Greek letters that have survived from literary sources are mostly addresses and long essays clearly meant for publication. The Latin letters, as we see it in the correspondences of Cicero and his friends, are true (private) letters of genuine correspondence, whether about personal or public matters (so concludes Sherwin-White, *Letters of Pliny*, p. 1). Nevertheless they contained much of the same high rhetoric. They were intended to demonstrate also the writer's rhetorical skills.

A second-century papyrus letter written to the town of Bacchias, Egypt (PMich. 8.507)

Julius Germanus to Tasoucharion, his sister, very many greetings. Before all else, I pray that you be well; I myself am well, and I make your obeisance before the local gods. I received your letter from Secundus and was greatly delighted about the health of the children, and do you watch over them. I shall go to the mill if I sift. For there are there two . . . for all to take. I shall take them, and I shall not let them be . . . Salute Ptolemais, our brother. I ask you, brother, keep watch over my sisters and Pais and my mother . . . Salute . . . Aunes and our friends. I pray for your health.[4]

It is fair to ask, If private letters merely repeated the same general phrases and expressions, why did anyone go to the trouble (and expense) to write at all? First and foremost a letter then often functioned like a phone call does today. I want my son to call when he travels to camp. Our telephone call will be nothing but the repetition of pleasantries.

Dad:	*"How are you?"*
Josh:	*"Fine."*
Dad:	*"How was the drive?"*
Josh:	*"Fine."*
Dad:	*"The cabins are okay?"*
Josh:	*"Fine."*
Dad:	*"How's the food?"*
Josh:	*"Fine."*

Since I can predict with astounding accuracy how our phone call will go, why do I want him to call? It assures me that he has arrived safely. Many ancient letters served the same general purpose. For example, PMich. 8.507 reads, "Artemis to Socrates, greeting. Before all else I pray for your health. I arrived in the city on the 9th."

Heikki Koskenniemi has documented this general purpose, outlining three common intentions in sending private letters in antiquity.[5] First, a letter was sent mainly to express a "friendly relationship" between the sender and the addressee. The importance was more in the act of sending the letter than in any particular content. He called this *philophronesis* ("a friendly frame of mind"). Second, a letter was often sent to serve as the "presence" of the sender when he/she was unable to come physically, whether merely to keep warm the relationship or to convey any directions (or commands or requests). He called this *parousia* ("presence"). Third, a letter could also be part of an on-going dialogue between the

---

[4]A strip of the papyrus is lost in the middle of the sheet, making it impossible to reconstruct some of the missing words.

[5]These terms come from Koskeniemi, *Studien*, pp. 34-47.

sender and the recipient, an individual letter being one-half of a conversation. This he called *homilia* ("dialogue").[6] All three of these purposes are evident in the two examples just cited.

The evidence clearly indicates that secretaries were used to write out private letters, and that private letters in antiquity were used for a variety of purposes. However, extremely private or personal matters were not usually written in letters. They either went unexpressed or were conveyed by the letter carrier.[7] As a result, it is not so surprising that ancients used a secretary to write even a private letter.

As mentioned in chapter four, Adolf Deissmann carefully differentiated between these occasioned papyrus letters and the literary epistles.[8] He then emphasized similarities between Paul and these occasioned papyrus letters, freeing Paul from the previous, unfavorable, comparisons to the literary epistles. Once Deissmann established what he saw as the obvious relationship, he drew several conclusions.[9]

1. These letters of Paul represented his genuine religious impulse at a given moment and contained none of the artificiality of the literary epistles; that is, they were artless and unpremeditated.

2. Paul's letters were concerned with matters of private (confidential, secret, individual, personal) interest and were not intended to be seen by the general public.[10]

3. They were a substitute for direct oral confrontation.

4. Since his letters were part of the occasioned papyrus letters, Paul must be placed with the lower ranks of society, not the well-educated upper classes.[11]

5. Since Paul's letters were not literary epistles, they cannot be treated as theological treatises, even if they later received canonical status.

Deissmann's work has done much to advance the study of Paul's letters. The study of the language of the papyrus letters has greatly aided our understanding of the Greek language. Paul wrote in the language of the common man of his day; a principle we would do well to remember. Deissmann forced us to recognize that Paul's letters addressed spe-

---

[6]It is difficult to find a good American English translation for this, but perhaps it would be "conversation."

[7]This aspect of letter carriers is discussed in chapter eleven.

[8]Deissmann, *Light,* pp. 290-301.

[9]Ibid.

[10]Deissmann's distinctions should be kept in mind when reading Paul's letters. "We may call it exegesis, but the common name for reading other people's mail is snooping" (McKenzie, *Light,* p. 12). He adds: "The moral principle involved illustrates the problems of reading the letters of perfect strangers, which is what Paul and the church of Corinth are to modern readers. We know little about them except from their letters. An epistle is addressed to us; a letter written from a naturally private situation. If the situation is not known, the letter is unintelligible unless the letter itself discloses enough of the situation."

[11]So Mary E. Andrews, "Paul, Philo, and the Intellectuals," *JBL* 53 (1934): 166, "Paul cannot be rated among the intellectuals of his day."

cific situations in specific places. Thus to understand what Paul was saying it is necessary to know the specific situation Paul was addressing.

Nevertheless, we cannot accept all the conclusions. Deissmann (and others) inferred too much from Paul's similarity to the papyrus letters. Although Paul's language was for the common man, his letters clearly indicate a powerful intellect backed by a solid education. He was not a Pliny, but neither was he to be ranked with scarcely literate soldiers and farmers.[12] Paul's letters were not written for the general public; nonetheless they were written for the Christian community. He wrote his letters to be read before congregations, and he encouraged communities to share letters.[13] He himself may have shared his letters with other communities.[14]

Luther Stirewalt[15] has correctly chastised me and others for drawing too much of a line between public and private letters. Perhaps it is an error to place Paul's letters as strictly in the private letters category. Stirewalt has demonstrated there is an improper emphasis on private letters, almost to the exclusion of seeing in Paul's letters any elements of the public treatise. It is not that the discussion should return to argue that Paul's letters were public letters. That would be to make the same mistake in the other direction. As L. T. Johnson demonstrates in his study of the Pastorals, an official type of letter, such as a "letter to a delegate," was also sent unofficially. Evidently the private sector felt free to make use of "public" letter forms when it suited their purpose. As in other aspects of Greco-Roman life, the lines between public and private were blurred.

It is now thought that Deissmann overstated his case. He has been critiqued for giving too "literary" a definition to an epistle[16] and for denying too much the literary worth of Paul's letters.[17] In fact Deissmann's entire distinction between letter and epistle is

---

[12]Stowers, *Letter Writing*, pp. 34-35, describes the world of Pliny: "The social context for such literary letters is a small circle of intimate aristocratic friends who shared advanced rhetorical educations. The purpose was aesthetic entertainment. As Pliny [the Younger] remarks, the first requirement for this kind of literary activity is leisure (7.2). Pliny notes that such letters should usually be brief and employ simple vocabulary in a direct style (7.9.8). The paradox is that Pliny employs elaborate structure and studied prose rhythm in order to achieve this simplicity and directness." Should we compare Paul's statements that downplay his rhetorical skills, often couched in the midst of a complex rhetorical argument?

[13]1 Thess 5:27; also Col 4:16. A parallel is seen in the use of Clement's letter; see Eus. *H.E.* 4.23. L. Hartman, "On Reading Others' Letters," *HTR* 79 (1986): 145, also argues Paul's letters were to be shared.

[14]If one accepts the common circular letter hypothesis for Ephesians or the less popular theory that the canonical letter to the Romans was a copy of the original letter (chaps. 1—15), to which Paul appended a final chapter, a commendation for Phoebe, who carried it to Ephesus.

[15]At the time I was finalizing this manuscript Luther Stirewalt published his excellent little book, *Paul, the Letter Writer* (Grand Rapids: Eerdmans, 2003).

[16]See A. T. Robertson, *A Grammar of the Greek New Testament in the Light of Historical Research*, 3rd ed. (New York: Hodder & Stoughton, 1919), p. 88.

[17]See, among others, Paul Wendland, *Neutestamentliche Grammatik: das Griechisch der neuen Testaments im Zusammenhang mit der Volkssprache dargestellt*, vol. 2, *Der urchristliche Literaturformen* (Tübingen: Mohr, 1912), p. 344; Henry Meecham, *Light from Ancient Letters* (New York: Macmillan, 1923), p. 101; and William Doty, "Epistle," p. 18.

strained.[18] Rather than view a letter as either literary or nonliterary, it is more accurate to see a spectrum ranging from the more literary epistles to the more occasioned private letters. The present conclusion about Paul's letters is that there is considerable variation among New Testament letters. But taken as a whole, they resemble neither the common papyri from the very lowest levels of culture and education nor the works of those with the highest levels of rhetorical training. They fall somewhere in between and have the cast of a Jewish subculture.[19]

Do Paul's letters fall in between merely because he was more educated than the common man but not educated enough to compose a literary epistle? A gradual transformation had been occurring in Latin letter writing.[20] Cicero, a generation before Paul, took what in Greek was the artless papyrus letter and elevated it somewhat, while nonetheless retaining the vitality and spontaneity of the Greek letter.[21] Pliny, a generation after Paul, completed the process, raising the private Greek letter to the literary level. Seneca, a contemporary of Paul, was somewhere in the middle, retaining the casual, situational element of the papyrus letter. In the form of letters to his disciple and friend, Lucilius, Seneca was able to teach his philosophy to Lucilius by reflecting on events in daily life. He combined elements of the philosophical treatise (without the lofty language and rhetoric) with the casual and seemingly spontaneous letter. Thus Seneca demonstrated that the letter was still a flexible form, which could be altered to meet the needs of a creative individual and could be used to discuss "theology," not in the form of a treatise but by casting it against the backdrop of daily life matters.

Paul, ministering during this same time, followed the same pattern. He took the popular, casual, brief Greek letter and modified it to suit his specialized purposes. W. G. Kümmel argued that Paul's letters were different because they were the instruments by which Paul conducted his missionary work. They were occasioned, responding to specific situations that arose in the church. Nonetheless, the tasks needed in missions, the care of souls, the protection against heresies, and the strengthening of the saints required more than could be said in the painfully brief, artless, stereotyped format of the papyrus letters.

PAUL'S LETTER AS A GRECO-ROMAN LETTER

To describe a Greco-Roman letter, it is customary to discuss structure and content, including formulae and epistolary rhetoric.

Structure. Greco-Roman letters had a basic structure of an opening, body and clos-

---

[18]See among others George Milligan, *New Testament Documents: Their Origin and Early History* (London: Macmillan, 1913), p. 95. Doty ("Epistle," pp. 9-22) offers a thorough analysis and critique of Deissmann.

[19]Stan Stowers, *Letter Writing*, p. 25.

[20]See the thesis of Catherine Salles, "Le genre littéraire de la letter dan l'antiquité," *Foi et Vie* 84/5 (1985): 41-47. Her thesis has not received the attention it deserves.

[21]Salles, "Le genre," p. 45.

ing. Paul's letter openings contained the usual information in the usual format: sender to recipient, greetings. Michigan Papyrus 513 begins: "Chairemon to Serapion, greeting." Paul used the same format. Yet, Paul also revised the format slightly. He modified the traditional word *chairein* ("greeting") to *charis* ("grace"), a subtle play on words. He then followed with the traditional Jewish greeting, "peace." For example, 1 Thessalonians 1:1 reads,

> Paul, Silvanus, and Timothy, To the church of the Thessalonians in God the Father and the Lord Jesus Christ: Grace to you and peace.

These addresses point out another interesting item. In the two examples above, the sender only used one name. This was most common when writing to family or where there could be no confusion as to who was writing. In the case of 1 Thessalonians, listing all three team members removed a chance of the Thessalonians wondering which Paul was writing to them.

It is commonly noted that a Roman name had three parts: a first name (*praenomen*), a family name (*nomen*), and a surname (*cognomen*). Paul, or *Paulos,* was likely his surname. Paul did not change his name from Saul to Paul when he began working with Gentiles.[22] Rather, he stopped using Saul, his first name and began using his surname when he moved into the Gentile world.[23] We cannot be sure why he made this change. Perhaps he was distancing himself from his Jewish heritage, but this is unlikely. We do not see Paul ashamed of his heritage. More importantly, it is unlikely that the typical person on the street had ever heard of the Jewish king Saul from a thousand years earlier. Paul likely avoided using Saul because of a very common problem in crosscultural work: one's name means something negative in another's language.[24] In his case, *Saulos* had a negative meaning in normal Greek; prostitutes were said to walk in a provocative, or *saulos,* manner.[25] Since his hearers were unlikely to have heard of *Saulos* as a name, they might make the unfortunate conclusion that it was some sort of nickname. Paul probably avoided this problem by using his surname, a common and quite reputable Roman name. In fact the Paulus clan was somewhat prominent in Asia Minor. It is even likely that Paul was related to Sergius Paulus, mentioned in Acts 13:6-14.[26]

We should notice another interesting facet of Paul's letter addresses. We would expect the address to read something like "Saulos Paulos of Tarsus to . . ." Since his family was somewhat prominent (or at the least was not disreputable), we expect him to iden-

---

[22]Although it is often suggested Paul changed his name from Saul to Paul, Acts 13:9 indicates he held both names simultaneously. See e.g., Pate, *End of the Ages,* p. 17 n. 19; also Donald Carson, Doug Moo, and Leon Morris (*An Introduction to the New Testament* [Grand Rapids: Zondervan, 1992,] p. 216).

[23]We actually do not know whether "Saul" was his *praenomen* or his *nomen.*

[24]My *supernomen,* "Randy," carries a similar problem in some countries. My colleague Bobby found a problem with his name when working among Muslims in Malaysia. His name phonetically means "pig."

[25]See LSJ: a "loose, wanton gait."

[26]See the arguments of Meeks, *First Urban Christians,* p. 218 n. 68; and Witherington, *Acts,* pp. 398-403.

tify himself by his family, as was customary. Paul however does not. Rather than using his earthly household, he identifies himself as a member of a new household: "Paul, an apostle of Christ Jesus" (1-2 Cor, Gal, Eph, Col, 1-2 Tim, Tit) or "Paul, a servant of Jesus Christ" (Rom, Phil). Instead of identifying himself as the son of a prominent household, he identifies himself as the slave of another. In most of Paul's letters he is either address-ing (or there is in the background) the tension between Jewish Christians and Gentile Christians. Paul is not merely remaining neutral by avoiding his Jewish name, Saul. He is aligning himself with a new household, the household of God. This is Paul's consis-tent solution to the Jewish-Gentile tension: we are all a new creation in which there is no longer "Jew" or "Gentile"; all of us belong to Christ (Gal 3:28). When members of warring groups became slaves in the same household, hostilities between them had to cease. They had new allegiances; the old differences had passed away. Paul indicates this understanding as early as his self-identification in his letter address: he is now of the household of Christ.

Greco-Roman letters usually followed the letter address with a supplication or thanks-giving to the gods for good health/safety[27] and a stereotyped phrase indicating that the writer held the recipient in his memory.

PMICH. 8.513

Chairemon to Serapion, greeting. Before all else I pray that you will be well, and I make your obeisance before the lord Serapis daily.

Jewish letters tended to elaborate the names of the sender and recipient more and often contained a prayer for peace as well.[28] Paul reflects this custom in 1 Thessalonians 1, add-ing a Christian flavor to it:

> We always give thanks to God for all of you and mention you in our prayers, constantly re-membering before our God and Father your work of faith and labor of love and steadfastness of hope in our Lord Jesus Christ.

Sometimes the only purpose of a Greco-Roman letter was to send greetings; hence there were ancient letters consisting of little more than an opening and a closing. None-theless, most Greco-Roman letters had some individualized content to share. This content was in the body of the letter, much the way we write letters today. Paul placed his content in the body of his letters.

Greco-Roman letters usually closed with a second health-wish. So Michigan Papy-rus 496 concludes "Salute Aunes and our friends. I pray for your health." After the

---

[27]See Weima, *Neglected Endings*, pp. 34-39.
[28]Bezadel Porten, "Address Formulae in Aramaic Letters: a New Collation of Cowley 17," *RB* 90 (1980): 398-413. See also the chart in Exler, *Form*, p. 61.

closing health wish, or sometimes in lieu of it, the letter ended with "farewell" (*errōso*), often abbreviated "*err*" (Greek, *EPP*). Paul closed with neither a second health-wish nor a farewell. Rather, he often used a benediction—though one might argue a benediction is only a Christianized health-wish—or a doxology. Yet even Paul's closings were not entirely in the "proper" place, since they usually did not end the letter.[29] Nevertheless, Paul's letters had a closing, even if he did not follow the traditional conventions.[30] Greco-Roman letters were also less consistent in the closing. In any event Paul's letters followed the typical structure of a Greco-Roman letter with an opening, body and closing.

Content. Although Paul's letters were quite long and detailed, the breadth and depth of Paul letters were not radically different from that of other substantive Greco-Roman letter writers.[31] As was typical of letter writers in his day, Paul expressed himself with the standardized phrases, often called stereotyped formulae, and the common ways of speaking, often called epistolary rhetoric, with of course a Christian flair.

Stereotyped formulae. Greco-Roman letters were filled with stereotyped formulae. For instance, when a writer wished to disclose some new piece of information, he would use a disclosure formula such as "I wish you to know, [name], that."[32] So Oxyrhynchus Papyrus 1493 states "I wish you to know, Brother, that . . ." So Paul wrote in Galatians 1:11: "For I want you to know, Brothers, that." Letter writers had standardized expressions for astonishment ("I am astonished that . . ."), joy ("I rejoiced greatly when . . . because . . ."), petition ("I beseech you, [name], in order that . . ."), thanksgiving ("I give thanks to [name of god] because . . . "), ironic rebuke, compliance, etc. All of these expressions had a standardized order for the words as well as a particular set of words that they used.[33] Paul used many of these same stereotyped formulae. For example, we find an astonishment formula in Galatians 1:6; a joy formula in 1 Corinthians 16:17; 2 Corinthians 7:9, 16; and Philippians 4:10; a petition formula in Romans 12:1; a compliance formula in Galatians 1:8-9; a statement of report formula in Galatians 1:13; and an ironic rebuke formula in 2 Corinthians 12:11-13.

Even the greetings were stereotyped. In Paul's letters, the location in the letter, the number of greetings and even the level of personalization were all typical for a letter of

---

[29]See, e.g., Phil 4:20; Eph 3:20-21; 2 Tim 4:18. Only Romans 16:27 is in the "proper" place, perhaps because Tertius was a professionally trained secretary and placed it properly.

[30]The best discussion at present is in Weima, *Neglected Endings.*

[31]This is not to try to squeeze Paul into the typical mold. Although *paranesis* (moral exhortation) may be found in other Greco-Roman letters, paranetic sections comprise a major element in Paul's letters and not merely a convention. Paranesis will be discussed later.

[32]T. Mullins, "Disclosure: a Literary Form in the New Testament," *NovT* 7 (1972): 47-48, gives many examples of "disclosure formulae" from the papyri. I also found disclosure formulae at the beginning of the letter body in POxy. 1155, 1481 and in the middle of the letter body in POxy. 1670.

[33]For a more complete list, including examples in Greek with references, see Richards, *Secretary,* pp. 204-5, or John White, *Light from Ancient Letters* (Philadelphia: Fortress, 1986).

his time. It was very common in even the everyday papyrus letters to include many greetings accompanied by personal descriptions. For example, in Oxyrhynchus Papyrus 533, the final 10 percent of the letter is greetings, with many personal descriptions. Paul's letter to the Romans contains the longest section of greetings, but they still only comprise 5.9 percent of the total letter.

Greeting formulae took three forms: a first-person greeting, where the writer greets someone, "I greet my father" (PTebt. 415); a second-person greeting, where the writer tells the recipient to greet someone, "Greet your mother" (PTebt. 412); and a third-person greeting, where the writer tells the recipient a third party greets someone, "Zanthilla greets her people" (POxy. 114).[34] Letters often had at least two if not all three of these types of greetings. In Romans, for example, all three types of greetings occur: the first person type in verse 22, the second person type in verses 3-16, and the third person type in verse 16.

Although most papyrus letters began with a formulaic statement of prayer, such as "I pray for your health daily," some began by giving thanks. Thanksgivings usually stated that the writer was thankful the recipient had been saved from some danger by the god(s) or that the god(s) had provided the recipient with continued good health or fortune.

On FEBRUARY 19, A.D. 107, A SOLDIER BEGAN A LETTER TO HIS FATHER:

I give thanks to Sarapis and Good Fortune that while all are laboring the whole day through at cutting stones, I as an officer move about doing nothing.
PMich. 8.465; see also POxy. 1299, 1070, 1481

Paul made much more frequent use of the thanksgiving formula, having one in all of his letters except Galatians and Titus.

Paul followed the traditional form of the thanksgiving,[35] with the following modifications:

1. In contrast to safety, health or good fortune, Paul was usually thankful for the congregation's continued faithfulness. Perhaps this was a sign the congregation was prospering, healthy and safe.

2. Paul usually blended an intercession into his thanksgiving (he gave thanks and then prayed it would continue), thus combining the more common opening prayer with a thanksgiving.

---

[34]These are my categories. Exler, *Form*, p. 116, first noted different types of greetings, but in a more general, less organized manner. Koskenniemi, *Studien*, pp. 148-50, suggested three different forms: (a) writer greets addressee, (b) writer greets others than addressee, and (c) writer sends greetings from another to addressee. Yet these categories fail to allow for several types including the common second person greeting.

[35]See T. Mullins, "Formulas in New Testament Epistles," *JBL* 91 (1972): 380-90.

3. Paul often previewed the contents of his letter in the thanksgiving. In 1 Corinthians 1:4-7, Paul gives thanks that the Corinthian church had been enriched in speech and knowledge so that they lacked no spiritual gift. Paul then spent substantive parts of the letter dealing with speech-related and knowledge-related spiritual gifts (tongues, prophecies, etc.).

Because he often used his thanksgiving to tactfully introduce themes for the letter, Paul had much longer thanksgiving formulae than the brief formulaic ones found in some Greco-Roman letters. He also placed his thanksgiving at the beginning of the letter (right after the "sender to recipient"), which was a less common location for a thanksgiving.[36]

As I noted, Paul included a thanksgiving in all of his letters except Galatians and Titus.[37] This is one of the ways the Pastorals vary from Paul's customary pattern. Although Paul expressed his gratitude in 1 and 2 Timothy, he did not follow his typical pattern. Galatians is the peculiarity. In other respects Galatians is a typical—some would say the proto-typical—Pauline letter. No scholars deny Pauline authorship because Galatians does not have a Pauline trademark: a thanksgiving. Why is it missing? If Galatians was Paul's first letter, as scholars often suggest, then perhaps Paul had not yet developed his practice. We have noted already that Paul had not crystallized his letter address at that point, saying "Paul . . . and all the brothers who are with me" instead of naming them as he did everywhere else.[38]

Yet, the lack of a thanksgiving may be more deliberate. If I received a letter that began:

Dear Randy,
What were you thinking? I saw . . .

I would be struck by its abruptness. Our American letters customarily have "How are you?" When I read a letter that has "How are you?" I don't think the writer is actually wondering how I am doing; it is just a part of American letter writing. If I receive a letter like the one above,

---

[36]There are examples of thanksgiving formulae at the beginning of the letter body (e.g., POxy. 1299), in the middle of the letter body (e.g., POxy. 1070), and at the conclusion of the letter body (e.g., POxy. 1481). Beda Rigaux, *The Letters of St. Paul: Modern Studies,* ed. and trans. S. Yonick (Chicago: Franciscan Herald, 1968), pp. 121-22, argues Paul has been influenced by the Jewish custom of beginning a speech with thanksgiving.

Paul Schubert in his extensive investigation noted well that it is sometimes difficult to find where Paul's thanksgiving ends and where the letter body begins; Schubert, *The Form and Function of the Pauline Thanksgiving* (Berlin: Alfred Topelmann, 1939). However, Jack Sanders suggested Paul had two distinctive phrases that show he was ending his thanksgiving; Sanders, "The Transition from Opening Epistolary Thanksgiving to Body in the Pauline Corpus," *JBL* 81 (1962): 352-62. These phrases have since been catalogued as disclosure and petition formulae. Sanders's system requires a truncated Pauline corpus, since Colossians, Ephesians, Titus and 2 Timothy do not follow his pattern. It seems best to say that Paul flowed from his thanksgiving into the letter body. The transition was often marked with a formula.

[37]Second Corinthians puts the form of thanksgiving into a stylized benediction.

[38]It has been suggested that Paul used this phrase to emphasize that *all* are supporting him; that is, the rest of Christendom. Yet, Paul's qualifier "all with me" seems to argue against this, especially given the emphatic location of "with me" in the phrase.

with no "How are you?" I am startled and have the impression that the writer is abrupt, perhaps even unhappy with me. In Paul's day people expected letters to have an obligatory "I pray daily for you" or perhaps "I thank the gods that you are in good health." When Paul begins his letter in Galatians 1:6, he does not start with "I pray" or "I am thankful," but rather "I am amazed you so quickly deserted your faith." The implication is that Paul was in a rush to get straight to the matter.[39] Once again Paul was previewing the contents of his letter.

Epistolary rhetoric. In addition to the standard stereotyped formulae, Paul also made common use of the typical literary and oratorical devices commonly used in Greco-Roman letters.[40] One would expect literary rhetorical devices in a written letter. Yet in antiquity, a well-written letter was supposed to sound like half of a conversation; that is, what the writer would have said were he there in person. Thus, Greco-Roman letters employed many of the rhetorical devices commonly used in speeches. Paul's letters were no exception, containing both *literary* and *oratorical devices.*

In the century before Paul, chiasm was much in vogue but had waned in popularity, leaving one Pauline scholar to pronounce that in Paul's day chiasm was "only to be noticed intermittently as a stylistic curiosity."[41] Joachim Jeremias, however, revived interest in chiasm by showing how Paul frequently used it. One example is sufficient. The well-known passage in Romans 10:9-10 reads:

> If you *confess in your mouth* that Jesus is Lord and *believe in your heart* that God raised him from the dead, you will be saved. For, *by the heart one believes* and so is justified and *by the mouth one confesses* and so is saved.[42]

This text contains a simple yet beautiful chiasm:

A = confess in your mouth
B = believe in your heart
C = you will be saved
B' = by the heart, one believes
A' = by the mouth, one confesses

---

[39]Among the private letters of the Michigan collection, those letters without a beginning prayer or thanksgiving were usually about a pressing matter, as seen in the letters' contents; see, e.g., PMich. 8.472, 485, 486, 493 and 496.

[40]This is a major point of debate. It is beyond the scope of this work to provide more than a brief summary.

[41]Rigaux, *Letters,* p. 127. Not all agree that chiasm had fallen out of use; see Welch, "Chiasmus," p. 258. R. B. Steele lists 1257 examples of chiasmus in Livy, 211 in Sallust, 35 in Caesar, 1088 in Tacitus, and 307 in Justinus; see Steele, "Anaphora and Chiasmus in Livy," *TAPA* 32 (1901): 166, and his *Chiasmus in Sallust, Caesar, Tacitus and Justinus* (Northfield, Minn.: Independent Publishing, 1891), pp. 4-5. Yet in most of his examples, the chiasm involves only pairs of words. Moreover, Steele noted that chiasm generally was absent in those letters of Cicero and Pliny that were less carefully crafted; see his "Chiasmus in the Epistles of Cicero, Seneca, Pliny and Fronto," *Studies in Honor of B. L. Gildersleeve,* ed. C. A. Briggs (Baltimore: Johns Hopkins University Press, 1902), pp. 339, 346-47.

[42]To see a chiasm usually requires following the Greek text a little more literally. Most translations obscure chiasms.

The chiasm was, however, actually more carefully crafted:

A = confess
B =   mouth
C =   believe
D =   heart
E =   saved.
D' =   heart
C' =   believes
B' =   mouth
A' = confesses

A passage that might seem to modern ears to be verbose or redundant was actually a chiasm. Other Pauline passages that seem difficult to modern readers may be a complex chiasm, not just in words but sometimes in sense lines or even ideas. So, Nigel Turner sees a chiasm in Colossians 1:13-20 and an elaborate treble chiasm in Ephesians 2:11-22.[43]

However, we must take care not to "find" what is not there. Sometimes an attempt to find chiasm in Paul demonstrated more the creativity of the modern writer than of Paul.[44] Nonetheless, ancients noticed and enjoyed chiasm much as we notice and enjoy rhyming sentences today. For us, rhyming makes something easier to remember and often gives us an appreciation that the writer thought carefully when constructing his material. It is important to note, however, that we do not dismiss the contents of the sentence just because the writer made them rhyme, nor do we assume the contents were trivial because the writer took the time to rhyme them. Readers in Paul's day viewed chiasm the same way.

In addition to chiasm Paul used other literary rhetorical devices. He made frequent use of analogy, although his particular handling of analogies was not typical. In fact, Paul has been criticized for having convoluted analogies, starting with one image, dropping it partway to pick up a second image. Sometimes he used a cluster of images to make a single point.[45] For example, in Romans 6—7, Paul argued that we are no longer bound to the Law. Our old self has died to the Law, having been buried with Christ in baptism (6:4). Since we have died with Christ, we are free from sin and the Law. He then began an analogy: the Law is binding on a person only during that person's lifetime (7:1). Thus, he continued, a married woman is bound by the law only until . . . and we expect Paul to say only until *she* dies, staying with his original analogy that the marriage laws were only binding while a person lived. However, Paul switched analogies and said

---

[43]Turner, *Style*, pp. 98-99. Scholars generally concede chiasm with pairs of words. The more elaborate the proposed chiasm, the more disputed it becomes.

[44]John Bligh's commentary on Galatians in the Householder Commentary Series (London: T & T Clark, 1969) may represent finding chiasm where it did not exist. He argues the entire letter of Galatians is one large chiasm centered around a smaller one in 4:1-10.

[45]So Doty, *Letters*, p. 45 n. 59.

only while *her husband* lives. When her husband dies, she is free from the law. We understand Paul's point, but he mixed his analogies. Why? Some have suggested that Paul was swept along by enthusiasm and failed to notice that he had switched metaphors. As we pointed out earlier, Paul's letters were not dashed off in haste during spare moments amidst a flurry of mission concerns. His letters were carefully crafted with multiple drafts and revisions.

I suggest Paul was fully aware of his change of metaphors. He was also confident that his readers would follow. (We did.) He was mixing his metaphors because we have left our slavery to sin (6:20) to become slaves of righteousness. We have left our old master and become married to Christ. He was cleverly weaving multiple metaphors together, fully expecting his readers to follow his meaning. His expectations were not misplaced. Even across 2000 years, readers have been able to follow his meaning. Paul's mixing of analogies was not a sign of careless haste but rather of thoughtful composition.

Paul also employed paradoxes and metaphorical imagery. He used pleonasm,[46] tribulation lists,[47] virtue/vice lists,[48] swearing one's message is God-given (e.g., Gal 1:12), curse pronouncements (e.g., Gal 1:8-9; 5:12) and moral imperatives (e.g., Gal 5:13-26), all of which were common literary devices. In Colossians 3, Paul made multiple use of vice and virtue lists, describing them with a clothing metaphor: there were things to "take off" as dirty clothing is cast off and other things to "put on" like clean clothing. He began in Colossians 3:5 by listing five vices they had already "put off," summarizing them with the word "idolatry." He then continued in 3:8 with five more vices they now needed to "take off," summarizing them with the word "lying." He then continued in 3:12 with five virtues to "put on," summarizing them with the word "love."[49]

Oratorical techniques were commonly employed both by the highly skilled rhetoricians in Rome and Athens and also by the lesser trained philosophers and preachers scattered across the empire. Even street preachers in the marketplace employed the less complex techniques, learning the techniques not from the classroom but from hearing others use them. In much the same way, modern oratorical techniques are learned more often by imitation than by classroom study. For example, it has become popular for politicians

---

[46]E.g., Gal 4:10: "you are observing special days and months and seasons and years." See also Cic. *Att.* 10.8: "Could there be a crime, deeper, greater, or baser?"

[47]For a simple tribulation list see Rom 8:35; 2 Cor 6:4-5; 11:23-29; 12:10. For antithetical tribulation lists see 1 Cor 4:10-13; 2 Cor 4:8-9; 6:8-10; Phil 4:12. 2 Enoch 66:6: "Walk my children, in long-suffering, in meekness, in affliction, in distress, in faithfulness, in truth, in hope, in weakness, in derision, in assaults, in temptation, in deprivation, in nakedness." Tribulation lists that include beatings, shipwrecks and nagging injuries can be found in Arr. *Epict. Diss.* 2.10.2; 2.10.3; and 6.4.2; TJos. 1:4-7; Sir. 39:28-34 (if not an antithetic parallel to vv. 21-27 as part of his theodicy); Jos. *BJ.* 4.3.10; *Ant.* 10.7.3; Plut. *Alex.* A-C. See also Hodgson, "Tribulation Lists," pp. 59-80.

[48]E.g., Gal 5:19-23. See also Arr. Epict. Diss. 2.16.4: "Expel . . . grief, fear, envy, malevolence, avarice, effeminacy, intemperance from your mind. But these can be no otherwise expelled than by looking up to God alone as your pattern."

[49]Vice lists often had five elements; see Richards, "Stop Lying," pp. 77-80.

to deflect accusations by seeming to accuse themselves and then responding: "Did I know that? No. Did I suspect that? Perhaps. Am I guilty? No!" This rhetorical technique is strikingly similar to the "imaginary interlocutor" of ancient rhetoric. As I was writing this chapter, I heard this technique used again last night on the evening news. Did the politician learn this in graduate school? No. It was picked up by imitation.

Educated persons were expected to speak eloquently in Paul's day. Some of the features of good speaking found themselves also in letters. For example, eloquence in speaking included common features, such as

(a) homiletic directness, as in Romans 14:12, "So then, each of us will be accountable to God";

(b) litotes (using a negative expression to say something positive), as in 1 Corinthians 1:25, "For God's foolishness is wiser than human wisdom"; and

(c) deliberate anacolutha (an abrupt change in grammar, usually smoothed over in a translation), as in 2 Corinthians 1:23, "But I call on God as witness against me: it was to spare you."

Many aspects of oration were unconscious, having become an integral part of one's speech-making. It was one of the indicators of a good speaker, a valued skill in antiquity. Of course, the most effective oratorical devices, such as controlling one's pitch or rate of speech, cannot be detected in a written letter.[50] Nonetheless, two major oratorical devices, used in speeches from the forum to the market, found their way into written letters including Paul's: paranesis and diatribe.

Paranesis (Greek for "exhortation") is usually connected with moral instructions. A paranetic section of a letter has a series of instructions, commands and exhortations to live a certain way. It is commonly noted that Paul's letters began with theology and ended with paranesis. This common pattern for Paul has been described with several clever expressions: Paul moved from "you are" to "you ought," or from the indicative to the imperative.

A common way to offer paranesis was through the use of a *topos* ("a common place"). A *topos* was a memorized short response to a commonly asked question, "miniature essays of stereotyped good advice"[51]—thus a place for the speaker to commonly return when answering a question. Ancient Greco-Roman street preachers (usually philosophers) had at ready a handful of memorized *topoi* to offer to those who responded to their preaching. A typical form was an injunction, a rationale, an analogous situation and a discussion. Romans 13 is a series of *topoi*.

---

[50]One variation, *numeris* (the succession of long and short syllables to give a pleasant musical cadence), can be seen in a letter such as 1 Cor 13:1-13.

[51]Doty, *Letters*, p. 39.

EXAMPLES OF A *TOPOS*

Sir 31:25-30:

Injunction: "Do not try to prove your strength by wine-drinking,"

Rationale: "for wine has destroyed many."

Analogous situation: "As the furnace tests the work of the smith,"

Discussion: "so wine tests the hearts . . . Wine is . . ."

Romans 13:1-5

Injunction: "Let every person be subject to the governing authorities;"

Rationale: "for there is no authority except from God."

Analogous situation: "Whoever resists authority resists what God has appointed,"

Discussion: "Do you wish to have no fear of the authority?"

Romans 13:6-7

Injunction: "Pay taxes"

Rationale: "for the authorities are God's servants"

Analogous situation: "Pay to all what is due them"

Discussion: "revenue to whom revenue is due, respect to whom respect is due, honor to whom honor is due."

Romans 13:8-14

Injunction: "Owe no one anything, except to love one another"

Rationale: "for the one who loves another has fulfilled the law."

Analogous situation: "You know what time it is, how it is now the moment for you to wake from sleep,"

Discussion: "Let us then lay aside the works of darkness . . ."

Although Paul used a standardized format, we do not mean to diminish the importance of his content. Often the paranetic material was a key—if not the key—thrust of Paul's letter.

The second common oratorical device was the diatribe.[52] The modern discussion of the diatribe began in the late 1800s among German classical scholarship. They concluded the diatribe was an established oratorical technique with several clear practices. The purpose of the diatribe was not technical discourse but rather for preaching, to persuade the common

---

[52]The diatribe remains hotly contested ever since Bultmann first contended that Paul utilized the diatribe. The very existence of the diatribe as an established form remains debated. Thomas Schmeller in a detailed investigation questioned the nature and use of the diatribe in Bion, Rufus, Epictetus and Paul. Schmeller, *Paulus und die "Diatribe": Eine vergleichende Stilinterpretation*, NTAbh 19 (Munich: Aschendorf-fsche, 1987).

man on the street to some philosophical or moral position. The goal of the diatribe was not enlightenment but conversion. Classical scholars argued that the diatribe did not have highly structured arguments, with a subordination of logical relationships, etc., but rather moved along by: a question and then the answer, a command followed by a question, a command followed by a statement, or some combination of these. The result was a lively conversational tone that had a flowing style (often with short sentences strung together). For example, the speaker seemingly interrupted himself with a question—one he anticipated his audience was thinking—and then answered his own question. This questioner, often called an "imaginary interlocutor," existed only in the mind of the speaker, for the purpose of bringing up a question the speaker wanted to answer. Teachers still use this technique today. I overheard a colleague begin a lecture: "Why should we study the Civil War? Because we can learn . . ."

Epictetus, a contemporary of Paul, used a format and vocabulary strikingly similar to Paul: "what then [*ti oun*], shall we . . ?" The response also had a standardized format, "By no means [*mē genoito*]," followed by explanation.

"What then [*ti oun*], would anybody have you dress out to the utmost? By no means [*mē genoito*], except . . ." (Epictetus *Diss.* 4.11.5; see also 1.10.2)

"What then [*ti oun*], should we sin because we are not under the law but under grace? By no means [*mē genoito*], do you not know . . ." (Rom 6:15; see also Rom 7:7)

In the case of Romans this issue is hotly debated, as seen in the classic collection of essays edited by Karl Donfried, still being reprinted: *The Romans Debate*. Were Paul and Epictetus the only two to use this form, or was this a popular style of preaching and this is why we see it in both of them? Why does it matter if Paul used the diatribe in Romans? (Note how I used an imaginary interlocutor to ask a question that I assumed you were thinking. Now I will answer it.) It becomes a keystone in the discussion of whether or not Romans was an occasioned letter. If Paul was responding to problems in the Roman church, then Romans cannot be used as a summary of Paul's theology. It was thus an occasioned letter and would function like the other letters of Paul, giving us a glimpse into the problems of the Roman church.

When Paul asked the question in Romans 6:15, was he responding to a question in the church? If so, then Romans is an occasioned letter, and there is no way to determine if the topic of Romans 6:15 was a key topic in Paul's thought or raised by Paul solely because someone in Rome was asking about it. However, the question in Romans 6:15 might be an imaginary question in the style of the diatribe. If so, then Paul was not responding to an actual question in Rome. Rather, he himself was using the question to introduce another element in the theology he wanted to proclaim.[53] Paul chose the subject. In this case

---

[53]So various authors argue in *The Romans Debate*. Günther Bornkamm argues that Romans uses the diatribe and the letter is not occasioned; Bornkamm, "The Letter to the Romans as Paul's Last Will and Testament," in *The Romans Debate*, ed. Karl Paul Donfried (Minneapolis: Augsburg, 1977), pp. 17-31. Karl Donfried strongly disagrees; "False Presuppositions in the Study of Romans," in *The Romans Debate*, ed. Donfried, (Minneapolis: Augsburg, 1977), pp. 132-41.

a theologian can argue Romans 6:15 was a key theme in Paul's theology.

Ultimately, we cannot solve the Romans debate with the diatribe. In fact, it is questionable how much the diatribe was a clearly defined technique at all. Many of the items identified as "diatribe" were techniques picked up from hearing street preachers. I used an imaginary interlocutor several times in the discussion above, but I am hardly trained in the use of a diatribe. Paul seems to be using common techniques of street preaching (techniques he learned from hearing other effective speakers), and it is unwise to conclude that he was deliberately employing a highly structured rhetorical technique.

Paul was not a trained rhetorician in the same class with Cicero or Seneca. Paul's anacolutha, or abrupt shifts in grammar, cannot always be explained as a deliberate use for rhetorical effect. At times it appears neither he nor his associates noticed the anacoluthon. We find very peculiar grammar in 2 Corinthians 14:7 and a (flawed) grammatical construction known as a *casus pendens* in Romans 8:3. Paul did not always finish his thoughts or his sentences neatly. He often diverted into parenthetical comments, sometimes never returning to the original thought. His pronouns did not always agree with their antecedents.[54] He used the wrong case for the direct object in Romans 2:8. Obviously, a lack of polish in Paul's grammar has no bearing upon the inspiration and the trustworthiness of God's Word—God is not bound to a society's grammatical rules. However, it does suggest that Paul was not highly trained in rhetoric, just as today it is often possible to determine the educational level of a writer from his or her writings.

A lack of rhetorical polish does not, however, imply a lack of careful thought. Paul did not feel himself bound by rhetorical conventions. Literary devices were merely tools for expressing the truths he wanted to proclaim. For example, the Rabbis spoke often of "blood and flesh." Paul and most others, however, used the more common word order of "flesh and blood," as in 1 Corinthians 15:50 and Galatians 1:16 (also in Mt 16:17 and perhaps Jn 1:13). However, in Ephesians 6:12, Paul writes "blood and flesh." Some have agonized over why Paul reversed the order:[55] was Paul wanting to use the rabbinic expression here in Ephesians, or was he thinking of the eucharistic language of the Last Supper (as perhaps seen in Jn 6:54, 56)? Neither is likely. If Paul and his colleagues had been trained rhetoricians, such a reversal of words would have fallen awkwardly on their ears and cried out for revision. Yet, in spite of multiple drafts, the word order "blood and flesh" never troubled them enough to warrant asking the secretary to reverse the wording in the next draft. Such fine rhetorical distinctions were not a concern for Paul and his team.

---

[54]The antecedent of *ho* (neuter) is masculine in Ephesians 5:5 and feminine in Colossians 3:14; see Turner, *Style*, p. 86.

[55]The same word order ("blood and flesh") occurs in Hebrews 2:14, and the unusual word order is discussed by Paul Ellingworth, *The Epistle to the Hebrews*, NIGTC (Grand Rapids: Eerdmans, 1993), pp. 171-72.

CONCLUSIONS FOR PAUL AS A LETTER WRITER

Paul's letters are neither public, philosophical treatises nor artless, spontaneous, private letters. Furthermore, a public versus private dichotomy is probably inappropriate for Paul's day. Letters fell on a spectrum ranging between these extremes, and Paul's fall closer to the middle of the spectrum and reflect a Jewish subculture.

Paul followed the standard format of an opening, body and closing, and used much of the standardized phrases, stereotyped formulae, of Greco-Roman letters. Paul's letters also used common rhetorical devices used by effective speakers and writers of his day, and while not in the same class as the premier rhetoricians of the classical age, they demonstrate a rhetorical sophistication that would have earned him respect as a persuasive speaker and letter writer.

9

ANALYZING PAUL'S WRITING STYLE

*A*nyone who writes has a writing style. Some writers have a distinctive style. Since we have copies of Paul's letters, can we determine his writing style? Why would we want to? Apparently a forged letter in Paul's name was possible (2 Thess 2:2). If we can accurately describe his style, then we can, perhaps, identify any forgeries.

THE WRITING STYLE OF PAUL

In the past, scholars sought to determine which letters of Paul were authentic and which were forgeries. Previous scholarship determined what they perceive as Paul's established theology, style and diction (although they frequently disagreed). To establish a "Pauline writing style" they usually began by assuming certain letters were unquestionably "Pauline." The theology, style and diction of these letters became the standard against which all the other letters were measured.

This approach has two significant weaknesses. First, the standard of "Pauline style" varies depending upon which letters are chosen as the starting point. Traditionally, the four "chief letters" (often called by the German term *Hauptbriefe*), Galatians, Romans, 1 and 2 Corinthians were the standard. Others have used a body of the "undisputed seven": the four plus 1 Thessalonians, Philippians and Colossians. Unfortunately, the "undisputed seven" were often disputed (e.g., some tossed out Colossians and added 2 Thessalonians).

This question of which letters to use is critical for this technique because the letters chosen determine the standard against which all other letters are measured. A starting point of four letters leaves a much more tightly drawn style and thus more letters are left outside. A wider starting point leaves a larger circle and fewer letters are left outside. Which letters are put in the "authentic" pile ultimately determines which letters then fall in the "inauthentic" pile. The starting point predetermines the endpoint.

The second weakness with this approach is that the so-called authentic letters vary considerably from each other. They were deemed similar because they are similar in "important areas," that is, what twentieth-century Western scholarship thought were important: Paul's teachings on justification by faith. This doctrine was vital to the Reformation. Many of us belong to denominations that fractured from the original church. I personally find it comforting to assume the church split over an essential, foundational element of the Christian faith and not merely over political and social issues. In seminary I was assured that the church split over the issue of "justification by faith,"[1] the central issue of the Christian faith. Yet justification by faith is not even mentioned in many of Paul's letters. While I believe a doctrine is true even if it is found in only one verse in one letter, it is more difficult to argue that it is the center of Paul's theology if it is found in less than half of his letters. One way to alleviate this problem is to accept as genuine only those letters that contain the ideas that were decided to be key to Paul.[2]

Using the absence of a theological theme as a measure of authenticity is a questionable methodology. The absence of a typical Pauline theme in a particular letter is probably only a sign that that particular church did not need the topic to be addressed.[3] After all, Paul's letters were occasioned,[4] and the letter's contents were first and foremost addressing that particular situation and only secondarily our situation. Because the contents of Paul's letters arose from specific situations we cannot presume a letter is inauthentic merely because a theme is missing.[5]

Can a Pauline style of writing be determined? In the past there have been some reasonably successful efforts to determine Paul's typical style of writing; however, the resulting description[6] was necessarily so vague or general that it was useless as a measure for rejecting certain letters as forgeries. There is now a more precise method that uses style and diction (not theology) to determine an author's writing style: statistical or stylometric analysis. This method, in theory, is effective in determining a writer's style and diction. All purported writ-

---

[1] This is not the place to argue the causes of the Reformation. It serves here only as an illustration.

[2] German critical scholarship, particularly that of the early 1900s, led this charge. It is possible they were still heavily under Luther's shadow.

[3] My students have asked, "What if we found a letter purportedly from Paul that didn't even mention Jesus?" Hypothetical questions can only receive hypothetical answers, but I believe even such a letter cannot be rejected outright. The absence of a theological theme is not the same as the presence of a conflicting theme. Cf. Esther.

[4] See the brief but excellent explanation in Scott Duvall and Daniel Hays, *Grasping God's Word: A Hands-on Approach to Reading, Interpreting, and Applying the Bible* (Grand Rapids: Zondervan, 2001), pp. 219-20.

[5] This is perhaps the reason the Romans Debate has continued to hold scholarship's attention. Holding the doctrine of "justification by faith" as the Pauline center becomes difficult if it is not even mentioned in many of Paul's letters. It is still true, though perhaps not the centerpiece of Paul's thought. What theological thought did Paul hold most dear? It might be difficult or even impossible to determine, if all of Paul's letters were occasioned. Paul wrote about an issue, not because it was dearest to his heart, but because it was crucial for dealing with the situation addressed in the letter. However, if we maintain that Romans stands apart from the rest, that Romans was *not* occasioned, then we can argue that Romans represents a summary of Paul's theology (what was dearest to his heart), and hence we can find the Pauline center. On the other hand, if the letter to the Romans was occasioned as all the other Pauline letters were, then Romans tells us much about the situation in Rome and of course unveils marvelous divine truths for us (as his other letters do), but Romans could not be considered a special window into Paul's theological soul. This is not the place to address the Romans Debate; however, the stakes are higher than merely determining the context of the Roman church.

[6] See, e.g., Turner, *Style,* p. 80.

ings are measured. It is an established approach and has been attempted by several.[7]

The most noted early attempt was by A. Q. Morton and James McLeman.[8] Their methods used the presence and/or absence of "significant words" as a sign that the letter was inauthentic. Attention was particularly placed upon words not found anywhere else in the New Testament (*hapax legomena,* often nicknamed "hapax"). The presence of multiple hapaxes was considered a sign that Paul did not write a passage.

A few words should be said about using the conclusions of these statistical methods for determining an author's writing style.

1. All these studies may be faulted for failing to recognize the presence of preformed tradition in Paul's letters. In this type of study, usually all the content of a letter was counted, including Old Testament quotations and quoted hymns, like Philippians 2:5-11. Much if not most of this type of material is non-Pauline; counting it "dilutes" the data.

2. None of these studies allows for any contribution by a coauthor; yet such material would naturally appear "dissimilar" to Paul.

3. Although Morton and McLeman recognize the possible influence of a secretary, they dismiss it without any serious consideration.[9] However, Josephus used secretaries in various roles, and scholars use this influence of secretaries to explain some of the stylistic differences between Josephus' writings.[10]

4. Scholars determined the "significant words," returning to the same problem of determining key Pauline theological themes. Although the presence of hapaxes is noteworthy, critics have pointed out both the body of Pauline literature used to determine a comprehensive vocabulary of Paul and the subject matter of a particular letter had a large influence on vocabulary. If all thirteen Pauline letters are used, there is probably a large enough sample to determine a Pauline vocabulary pool. Of course, then all thirteen letters fit. If the pool is reduced to four or seven letters, the amount of vocabulary

---

[7]The first major work to use statistical analysis to determine style was P. N. Harrison, *The Problem of the Pastorals* (London: Oxford University Press, 1921).

[8]Andrew Morton and James McLeman, *Paul, the Man and the Myth* (London: Hodder & Stoughton, 1966).

[9]*Paul,* p. 94. Morton and McLeman are seemingly eager to dismiss any possible influence of a secretary. Their studies found numerous divergences from their perceived standard of Pauline style. Why not place the blame for these divergences at the feet of coauthors and secretaries? The motives of Morton and McLeman are suspect. They claim the differences prove that Paul was not the author of many of the letters credited to him. They assert Pauline authorship for the *Hauptbriefe* (Rom, 1-2 Cor, Gal) only. The rest of Paul's letters came from six different authors. Yet, Pauline authorship of the *Hauptbriefe* can be maintained in their study only by eliminating a large number of what they termed "anomalies," places where even these letters were quite dissimilar.

[10]Josephus uses a general term *synergoi* ("fellow workers") who aided him in translating his work, but scholars say their role extended well beyond mere translation. His work on the *Antiquities of the Jews* displays well his lack of skill in Greek and in Hellenistic historiography. Yet his work on the *Wars of the Jews* is well written. "The immense debt which he [Josephus] owes to these admirable collaborators [the *synergoi*] is apparent on almost every page of the work"; so Thackeray, "Introduction," 1:xv.

is too small to determine the length and breadth of Paul's vocabulary. It is not an adequate sampling to conclude that some other letter of Paul is inauthentic because it used words not found in the other letters.[11] To illustrate this weakness, Acts 27 could be dismissed as not Lukan, since nowhere else does Luke use technical nautical vocabulary. Yet, all would agree the subject matter of Acts 27 (Paul's voyage to Rome) is the reason Luke used so many nautical terms.

Some methodological problems with the earlier statistical studies have been corrected by the work of Anthony Kenny, by using a better statistical method.[12] To avoid the weaknesses of previous works, Kenny did not center upon unusual vocabulary (hapaxes). Rather his study used elements not normally effected by subject matter, such as the frequency of subordinate clauses, the frequency of coordinating conjunctions (such as *and* or *but*). Studies have shown that this type of stylometric analysis is remarkably accurate for determining if certain letters are statistically "similar enough" to cluster together and if other letters stand too far away from the cluster and are "too dissimilar." The results of his study are worth noting: there is a great deal of diversity among the thirteen letters of Paul, and all thirteen letters share about the same amount of commonality. Kenny concludes:

> There is no support given by [the data] to the idea that a single group of Epistles (say the four major Tübingen Epistles [*Hauptbriefe*]) stand out as uniquely comfortable with one another; or that a single group (such as the Pastoral Epistles) stand out as uniquely diverse from the surrounding context.[13]

Kenny sees only two options: either there were thirteen different authors (each letter had a different author) or there was one very diverse writer. For the thirteen letters of Paul there is no statistical case for arguing one man was responsible for a small cluster of letters and not for the other letters. Kenny tentatively separates Titus from the others, since it is

---

[11]G. U. Yale, *The Statistical Study of Literary Vocabulary* (Cambridge: Cambridge University Press, 1944), p. 281, sounded what became the rallying cry for many who opposed statistical analysis: for a proper comparison, the samples must be larger than 10,000 words and be similar in length and subject matter; see, e.g., E. E. Ellis, "The Authorship of the Pastorals: a Resume and Assessment of Recent Trends," in *Paul and His Recent Interpreters* (Grand Rapids: Eerdmans, 1961), p. 54. More recent works profited from Type-Token-Ratio analysis used in other fields and have avoided some of the pitfalls of the older studies. E.g., W. C. Wake, "Numbers, Paul and Rational Dissent," *Faith and Freedom* 37 (1984): 59-72, uses statistical criteria like sentence length, distribution of *kai* ("and") and word position within sentences. His work is not without critics, though; see P. Trudinger, "Computers and the Authorship of the Pauline Epistles," *Faith and Freedom* 39 (1986): 24-27.

[12]*A Stylometric Study of the New Testament* (Oxford: Clarendon, 1986). Kenny also used a better text (Aland's) and technique (see, e.g., Kenny, *Stylometric*, 80 and his table 14.2, pp. 107-10). Kenny's lack of the hostility so quickly evident in Morton and McLeman also enabled him to be more objective. Kenny was also much more hesitant to draw sweeping conclusions even when he had considerably more data (e.g., p. 95). See also Kenneth Neumann, *The Authenticity of the Pauline Epistles in the Light of Stylostatistical Analysis*, SBLDS 120 (Atlanta: Scholars, 1990).

[13]Kenny, *Stylometric*, pp. 99-100. Neumann, *Authenticity*, p. 217, reaches a similar conclusion: "there is little reason on the basis of style to deny the authenticity of the disputed letters."

the furthest from the center. However, he concludes, "twelve of the Pauline Epistles are the work of a single, unusually versatile author."[14]

While the Apostle to the Gentiles may have been an "usually versatile author," there may be a more reasonable explanation. Kenny's study, like most of the other statistical studies, does not allow for the influence of coauthors and secretaries.[15] I suggest Paul was the Patriarchal Voice of a letter that still had input from coauthors and a secretary. What effect would this have on a statistical study? First and foremost, one would expect results like that described by Kenny. Paul, as the dominant (often domineering) author, was the common thread that provided the similarity, while the various coauthors and secretaries provided enough input to prevent a clear style from emerging.

There are two ways to illustrate how coauthors and secretaries would better explain Kenny's data. First, if (as argued in chapter seven) Sosthenes played a major role in parts of 1 Corinthians, then 1 Corinthians should score farther from the Pauline "center," rather than as one of the four main letters, the *Hauptbriefe*. Second, if (as noted in chapter five), two of Paul's letters have less influence from a secretary (Philippians and Romans), then these two letters should be more similar to each other statistically and both be closer to a perceived Pauline center. Neither of these two elements would be expected in most typical analyses of Paul's letters.

How do these expectations match the results of Kenny's study? According to Kenny's research, the following ranking indicates how well each of the thirteen letters is "at home" in the Pauline corpus (from most comfortable to least): Romans, Philippians, 2 Timothy, 2 Corinthians, Galatians, 2 Thessalonians, 1 Thessalonians, Colossians, Ephesians, 1 Timothy, Philemon, 1 Corinthians and Titus.

Kenny's data found no *Hauptbriefe*. The style in all of Paul's letters has been sufficiently "diluted" (I would argue by the influence of team members and secretaries), and thus all letters are somewhat dissimilar. Yet, as suspected, 1 Corinthians is much further from the Pauline center than is normally suggested, while Romans and Philippians are the most similar and the closest to the Pauline center.

The conclusion we must reach is that style analyses are not effective in determining the authenticity of a Pauline letter. Our modern, Western, individualistic perception of a solitary writer cannot be cast back upon Paul. His letters are too filled with Old Testament material, quotes, coauthors and secretarial influences to root out a "pure Paul" litmus test for other letters.

Must we then accept as authentic any letter purported to be from Paul? Even Paul rejected this option (2 Thess 2:2); he told them his handwriting when he "signed" his letters was determinative.[16] Since there are no original copies of Paul's letters, only cop-

---

[14]Kenny, *Stylometric*, p. 100.

[15]Neumann, *Authenticity*, p. 218, noted that the variations in style could be the result of "Paul's amanuenses or co-senders."

[16]For signing letters, see chapter eleven.

ies of copies, it is not possible to compare handwriting. Forgeries usually were circulated to damage someone's reputation or cause, as was apparently done to Paul (2 Thess 2:2). In antiquity, ancients determined a letter's authenticity by the handwriting and the letter's seal (in the case of the upper class). An autographed signature was the customary means of avoiding the problem of forgeries, if the recipient knew the writer's handwriting. To avoid this problem further with the Thessalonians Paul indicated that the handwriting at the end was his, and that all of his letters (to them?) would have an autographed subscription. Thus when Cicero was trying to disguise his letters, he wrote Atticus: "I won't use my own handwriting or seal."[17] Although pseudonymous letters with forged handwriting were known,[18] the typical writer had no reason to fear forged handwriting.

What did ancients do when they read a copy of a letter? They could not verify the handwriting or the seal. Their plight was similar to ours. They used two criteria: the letter was considered authentic if (1) the copy was in the handwriting of a trusted colleague, or (2) the content, tone and argument were recognizably the author's. The first criterion is seen when Cicero accepted a letter as from Pompey because he recognized the handwriting of Sestius: "You should know already the reply that Pompey is sending by Lucius Caesar. . . . I have never seen anything more Sestian in its style."[19] While valid at the time, this criterion is of no benefit today.

The second criterion needs further explanation. In antiquity, a letter was accepted as authentic if it claimed to be from the author and had a reasonable chance of being so (i.e., not written fifty years after his death) and contained larger aspects, such as argumentation, tone or content that was consistent with the author. While a secretary could account for other elements of style, it was assumed an author exerted sufficient control to prevent these elements from becoming too dissimilar to his own. Two examples will suffice to show that ancients used this criterion.

First, Atticus received a letter from Caesar that he suspected was a forgery. He apparently sent a copy to Cicero without comment to see if Cicero drew the same conclusion. He did, declaring:

> the letter you send does not give me any consolation. For it is grudgingly written, and raises great suspicion that it is not by Caesar; I expect you noticed that too.[20]

Although he was quite familiar with Caesar's writing style, Cicero made no appeal, for instance, to deviations in the letter's vocabulary or grammar as evidence of the letter's inauthenticity. Rather, he appealed to its "out of character" nature.

---

[17]Cic. *Att.* 2.20.
[18]Jos. *BJ.* 1.31.1; Suet. *Aug.* 51.1. There were persons adept in the art of forging handwriting; see Suet. *Tit* 3.2; *Vesp.* 6.4; Jos. *BJ.* 1.26.3.
[19]Cic. *Att.* 15.3. Cicero accepts the letter's contents as being what Pompey wanted.
[20]Cic. *Att.* 11.16.

Second, Tyrrell and Purser, the noted authorities on Cicero, used this criterion to reject the supposed letter of Cicero to Octavian:

> That this letter is the work of a rhetorician, and a very foolish one too, is evident. The complete lack of dignity, the feeble impotent abuse, and the utter aimlessness of the whole production stamp it at once as entirely alien from Cicero's style.[21]

Again, such things as hapaxes, variations in diction or established phraseology were not considered. The reason is clear: a secretary easily accounted for such differences. Hence the presence of such variations was not necessarily a sign of a forgery. This is, however, a one-way street. The presence of an author's typical diction, grammar and phraseology was used to support authenticity.

Many scholars today consider some letters of Paul to be forgeries. Yet, the role of a secretary can account for many of the factors they use to reject these letters. For example, in a little book on the letters of Paul, Leander Keck lists four typical reasons for rejecting some of Paul's letters:

1. numerous differences in form, function, style, vocabulary and theological point of view;

2. in at least one case (2 Thess) there is a clear literary dependence upon the apostle's own writing;

3. certain issues and situations addressed in these letters do not correspond with those Paul is likely to have confronted; and

4. it is virtually impossible to fit some of the letters (notably the Pastorals) into the chronology implied by the authentic letters.[22]

The last two reasons are disputed, and are maintained only if the letters are already considered inauthentic. They are supporting arguments only and cannot independently demonstrate inauthenticity.

Although I would dispute there are any significant differences in form and function, Keck seems correct in his first point, that there are significant differences in style, vocabulary and theological point of view. By "style" he means some specific stylistic issues, such as the use of coordinating conjunctions, etc. By "vocabulary" he is referring primarily to hapaxes, as well as some examples of synonyms. He also cites examples of passages having a different (though not necessarily contradictory) theological point of view. However, these reasons are inadequate to argue certain letters are forgeries. A secretary and coauthors can easily account for the style and vocabulary differences. More than that, these are the very types of differences one would expect from coauthors and a secretary. Differing theological viewpoints may have come from a coauthor, as illustrated in chapter seven (for

---

[21]Tyrrell and Purser, *Cicero*, 5:338-39.
[22]Leander Keck, *Paul and His Letters*, Proclamation Commentaries, 2nd ed. (Minneapolis: Fortress, 1988).

1 Cor 8 and 10). Keck also contends that at least 2 Thessalonians contains material reused from another letter of Paul. The same can be maintained for Ephesians. I will demonstrate in chapter ten that authors reused material from their other writings; it was not necessarily a sign of inauthenticity. Finally, analyses based upon the writing style of Paul are not a reliable measure of authenticity. Thus, we do not find adequate evidence for maintaining certain Pauline letters as forgeries, or pseudonymous.

STYLISTIC DIFFERENCES BECAUSE PAUL USED A SECRETARY

The length of the letter. On more than one occasion Cicero commented, "My letter would be longer, if I could write myself."[23] Such statements are commonly used to assert that a secretary caused a letter to be shorter, that an author tended to write longer letters when writing in his own hand.[24] While a surface reading of Cicero's comment suggests this, a more careful look indicates otherwise.

Atticus preferred letters in Cicero's own hand; it was proof of Cicero's appreciation of their relationship. Cicero honored this except when he was very busy. In letters to Atticus, he noted that he was using a secretary because of his busy schedule.[25] The availability of extra time, indicated by the opportunity to write in his own hand, is probably the larger factor in why at least some of the letters in his own hand were longer. Another short letter was blamed on the use of a secretary: "were I writing myself, this letter would have been longer." Later in the letter, though, he stated "I dictate it owing to inflammation of the eyes."[26] Furthermore, from the date of the letter (January 23, 49 B.C.), it can be determined that Cicero's usual secretary, Tiro, was absent. Cicero was using an unfamiliar one.[27] Since this letter was rather "flat" stylistically, lacking Cicero's usual spontaneous energy, anacolutha, exclamations, short quotations, or witticisms, it is not clear what caused the letter to be shorter: the use of a secretary, the use of an unfamiliar secretary, or ill health (inflammation of the eyes). In another letter Cicero explained "Let my secretary's handwriting be proof I am suffering from inflammation of the eyes, and that is the reason for brevity."[28] In reality Cicero's longer letters were written with secretarial help, but was this the reason they were longer or because they were sent to strategic individuals? The evidence is contradictory. I must conclude that using a secretary had no consistent effect upon the length of a letter.

The rhetorical content of the letter. Did using a secretary make a letter less rhetorical? Quintilian denounced the fashionable use of a secretary, arguing the very presence of a

---

[23]Cic. *Att.* 8.15.
[24]This is the conclusion of Bahr, "Letter Writing," p. 475.
[25]Cic. *Att.* 1.19; 7.13a; also *QFr.* 2.16.1.
[26]Cic. *Att.* 7.13a.
[27]I surmise this because Cicero was traveling at the time and would not have brought spare secretaries. Tiro had been left behind at an earlier stop because he was sick.
[28]Cic. *Att.* 8.13.

secretary was a rhetorical disadvantage: a secretary could neither keep pace with him nor truly understand him.[29] This was certainly the meaning of Seneca's comment that the speech of Janus was so eloquent "the secretary is not able to follow him."[30] Yet such boasts were intended to indicate the skill of the rhetorician rather than to indicate any real disadvantage to using a secretary.[31] Quintilian was advising the elite rhetoricians of Rome not the commonplace letter writers. The fashionable use of a secretary, Quintilian argued, was unbecoming of a true rhetorician. For Quintilian, the purer a letter, the better it was. The influence of anyone, secretary or other, had a polluting effect, since Quintilian and his colleagues stood at the apex of the rhetorical art.

This is another one of the many ways in which the Roman rhetoricians were not analogous to the typical letter writer. While a secretary was less skilled than Quintilian, he was usually more skilled than most letter writers. The use of a secretary usually improved a letter. Quintilian's comments give implicit support that ancients recognized using a secretary influenced the letter. Yet what of Paul who was better trained rhetorically than a typical letter writer but well below the level of Quintilian? We cannot be sure how much of Paul's rhetorical skill was lost through the use of a secretary. However, since his letters were considered weighty compared to his speeches (2 Cor 10:10)—a rhetorical device in of itself—it seems wise to conclude that Paul was content with the final draft of his letter. Using a secretary did not have a consistent effect upon the rhetorical content of a letter of Paul in any way that I can determine.

The flow of the letter. Because secretaries and coauthors had other duties and schedules, and because visitors came and went, the drafting of a letter was not the solitary project of a long afternoon. In the ancient Mediterranean world, visitors were to be received, proprieties to be observed. The concerns and duties of everyday life intruded into a writer's space. It is unwise to suggest Paul and his team had unbroken solitude to write a letter. Even the very wealthy aristocracy did not have such luxuries.

Drafting a letter over a period of time allowed for possible disjointedness. The writer's mood could change. The situation could change, additional news could arrive. The peculiar shift in 2 Corinthians 10—13 from thankfulness to what seems to some to be a harsher tone can be explained by writing over a period of time. The letter was likely in the hands of Paul and his team for days, perhaps weeks, even a month or two. Suggesting that the flow of a letter was affected by breaks in the writing process is more than just plausible; there is evidence. Realistically, it is not the type of situation where one would expect evidence. How would we ever know today that an ancient letter was written over

---

[29]Quint. *Inst.* 10.3.20. He actually speaks out of both sides of his mouth for he also lists the problem of a secretary recording so quickly that the speaker rushes, lest he seem hesitant, and thus doesn't consider his words carefully enough.

[30]Sen. *ApoloCol* 9.2 (shortly after the death of Claudius in A.D. 54).

[31]This is also the likely meaning of Philostratus' comment that letters written by Marcus himself had his "divine imprint" while those written with a secretary did not; 2.257.29-258.

a period of time? Cicero, with his love for writing about even mundane matters, once again gives insight. Cicero began a letter to his brother Quintus.[32] He began the letter using a secretary[33] and discussed various topics at great length. After mentioning business at home, he began responding to a series of letters he had received from his brother, answering them in order: "I come now to your letters . . ."; then "I have answered your longest letter; now hear what I say about your very little one . . ."; then "I come to your third letter"; then "your fourth letter . . ."; then "I have also received a very old letter . . ."[34] We see a similar pattern as Paul addressed a series of questions from the Corinthian church in 1 Corinthians: "Now concerning the matters about which you wrote . . ."; "Now concerning virgins . . ."; "Now concerning food sacrificed to idols . . ."[35]

After Cicero's long section responding to his brother's letters, he added the remark: "Just as I was in the act of folding this letter, there came letter-carriers from you and Caesar . . . How distressed I was! [over news of the death of Caesar's daughter Julia]."[36] Yet the letter did not end with these short remarks, for he then added "After I had written these last words, which are in my own hand, your son Cicero [Cicero's nephew] came in and had dinner with me."[37] The news of the death of Caesar's daughter had led him to add a postscript in his own hand. Before he could seal and send the letter, his nephew arrived with yet another letter from his brother. He responded to this letter during the meal he shared with his nephew by dictating to Tiro, his personal secretary.[38] After finishing this section, Cicero appeared ready to put a final postscript on the letter and seal it, for he wrote: "Because I have had a letter on my hands for many days on account of delay on the part of the letter-carriers, many things have been jumbled up in it, written at various times." Before the letter could be sealed, however, yet another letter arrived to which Cicero hastily scratches a short response. The letter is then ended.

The letter gave no indications of an extended period of time. There was nothing in it that prevented seeing it as written during a long afternoon and evening. It was only his concluding comment "because I have had a letter on my hands for many days" (and the shifts in handwriting) that indicate there were multiple breaks in the writing process. In Cicero's case, this long letter would normally have been broken into multiple letters, sent as each was finished, a luxury available to him because he maintained teams of private

---

[32]Cic. *QFr.* 3.1.

[33]He does not state this but it can be inferred since he notes the next section (3.1.19) was written in his own hand.

[34]Cic. *QFr.* 3.1.1-7, 8, 11, 12, 13, 14.

[35]1 Cor 7:1, 25; 8:1. It is less clear if Paul was responding to questions or to reports of problems when he began addressing other issues in 11:17; 12:1; 15:12; and 16:1. Cicero and Paul both used a recurring *de . . . de . . .* when listing the responses; see Cic. *Fam.* 12.30.

[36]Cic. *QFr.* 3.1.17.

[37]Cic. *QFr.* 3.1.19.

[38]Cic. *QFr.* 3.1.20: "I dictated this to Tiro during dinner, so do not be surprised at its being written in a different hand."

letter carriers. In this instance his carriers were temporarily delayed and he was not able to send multiple letters. His situation momentarily became more like that of Paul and other typical letter writers. When additional news came before a letter was dispatched, a reaction was appended to the current letter in progress rather than ending the one and starting another.

The addition of details. In a very personal letter to his friend Atticus, Cicero wrote in his own hand, apologizing for offending his friend over a matter. He concluded with a few brief comments, including: "Your men have beautified my library by binding the books and affixing title-slips. Please thank them."[39] Later that day or perhaps the following, Cicero sent another letter to Atticus, using a secretary. He repeated the matter of Atticus' kind provision of library slaves to organize his scrolls, but this time with considerably more detail:

> Since Tyrannio has arranged my books, the house seems to have acquired a soul; and your Dionysius and Menophilus were of extraordinary service. Nothing could be more charming than these bookcases of yours now that the books are adorned with title-slips. Farewell.[40]

The second letter repeated the same sentiments but did so more eloquently and with more details, including the names of the slaves. In the earlier letter, Cicero dashed off a note in his own hand to apologize to his friend. He included a brief thank you for the loan of the library slaves, but like many powerful men he did not know their names (or care to know them). Later Cicero sent a formal letter of thanks, no doubt telling the secretary to fill in the details, including finding out and recording the names of the slaves.

In Paul's letter to the Romans he concluded by greeting a large number of people by name, all in the Roman church. It has been questioned how Paul came to know so many when he had never visited the church. In Paul's day, however, people traveled extensively, so it was not impossible. Yet there is another explanation. Paul used a secretary, Tertius (Rom 16:22), who apparently was not a member of his band. Tertius, a Roman name, was also a believer for he sent greetings "in the Lord." Secretaries did not send greetings in a letter written for another, with the rare exception where the secretary was also known to the recipients. The few examples of a secretary squeezing in a greeting are only where the secretary was well known to the recipient.[41] Most likely Tertius was a member of the Roman church. Paul customarily put greetings at the end of his letters, but not to the length found in Romans. In fact, Paul would have been considered a poor role model for sending greetings. Most of his letters compare poorly with the amount of greetings found in the typical papyrus letter. Paul spent considerable time in Corinth, knowing that church bet-

---

[39] Cic. *Att.* 4.5.

[40] Cic. *Att.* 4.8.

[41] Thus Alexis, the secretary for Atticus, often sent a word of greeting to Cicero; Cic. *Att.* 5.20: "I am pleased that Alexis so often sends greetings to me; but why cannot he put them in a letter of his own, as Tiro, who is my Alexis, does for you?"—a frivolous expense, such as Cicero would think nothing of asking.

ter than perhaps any church but Ephesus, and yet he sent no personal greeting, only a generic "Greet one another with a holy kiss" (1 Cor 16:20 and again in 2 Cor 13:12, also in 1 Thess 5:26 and Tit 3:15). He sent no greetings at all in Galatians, Ephesians, 2 Thessalonians and 1 Timothy. The Philippian church was dear to his heart; yet he sent only a generic greeting: "Greet every saint in Christ Jesus."

It cannot be argued that Paul avoided names because he feared offending someone he omitted or because he did not want to single out individuals, for he singles out individuals in Colossians 4:15 and 2 Timothy 4:19. Paul's custom was to offer cursory greetings and any greetings with names were always in the section before he personally picked up the pen. In contrast to his usual custom, the letter to the Romans has extensive greetings, listing many people by name. Given the evidence, I suggest as explanation that Paul instructed Tertius to greet the leaders of the church in Rome. Tertius either knew or researched whom to greet. The use of a well-trained secretary may have resulted in a more complete list of greetings.[42]

Corrections. In chapter four we saw that secretaries often corrected (edited) the letter. In a letter to Atticus, Cicero concluded with a customary comment, "Please arrange my affairs." Then he adds, "Oh, I forgot to answer one question about the brickwork . . ."[43] This is unique in the letters of Cicero. While this could be the single time Cicero had a momentarily lapse of memory, there is a more likely explanation. When this letter was written, Cicero was at sea and had no secretary with him.[44] Forgotten remarks appended to the end of a letter are not found in Cicero's letters, I conclude, not because they never occurred, but because normally Cicero required the secretary to move the material up into the letter in the next draft (or final copy). He did not wish to seem scatter-brained. This particular letter had no subsequent revision. It was dispatched when the ship landed in port.

Paul's letters (and Cicero's), however, contain what appear to be spontaneous corrections, suggesting that perhaps there was no editing. The presence of these phrases in Paul's letters has been used by a few to argue against the view that Paul's letters were edited, saying these comments are clear signs that Paul's letters had no editing after the first draft. We can see an example in 1 Corinthians 1:13-17.

> Has Christ been divided? Was Paul crucified for you? Or were you baptized in the name of Paul? I thank God that I baptized none of you except Crispus and Gaius, so that no one can say that you were baptized in my name. (I did baptize also the household of Stephanas; be-

---

[42]Only Romans has all three forms of "greeting formulae"; see the discussion of greetings in chapter eight. The role of Tertius in Romans is visited again in chapter thirteen.

[43]Cic. *Att.* 5.12.

[44]Cicero does not state he was writing in his own hand; Atticus knew his handwriting. He also does not state there was no secretary present; however, I deduce this from his correspondence: Tiro, his secretary, had been left behind, ill in Athens, partway through the voyage. Tiro was expected to catch up, but inclement weather had prevented his arrival up to that point.

yond that, I do not know whether I baptized anyone else.) For Christ did not send me to baptize but to proclaim the gospel, and not with eloquent wisdom . . .

The comment about Stephanas does appear to our eyes to be an after-thought, a spontaneous correction. While dictating, Paul suddenly realized that he had forgotten the household of Stephanas and added the comment. Bible translators commonly add parentheses to accentuate this. Such a correction, some argue, would obviously have been smoothed over if there had been a second draft.[45] Thus the text here in 1 Corinthians suggests the letter had no subsequent editing, since the "spontaneous correction" remained apart and was not incorporated into the earlier statement.

Likewise, Cicero wrote: "Well, then, his arrival—I mean Caesar's—is being eagerly awaited." In Cicero's case, it appears that he realized the antecedent of "his arrival" was not clear and so he spontaneously corrected it. It would seem the secretary merely recorded the correction "as is." This would seem to argue that the letters of Cicero (and, similarly, of Paul) were not edited. The premier authorities on Cicero, however, advise caution:

> But it is a serious error to ascribe carelessness to [the letters of Cicero]. His style is colloquial, but thoroughly accurate. Cicero is the most precise of writers. . . . Every adjective is set down with as careful a pen as was ever plied by a masterhand; each is almost as essential to the sentence as the principle verb.[46]

Perhaps Paul's comments about Stephanas were not so extemporaneous. Paul was quite subtle in his rhetoric here (an ironic critique of those who thought they were "wise" in such ways). Paul argued, "Were you baptized in my name?" He then added that he was glad he had not baptized many, for it was not important which Christian leader baptized which individuals. The addition of the household of Stephanas in verse 16 was not a last minute "correction" but rhetoric, as if the topic of who baptized whom was so minor Paul had trouble even remembering whom he had baptized. He then excused his apparent forgetfulness over whom he had baptized by saying that he was not called to baptize but to proclaim the gospel, and not with wisdom. This then introduced his argument in 1 Corinthians 1:18-31.[47]

Obviously, it is not possible here to delve into a detailed description of Pauline rheto-

---

[45]Luther Stirewalt sees this and other similar "corrections" and "clarifications" as evidence of extemporaneous composition (with no subsequent editing); *Paul, the Letter Writer,* pp. 20-21. I must respectfully disagree.

[46]Tyrrell and Purser, *Cicero,* 1:76. See also Sen. *Ep.* 75.1 where Seneca calls his letters "carelessly written"; yet Richard Bummere, the LCL editor for Seneca, warns that this remark is by no means to be taken literally: "the ingenious juxtaposition of effective words, the balance in style and thought, and the continual striving after point, indicate that the language of the diatribe had affected the informality of the epistle" (LCL 1:x).

[47]The main argument, vv. 18-31, is a proem midrash, where an Old Testament text was quoted (or paraphrased), followed by a second text, which has one or more catchwords in common with the first text. Commentary followed with a final, concluding text.

ric, but this supposed "spontaneous correction" is not necessarily evidence that Paul did not edit or revise his first draft. Rather, I suggest it was part of his rhetorical argument. First Thessalonians 2:18 reads:

> For we wanted to come to you—certainly I, Paul, wanted to again and again—but Satan blocked our way.

Was this a parenthetical clarification[48] and therefore an indicator that there was no subsequent editing? I argue it is a subtle rebuttal to the Thessalonian criticism that Timothy and Silas cared for them but Paul did not wish to visit them again.

Stylistic differences. The tone and broad style of a letter remained consistent for most authors, whether they used a secretary or not. For example, the letter of Ignatius to the Tragellians was written with a secretary through 13:2. The final section was from the hand of Ignatius himself; yet as William Schoedel indicates, the self-deprecating language of this postscript was characteristic of the entire letter's style.[49]

Although the broad style, themes and tone remained consistent, more specific indicators of style could vary. For example, Cicero wrote some letters in language analogous to his speeches and philosophical treatises.[50] Every word, every particle was chosen with the utmost care. Yet, many other letters were more conversational, far less formal and studied.[51] In his casual letters to his friends, Cicero evidently did not exercise minute control over every word choice.

Tyrrell and Purser assert Cicero's letters to his friends are more like the letters of other writers than like his own speeches.[52] Their claim that Cicero's letters to his friends were stylistically more similar to letters by other writers than to his own speeches is an astounding statement. Yet, this claim has been supported by a meticulous examination of the way Cicero ended his clauses. Tadeusz Zieliński demonstrated that Cicero preferred to use particular types of clause endings and avoided other types he termed "poorly selected endings."[53] The ratio of each type of clause ending remained constant throughout the speeches of Cicero. This celebrated "law of clause endings" has been demonstrated to be remarkably accurate; that is, all the formal, carefully composed works of Cicero conform. This "law" is accurate enough, according to Tyrrell and Purser, to be used to determine which of several variant readings among Cicero's speeches is authentic.[54] However, other ancient writers do not demonstrate a similar degree of conformity; thus this "law of clause

---

[48]Stirewalt, *Paul, the Letter Writer,* p. 20, calls this a correction made "in passing."

[49]Schoedel, *Ignatius,* p. 13.

[50]E.g., his first letter to Quintus, his famous letter to Lucceius (*Fam.* 5.12), and many of the "Consolation Letters."

[51]See the criteria listed by Tyrrell and Purser, *Cicero,* 2:lxv-lxvii.

[52]Tyrrell and Purser, *Cicero,* 2:lxix-lxx.

[53]T. Zieliński, *Das Clauselgesetz in Ciceros Reden: Grundzüge einer oratorischen Rhythmik,* Philologus Supplementband XIII, 1a (Leipzig: Dieterich, 1904).

[54]Tyrrell and Purser, *Cicero,* 2:lxvi-lxvii n.

endings" is only an appropriate measure of subtle Ciceronian style. What is significant for the study of Paul, however, is that while Cicero's speeches and formal letters conform, his letters to friends do not. These letters have a much higher proportion of what Zieliński termed "poorly selected endings."

How should this be interpreted? Did Cicero have two writing styles or did a secretary exert enough influence as to obscure this subtle measurement? While Cicero carefully oversaw the correct recording of every particle and adjective in an oration and in his formal letters, a private letter to a close friend was evidently less of a concern. In Cicero's mind, a published speech or a formal letter was well worth the time and expense caused by rewriting in order to make even subtle changes in particular sentences. Letters to friends were more casual. More of the secretary's style leaked into the letter, obscuring these very subtle and unique aspects of Ciceronian style. The use of a secretary usually resulted in enough minor changes that a highly specialized criterion like clause endings can detect the difference, even though the letter was still quite Ciceronian in content and in broad style, tone, and argumentation.[55]

Few ancient writers have been scrutinized as painstakingly as Cicero. However, Paul has been. Paul's letters have likewise been subjected to detailed analyses, and some of his letters are inconsistent when measured with a highly specialized criterion. Many New Testament scholars have argued the results indicate the letters are not from Paul. Would they argue the same for Cicero's letters to his friends? Classical scholars have long recognized the influence of a secretary upon a letter's style.

CONCLUSIONS FOR PAUL AS A LETTER WRITER

Because Paul used coauthors and a secretary, his writing style was "diluted." His letters were team letters, so statistical measures of style are not effective in determining authenticity. Using a secretary affected a letter in more ways than just style. Often letters written with a secretary were longer, but not always. Often they had more rhetorical elements and better organization, but the reason for this is not certain. Perhaps secretaries made better letters. Perhaps better writers used secretaries. In Paul's case, it is more likely that the improvements were the result of editing rather than secretarial mediation. Secretaries were, however, more likely to include details, such as names or a detailed description of an item for sale.

Finally, using a coauthor had an even greater possible influence upon a letter (see chapters six and seven). Non-Pauline but pre-dispatch—and thus authorized—interpolations can result from the presence of a coauthor. Jerome Murphy-O'Connor is justified in challenging New Testament scholarship to make distinctions between those letters from Paul (and his secretary) and those that include a coauthor.[56]

---

[55]A similar analysis of the letters of Trajan to Pliny has been done. Sherwin-White concludes, "The hand of Trajan cannot easily be detected by formal stylistic analysis." Nevertheless, Trajan's hand can be seen in the content of the letter, the way certain issues were handled, the fiery language used on occasion, the exceptions to precedence, etc., *Letters of Pliny*, p. 541. See also, Richards, *Secretary*, pp. 125-26.

[56]Murphy-O'Connor, *Paul the Letter Writer*, p. 16.

10

PREPARING A LETTER FOR DISPATCH

$\mathcal{W}$e began this book by looking at the practical logistics of how letters were scratched onto a papyrus sheet. After looking at several aspects of this process, including coauthors, rough drafts and secretaries, we spent several chapters looking at the actual letters of Paul. We examined more technical matter like epistolary genre (classifying letters), rhetoric and style analyses. Now we turn our focus once more back toward Paul's historical situation.

Once a letter was finished, how was it "mailed"? This leads us to ask about how the dispatched (mailed) copy was prepared and even how much it would have cost. For my generation, preparing a letter was a bit of trouble—as evidenced by how hard my mother nagged me to send those "thank you" notes. Mailing the letter, however, was an insignificant expense. For my students' generation, preparing a letter (an e-mail) is *very* little trouble, and there is really no perceived expense to "mail" it. But Paul's situation was different.

MAKING A COPY

Modern classical scholarship generally agrees that ancient letter writers kept copies of their letters. R. Y. Tyrell and L. C. Purser, the translators of seven volumes of Cicero's letters, comment: "There seems considerable evidence that the senders of letters . . . were accustomed to keep copies of letters, even, perhaps, letters which might seem to us to be of no great significance."[1] Indeed, secretaries often were hired to make copies as well as to write letters.[2]

From incidental remarks in ancient letters it becomes clear that letter writers made copies of letters[3] for three reasons: (1) multiple copies were made and sent via different

---

[1]Tyrell and Purser, *Cicero,* 1:59.

[2]In Hebrew (*sofer*), Greek (*grammateus*) and Latin (*librarius*), the same term was commonly used to designate a "secretary" or "copyist."

[3]The practice of making copies is not the subject of any ancient writing. It is discerned from incidental comments. For this reason, one of the best ancient sources is Cicero. I am not, however, arguing that the letters of Cicero, Seneca and their peers are analogous to Paul's, but rather that copy-making was a part of basic letter-writing conventions, for we can find evidence for the custom across the literary spectrum, in Cicero (*Att.* 3.9), in his friends (Cic. *Att.* 1.17) and also in the papyri (PZen. 10). We therefore conclude that this was a common enough practice.

carriers to help insure the safe arrival of the message, (2) a copy of a letter was made to be shared with another, (3) a copy was made to be retained by the author.

To dispatch multiple copies. Authors were known to dispatch multiple copies of a letter.[4] In this particular scenario the multiple copies were dispatched with different carriers and often different routes, in order to ensure the letter's safe arrival.[5] The most common examples of this practice come from the Roman aristocracy during the political intrigues of the last days of the Republic, when various factions were intercepting carriers, sending false messages, etc.[6] It is scarcely plausible that Paul practiced this custom. It was expensive and unnecessary. The practice of sending multiple copies to one location must be contrasted with sending one copy to multiple locations, such as Paul did with his letter to the Galatians.[7] Clearly Paul dispatched one copy that was carried to the various churches of Galatia.[8]

To share a copy. Letter writers were known to make copies of a letter to be shared with another person. For example, Pollio wrote to Cicero: "I am sending you for your perusal a letter I have written to Balbus."[9] Brutus wrote: "I have read the short extract from the note you sent to Octavius: Atticus sent it to me."[10] Cicero urged his friend Atticus: "Be sure you send me a line as often as you can, and take care that you get from Lucceius the letter that I sent him."[11] The parallel to Paul is obvious. He urged the church at Colossae to read the letter he had sent to Laodicea (Col 4:16).[12]

At the end of his own letter, a writer sometimes copied another letter. For example:

> Antimenes to Zenon greeting. If you are well, it would be excellent. I too am in good health. I have written for you below a copy of the letter which came to me from Sosipatros in order that you may take note . . .[13]

Cicero ended a letter to Atticus by saying "I have sent you a copy of the letter I wrote

---

[4]Cicero once chided a young lawyer-friend for making multiple copies of a letter in his own hand. Evidently Cicero considered such a task to be secretarial work (Cic. *Fam.* 7.18.2).

[5]This concern can be seen in the comments by the sender of a second-century papyrus letter to Karanis, PMich. 8.500.

[6]Among many examples, see Cic. *Fam.* 9.16.1; 10.5.1; 11.11.1; and 12.12.1.

[7]The carrier no doubt followed the Roman highway, stopping at each town in succession. Silvanus, the carrier for 1 Peter, did the same thing, with the letter address indicating the order of delivery; see C. J. Hemer, "The Address of 1 Peter," *ExpT* 89 (1978): 239-43. In the case of 1 Peter, the listing of provinces was to legitimize the carrier's need to visit each place (and perhaps to request from each church the assistance needed to reach the next destination).

[8]Paul drew their attention to his handwriting at the end of the letter (Gal 6:11). Such a comment would have no meaning if they were reading a copy.

[9]Cic. *Fam.* 10.32.5.

[10]Cic. *Br.* 1.16.1.

[11]Cic. *Att.* 4.6.

[12]Paul could have meant only for the church to borrow the other's letter for reading, but given the proclivity for making copies, it is less likely. Paul chose this wording as less presumptuous than "you will want to spend the money to make a copy of my letter."

[13]PZen. 10 (dated April 1, 257 B.C.). See also another example, PZen. 43 (dated October 26, 253 B.C.).

to Pompey."[14] Evidently Atticus had the same custom. Cicero commented, "Your letter and the enclosed copy of one of my brother Quintus' letters show me . . ."[15] Sharing copies of letters was commonplace.[16] Copies of letters were desirable in the ancient world.[17] Cicero frequently read letters to his dinner guests, both those he himself wrote as well as those he received. When a guest particularly enjoyed a letter, he requested a copy.[18] Ancients often sought copies of material they liked.[19] This is commonly suggested as the reason for the widespread copying of Paul's letters.[20] A Christian visiting a church in another town heard a letter of Paul and requested a copy to take home to his church.

To retain a copy. Letter writers kept copies of their letters. In a chatty letter, Cicero remarked casually that he was scratching off a copy of a letter into his "notebook" while he was reclining at the meal table.[21] Dolabella, a friend of Cicero, asked for a copy of something Cicero had written. Cicero dismissed it as a "little nothing he had written"; nevertheless, he had a copy of it at his residence in Pompeii and was able to send Dolabella a copy.[22] Cicero dashed off a note in a hurry during a meal; yet he retained a copy.[23]

Because retaining copies of a dispatched letter was routine practice,[24] letter writers usually did not mentioned it. We typically read about it only when a letter was lost or damaged and a replacement was sent. Nevertheless, since letters were often lost, there are still numerous references to this practice.[25] For example, in a letter to his brother, Cicero told of a mishap with a letter to Caesar. The packet of letters had become so wet as to be unreadable; therefore Cicero sent another copy.[26] The damage was not always accidental. Cicero commented, "You are sorry the letter has been torn up; well don't fret yourself; I have it safe at home; you may come and fetch it whenever you like." The Loeb translator noted he was probably referring to the preceding letter in which Tigellius was severely criticized. Cicero told him "I have it safe at home." Obviously this was not the original letter; it had been sent—and torn up! What Cicero had at home was a copy of

---

[14]Cic. *Att.* 3.9.

[15]Cic. *Att.* 1.17.

[16]See, e.g., Cic. *Fam.* 3.3.2; 10.12.2; 10.33.2; *Br.* 1.16.1.

[17]Ancient historians also preferred them as sources; see, e.g., Plut. *Alex.* 47.3; 54.2; 57.4; 60.1.

[18]Cic. *Att.* 8.9.

[19]Cicero attempted to squelch one letter he regretted writing, but even he was unable. He complained to Atticus how he failed to stop its spread; Cic. *Att.* 13.21a.

[20]See, e.g., Harry Gamble, *New Testament Canon: Its Making and Meaning,* Guides to Biblical Scholarship, New Testament Series (Philadelphia: Fortress, 1985), pp. 36-43.

[21]Cic. *Fam.* 9.26.1.

[22]Cic. *Fam.* 9.12.2.

[23]He dashed off (*exaravi*) the letter but retained a copy in his notebook (*in codicillis*); Cic. *Fam.* 9.26.1.

[24]"For there seems considerable evidence that senders of letters, or, at all events, Cicero and Tiro, were accustomed to keep copies of letters, even, perhaps, letters which might seem to us to be of no great importance; and this is probably one of the reasons why we have such a rich collection of the correspondences of Cicero"; Tyrell and Purser, *Cicero,* 1:59.

[25]For a lost letter see Cic. *Fam.* 7.25.1.

[26]Cic. *QFr.* 2.12.4: "So later on I sent Caesar an exact duplicate of my letter."

the letter he had made before dispatching the original.[27]

While Cicero mentioned letter copies the most, the references are not restricted to him. According to Plutarch, when Alexander the Great in a fit of rage set fire to his secretary's tent he later regretted that the copies of his letters had been destroyed as well. Alexander felt their loss keenly, and wrote to all his recipients to request that they send him copies of the dispatched letters to replace his lost copies.[28] Cicero wrote his brother, Quintus, complaining of the "brutality of language" used in a letter supposedly written by Quintus;[29] however, Cicero could not be positive it was from Quintus. Yet Cicero knew well not only Quintus' handwriting but also that of Statius, Quintus's secretary. Apparently it was a copy circulating around that Cicero had seen.[30]

Was this practice limited to only the wealthy aristocracy? In the painfully brief papyri, as might be expected, there are no references to retaining a copy of the letter. It would be a weak argument from silence to argue they retained no copies of their letters; many papyri do not refer to using a secretary, but the changes in handwriting clearly indicate a secretary was used.[31]

Nonetheless, the sands of Egypt have produced some evidence that even poorer letter writers kept copies of important letters. An Egyptian letter writer from the time of Paul, wanting to impress how diligent he had been, complained he spent two drachmas to have a copy made of a letter.[32] Among the Zenon papyri, there were several identical copies of a letter circulating around.[33] In the case of the letters of Ignatius, the collection of his letters was made from the copies he had kept of his letters.[34] There are numerous references in the papyri to a writer sending copies of other letters.[35] As with other letter writing customs, the papyri provide evidence but always more scanty. Nevertheless, the practice is adequately documented. Harry Gamble concludes:

> Ancient writers often kept copies of their private letters even when no particular literary merit or topical importance was attached to them; and copies of instructional, administrative letters

---

[27]Cic. *Fam.* 7.25.1. LCL editor W. Glynn Williams noted that Cicero was speaking of a copy of the letter (p. 2:101).

[28]Plut. *Eum.* 2.2-3.

[29]Cic. *QFr.* 1.2.6: "That letter you sent by way of a jest to C. Fabius (if indeed it is yours) conveys to the reader an impression of brutality of language."

[30]In addition to the unfamiliar handwriting, it is very unlikely those circulating the letter could have secured the original anyway.

[31]See among *many* examples, PMich. 8.486.

[32]H. C. Youtie, "P.Mich.Inv. 855: Letter from Herakleides to Nemesion," *ZPE* 27 (1977): 147-50. See the excellent discussion in Millard, *Reading and Writing*, p. 165.

[33]So the editors, p. 114. PZen. 43 has one copy appended to it. For another papyrus indicating the use of copies, see PTebt. 32.

[34]See the argument in chapter fourteen.

[35]See, e.g., PMich. 8.498: "And I ask, brother, that you make acknowledgment to Rufus if you write to him. I sent you the letters of Aemilianus and Rufus and Chariton. Write me how you are and what you want." So also PZen. 10.

were all the more likely to be kept. In antiquity, collected editions of letters were nearly always produced by their author or at their author's behest, often from copies belonging to the author.[36]

Although most references to copies of letters are found when the dispatched letter was lost or damaged—the ancients also knew the wisdom of having a backup copy. Letter writers also retained a copy of their letters in order to reuse all or part of one letter in a different letter to a different recipient. This practice appears to have been quite acceptable. It was commonly practiced and commonly noted. The only place I noticed where it was spoken of disparagingly was a letter in which Cicero sheepishly confessed to Atticus that he had carelessly used the same preface in two different works. This was a problem, though, not because it was reused, but because the works were too similar to allow this (according to Cicero).[37] The problem then was not that he had reused some material, but that he had not done it correctly.

From the evidence we can infer that material was recycled from one letter to another in two common scenarios. First, if a writer had written a lengthy account and then later wanted to send the information to another recipient, he would recopy that section into the new letter. We would never know this (nor would the original recipients) without some extenuating circumstance. Fortunately, there are a few examples. Cicero was providing funds for his young nephew's education. Because of this, he took great interest in his nephew's affairs and frequently commented when he felt his nephew's education was lacking. He also expected reports on his nephew's activities. On one occasion, his nephew sent a lengthy letter including an extended recounting of some adventures. Cicero's friend, Atticus, also took interest in (and perhaps contributed to) the affairs of the young man.[38] Apparently the nephew, trying to kill two birds with one stone, sent the same extended account in a letter to Atticus. This might seem like a faux pas, but there was no hint that this was viewed as inappropriate. Cicero merely commented in a letter not long afterwards to his friend Atticus: "I am sending you young Quintus' letter. . . . I have sent you half the letter. The other half about his adventures I think you have in duplicate."[39] Since Cicero knew that Atticus had an interest, he sent a copy of the nephew's letter to Atticus. He did not, though, recopy the second half since Atticus already had it. There is no sign the reuse of the material was seen negatively.[40]

A second common reason for reusing material in another letter was when the writer wanted to send a well-written passage to another. For example, Atticus had written a letter to Cicero with a cleverly written passage about Atticus' sister. Atticus then repeated the pas-

---

[36]Harry Gamble, *Books and Readers,* p. 101.

[37]Cic. *Att.* 16.6.

[38]Cicero had likely arranged the marriage of his younger brother, Quintus, to the sister of his friend Atticus. This unhappy marriage produced this one son, Tullius Cicero Q. He was thus the nephew of both Cicero and Atticus.

[39]Cic. *Att.* 13.29.

[40]Cicero mentioned it to explain the abrupt ending of the copy.

sage in a letter he sent to another. Cicero became aware of this only because the other recipient happened to share the letter with Cicero and Cicero noticed the repetition. He in no way chided Atticus for reusing the material, only commenting: "The letter contained the same passage about your sister that you wrote to me." Following the assassination of Caesar and the survival of Anthony, Cicero wrote: "I should like you to have invited me to your banquet on the Ides of March; there would have been no leavings [Anthony]." Cicero reused that clever bit of prose in a different letter to another man.[41] There is actually a third scenario where material from one letter was reused in another: the commendation of the letter carrier. Paul's identical commendations of Tychicus (Eph 6:21; Col 4:7-8) and Ignatius's identical commendations of Burrhus (*Phld* 11:2; *Smyrn* 12:1) are our best examples.[42]

Thus, ancients kept copies of their own letters for several different purposes. That Paul retained copies of his letters seems a matter of course to scholars of Greco-Roman letter writing.[43]

PREPARING THE DISPATCHED COPY

In the case of the brief, strictly private letters, one might expect the dispatched letter to be scrawled hastily across a papyrus sheet. Yet, editors of papyrus collections often comment upon the neat handwriting and careful preparation of a letter. Even in a letter (PMich. 8.514) where the original draft was dispatched, the handwriting was neat and professional. Letters to be read publicly were given more care. Preparing the copy of the letter for dispatch was the culmination of the secretary's work.

Preparing a copy for public reading. It is difficult for modern Westerners to separate literacy from the ability to write. The English verb "to write" implies both literacy (a knowledge of how written letters produce words) and also handwriting (the ability to write letters down). To understand the ancient situation better, let us think about two modern analogies: typing and calligraphy. We can all read typing; yet not all of us can actually type. For some, typing an essay would require pecking out each letter slowly with one finger. It can be done, but not with any speed. This may well describe the typical literate person of the first century. He or she could write but often only slowly.[44]

---

[41]Cic. *Fam.* 12.4.1 and *Fam.* 10.28.1.

[42]The paucity of evidence is explainable. First, I am aware of no other examples where we have two recommendation letters for the same individual written by the same person to different recipients. Second, no author would want to say in a recommendation letter that he was merely reusing something he had written to another. However, Cicero laments having to write the same thing over and over. See the discussion in chapters eleven and fourteen.

[43]See, e.g., the earlier studies of Hermann von Soden, *Griechisches Neues Testament* (Göttingen: Vandenhoeck & Ruprecht, 1913), p. vii; T. Henshaw, *New Testament Literature* (London: Hodder & Stoughton, 1963); and Hartman, "On Reading Others' Letters," p. 139. Cf. O. Roller, *Formular,* p. 260. More recently see, e.g., E. E. Ellis, *The Making of the New Testament Documents* (Leiden: Brill, 2002), p. 86; Gamble, *Books and Readers,* p. 101; Murphy-O'Connor, *Paul the Letter-Writer,* pp. 12, 36-37; and Witherington, *Paul Quest,* p. 102.

[44]This is Deissmann's conclusion, citing as one example: "Written for him hath Eumelus the son of Herma . . . , being desired to do so for that he writeth somewhat slowly"; Deissmann, *Light,* pp. 166-67.

Handwriting in the first century can also be compared to modern calligraphy. We all can write, but most of us have no skill at calligraphy. We actually consider literacy and calligraphy distinctly separate skills. Ancients who were literate often had no particular skill with handwriting. Like modern calligraphy, they considered it a separate skill only somewhat related to literacy. The art of scoring paper, mixing ink, sharpening reeds, and writing beautifully upon the rough surface of a sheet of papyrus, perched upon one's knees were the trained skills of a secretary.

The typical literate person of the first century had a handwriting often described by modern scholars as "cramped." For example, the handwriting of PMich. 8.496 is described by the editors as "large and elegant, with a very slight slant to the left and no linking of letters," but the handwriting of the postscript is "in small, very cursive writing."[45] The author's own writing at the end of the letter often demonstrated that his own handwriting was much inferior to that of the secretary.

The collection of papyrus letters from Karanis (many dating to a generation after Paul) contains many examples of the letter writer using a skilled secretary with fine handwriting. According to the editors, several letters from an Egyptian named Terentian show he usually hired secretaries to write his official letters.[46] The secretaries were presumably contracted workers since they vary from letter to letter. For example, the editors compare the handwriting of the secretaries of several of Terentian's letters:

> The hand [of PMich. 8.468] is a fairly large cursive with well-formed letters and even alignment; it creates an impression of skill and long practice. It resembles somewhat the hand of 472, but is heavier and more forceful. It differs in a marked degree from 467, which is lighter, more upright, and rather calligraphic. *Terentianus undoubtedly made use of professional scribes,* as he did also for his Greek letters.[47]

When Cicero wanted a beautiful letter, he troubled to use fine, large paper (*macrocolla*) and a different secretary than Tiro, whose skills apparently lay in the ability to write quickly rather than beautifully.[48] When an ancient wished his letter to be well received, he used a good pen and nice paper.[49] It is often incorrectly assumed Paul merely signed the last working draft and dispatched it. His letters do not evidence such casualness.[50] Those who received his letters considered them "weighty and strong" (2 Cor 10:10). They were of course referring to the rhetorical strength of Paul's letters. Yet rhetoricians considered appearance to be an integral part of rhetoric, as seen in the assessment of Paul's oral rhetoric: "his bodily

---

[45]Herbert Chayyim Youtie and John Garrett Winter, eds., *Papyri and Ostraca from Karanis*, 2nd series, Michigan Papyri 8 (London: Oxford University Press, 1951), p. 109.

[46]Youtie and Winter, *Papyri from Karanis*, p. 16.

[47]Ibid., p. 24 (emphasis mine). See also PMich. 8.471 and 514.

[48]Cic. *Att.* 13.14-25.

[49]Cic. *QFr.* 2.15b.1: "For this letter I shall use a good pen, well-mixed ink, and ivory-polished paper too." Cicero is jesting with his brother; nevertheless, the point remains.

[50]So, e.g., Gamble, *Books and Readers*, p. 95.

presence is weak, and his speech contemptible" (2 Cor 10:10). Part of his oratory was bodily appearance. It is unlikely a letter scribbled in a poor, cramped hand would have been considered "weighty and strong." Or at the very least, Paul's opponents would have added the insult of ridiculing the letter's appearance to their list of insults of Paul.

Since most writers had poor handwriting, aside from quick notes dashed to family, ancients (if they could afford it) paid to have the dispatched letter written in a pleasing script. There is no reason to assume Paul was the exception to the rule. Since the skills to prepare a letter pleasing in appearance were usually limited to those trained in the craft, we should assume Paul paid to have a dispatched copy prepared in pleasing script and on good quality papyrus. Ancients differentiated these. We will see later in this chapter that good quality handwriting commanded a higher rate. Papyrus was sold in several grades.

A secretary better skilled in penmanship and the other arts of ancient writing did not necessarily possess more rhetorical skills or even better grammatical skills. For example, in a letter dating to a generation after Paul, the editors comment, "The rather heavy hand is skillful and competent; the alignment is even and the letters are of uniform size, with very little real linking." Obviously the secretary was skilled to the level (and perhaps even above the level) of most of the other secretaries used in the letters of this collection. Yet, the editors remark that the story "in this letter becomes at times somewhat incoherent because of careless spelling and indifferent syntax."[51] Here "a good writer" (penmanship) did not also mean "a good writer" (grammatically); in much the same way today a skilled calligraphist may well write a letter with misspellings and poor grammar.

Writing out long letters. Writing out a dispatched copy of a letter of Paul was complicated by the fact that Paul's letters were inordinately long. The typical papyrus letter was one papyrus sheet. In the approximately 14,000 private letters from Greco-Roman antiquity, the average length was about 87 words, ranging in length from 18 to 209 words. The letters of the literary masters, like Cicero and Seneca, were considerably longer. Nonetheless, Paul stands apart from them all.[52]

Table 10.1. A Comparison of Letter Length

Author	Shortest Letter (number of words)	Longest Letter (number of words)	Average Length (number of words)
All extant papyrus letters (~14,000)	18	209	87
Cicero	22	2,530	295
Seneca	149	4,134	995
Paul	335	7,114	2,495

[51]PMich. 8.471. So Youtie and Winter, *Papyri from Karanis*, p. 37.
[52]These approximations were originally from Alfred Wikenhauser and Josef Schmid, *Einleitung in das Neue Testament* (Freiburg: Herder, 1973), p. 245, and are sufficiently accurate. His figures for Paul's letters have been adjusted to reflect the text of NA[27].

Philemon, as noted, was a typical length, perhaps even a bit long. The church at Rome, when it first received Paul's letter, was probably more stunned by the letter's length than by its content.

How long did it take Paul (and his team) to write these long letters? Of course, we have no idea. I find it impossible to predict how long it will take me to write something; interruptions and rewrites can add extra time. However, the logistics of dictating and writing out a draft require certain minimums of time. Why bother to estimate at all? These estimates can help us avoid imagining a scenario that is completely unreasonable.

I will not venture to guess how long it took Paul to compose a draft of any letter, nor am I so bold as to predict how long any editing took. It is possible, however, to make some rough estimates for how long it took a secretary to prepare each written draft. Certainly a rough draft was completed more quickly, while a polished draft on fine papyrus was written more slowly and carefully. Nonetheless, I will make some rough estimates. In literary works, copyists maintained an average hexameter line, composed of sixteen syllables with a total of about 36 letters. This line was called a *stichos*. It was a standard measurement. Copyists charged by the number of lines, or *stichoi*. Books were priced this way.[53] Although private letters did not have to conform to this standard, it appears to have become custom.

According to the calculations of Eduard Strange, a secretary could write about 85 lines per hour (about 1.5 lines per minute).[54] As we will see, his estimate seems reasonably accurate, although secretaries probably did not sustain this rate consistently for hours. Allowing secretaries time to prepare the papyrus sheets, score the lines on the sheets, mix the ink, etc. (we should not forget to factor in time to travel, the inevitable interruptions, and the amount of daylight), it seems wise to suggest no more than five hours of actual steady writing per day. While I am certainly open to being criticized from several directions, I think these rough estimates here allow us a general impression of how long it took to prepare each draft of a letter.

These estimates are for each time a secretary wrote out a draft. We have no idea how many times Paul had a letter rewritten.

I feel confident in expressing a *minimum* number of drafts: the initial draft was prepared from notes, surely there was at least one revision, the polished draft was prepared for dispatch on quality papyrus and a copy written in Paul's notebook, which would result in a minimum of four drafts. Thus Paul's letter to the Romans needed twelve days just for the secretary to prepare his drafts. This does not include any time for composition or note-taking sessions. The estimates in the table tell us nothing about how many weeks or

---

[53]The definitive discussion of stichometry remains Kurt Ohly, *Stichometrische Untersuchungen* (Leipzig: Otto Harassawitz, 1928); see esp. pp. 88-89.

[54]Strange, *Diktierpausen*, pp. 109-17. He does not use these terms or rates. I have calculated them based upon his total estimates for each letter, divided by the length of each letter. I took the average of these. His estimates seem reasonable, although perhaps a bit fast.

Table 10.2. Estimating the Time Needed to Write Each Letter of Paul

Letter	Number of Lines in the letter[a]	Number of Hours Needed	Number of Days Needed for Each Copy
Romans	979	11.5	2-3 days
1 Corinthians	908	10.7	2 days
2 Corinthians	607	7.1	$1\frac{1}{2}$ days
Galatians	311	3.6	1 day
Ephesians	331	3.9	1 day
Philippians	221	2.6	$\frac{1}{2}$ day
Colossians	215	2.5	$\frac{1}{2}$ day
1 Thessalonians	207	2.4	$\frac{1}{2}$ day
2 Thessalonians	111	1.3	$\frac{1}{2}$ day
1 Timothy	238	2.8	$\frac{1}{2}$ day
2 Timothy	182	2.1	$\frac{1}{2}$ day
Titus	100	1.2	$\frac{1}{2}$ day
Philemon	44	0.5	

[a]For the number of lines of text for Paul's letters, I used the list conveniently summarize in McRay, *Paul,* pp. 276. I chose this list for it gives numbers slightly lower than those found in P[46] and Codex Claromontanus (in order to err on the side of caution). See also the list provided in Murphy-O'Connor, *Paul the Letter Writer,* p. 121.

even months it took to compose a letter. The estimates do, though, keep us from suggesting that Paul easily dashed off a letter over the weekend.

ESTIMATING PAUL'S COST TO WRITE A LETTER

As we have seen, our data from the time of Paul is too thin to draw any conclusions about the cost Paul incurred in writing and sending letters. All estimates are filled with guesswork. Some scholars will say that any attempts to estimate Paul's cost should be avoided altogether. Nevertheless, many today could not even venture a guess as to the cost. We often have a vague impression that the cost to write Paul's letters was insignificant, and such an impression is misleading. For this reason, an educated guess is helpful.

The cost of supplies. The secretary usually took the initial notes and prepared the first draft on tablets or washable papyrus notebooks.[55] We may assume these materials were

---

[55]E. G. Turner, *Greek Papyri: An Introduction* (Oxford: Clarendon, 1968; reprint, 1980), p. 6, notes the primary function of these "folded tablets" was "above all, for first drafts."

not charged to Paul. The dispatched copy was written on papyrus, as was the copy Paul retained. Paul would have been charged for the papyrus for both copies. According to Pliny the Elder, papyrus sheets came in multiple sizes, ranging from *Augusta,* which was "13 digits" wide (about 10 inches) to *emporetica,* which was "6 digits" wide (nearly 5 inches). A standard roll, according to Pliny, was manufactured by joining 20 sheets, making a roll nearly 12 feet long.[56] Longer rolls were custom-made by buying up to three standard rolls and joining them together.[57] At the time of Paul, a standard papyrus roll cost about four denars.[58]

Some secretaries wrote with large letters; some wrote in a small, cramped hand. We, of course, have no idea the penmanship used by Paul's secretary. Judging from the papyri, a medium hand was the most common. Since Paul called his penmanship "large letters" in comparison to his secretary's (Gal 6:11), it seems most advisable to assume his secretaries used a medium script. Three of the oldest manuscripts of the New Testament (papyri 46, 66 and 75) have one column per page with an average of about 25 letters per line.[59] Secular papyri often followed the same pattern. Among the papyri from Karanis (PMich. 8), papyrus 466, 468, 478, 486, 490, 491 and 499 average 36 letters per line; 465, 472, 482, 484 and 487 have lines a little shorter (about 26 letters); while 467, 471, 477 and 492 have lines a little longer (about 45 letters).[60]

Using these and other early examples of papyri, thirty lines of writing per page seems typical.[61] I estimated the cost of papyrus by assuming an average of about 30 lines per column, with columns being about 5 inches wide, with about 35 letters per line. Thus a

---

[56] Pliny *N.H.* 13.11. See Turner, *Greek Papyri,* p. 4.

[57] Especially for books, papyrus rolls could reach as much as 30 feet; see Gamble, *Books and Readers,* pp. 45-47.

[58] So Millard, *Reading and Writing,* p. 165; and Harris, *Ancient Literacy,* p. 195.

[59] Codex Alexandrinus has a larger page with two columns, but still averages about 25 letters per column. The best parchments, Sinaiticus and Vaticanus, have 3 and 4 columns per page (respectively) and thus smaller columns (10-15 letters per column).

[60] This is according to my rough counts. There were some papyri with considerably shorter lines (10-15 letters), but the papyrus sheet itself was small and forced short lines.

[61] P[66] (A.D. 200) was written in a medium hand and averaged 17 lines per page, but had pages half the height of a normal page (about 6 inches high by 5 inches wide). P[75] (early third century) had a smaller hand and averaged 42 lines per page with typical page sizes (about 10 inches high by 5 inches wide). See Metzger, *Manuscripts,* pp. 64, 66, 68. PMich. 8.468 (early second) had 30 lines in two columns (about 10 inches high by 8 1/2 wide). P[46] (A.D. 200) began in a medium hand and initially averaged 30 lines per page with typical page sizes (about 11 inches high by 6 inches wide). P[46] is a difficult manuscript and scholars are currently reassessing it. Apparently, the copyist reached the middle of his codex and realized he was not going to have room for all the letters of Paul. He then began to write with increasingly smaller script and margins. See Eldon Epp, "Issues in the Interrelation of New Testament Textual Criticism and Canon," *The Canon Debate,* ed. L. M. McDonald and J. A. Sanders (Peabody, Mass.: Hendrickson, 2002), pp. 498-501. Epp's painstaking and careful research has demonstrated the difficulty in estimating how much papyrus a writer would need. His cautions are well advised. Nonetheless, a scribe copying a book of set parameters was different from a secretary writing a letter. We seem justified in assuming a medium script with standard spacing.

standard papyrus roll accommodated about 24 columns with about 720 *stichoi*.[62] Ink (and the pen), I assume, was not a separate expense but was included in the secretary's basic charges.

The cost of labor. The writer of an Oxyrhynchus papyrus from the early third century paid to have copies made of two books.[63] The writer of the papyrus mentioned paying two rates, 28 drachmas and 20 $^2/_3$ drachmas per 10,000 *stichoi*.[64] This rate received indirect confirmation from an imperial edict of Diocletian in A.D. 301.[65]

These rates were for copies of literary works prepared by professional secretaries. Perhaps a local secretary charged considerably less; however, then as now, smaller projects often commanded rates similar to (or even higher than) large projects. A man in Egypt at the time of Paul paid two drachmas for a copy of a letter.[66] We do not know the number of lines nor if the fee included some sort of official charge, since the letter was probably an official document; nevertheless, the man did pay the rate and did not describe it as excessively expensive.[67] It seems reasonable that secretaries probably charged the standard rate for copying letters[68] and perhaps a higher rate for writing them. For the sake of caution, I will again assume the lower rate, twenty-five denars per ten thousand lines. The secretarial cost was labor and did not include the cost of papyrus.[69]

---

[62]Assuming a column of about 5 inches, with a small space between the columns and some loss for the overlap when the sheets were glued together.

[63]PLond. Inv. 2110. This papyrus is often cited with a second century date, following the editor's (H. I. Bell) original estimate. Ohly, *Stichometrische*, p. 88 n. 4, states that Bell told him he had since changed his mind and dated the document confidently to the early third century.

[64]PLond. Inv. 2110. E. G. Turner, *Greek Papyri*, p. 88, lists the second rate at 20 $^1/_3$, citing this papyrus. Bell's original calculation was 20 $^1/_2$; see Ohly, *Stichometrische*, p. 89. This discrepancy is because the letter writer actually stated (according to Bell's reconstruction) that he paid 47 drachmas for one book (of 16,600 lines) and 13 drachmas for the second book (of 6,300 lines). The discrepancy between 20 $^1/_2$ and 20 $^2/_3$ is a difference of math.

[65]Gamble, *Books and Readers*, p. 275 n. 110 and Catherine Hezser, *Jewish Literacy in Roman Palestine* (Tübingen: Mohr Siebeck, 2001), p. 125, both cite the Edict of Diocletian (A.D. 301) *De pretiis rerum venalium* 7.39-41, and state the rate was 20 and 25 denars per *hundred* lines—100 times more expensive! Here the discussion becomes muddled. Gamble lists the Edict as *CIL* 3.381, while Hezser writes *CIL* 3.831. I could not find it under either reference or anywhere else in the entire volume. The inscription is recorded, however, in Ohly, *Stichometrische*, p. 88. The Edict lists three rates: 25 denars for 100 lines of beautiful script (*kalligraphos*), 20 for 100 lines of secondary script, and 10 for 100 lines by a notary. (The term *agoraios* normally means a shorthand writer but here H. I. Bell says it means a notary making an official but plain copy.) Bell explained this enormous price difference by noting that the denar had slipped to $^1/_{36}$ of its value by the time of the decree. Since the drachma had already slipped against the denar—the rate was already 3 denars = 4 drachma by Paul's time—the two rates in the Edict do not seem terribly out of line with the Oxyrhynchus papyrus.

[66]See Youtie, "PMich.Inv. 855," pp. 147-50.

[67]Millard, *Reading and Writing*, pp. 164-65, comments "that seems a large sum" and does not use this data in his calculations. However, Millard is discussing the cost of copying books, which should be distinguished from the costs of preparing and copying letters.

[68]This is the conclusion of Ohly, *Stichometrische*, p. 89.

[69]So Millard, *Reading and Writing*, p. 164

Unlike merely preparing a new copy of an existing work, secretarial costs for preparing a letter needed to include the cost of writing out all the drafts and revisions. Since we have no idea how many times Paul had a letter rewritten, I cannot estimate this very well. I can, however, make some attempt to estimate the number of lines a secretary charged for a letter. For example, the letter to the Romans was about 1,000 *stichoi* long. The taking of notes and the writing of an initial draft of Romans were probably one charge since most letters written by a contracted secretary included these two steps. After the preparation of an initial draft, there was probably at least one revision. To err again on the side of caution, I have said that for most of his letters Paul paid for a minimum of the initial draft and one revision, both done on tablets or washable notebooks, then paid for a copy to be dispatched (with nice script on good papyrus) and a copy to be retained. This means that for Romans, Paul probably paid a secretary for about four thousand lines, or roughly, eight denars. This estimate seems somewhat in keeping with the scant evidence we have. For example, Alan Millard estimated a copy of Isaiah cost about six to ten denars at the time of Paul.[70]

The cost of each letter. The estimates given below in denars are educated guesses and err on the side of caution. Attempting to convert ancient denars to U.S. currency is a difficult matter. Some scholars choose to use commodities like grain prices or gold prices, yet ancients held such commodities in different esteem than we do. Once again, to gain the same "emotional" equivalent for currency, we shall return to the "workers conversion rate" used in chapter three. An unskilled laborer in the time of Paul earned a half-denar per day,[71] or $60 in today's currency. Since the drachma had devaluated some during Paul's time[72] and to err again on the side of caution, an additional 10 percent was removed from Paul's rate, settling on a conversion rate of one denar = $110.

Paul's cost to write each letter does not include the price of sending someone to deliver the letter.

It is important to notice that I estimated a copy of Romans would take two to three days to write out, based upon how fast a secretary would ordinarily write. The figure in Table 10.2 matches well the scribal rate from antiquity, for one copy of Romans would cost 2 1/2 denars.[73] The fact that these calculations independently arrive at an amount that is very similar provides added assurance that the estimates here are reasonable. The best test for these estimates, however, is to use this method to calculate how much a typical letter cost. Evidence indicates that ordinary people in Paul's day wrote letters. My es-

---

[70]Millard, *Reading and Writing*, p. 165. Millard's estimate included the materials, but was also for a copy of an existing work, where there were no revisions. This is a bit like comparing apples and oranges, but at least the two figures are in the same ballpark.

[71]Millard, *Reading and Writing*, p. 165, also estimates a half-denar per day.

[72]Four drachmas to three denars, but it is unclear how this affected local wages.

[73]This would place secretaries in the pay scale of skilled laborers, as would be expected. The papyrus rate of 25-28 denars per 10,000 *stichoi* converts to about 400 *stichoi* per day. My estimate of 85 *stichoi* per hour makes a five-hour day of writing. Once again, the various pieces of evidence converge.

Table 10.3. Estimating the Cost to Write Each Letter of Paul[a]

	Number of Lines	Percentage of a "Standard" Papyrus Roll Needed Per Copy	Cost of Papyrus Per Copy in Denars[b]	Cost of Secretarial Labor Per Copy in Denars[c]	Total Cost in Denars for the Finished Letter[d]	Cost in Today's Dollars
Rom	979	136%	5.44	2.45	20.68	$2,275
1 Cor	908	126%	5.04	2.27	19.16	$2,108
2 Cor	607	84%	3.36	1.52	12.8	$1,408
Gal	311	43%	1.72	0.78	6.56	$722
Eph	331	46%	1.84	0.83	7.00	$770
Phil	221	31%	1.24	0.55	4.68	$515
Col	215	30%	1.20	0.54	4.56	$502
1 Thess	207	29%	1.16	0.52	4.4	$484
2 Thess	111	15%	0.6	0.28	2.32	$255
1 Tim	238	33%	1.32	0.60	5.04	$554
2 Tim	182	25%	1.00	0.46	3.84	$202
Tit	100	14%	0.56	0.25	2.12	$233
Philem	44	6%	0.24	0.11	0.92	$101

[a] I am calculating the cost for one copy of a letter ready for dispatch, along with one copy to be retained by Paul.

[b] As shown above, I am calculating 30 lines per 6 running inches of papyrus, with a standard 12 foot roll costing 4 denars.

[c] I am using the lower rate of 25 denars per 10,000 lines of text. This rate is probably low for secretarial labor since it was the standard rate for copying large works. PMich. 8.855 implies a *higher* rate; nevertheless, I chose to err on the side of caution.

[d] Since I am estimating papyrus for only one dispatched copy and one retained copy, the drafts are assumed to be upon reusable material, not charged to Paul. I am estimating labor at being written out four times: initial draft, one revision, the finished (dispatched) copy and a retained copy (in Paul's notebook). If a letter underwent more revisions, then the cost obviously was higher.

timates would have to place a typical letter within their reach. Although even Philemon is a trifle long for a Greco-Roman letter, a single dispatched copy (one without revision or a retained copy) would have cost approximately a third of a denar, a notable expense, but one well within the reach of those living above the mere subsistence level.

Conclusions for Paul as a Letter Writer

The estimates given above are rough and easily critiqued, although if anything they are likely to be low. The purpose here is not to give precise figures but to aid us in seeing that writing Paul's letters was no insignificant expense. We have already seen that weeks, if not months, of work likely went into a letter; we can now see that considerable expense also was involved. While not prohibitive, sending such long letters was certainly an undertaking for the team. Since Luke and Acts each are about twice the length of Romans, it is understandable why Luke needed a patron, "Theophilus," to underwrite the expense of publishing his work.

How was it that Paul paid for his letters? It is possible that the church where he was serving or a patron in the church paid the expense. It is less likely that Paul paid for the letters from his income as a tentmaker. Paul's work as a tentmaker has been exaggerated in modern times, particularly in discussions of modern mission methodology. As a traveler, Paul did not carry the supplies necessary to conduct a significant business as a tentmaker. It is true today and even truer in antiquity that one did not enter a town and immediately open a profitable business. In the ancient Greco-Roman world, it took considerable time to establish the necessary relationships in order to gain the necessary permissions to conduct business in a city, both from city leaders as well as the appropriate guilds. Paul was able on occasion to enter into business, but only in situations such as Corinth, where he was actually assisting in an established business with an established shop with regular suppliers, owners with memberships in the appropriate trade guilds and a regular clientele. While he and his team may have done some minor contract work (repairing tents perhaps) in order to gain food and lodging, Paul was primarily dependent, as were all travelers, upon hospitality and patrons.

11

DISPATCHING THE LETTER

*W*hen we finish a written letter today, we sign it, fold it (usually in thirds) and place it in an envelope. We use adhesive to seal the envelope (for privacy). We write the address in a standardized location on the outside of the envelope using a standardized format (name; street address; city, state and zipcode; each having its own lines and standard abbreviations). The cost of delivering the letter is paid to the government (in the form of stamps). Ancient letter writers shared many of these same needs (authentication, privacy, instructions about where to deliver the letter) and they used similar solutions.

SIGNING THE LETTER

Once a copy of the letter was ready, an ancient writer did not "sign" a letter as we do today. We use our "signature," our personal name written in a distinctive cursive script, as a sign of authenticity. Ancients did not do this. However, they did authenticate letters in three ways, listed here in descending order of value:

1. The use of a seal (signet) pressed in clay.

2. A summary of the letter's contents in the author's own handwriting at the end of the letter.

3. A word of farewell in the author's own handwriting at the end of the letter.

While the list appears in descending order of value, it is an ascending order of usage. A concluding word of farewell in the author's hand was the most common; seals were the rarest. Sealing a letter with a personal signet was the most secure means of authenticating a letter, and will be discussed momentarily, but the other two means were much more common.

All three ways of authenticating a letter involved the author doing something to the letter after the final draft was prepared but before the letter was dispatched. As I noted earlier, an author was held responsible for every word of the letter. The personal handwriting at the end of a letter indicated the author had seen the letter and consequently assumed responsibility for its contents. In two of the cases, the author wrote something to the end of the final draft of the letter. This is most easily seen in the papyri because we have the originals and can see that the handwriting changed.[1]

---

[1]E.g., POxy. 2985; 113; 394; 530.

Often at the end of a Greco-Roman letter there is a postscript. This postscript could contain two types of material, either a summary of the letter or some additional material. The first, summary postscripts (or "summary subscriptions," as they were originally called[2]) were more common in business records than in private letters. A record was a written account of an oral agreement, usually a contract or other legal arrangement. A contract from Oxyrhynchus for the sale of a weaving loom, dated A.D. 54, is commonly cited.

POxy. 264

Ammonius, son of Ammonius, to Tryphon, son of Dionysius, greeting. I agree that I have sold to you the weaver's loom belonging to me, measuring three weavers' cubit less two palms, and containing two rollers and two beams, and I acknowledge the receipt from you through the bank of Sarapion, son of Lochus, near the Serapeum at Oxyrhynchus, of the price of it agreed upon between us, namely 20 silver drachmae of the imperial and Ptolemaic coinage; and that I will guarantee to you the sale with every guarantee, under penalty of payment to you of the price which I have received from you increased by half its amount, and of the damages. This note of hand is valid. The 14th year of Tiberius Claudius Caesar Augustus Germanicus Imperator, the 15th of the month Caesareus.

[2nd hand] I, Ammonius, son of Ammonius, have sold the loom, and have received the price of 20 drachmae of silver and will guarantee the sale as aforesaid. I, Heraclides, son of Dionysius, wrote for him as he was illiterate.

We notice several things about this very typical postscript. (1) It repeated all the important points, while omitting details like the size of the loom or the identity of the banker. (2) Postscripts usually repeated the material in the same order as the body of the letter. (3) It rarely added any information not already in the body of the letter. (4) The postscript was in a different handwriting (a second hand), as a sign of authentication. When the author of the letter was so illiterate that he could not write at all, he needed a third person to write the postscript rather than have the secretary prepare it. The postscript needed to be in a second hand in order to authenticate (verify and legalize) the agreement, which the secretary had prepared in the appropriate legal language, including legal details like type of coinage and penalties for non-compliance. The summary demonstrated that the author agreed to the contents of the letter even though he did not write the letter himself. The fact that the summary was in his own handwriting (or at least not

---

[2]The foundational work on these was Bahr, "Subscriptions," pp. 27-41.

in the same handwriting as the body of the letter, in the case of an illiterate author) was a vital part of the authentication.[3] Summary postscripts could vary from an elaborate and thorough summary of the letter[4] to only a brief sketch.[5] Brevity even reached the extreme of "as above," a summary that maintained the convention but defeated its purpose.[6]

Only copies of Paul's letters still exist today, therefore, it is impossible to verify a postscript in his own handwriting. Paul, however, on more than one occasion drew attention to his handwriting. Since the original readers were able to see this change in handwriting for themselves, it seems a rhetorical emphasis.[7] There is one clear example of a *summary* postscript among the letters of Paul (Philem 19-21): "I, Paul, am writing this with my own hand: I will repay it." Since this type of postscript was used primarily in legal records and not personal letters, the rhetoric is more striking, for a postscript was not expected. Paul's use of a custom normally reserved for legal documents was to underscore his wishes, implying an almost legal contract between him and Philemon. His repeated references to repayment and Philemon's debt to Paul, etc. emphasized this. This was yet another piece in the rhetorical arsenal which Paul wielded to influence his friend.

Yet, the postscript in Philemon was more than a mere summary. This highlights that Paul typically used postscripts for the second purpose; that is, to provide additional material. In Greco-Roman letters, this postscripted material took two forms: secretive (or sensitive) material and new (or forgotten) material. In the first scenario a writer added material in an autographed postscript because the information was secretive or sensitive. Obviously, if the author feared a lost or intercepted letter, putting the information in a postscript changed nothing. Such highly sensitive information was entrusted verbally to the carrier (discussed in chapter thirteen).

There was also sensitive information that one did not wish to become public knowledge (or gossip) in one's own household. Dictating it to a secretary resulted in, at the very least, the secretary knowing the material, and probably being overheard by all nearby. Ancients did not share our love for privacy. Cicero added a comment at the end of a letter to his friend Atticus. He explained the inclusion written in his own hand:

> For our letters are not such that it would do no harm to us if they are not delivered. They are full of secrets so that we cannot even trust an amanuensis as a rule, for fear of some jest leaking out.[8]

---

[3]If someone prepared a copy of an agreement, then obviously both parts would be in the handwriting of the copyist. Ancients recognized this problem and so the copyist would title the agreement *antigraphon* (copy) and then repeat the word *antigraphon* (copy) before copying the postscript; see, e.g., POxy. 1453.

[4]E.g., *BGU* 910 (Aug. 23, A.D. 71); *BGU* 183 (A.D. 85); *BGU* 526 (Oct. 12, A.D. 86); see Bahr, "Subscriptions," p. 28 n. 6.

[5]E.g., *BGU* 713 (A.D. 41/42); *BGU* 636 (Nov. 5, A.D. 20).

[6]*BGU* 526 (Oct. 12, A.D. 86).

[7]Although the "hearers" could not see the change, the "reader" could.

[8]Cic. *Att.* 4.17.1.

Cicero feared an intercepted letter, but here he also feared indifferent gossip. His letters often contained postscripts with politically sensitive material, as might be expected of Roman leaders during the final intrigues before the collapse of the Roman Republic. Cicero wrote these comments in his own hand to prevent their becoming common knowledge in his own household. His clever but biting jokes were choice morsels for gossip. Apparently Paul felt no need to write personally secretive material at the end of his letters, for we find none.

Autographed postscripts were also used when new material arrived after the final draft of the letter was finished, somewhat like our "P.S." today. For example, "Since writing this letter I have been told . . ."[9] indicates that the author received new information after the letter was ready for dispatch. If this information arrived before the final draft, it was merely incorporated into the main body of the letter during a subsequent draft. How likely was new information to arrive after a letter was finished and before it was sent? Actually, it was more common than might be thought at first glance.

Time was required for a secretary to prepare a final copy. On other occasions a letter carrier was not immediately available, so the letter remained in the writer's custody. We will see in a moment that an author did not sign and seal the letter until the carrier was actually ready to depart, for the very reason that some new bit of news could arrive and necessitate changes in the letter. A last-minute change in loyalties among Roman politicians caused Atticus to add a comment to the end of one of his letters: "Curio is now defending Caesar."[10] Atticus apparently heard this juicy bit of political maneuvering after he had written the letter but before he dispatched it. We noted earlier that Cicero observed it was common practice for writers to change the date at the end of a letter if a delay occurred before the letter was sent.[11]

As a point of comparison to Paul we suggest that 2 Corinthians may fit this scenario. Scholars have long noted the differences between chapters 1—9 and 10—13, even suggesting that 10—13 was once a separate letter that in later copies became attached to 2 Corinthians.[12] There is a shift in tone at the beginning of chapter 10. Even the wording "I myself, Paul, appeal to you" suggests to some a letter opening, but as we have seen, this was not the way to begin a letter.[13] This wording, however, was not unusual for a post-

---

[9]Cic. *Fam.* 12.12.5.

[10]Cic. *Fam.* 2.13.3.

[11]Cic. *QFr.* 3.1.8.

[12]The differences between 1—9 and 10—13 were first noted by J. S. Semler (1776). The view of 10—13 as a separate letter has two variations: either 10—13 was written after 1—9 (so Semler, Bruce, Barrett, Windisch) or written after 1 Corinthians and before 2 Corinthians, as the so-called harsh letter (so Wanson, Filson, Héring, Marxsen, de Zwaan, Bultmann, Dodd, Georgi, Schmithals, Klijn). See the discussion in Werner Kümmel, *Introduction to the New Testament,* rev. ed., trans. H. C. Kee (Nashville: Abingdon, 1975), pp. 289-90.

[13]Some may suggest that the epistolary garb has been stripped away, but we still have the unexplained emphasis on Paul as the author.

script—they usually began with an emphasis on the unmediated input of the author, such as "I am now writing . . ." The relative length (33%) of this section was not inappropriate. There are examples with postscripts of a longer relative length. The abrupt shift in tone was also not unusual for a postscript. Furthermore, in other Pauline postscripts (Philem 19-25; 1 Cor 16:22-24; Gal 6:12-18 and Col 4:18), there is a tendency for the language to be more abrupt and stern than that found in the body of the letter. It is quite possible that "pure Paul" tended to be more blunt and that his coauthors (and secretaries) tended to moderate his tone.

A larger role for Paul in 2 Corinthians 10—13 may also be seen in the use of "I" and "We." It is often disputed what was meant when the letter has "we." Nevertheless, looking at the frequency of these words, there seems a shift in emphasis between these two sections.

Table 11.2. "I" vs. "We" in 2 Corinthians[a]

	"I"	"We"
2 Cor 1—9	81 (26%)	255 (74%)
2 Cor 10—13	147 (74%)	51 (26%

[a]Adapted (and corrected) from M. Carrez, "Le 'nous' en 2 Corinthiens: Contribution à l'étude de l'apostolocité dans 2 Corinthiens," *NTS* 26 (1980): 475.

Jerome Murphy-O'Connor, in his delightful little introduction to the letters of Paul, carefully outlined how 2 Corinthians maintains the "I" and "we" in alternating blocks, arguing that the "we" blocks corresponded largely to material with which Timothy (the coauthor) was familiar.[14] This is not the place to analyze his thesis, but it is noteworthy that the emphasis shifts from "we" to "I" in chapters 10—13, a shift expected in a postscript. The possibility that 2 Corinthians 10—13 was a postscript precipitated by additional news from Corinth is an option that scholars should not summarily dismiss.

Whether or not 2 Corinthians 10—13 is a postscript, there are ample examples that Paul used a postscript as a "signature" to his letters. Galatians 6:11-18 is the most commonly cited example in Paul. Other than the Christian terminology, most of his postscripts were typical, containing a final salutation, an authenticating remark about writing in his own hand, and a closing list of greetings. He also added on occasion a reference to a "holy kiss" and a final blessing. This final blessing is one of the most consistent epistolary conventions in Paul's letters, being found in all thirteen letters.[15] The major purpose of the postscript, though, was to authenticate the letter, as seen in 2 Thessalonians 3:17: "I, Paul, write this greeting with my own hand. This is the mark in every letter of mine; it is the way I write."

---

[14]Murphy-O'Connor, *Paul the Letter-Writer,* pp. 24-31.
[15]See Weima, *Neglected Endings,* pp. 78-87.

FOLDING AND SEALING THE LETTER

Once a letter was ready to be dispatched, it was folded and sealed. Since most papyrus letters were a single page, the sheet was folded, accordion-style, in a strip about an inch wide, much as children make a paper fan from a sheet of paper. Once the page was folded in this manner it was then doubled-over once lengthwise (to make peeking into the letter difficult).[16] A string, often a fiber pulled off the edge of the papyrus sheet itself, was tied about the bundle and a lump of clay was pressed over the knot. If the sender had a seal it was impressed into the clay. We have no way to know if Paul possessed a signet. Even if he had, his recipients would not have recognized it. Seals were extra security measures taken by the upper classes.[17]

The recipient's name/address was written on the outside, for example: "Deliver to Claudius Tiberian, my father, from Claudius Terentian, his son."[18] A hired secretary often had the recipient's name and address already written on the back of the papyrus sheet so that once the letter was folded, the address was already in the proper place.[19] Sometimes the address also contained additional instructions, such as "Deliver to Arrian, soldier of the legion XXII Deioteriana."[20]

In the case of longer letters such as Paul's, the papyrus was multiple sheets glued together as a long roll. The roll was scrolled up. If the roll was only a few sheets long, the roll was folded over and tied. If the roll was longer, it was only tied.

To speak of a finished letter did not necessarily mean the letter was already "folded and sealed." Cicero complained to his brother about a mutual friend, Oppius:

> when he [Oppius] has decided to send letter carriers . . . something unexpected hinders him, and he is unavoidably later than he intended in sending the carriers.[21]

This might have meant that there was a letter carrier with a finished, sealed letter when something delayed the carrier's departure. However, from Cicero's later comments it becomes clear that once the carrier was able to leave, Oppius corrected the date at the end of the letter, meaning that the letter had not yet been folded and sealed.[22]

---

[16]PMich. 8.471. According to the editors: "The papyrus shows seven vertical folds, and the address, which is now very faint, was written on the verso, from the bottom of the sheet toward the top, on the fourth panel from the left edge of the recto." PMich. 8.492 was done by a skilled secretary who apparently folded the letter from both the left and right sides so that when finished only the backs of the center panels were exposed, providing a more durable and private cover.

[17]On one occasion Cicero had opportunity to intercept two letters he suspected spoke badly of him. After reading the letters he realized they did him no harm, so he sent them on to Atticus to be delivered. Cicero (*Att.* 11.9) added, "Though the seals are broken, I think Pomponia has his signet." Evidently, in the upper levels of Roman aristocracy, even seals did not guarantee a safe letter.

[18]PMich. 8.469.

[19]This is clear in PMich. 8.492, where there is a final word of greeting in a second hand, but the address on the verso is in the secretary's (the first) hand.

[20]See PMich. 8.483 and 484.

[21]Cic. *QFr.* 3.1.8.

[22]Cic. *QFr.* 3.1.8.

Cicero once wrote that, "Just as I was in the act of folding this letter, there came letter-carriers from you and Caesar. . . . How distressed I was [to hear of the death of Caesar's daughter]."[23] Although he says he was folding the letter, there were no closing comments at this point in the letter. Evidently closing comments in the author's own hand (such as final greetings, a health-wish, a date) were written when the letter was actually being folded to be sealed and sent. He was about to add those things when news arrived.[24] His comment "I was in the act of folding the letter" must include all the final actions of finishing a letter.

Opening a sealed letter compromised it and made its contents suspect. When ancients traveled to new places, they sought someone of status in the new location to facilitate the visit. Ideally they asked an acquaintance of status from their hometown to write a recommendation letter. Travelers carried such letters with them as a way to introduce themselves and to gain assistance. Cicero sent a sealed letter of recommendation to be carried by the recommended person, Caecina, to be given to Furfanius. Cicero also provided Caecina with a copy of the recommendation letter (Cic. *Fam.* 6.8) so he would know what Cicero had written. Caecina came from an important family and Cicero no doubt wanted his family to know what a kind letter he had written for Caecina. Providing an unsealed copy was the only means to do this and still leave the original letter sealed and thus useable. It must also be noted that Cicero's collection had a copy of the letter Caecina had carried to his benefactor, Furfanius, yet another example that letter writers kept personal copies of letters they dispatched.

Carrying the Letter

Once the letter was finally signed, folded and sealed, it was "mailed." Letters were carried to their destination. The Roman Empire maintained an official postal system, but private individuals were not permitted to use the Imperial Post. All private letters were delivered by private arrangements, carried by family members, slaves and friends, as well as acquaintances and even total strangers. Businessmen and soldiers frequently carried letters that had no connection to their travel. This impromptu postal system gave rise to three different types of letter carriers.

Types of letter carriers. Imperial letter carriers. The Roman imperial postal system (*cursus publicus*) was patterned after the older Greek (Ptolemaic) system, which in turn arose from the Persian system of mounted horsemen operating between relay stations. Our Pony Express system during the early days of the American West was a modern link in an ancient chain.

There is no data to determine how speedy the Persian mail system was; there is, how-

---

[23]Cic. *QFr.* 3.1.1.
[24]Cic. *QFr.* 3.1.19 notes that he had written those final comments in his own hand. In this particular letter, additional carriers brought even more news causing him to delay again the dispatch of this letter while he added even further comments.

ever, data for the Greek and Roman systems.[25] Archaeologists have found the remains of
a record book dating about 255 B.C., from one of the government relay stations. Postal
items were individually logged, recording the name of the sender and recipient, the previous carrier and the subsequent carrier, and the day and hour the letter arrived, rather
like the tracking system used by UPS or FedEx.[26] This (and other sources) indicate a
Greek Imperial letter could travel as fast as 100 miles per day.[27] One Roman Imperial letter
arrived 125 miles away on the same day it was sent![28]

The Imperial Post used mounted carriers, ships, and foot messengers, often in combination. Since the government often sent multiple copies of important letters to insure safe
delivery, copies were often sent by divergent means; in other words, a letter might be sent
by sea and also by land. Despite its impressive speed and efficiency, the Imperial postal
system is of no relevance to our study here; Paul was not permitted to use this system
since it was restricted to government purposes. Furthermore, the speed and efficiency of
the Roman system cannot be used to describe the private system. It would be quite in error to say Paul's letters traveled 100 miles per day.

Happenstance letter carriers. A private letter writer had to find his own letter carrier.
Letters in the Greco-Roman period were commonly carried by family members (including
slaves and employees) or friends who were traveling for other purposes; however, letters
were also entrusted to acquaintances and even total strangers, such as soldiers, businessmen, even a passing traveler. "Having had the luck to find someone going up to you, I felt
obliged to address you. I am much surprised, my son, that to date I have received from
you no news of your welfare."[29]

This system seems haphazard and completely unreliable; however, ancients understood
the system and travelers took the extra task as a matter of course. This procedure is still in
practice in a few places in the modern world. For many years I worked as a missionary-
teacher on a remote eastern island of Indonesia. Church business often required traveling
among isolated mountain villages. When word spread that I was making a weekend trip to
a particular area—it was impossible to keep such matters secret—students and neighbors
began appearing on my doorstep the evenings before I left. They had in hand a letter with
the name of the recipient and the village scrawled on the outside of the folded sheet. When
I arrived at the village, I gave my stack of letters to the local pastor to distribute. This was
the accepted system. Although the sender always asked politely if I would mind carrying
a letter, it was only a token request. He already had the letter prepared.

Ancient letters reached their destination in a strikingly similar fashion. The carrier

---

[25]I am dependent upon the data and description of Turner, *Greek Papyri*, pp. 139-40.
[26]A. S. Hunt and C. C. Edgar, *Select Non-Literary Papyri*, 2 vols., Loeb Classical Library Greek Series (Cam-
    bridge, Mass.: Harvard University Press, 1932-34), p. 397.
[27]So concludes Epp, "Letter Carrying," p. 52.
[28]*PBeatty Panopolis* 2; see the text and description in White, *Light*, pp. 214-15.
[29]POxy. 123.

spoke to the elders of the city at the gate or more likely to someone in the market. The carrier was pointed along until he or she met someone who knew the recipient and could delivery the letter. It is unlikely that a happenstance carrier delivered a letter all the way to a recipient's home.

On occasion the letter address gave more specific instructions, presumably because the recipient was harder to find: "To Dionysius, who is also called Amois, son of Ptolemy and brother of Apollonios the village secretary of Tholthis, who is staying near Theon, the son of Ischyrion."[30] Sometimes a letter writer gave advice about how to address a reply, such as in the letter from a son to his father in the early second century: "And if you write me a letter, address it: 'on the liburnian of Neptune.' "[31]

In the case of frequent correspondence it was quite common for a letter writer to mention previous letters so that the recipient could determine if an intervening letter had been lost. To help identify letters, the name of the carrier was often mentioned, as in this letter dated A.D. 41:

> Serapion to our Heraclides, greeting. I sent you two other letters, one by Nedymus and one by Cronius the sword-bearer. For the rest, I received the letter from the Arab, read it, and was grieved.[32]

In another letter the writer noted: "I rejoiced greatly on receiving your letter which was given to me by the cutler, though I have not yet received the one which you say you have sent me by Platon the dancer's son."[33] Apparently the cutler was more reliable than the dancer's son.

Sometimes in Indonesia I was asked to drop off a letter in a village to be forwarded to another village. This was possible because the sender knew there was regular traffic between his target village and the village where I was visiting. The same situation occurred in the first-century world. A letter was sent to a place, usually a specific person at an intermediary place, in order for the letter to be forwarded. This intermediary place was often a larger, busier town that was a "hub" for a cluster of smaller towns around it. We find Greco-Roman letters with the original recipient on the outside address, for example, "To Tasoucharion, my mother." Someone else then later added (in another hand) a secondary address, "Deliver to Julia . . ." followed by the location where Julia could be found.[34] Presumably, Julia made the arrangements for the continuation of the letter.

Sometimes, the original carrier needed to entrust the letter to another; perhaps the carrier was not able to finish the journey or his plans had changed. When a letter was handed from one carrier to another, additional directions were added to the letter address to help

---

[30]POxy. 1061 (22 B.C.).

[31]PMich. 8.467.

[32]*BGU* 1079; PFay. 123; PLond. 42; PCol. 3.6; see the discussion in Epp, "Letter Carrying," p. 45. There are numerous examples from Cicero's letters.

[33]POxy. 1676.

[34]PMich. 8.466. The papyrus is damaged after Julia so we can't determine where this intermediary lived.

the new carrier know where to take the letter. The address of the papyrus letter then had additional lines added in a handwriting that was neither the secretary's nor the author's.[35] The additional name provided was probably someone better known, someone to whom the letter could be delivered in order to be forwarded to the recipient. It might surprise us since this entire arrangement seems somewhat haphazard and loosely structured, but ancient letters commonly arrived at their intended destination within a reasonable time.

Not having a carrier kept many from writing letters, but it was also quite common to claim "there was no carrier" as an excuse for why they had not written.[36] To use my personal experiences again, once letters were handed out in an Indonesian village, on occasion someone would ask me directly if I had a letter for him. This particular person could not imagine how I could have been coming and their family member not have sent a letter. He was hoping the problem was that somehow I had forgotten to give it or perhaps had lost it, rather than the possibility that the family member had failed to write. In such a case, it was almost "rude" not to have sent a letter. The same was apparently true in antiquity, to judge from this complaint:

> Julius Clemens to Arrianus his brother, greeting. This is now the third letter I am writing you, and you have sent me no reply, although you know that I am worried if you do not write me frequently about your affairs, and in spite of the fact that many persons come here from your vicinity.[37]

A pregnant woman wrote two letters to her family and in the second letter she complained that several people had been available to carry a letter to her and yet, "You have not even thought fit to write me one letter."[38] How did one respond to such an accusation? The negligent letter writer had to provide an explanation of why he hadn't written when a carrier was available.

A common excuse for ancient letter writers was to claim a letter had been written and must have been lost by the carrier: "I have written to you often, and the negligence of those who carry the letters has slandered us as negligent."[39] This writer, like many, found the most plausible excuse was to blame the carrier. It was a flimsy lie, and both parties knew it, but it was a polite and handy way to avoid a social faux pas.

The availability of a carrier often prompted someone to write. Similarly, since an ancient letter writer could have a letter in his hands for quite some time, most did not write until a carrier was available. If someone needed to send a letter, officials had the Imperial postal system; private individuals were left to the whims of chance—unless they had the financial resources to pay the expenses of someone to carry a letter.

---

[35]PMich. 8.465.
[36]Turner, *Greek Papyri*, p. 130, lists the two greatest challenges of letter writing to be finding a carrier and then keeping the letter from going astray.
[37]PMich. 8.484.
[38]PMich. 8.508.
[39]PMich. 8.499.

Private letter carriers. The wealthy elite were not privy to the Imperial Post. Although the volunteer post (with happenstance carriers) functioned rather well, the wealthy often used personal slaves to carry letters. The wealthy Epicurean Papirus Paetus had two slaves retained solely for carrying letters.[40] Cicero and Atticus also used slaves for carrying letters. When Paul says he received news of the Corinthian church from "those of Chloe" (1 Cor 1:11), he is likely referring to Chloe's slaves who carried the letter.

I call these carriers "private" in the sense that their primary task was to deliver letters. One hoped a letter was more likely to arrive safely and expeditiously when a private carrier was used. Sending someone on a journey merely to carry a letter might seem simply another example of the extravagance of the Roman aristocracy, but in actuality there was some justification. We think of the usual expenses of a traveling businessman: salary, transportation, lodging and food. Slaves received no salary. They usually walked. They often slept outside or as the guest of another slave. Slaves were fed and clothed whether they were working or not. Much the same would be true of an apprentice or junior team member. The leader of the team was responsible for the expenses of his team. In reality, sending a slave (or apprentice) was not prohibitively expensive.

Although sending a slave or apprentice to carry a letter might not add much additional expense, why bother at all, if a happenstance carrier was available and willing? Private carriers were used when the sender wanted someone more reliable. Letters were lost. Sometimes they just never arrived.[41] Sometimes they were damaged in transit.[42] A carrier admitted being given a letter but confessed it had been "lost on the way."[43] Unreliable carriers are illustrated well by comparing two letters of Cicero to his friend Atticus. In the first one, Cicero noted he was giving the letter to the first available person. He did not want to delay sending it while he waited for a trusted carrier.[44] In the following letter to Atticus, Cicero lamented that the previous letter had not arrived.[45]

Sometimes letters were read by others, even by the carrier himself:

> I have been rather slow about sending one [a letter], for lack of a safe messenger. There are very few who can carry a letter of weight without lightening it by a perusal.[46]

---

[40] Cic. *Fam.* 9.15.1.

[41] We have numerous references to lost letters. Even Cicero was not amazed when letters were lost, only annoyed; see Cic. *Att.* 2.8.

[42] See Cic. *QFr.* 2.12.4.

[43] Cic. *Att.* 2.13.

[44] Cic. *Att.* 2.12.

[45] Cic. *Att.* 2.13. Again it is noteworthy that although Atticus never got the letter, *we* have it; it is in the collection of Cicero's letters. Even though the dispatched copy was lost in transit to Atticus, Cicero kept a copy. Again we see signs that a published collection of an author's letters made use of the author's retained copies rather than collecting the dispatched copies. (This is discussed in more detail in chapter fourteen.)

[46] Cic. *Att.* 1.13.

When opponents were involved, letters were even intercepted and destroyed.[47] While this was common for political intrigues, does it have any relevance to Paul? Paul's opponents were not above sending forged letters in Paul's name (2 Thess 2:2). It is not unreasonable to assume they would destroy any letters of Paul they managed to intercept.

Private letter carriers often expected to carry a response back. Cassius sent a letter to Cicero by means of one of his slaves. Cicero complained to Cassius that the slave was rushing Cicero to finish a reply letter so that he could be on his way.[48] If the availability of the carrier made it appear rude not to send back a reply, it was even more so with a private carrier.

Other common tasks of the letter carrier. Someone who was traveling and could carry a letter could also on occasion carry other materials as well. Sending the letter by a private carrier, however, allowed two additional benefits: the carrier could provide additional "insider" information and could read the letter to the recipient.

Bringing material or supplies. There are numerous examples of letters mentioning that the carrier was also bringing various supplies to the recipient. For example: "Know that everything is going well at home, through the beneficence of the gods. I sent you two jars of olives, one in brine and one black."[49] A fifth-century B.C. letter ended: "Please ask the letter carrier for six melons."[50] Often, as in the examples above, the letter specifically mentioned the carrier was bringing this material as a means of keeping the carrier honest. A letter to Apollinarius (second century) contained a word of greeting but mostly was a list of items as if to insure the carrier delivered all the supplies:

> Apol . . . to Apollinarius, his brother, greeting. Having learned you are in Bacchias I salute you, brother, . . . I received barely one letter from you, in which you informed me that I should receive the cloaks and the pig. The pig I did not receive, but the cloaks I did get. Farewell. Pharmouthi 4.
>
> [2nd hand] I pray for your good health and pleasure, brother. Do you receive four good lettuces, a bundle of beets, 21 bulbs, 16 greens, and three good semi-salted fish. Theon, my brother, salutes you and urges you to come to us from Bacchias . . .[51]

Apparently it was sometimes necessary to encourage honesty on the part of the carrier, as seen in an early second-century Greek letter of a sick son, Terentian, to his father: "You write me that you have sent . . . through Anubion, but he does not know that you wrote

---

[47]Cicero complained of Lepidus intercepting his letters (Cic. *Fam.* 10.31.4); yet he himself also intercepted a few letters of others (see Cic. *Att.* 11.9).

[48]Cic. *Fam.* 15.17.1-2.

[49]PMich. 8.467. PMich. 8.468 has quite a long list of supplies sent along.

[50]PMich. Inv. 497.

[51]PMich. 8.496. It is interesting to note that the man did not include the list of what he was sending back in the letter proper. Since it was, in the opinion of the editors, prepared by a rather skilled hand, no doubt a secretary had the letter prepared in advance. Apparently, the writer did not want to commit himself in advance. He waited until a carrier was ready to decide what supplies he was sending.

to me here and has given me nothing."[52] Evidently Terentian believed that Anubion kept the material for himself, thinking that he would never know that his father had sent something. If Terentian was as sick as he claimed in his letter, Anubion had even more motivation to keep the items for himself.[53] On another occasion a son in the Alexandrian navy wrote to his father (in Latin): "And if you are going to send anything, put an address on everything and describe the seals to me by letter lest any exchange be made en route."[54] Evidently it was not unheard of for a ship's crew to open packages, pilfer some contents, and then reseal the package and place another seal on it.

A happenstance carrier was unlikely to be given something of value to carry, unless the sender or recipient knew him. A daughter had written and asked her mother to send a chiton (garment) for her baby—even in the ancient empire, grandmothers gave gifts to grandbabies. The grandmother wrote back: "In regard to what you said: 'Send a chiton for the little one,' if I find a trustworthy person I will send it; and if the god wills I come to join you."[55] Sending an item of any value required a more trustworthy carrier.

Providing additional information. Private carriers brought the letter directly to the recipient. Thus, the carrier was a personal link between the sender and the recipient. As such, the carrier was often expected to elaborate further the contents of the letter. In fact there are many examples of letters that describe the situation briefly and give the writer's conclusion. The carrier was then expected to elaborate all the details for the recipient. For example, a woman sought the help of Zenon against someone mistreating her son. She briefly described her grievance and then added: "The rest please learn from the man who brings you this letter. He is no stranger to us."[56]

This can also be seen in a complaint of Cicero. The carrier did not come personally and provide the missing details:

> I received your letter . . . and on reading it I gathered that Philotimus did not act . . . [on] the instructions he had from you (as you write) . . . [when] he failed to come to me himself, and merely forwarded me your letter; and I concluded that it was shorter because you had imagined that he would deliver it in person.[57]

The letter was shorter because the sender had expected the carrier to provide the details. The sender did not usually state that the carrier had additional news; it was expected.

The fact that the carrier had news was specifically noted only when the matter was urgent or secretive. For this reason, the clearest examples of the carrier having addi-

---

[52]PMich. 8.477.
[53]In actuality, Terentian's suspicions were unjustified, for we later read that Anubion did send the items on.
[54]PMich. 8.467.
[55]PMich. 8.514.
[56]PCol. 3.6. See also PMich. 8.492: "I also gave Coprous all this information by word of mouth, so that she might tell you."
[57]Cic. *Fam.* 4.2.1. There are many other examples; see Cic. *Fam.* 3.5; 10.7; 1.8.1; 3.1.1.

tional information come from the days of furtive intrigue during the collapse of the Roman Republic. Thus Brutus wrote to Cicero,

> Please write me a reply to this letter at once, and send one of your own men with it, if there is anything somewhat confidential which you think it necessary for me to know.[58]

The normal action would have been for Cicero to send his reply back with the carrier that brought Brutus' letter to him. Brutus' carrier, however, would not have known any special insights; therefore, Brutus specifically asked Cicero to send one of his own men. In another example, the carrier, Arruntius, told the recipient, Cicero, that the sender, Trebatius, wished the letter destroyed after it was read. We happen to know this because Cicero complained in his reply:

> Your letter, delivered to me by L. Arruntius, I have torn up, though it did not deserve such a fate; for it contained nothing that might not have been quite properly read out, even at a public meeting. But not only did Arruntius say that such were your instructions, but you yourself added a note to that effect.[59]

Evidently the sender feared the instructions to destroy the letter might be forgotten by the carrier, so he explicitly stated it in a postscript.

In rare instances the carrier might contradict the contents of the letter. Today we might be inclined merely to dismiss the carrier's comments, but ancients did not, as seen in a letter written to Cicero. The written letter contradicted the oral report. The contradiction was deemed important and required resolution.[60] For this reason also, private carriers had to be trustworthy, for their reports were believed. It was expected private carriers would have added information.

Even if there was no specific news the sender wished conveyed, the sender knew the carrier would nevertheless chat about the situation, provide minor details, etc. (Sometimes the carrier provided more news than the sender might have wished shared.) If the sender wanted the recipient to know that such information was reliable he added a note that the carrier was trustworthy.

Reading the letter. Reading was always aloud. For example, Acts 8:28-30 tells us that Philip heard what the Ethiopian was reading in his chariot. Ancients preferred to have a letter read aloud to them rather than reading it aloud to themselves. When an ancient text said "I read your letter," this was not meant in the modern sense of reading, but as "I heard your letter read."[61] In Plutarch's story of Alexander the Great, Alexander "read" the inscription on Cyrus' tomb; in actuality it was a translation read aloud to

---

[58]Cic. *Fam.* 11.20.4. Cicero does a similar thing; *Fam.* 11.26.5.
[59]Cic. *Fam.* 7.18.4.
[60]Cic. *Fam.* 5.6.1.
[61]Often the same slave was used as "reader" and secretary; see Sherwin-White, *The Letters of Pliny*, pp. 225 n.15, 515-16.

Alexander, for he could not read the original inscription.[62]

Rhetoric, the art of public speaking, was prized in the Roman forum and trickled down into the streets of the provinces. In a world that so valued oratory, reading the letter was more like performing the letter. This is why the wealthy owned slaves whose duty was reading; there are numerous references to Caesar, Pliny and Cicero having letters read to them.[63] The majority of recipients, of course, did not have private readers. If the private carrier was literate (and privy to the letter's situation), he was the logical choice to read the letter. He knew the details of the situation and could provide the nuances of voice and expression that best conveyed the author's intents. This was an advantage to both the sender and the recipient. It seems likely that the recipient (excluding the wealthy rhetoricians) had the letter read aloud by the carrier if the carrier was able.

CONCLUSIONS FOR PAUL AS A LETTER WRITER

Many of the points of this chapter have specific applications to Paul. They are the subject of the next chapter. By way of conclusion here, the papyrus letter below illustrates well several of the points made in this chapter. It is the letter of a young man, Apollinarius, newly enlisted in the Roman army, written to his mother.

PMICH. 8.490 (SECOND CENTURY)

Apollinarius to Taesion, his mother, many greetings. Before all else I wish you good health and make obeisance on your behalf to all the gods. From Cyrene, where I found a man who was journeying to you, I deemed it necessary to write to you about my welfare. And do you inform me at once about your safety and that of my brothers? And now I am writing to you from Portus, for I have not yet gone up to Rome and been assigned. When I have been assigned and know where I am going, I will let you know at once; and for your part, do not delay to write about your health and that of my brothers. If you do not find anybody coming to me, write to Socrates and he forwards it to me. I salute often my brothers, and Apollinarius and his children, and Kalalas and his children, and all your friends. Asclepiades salutes you. Farewell and good health. I arrived in Portus on Pachon 25.

[2nd hand] Know that I have been assigned to Misenum, for I learned it later.

This papyrus letter illustrates seven things that summarize well our findings here:

---

[62]"After reading the inscription upon this tomb, he ordered it to be repeated below in Greek letters" (Plut. *Alex.* 69.2).

[63]See esp. Pliny *Ep.* 8.1, who laments at length over the temporary loss of his reader. Furthermore, for proper reading, a reader needed to go over the document first. Ancient Greek was written without spaces between the words and with little or no punctuation; see Stirewalt, *Paul the Letter Writer*, pp. 16-17.

1. The young recruit wrote twice to his mother, even though he did not yet have the information she wanted. When he learned of someone headed to Karanis, where she lived, he sent a letter. He knew she would want to know he was alive and well, even if he had no particular news.

2. He complained because he had not received a reply from his mother. Ancients loved sending and receiving letters.

3. He suspected (hoped?) his mother had not yet sent him a letter because she was unsure where to address it, so he suggested she send it to Socrates, an intermediary, who would forward it to him.

4. He used a secretary even for this brief letter.[64] This is also discernible because there is a change in handwriting at the end of the letter. A young recruit would have no personal secretary with him. It is unlikely a friend wrote it instead of a hired secretary, for the writing is moderately skilled and the vocabulary and syntax is adequate; a fellow recruit was unlikely to be this skilled in writing. The secretary was probably hired in the market. The cost of preparing several brief letters was within the grasp of even a young recruit, although it was not an insignificant or trivial expense.

5. The secretary prepared a complete letter, ready for dispatch. The letter's address was, as customary, written on back and at right angles to the letter. This placed the address on the outside of the final fold once the letter was folded. The address, however, was in the first handwriting; that is, the secretary completely finished the letter, leaving only Apollinarius to check, sign, fold and seal it.

6. This letter is a good example that writers did not fold and seal letters until a carrier was actually ready to take it, since something could come up that needed to be added. Evidently Apollinarius' carrier did not leave immediately. Apollinarius did not know his place of assignment when he instructed the secretary to write the letter; he was in the port Ostia awaiting transfer up to Rome. Before he found a carrier he reached Rome and was assigned to the fleet at Misenum. Since a letter carrier had not yet taken the letter, the letter had not yet been sealed; thus Apollinarius was able to add this new information to the bottom of the letter before sealing and sending it.[65]

7. The letter arrived safely since it was found in the ruins of Karanis (Egypt), where his mother lived.

---

[64]This is also the editors' conclusion. H. Youtie and J. Winter, *The Michigan Papyri*, vol. 8, *Papyri and Ostraca from Karanis* (Ann Arbor: University of Michigan Press, 1951), p. 92. There are two letters from this son to his mother (PMich. 8.490 and 491), in two different handwritings for the bodies of the letters.

[65]He probably added this note himself, although the fact that the original letter had even the final greeting in the secretary's handwriting could be evidence that he was completely illiterate. Secretaries often added even the closing greeting; see, e.g., POxy. 1491. If he was illiterate, then he found someone else to add the final message.

We have seen that, despite occasional difficulties and mishaps, ancient letters flowed rather freely and smoothly across the empire.

> If papyrus was needed, it could be sent; if forwarding was required, that could be arranged; if detailed delivery instructions were essential, they could be provided; if a reply was urgent, a return letter carrier might be designated. Apparently addressees were easily enough located, both by the letter writer and the carrier.[66]

There are sufficient examples for us to agree with Eldon Epp that the challenges of letter writing in the Roman Empire were usually met. When Paul and his team sent a letter, they could feel fairly confident that it would arrive safely and in a timely manner.

---

[66] Epp, "Letter Carrying," p. 51.

12

PAUL'S LETTER CARRIERS

*I*n the last chapter, we discussed ancient letter carriers. Paul had his choice of two kinds of letter carriers. Since carriers often did more than merely deliver the letter, some interesting possibilities arise for Paul.

IDENTIFYING PAUL'S CARRIERS

We have seen that it was common in antiquity to identify the carrier of the letter. In this way the recipient would know if the letter had changed hands and was being delivered by a different carrier. For example, Julius wrote: "A number of times I asked Longinus, who brings you the letter, to take something for you, and he refused, saying he was unable."[1] Even in the case of a carrier who was not known to the recipient, the letter writer often identified the carrier in some way, as in: "From Cyrene, I found a man who was journeying to you."[2]

Unnamed carriers. In Paul's case he never described an unnamed carrier. For example, he did not say anything about who carried Galatians and 1 and 2 Thessalonians, his early letters. Since the letter carrier was not named or described in any way, it is most likely Paul used a happenstance carrier who was traveling that way and who may well have been a convert. It is impossible to ascertain. However, it is most likely the carrier had no particular relationship to Paul.

Named carriers. Since happenstance carriers were by far the predominant method[3] one might assume Paul always used them. However, we see from his letters that Paul's custom was to use a private carrier. This carrier was not a slave but a member of his mission team. He or she was sent for the expressed purpose of delivering a letter, for example: "Tychicus will tell you all the news about me. . . . I have sent him to you for this very purpose, so that you may know how we are" (Col 4:7-8).

Paul chose this option for all the benefits a private carrier provided. First, the cost was not prohibitive; Paul was already responsible for the team member's expenses. The letter also was less likely to be lost or intercepted if Paul used a member of his team, one who

---

[1]PMich. 8.466 (March 26, A.D. 107).
[2]PMich. 8.490.
[3]This is also the conclusion of Witherington, *Paul Quest,* p. 102.

knew who the enemies were to avoid. Finally, the letter was less likely to be opened and read during the journey; an associate had probably heard at least parts of the letter during the writing and rewriting process.

A formula for identifying the carrier. In antiquity a letter sometimes ended with "I am writing through . . ." as a means of identifying the letter carrier. First Peter 5:12 used the same formula to identify Silvanus as the letter carrier. Although commentators often misunderstand this verse as identifying Silvanus as the letter's secretary, it has been demonstrated that this formula was used only to identify him as the letter carrier.[4] Although Paul often named his carrier, he did not use this or any other standard formula. Paul's citation of his carrier was never merely formulaic; he commended the person more than was common and in ways that were not common.

THE LOGISTICS OF CARRYING PAUL'S LETTERS

The interchange of letter and letter carrier in Paul's correspondence is seen clearly in the case of Colossae, the location of both a church and the home of Philemon. When Paul decided to send Onesimus back to his master, Philemon, he sent with him a recommendation letter of sorts, a letter of restoration. Paul had Tychicus escort Onesimus home, to increase the likelihood of restoring this runaway slave.

Paul, though, could not write only to Philemon. As seen in the last chapter, it was often awkward not to send some type of letter if a carrier was available, all the more to the Colossian church, since it may well have met in Philemon's home. Since Paul knew of the problems in Colossae (from Epaphras), he took the opportunity to address those issues. In the letter to the church, Paul mentioned Tychicus escorting Onesimus home (Col 4:9), making the private matter public, and thus adding additional pressure to Philemon to restore Onesimus. Since Epaphras had brought news of the Colossian church to Paul, Paul also needed to explain why Epaphras was not returning with the letter. Not sending Epaphras could have raised concerns: Did Paul distrust Epaphras? Had there been a rift? Paul eliminated any doubts by praising Epaphras, while also explaining his delay in returning to Colossae (Col 4:12-13).

Traveling (then and now) required peace, relative freedom from robbers and coinage that was accepted everywhere. For two hundred years, beginning with Caesar Augustus in 30 B.C., members of the Roman Empire enjoyed the means and freedom to travel.[5] Lionel Casson described the time of Paul as unusually beneficial for the private traveler:

> He could make his way from the shores of the Euphrates to the border between England and Scotland without crossing a foreign frontier, always within the bounds of one government's

---

[4]See the arguments in Richards, "Silvanus was not Peter's Secretary," *JETS* 43 (2000): 417-32.

[5]The best concise discussion of travel in the Roman Empire for those interested in Paul is Brian Rapske, "Acts, Travel and Shipwreck," in *The Book of Acts in Its Greco-Roman Setting*, David Gill and Conrad Gempf, eds., vol. 2 in The Book of Acts in Its First Century Setting series (Grand Rapids: Eerdmans, 1994), pp. 1-48.

jurisdiction. A purseful of Roman coins was the only kind of cash he had to carry; they were accepted or could be changed everywhere. He could sail through any waters without fear of pirates, thanks to the Emperor's patrol squadrons. A planned network of good roads gave him access to all major centres, and the through routes were policed well enough for him to ride them with relatively little fear of bandits. He needed only two languages: Greek would take him from Mesopotamia to Yugoslavia, Latin from Yugoslavia to Britain.[6]

Eventually the Romans provided its citizens over 50,000 miles of main military highways and 200,000 miles of secondary roads. Many of these roads arose from public building projects imposed on local towns and communities by the Roman government. The roads of the empire quickly filled with travelers on government business, personal business, pilgrimages to shrines and festivals, etc.

Travel by land and sea. It is commonly thought that Paul traveled about 6,200 miles in his journeys, as described in Acts, for Paul is seen frequently on the road. One common modern mistake readers make is to assume year-round travel. In general, ancients were fair-weather travelers. Most travelers went by land from June to September. Travelers avoided journeys involving mountain passes or high plateaus during the rainy seasons of April and May in the spring and October in the fall, because run-off was dangerous. Many of Paul's journeys involved high elevation passes (e.g., the very dangerous "Cilician Gates," a narrow mountain pass through the Taurus Mountains; see Acts 13:14; 14:24; 16:1; 18:23). Roman roads were considered closed from November 11 until March 10 each year, especially in areas of higher elevation, where plummeting temperatures and heavy snowfalls made travel perilous. Most people cautiously restricted their land travel to the summer months.

Traveling by land almost always meant walking. Using the distances between ancient stopping places, travel records, as well as comments found in literary sources, scholars have reached a general consensus that on a normal day a traveler in Paul's day walked about 20 miles.[7] Peter's trip from Joppa to Caesarea (about 40 miles) took two days (Acts 10:23-30). Travelers who used donkeys or camels to carry loads generally still covered about the same distance. Wagons and chariots tended to average a little more, about 25-30 miles per day; while on horseback, a traveler could easily average 50 miles a day.[8] We can feel quite confident, however, that Paul and his letter carriers walked.

Traveling by land necessitated lodgings. The wealthy aristocracy of Rome often maintained a number of homes along the common routes they plied. A slave would run ahead to announce the arrival of the master so that the home could be made ready by the slaves

---

[6]Lionel Casson, *Travel in the Ancient World* (Baltimore: Johns Hopkins University Press, 1994), p. 128.

[7]So Jerome Murphy-O'Connor, "Traveling Conditions in the First Century: On the Road and On the Sea With St. Paul," *BR* 1 (1985): 40. See also Rapske, "Acts, Travel and Shipwreck," p. 6 (17-23 miles per day). Scholars from the late 19th (Ramsay) and early 20th (Charlesworth) centuries tended to estimate 15-20 miles per day.

[8]See the discussion by Rapske, "Acts, Travel and Shipwreck," pp. 7-14.

who serviced the residence. Someone traveling on the business of his master would also be permitted to stay overnight in these homes. In situations where neither the master nor his friends owned a home, an aristocrat often traveled with a retinue of servants, carriages, tents and donkeys to enable a well-equipped camp each evening.

The ordinary person traveling on matters of personal business had no such options available. Often such a traveler had no recourse but the roadside inn. A Roman writer, Petronius, recounted a seamy story of misadventures in the roadside inns of his day.[9] Archaeological remains and ancient descriptions paint a picture of "dilapidated and unclean facilities, virtually non-existent furnishings, bed-bugs, poor quality food and drink, untrustworthy proprietors and staff, shady clientele, and generally loose morals."[10] It is not surprising then that early Christian writings emphasized the importance of hospitality. Christian hospitality was essential to the work of Paul and any team members he sent on errands, such as letter carrying.

A modern reader might be tempted to calculate the distance between two cities visited by Paul, divide the distance by 20 miles per day and conclude that it took X number of days for a particular journey. While such a method may be reliable for a journey of one or two days (e.g., Peter's trip from Joppa to Caesarea), there were several factors that suggest any journey of distance took considerably longer. Certainly Jewish travelers were affected by the Sabbath. Not only did they not travel on the Sabbath, they also likely delayed a departure in order to remain in a place where there was a synagogue if the Sabbath were near.

A far more serious travel interruption was caused by the seasons. When Roman roads closed in November, a traveler was forced to spend the winter wherever he was at that time, something that seems inconceivable to us modern Westerners but was an accepted reality for ancient travelers. Furthermore, they did not leave such matters to chance but planned where they would spend the winter. Thus Paul on one occasion planned to spend the winter in Nicopolis (Tit 3:12) and on another occasion urged Timothy to hasten so as to arrive in Rome before winter closed travel (2 Tim 4:21). The time required for a journey was four months longer if winter struck before reaching their destination.

Although seasons were the major factor in how long a journey took, traveling times were also affected by terrain. In today's era of bridges, tunnels and superhighways, the distance one actually travels is often scarcely further than the distance "as a crow flies." In ancient times walkers often took the easier even though longer path. Anyone who has followed a cow's trail from pasture to barn has noticed this phenomenon. Today, tourists to Asia Minor (modern Turkey) are often struck by the towering mountains that seem to

---

[9]Petronius *Sat.* 94-7. Similarly, many an English writer found the setting of an 1800s wharf-side inn the perfect context for a story of danger and intrigue. Rapske, "Acts, Travel and Shipwreck," p. 15, argues that Petronius' tale, though exaggerated, was not overly hyperbolic. Petronius assumed his tales would resonate in the hearts of his audience who had their own misadventures in these inns.

[10]Rapske, "Acts, Travel and Shipwreck," p. 15.

block travel in all directions. Long, uphill journeys, snow-blocked passes and flash floods all slowed the ancient traveler. Even in America, as recently as a generation ago it was common to hear directions such as "after crossing the third creek, turn left on the next road." Today we hardly even notice creeks and rivers as we hurl over them on seamless bridges. In antiquity, a creek meant, at the very least, wet feet. Larger rivers and creeks swollen from rains posed serious obstacles and even hazards for the traveler. One knew well how many creeks would have to be crossed between here and there.

Seasons and terrain were not the only delays a traveler faced. The blessing/burden of hospitality also slowed the traveler. Even today, when I travel in remoter parts of Asia, I cannot pass through a village without stopping to greet the pastor of the village church. If the pastor found out I had passed through his village without stopping he might never forgive the insult. Stopping to greet the pastor is not a ten-minute visit. Rather, I (and the others in my car, for no one travels alone in rural Asia unless it is unavoidable) stop the car and enter his house. He retires to the back of his house to bathe and change clothes while the women scurry about in the kitchen to prepare tea and some kind of snack. (How could he dishonor his guest by doing less?) When he reappears, we visit for at least an hour and then he walks me to visit the home of at least one leader in the church, where the process is repeated. (The pastor could not have an important guest in his home without taking the guest to visit the church leader. It would insult the church leader, implying that the pastor was ashamed of his congregation.) This process continues until the time comes for either lunch or dinner, depending upon what time I had arrived in the village, at which point the pastor, the church leader and I return to the parsonage to eat together. After the meal and further conversation, I can press the urgency of my travel needs and be allowed to continue on my way, that is, until I reach the next village with a church. Before the advent of automobiles, the traveler would have spent the night in each village. If the traveler was a minister and Sunday was near, the church would insist that he stay and preach. Traveling in the remote villages of Asia takes considerably more time than merely calculating the distance.

Towns in the ancient world were commonly spaced a day's walk apart. It is unwise, however, to suggest that a traveler left the next morning. In modern America, where efficiency often outweighs relationship, we think in terms of arriving at someone's home in the late afternoon and departing the next morning. Anyone who has lived in the Middle East knows the impossibility of such a scenario. Only in the case of an emergency or extreme urgency would such a serious breach of etiquette be forgiven.

Which culture is closer to the world of Paul? Jesus warned his disciples against such rudeness as merely greeting someone on the road and then moving on (Lk 10:4), and gave clear instructions to those he was sending (Lk 10:3-12). Word would quickly spread if someone was rude enough to arrive in the evening and then leave the very next morning. Moreover, the host likely provided the food supplies and extra funds needed for the traveler's next walk. In the case of the early years of the church, a traveling Christian was likely asked to share at a meeting of the local church, as we see was expected of Paul (Acts 20:5-7). It is often thought Paul avoided Ephesus on his final trip to Jerusalem because a stop-over in Ephesus would require too long a stay. Objectors have pointed out that stopping in Miletus and summoning the elders down from Ephesus would take five days, arguing a stop in Ephesus would have been faster. Witherington points out that

> it is possible the ship's schedule did not include a stop in Ephesus, but that may not have been Paul's rationale: More probably, Paul's view was that though he would lose five days by meeting the elders at Miletus, he would lose even more if he went to Ephesus, in view of all the friends, supporters, acquaintances, and enemies he made there during his almost three years in that city.[11]

Stopping in Miletus allowed Paul the haste he needed without offending his friends in Ephesus, an arrangement the Ephesian Elders would well understand.

There were times when haste was necessitated, such as when the traveler was trying to clear a pass before the snows, or reach a town in time to winter there (Acts 27:12), or to reach a pilgrimage site in time for a festival (Acts 20:16). Ancients also recognized a ship's scheduled departure required haste on the part of a traveler (Acts 20:7, 13). Ancients recognized these as unusual situations that excused any rudeness from haste. In general, ancients did not share our love for speedy travel. Seasons, Sabbaths, swamps and stopovers were all perils for the foot traveler, resulting in longer traveling times than a hypothetical 20 miles per day.

The hassles and dangers of foot travel caused many ancients to brave the sea. Before Paul's day, pirates had made sea travel too risky for most; however, the Roman Empire made great strides in domesticating the sea. The Mediterranean Sea became, in the words of Steve Vinson, "a Roman lake."[12] It is not possible to estimate the number of ships plying the Mediterranean waters, but the number of grain ships alone required to maintain the supply of grain needed by Rome has been estimated in the thousands.[13] Convoys of ships made regular trips as far as India. Harbors were bustling centers of activity, offering travelers many options. Most ships carrying passengers were about one hundred feet long with two masts. The larger grain ships were 130-150 feet long with three masts. Josephus, on an unsuccessful attempt to sail to Rome, was on a ship with six hundred passengers.[14] Paul's ship to Rome had 276 onboard.[15]

Sea travel had several immediate advantages over land travel. Obviously, it was easier on one's feet. In the case of sick, weak and older travelers this was an important consid-

---

[11]Witherington, *Acts,* p. 609.

[12]Steve Vinson, "Ships in the Ancient Mediterranean," *BA* 53 (March 1990): 17-18.

[13]See the discussion in Rapske, "Acts, Travel and Shipwreck," p. 2, esp. n. 6.

[14]Jos. *Vit.* 15.3.

[15]Acts 27:37. According to Luke, this ship left too late in the season. Aside from those compelled by Rome, only the brave or desperate of souls would likely book this passage. Thus it seems probable that the ship could carry a larger number of passengers.

eration. The large number of ships plying the sea routes provided travelers with the opportunity to purchase a fare to most destinations. Ships usually hugged the coastline and
anchored nightly, either in a port or merely offshore. The moderate weather of the Mediterranean (during sailing season) made sea travel a reasonable, if not comfortable, option.
Sea travelers also were usually spared the problems of lodging or a prolonged stay required by hospitality. The ship's schedule, determined by her captain, kept one from ex-
cessive delays.

Nevertheless, sea travel had its own difficulties. In the Mediterranean, travel was usually in a clockwise flow around the edges of the sea (Rome to Greece to Turkey to Palestine
to Egypt and back to Rome). Thus, a traveler often had to take a rather circuitous path.
On the first missionary journey, when Paul and Barnabas finished on Cyprus, they were
likely headed back to Syrian Antioch when their ship sailed toward the port of Attalia
(Perge). The ship's route was probably northwest from Cyprus to the Turkish coast, then
sailing east down the coast back to Antioch. When John Mark "deserted" Paul, he likely
remained with the ship, for which they had probably paid a fare to Antioch. Paul and
Barnabas left the ship and took the land route home.[16] Ships could sail against this clockwise pattern but normally only by hugging tightly against the southern coasts of Greece
and Turkey.[17]

Ships with favorable winds could average up to 7 miles per hour. Thus, grain ships
from Egypt to Rome, during the fair sailing season, took 10-20 days. However, with unfavorable winds, the trip took twice as long or even longer.[18] If the ship required the zig-
zag course of tacking against the wind, then the trip was considerably longer.

To travel by sea a person walked the piers asking captains their next port of call and if
there was passenger space. Should a reasonable fare be arranged,[19] the traveler inquired
when the ship was due to leave port. Most ships plied a standard route. Unfamiliar seas
were a danger to ship and crew. Within this standard route, however, there was room for
variance. Since a sea captain was dependent upon cargo, he might skip port if his holds

---

[16]The *Via Sebaste* road was the land route home from Perge to Syrian Antioch. It was about 50 years old
by Paul's time. This land route to Syrian Antioch was also quite circuitous, since it involved first traveling
north though the mountains, then east and south through the mountains again. There was no Roman
road following the Turkish coast to Syrian Antioch. (Even today there is not much of one.) For a good
description of the *Via Sebaste*, see David French, "Acts and the Roman Roads of Asia Minor," in *The Book
of Acts in Its Greco-Roman Setting*, ed. David Gill and Conrad Gempf, vol. 2 in The Book of Acts in Its
First-Century Setting (Grand Rapids: Eerdmans, 1994), pp. 49-58, esp. pp. 50-53.

[17]So Rapske, "Acts, Travel and Shipwreck," p. 37 and others.

[18]See ibid., p. 36.

[19]I found no data to determine average fares or if there were even standard fares. I know of only one papyrus, *PZen.* 10 (April 1, 257 B.C.), where it mentioned Ariston and his sister (?) Doris paid 35 drachmas
to hire a boat from Patara to Arsinoë in Cilicia. This seems exorbitantly high. Yet, Doris was a "lady." The
captain had done "everything necessary for her comfort" (according to the editors, p. 69). It is unclear
from the letter but it is possible they hired the entire boat. In any event, it seems unwise to draw any
conclusions for Paul from this data.

were full; if he had no cargo to deliver or pick up, why pay the harbor fees for a stop? However, a captain might remain longer in port if he were seeking a cargo. Should opportunity arise for a good profit, he might shift his route or even reverse his course. Should the ship be excessively delayed or alter the route too much, a passenger had to disembark and try another ship.

When a ship arrived in port, the captain went ashore to make arrangements to sell and buy cargo. In the case of larger grain ships, unloading the cargo could take up to twelve days![20] Seeking buyers and sellers of cargo, arguing with dock crews, dealing with greedy port officials, all led to time in harbor.

Sea travel was also subject to seasonal restrictions. For sailing, the "safe season" was June through mid-September. A month and a half on either side was considered the "risky season." The winds shifted about; sudden squalls and fierce storms were common. Stormy weather wasn't the only risk to winter sailing; the Mediterranean skies tend to remain cloudy during the winter, obscuring the sun during the day and the stars at night. During Paul's day, sailors did not even have a compass, so visibility was essential to navigation.[21] Travelers did not generally have the option of sailing in the winter. The government discouraged official shipping (with the exception of the grain ships), and private vessels were not usually willing to risk life and fortune.

Sometime during the month of October, or early November at the latest, a captain picked a harbor in which to winter. It was an important decision. A good harbor needed to provide not only a safe haven for the ship from the weather, but also adequate housing (and entertainment) for the crew; otherwise, the captain could find himself without a crew by springtime.

The perils of travel. Sea travel was not without its own problems. While Roman ships were quite advanced for their time, these ships were plowing the furrows of the Mediterranean a thousand years before the Vikings. The sea was full of dangers. If a pirate captured the ship, passengers often ended up as slaves. If a storm captured the ship, passengers often ended up as fish bait.

Weather and pirates were not the only danger. A man cautioned his wife in a letter, "When you come, bring your gold ornaments, but do not wear them on the boat."[22] Terentian wrote his father that he had purchased quite a bit of supplies for his father. Some he sent by way of Martialis and some he planned to send later; however, misfortune struck:

> I have sent you, father, by Martialis a bag sewn together, in which you have two mantles, two capes, two linen towels, two sacks, a wooden bed. I had bought the last together with a mattress and a pillow, and while I was lying ill on the ship they were stolen from me.[23]

---

[20] Ernst Haenchen, *Acts of the Apostle*, trans. B. Noble and G. Shinn (Oxford: Basil Blackwell, 1971), p. 704 n. 2.

[21] L. Casson, *Ships and Seamanship in the Ancient World* (Princeton, N.J.: Princeton University Press, 1971), p. 271. His is the best concise description of Roman shipping.

[22] PMich. 3.214 (A.D. 296).

[23] PMich. 8.468 (early second century).

Paul and other travelers had to exercise caution when traveling because travelers made easy prey for thieves.

One might assume letter writers had little to fear from thieves. A carrier's valuables might be taken, but who would steal a letter? In a different letter, Terentian warned his father that the contents of packages were sometimes pilfered or switched while aboard ship: "Describe the seals to me by letter lest any exchange be made en route."[24] Someone wanting to steal Terentian's belongings would do well to steal any letters as well. Terentian's advice was no doubt standard, since there are numerous examples of letters describing the contents of the accompanying packages. Someone wishing to steal the valuables of one of Paul's letter carriers might well take the letter also.

Traveling by ship posed another peril for letter carriers. Letters were lost when a ship sank. Some scholars have maintained that all of Paul's letters would have been lost in the shipwreck on Paul's journey to Rome. As Brian Rapske pointed out, ancients knew to take precautions when carrying valuable papers aboard ship. Furthermore, ancients took care to try to rescue valuables, as a story of Julius Caesar illustrates:

> [He] plunged into the sea, and after swimming for two hundred paces, got away to the nearest ship, holding up his left hand all the way, so as not to wet some papers which he was carrying, and dragging his cloak after him with his teeth, to keep the enemy from getting it as a trophy.[25]

It is doubtful Paul took many papers with him on this final voyage, since he was aware that it was well past the safe time to travel by ship.[26] Other colleagues, who planned to join him in Rome later, were no doubt entrusted to carry the bulk of his supplies. Furthermore, in the case of Paul's shipwreck the passengers and crew had time to make preparations for landfall.

As we see, travel was perilous. The dangers of travel discouraged many from venturing far from home (Prov 27:8). Nevertheless, many ancients braved the roads and sea lanes. In fact, for most, travel was relatively safe if one took two routine precautions: travel during the open season (which we have just discussed) and travel in groups.

Traveling alone was dangerous. In Jesus' story of the Good Samaritan, the poor victim was apparently traveling alone. Jesus' hearers on that day included some listeners who were not supportive of him but were probably traveling with him that day because ancients traveled in groups. In most towns, travelers gathered in the early morning in the center market to purchase supplies they might need for the day but also to join up with other travelers. They walked together for safety, and also because ancients preferred community.

Paul was what ancients called a professional traveler, someone willing to face the hard-

---

[24]PMich. 8.467.

[25]Suet. *Jul.* 64. This story is likely mythic, designed to amaze the readers with Julius' skills. Nonetheless, even assuming it an exaggeration, one may still draw the inference that ancients were cognizant of the risks sea travel posed to documents.

[26]It may well be a concession by Festus to the Jews that he sent Paul on a ship that was leaving late enough in the year to be ill-fated, a ship that Paul's opponents chose not to board.

ships of traveling out of season.[27] We read of Cicero also being willing to travel out of season, crossing through the Cilician Gates (the Taurus mountain pass used by Paul on several occasions) in November 51 B.C. and again in April 50 B.C. Yet, this pass was often closed by snow and perilous in the winter.[28] In one letter Paul recounted a list of his tribulations, many of which refer to traveling:

> Three times I was shipwrecked; for a night and a day I was adrift at sea; on frequent journeys, in danger from rivers, danger from bandits, . . . danger in the wilderness, danger at sea, . . . through many a sleepless night, hungry and thirsty, often without food, cold and naked. (2 Cor 11:25-27)

Sleepless nights, hunger and thirst were results of his overland journeys. As Murphy-O'Connor concludes:

> it is obvious that on occasion [Paul] found himself far from human habitation at nightfall. He may have failed to reach shelter because of weather conditions; an unusually hot day may have sapped his endurance; mountain passes may have been blocked by unseasonably early or late snowfalls; spring floods may have made sections of the road impassable (he claims to have been "in danger from rivers").[29]

Although Paul was a professional traveler, this may not have been true of his letter carriers. Some may have been as determined as Paul, but most were probably what Ramsay and Jewett call "fair-weather travelers."[30] The church father Basil of Caesarea (ca. A.D. 350) has been cited as such an example, for Basil restricted his travel to the open season, and then only in mild weather. He frequently refused to travel at all. Nonetheless, as Rapske points out, Basil's letters also mention various government and business personnel who were traveling, often during the closed season, whom Basil used to carry his letters.[31] Paul was not unique in traveling out of season, hardy but not unusual.

Distances and traveling times. As we have seen, estimating travel times is a dubious endeavor. Too many factors could lengthen a trip. For land travel, unplanned factors like flash floods, civil unrest, bandits, and hospitality demands easily lengthened the time it took travelers to reach their destination. For sea travel, loading/unloading cargo, winds and waiting for a connecting ship easily lengthened a journey, quite apart from seasonal delays.

Although we cannot determine how long it took a particular letter to arrive, it is pos-

---

[27]Witherington, *Acts,* p. 636, objects to classifying Paul as a "professional traveler," which he equates with those who traveled in order to publish observations. He prefers the term "veteran traveler." Witherington means Paul was not merely a "fair-weather traveler."

[28]Antigonus lost many soldiers in the snow when he attempted to cross in 314 B.C.

[29]Murphy-O'Connor, "Traveling Conditions," p. 41.

[30]E.g., Robert Jewett, *A Chronology of Paul's Life* (Philadelphia: Fortress, 1979), pp. 55-58, classifies Paul also as a fair-weather traveler, but he and the others are probably reading too much into 1 Cor 16:5-6; see the critique by Rapske, "Acts, Travel and Shipwreck," pp. 4-5.

[31]See Rapske, "Acts, Travel and Shipwreck," pp. 4-6, for an excellent summary and critique of the "fair weather traveler" argument.

sible to give some general indicators. In the case of sea travel, a letter in 257 B.C. took two months to travel from Cilicia in southern Turkey around the Mediterranean to Alexandria in Egypt.[32] A happenstance carrier on a boat no doubt carried the letter. This was quite a speedy delivery; the ship was, however, sailing in favorable winds. Luke reported that the journey from Troas to Philippi took two days (Acts 16:11), but a later return journey took five days (Acts 20:6).

In the case of land travel, which often included short trips by boat, it is a little easier to estimate traveling times. The best source for this type of data comes from the letters of Zenon. Zenon was the manager of a large estate (6,800 acres) in Egypt owned by the finance minister under Ptolemy II. Zenon kept records of the various transactions of this estate. Archaeologists uncovered his archives, the largest papyrus collection ever found, consisting of nearly 2,000 records covering the period 260-240 B.C. Zenon kept inventories, receipts, accounts, records of deposits and letters.

What makes Zenon's collection significant for our discussion is that he recorded the date and place he received the letter on the outside of about 150 letters. Many letters themselves also mentioned the date and place of writing. Eldon Epp has painstakingly analyzed this data.[33] From his observations we can calculate the distance between the place of writing and its destination and the time the letter took. Two different letters were sent in different years from the same town down to Alexandria, 150 miles away. One letter (*PSI* 5.514) arrived in four days, traveling upstream. The other letter (*PCairoZen.* 59154), traveling downstream, took 25 days. One would expect the letter traveling downstream to arrive faster; however, this second letter was a request for wood to be delivered for a festival. Apparently, the writer also assumed the letter would arrive expeditiously (within a week or two), since the festival was imminent. In this case, the letter did not arrive in time (or at least the recipient claimed it did not arrive in time to send the wood). It seems wise to exclude this letter. *PSI* 5.502 made the same journey in seven days; while PMich. 1.48 made the trip in six days.

In the Zenon papyri, letters traveling relatively short distances seem to follow the pattern of approximately 15-20 miles per day. Longer journeys were less standard. Two letters (*PCairoZen.* 59075 and 76) traveled 350 miles from the Transjordan in Palestine to Alexandria in 36 days (about 10 miles/day). It is not, though, possible to make these standard. PMich. 1.28 went 15 miles in one day. Yet, PMich. 1.10 took 19 days to travel 80 miles (4 miles/day!). Happenstance carriers had other business that could delay a letter. The perils and hassles of traveling also delayed letters. A letter from Zenon's collection tells us of Ariston and his sister Doris, who traveled from Alexandria to Cilicia (southern Asia Minor). Unfortunately, we are not told how long the trip took, but we are told that their journey was interrupted by an unexplained delay of two months, another indicator

---

[32]PZen. 10. The dates and traveling time are given by the editor, C. C. Edgar, p. 71.
[33]Epp, "Letter Carrying."

of the perils of traveling. When they finally arrived safely, a letter (*PCairoZen.* 59029) was sent from Cilicia to Alexandria (about 800 miles) and it arrived in only two months.

Once a carrier left Corinth with Paul's letter to the Romans, he needed only 10 days by ship to reach Rome. This assumes favorable winds, minimal stops, no delays in loading/unloading cargo, and a ship that was heading from Corinth westward to Rome, and not eastward around the Mediterranean. Carrying a letter from Ephesus to Corinth took a week, maybe two, if carried by ship. If the carrier was going by land, the letter took the time needed to walk, plus all the stopovers for hospitality concerns.

Luke's travel narrative of Acts 20:3—21:8 provides an excellent description of the hazards of setting timetables. Paul left Corinth with the intention of hurrying to celebrate Pentecost in Jerusalem; he was willing to push the limits of hospitality in order to expedite his travel (Acts 20:16). Yet Luke speaks of numerous delays and mid-stream adjustments.

Paul had planned to go by sea but had to switch to a land route (Acts 20:3). The trip through the cities of Macedonia required additional stops to greet each church. It appears significant that Luke mentioned how the team left Philippi after Passover, probably indicating they had celebrated in Philippi. If Passover were near, the church (Lydia?) no doubt prevailed upon Paul and his team to delay and celebrate with them, since there was no Jewish community in Philippi. Once moving again, the sea journey between Philippi and Troas, which on one occasion had taken two days, this time needed five (20:6). When they reached Troas their voyage was delayed seven days. The most likely explanation was their ship was unloading and loading cargo. These unexpected delays may have influenced his decision to bypass Ephesus. The ship made good time until arriving in Tyre. There Luke specifically noted a delay of seven days for unloading cargo. Once reaching Caesarea (only three to four days' walk from Jerusalem), they were again delayed by the requirements of hospitality in Philip's home (Acts 21:15). As modern readers we are apt to see a story filled with frustrating obstacles and irritating delays. However, it is likely that Paul, Luke and the readers of Acts all viewed this as a rapid journey, since they had no extended stays and did not need to spend the winter anywhere.

This analysis leads us to two conclusions. First, it is not possible to declare a standard timetable for letter deliveries. While very rapid deliveries did occasionally occur, most letters traveled no faster than 15 miles a day and often took considerably longer. Second, letters crisscrossed the ancient world, traveling great distances with relative ease and a fair degree of success.

Multiple deliveries or destinations. Obviously a letter carrier could handle more than one letter at a time. There are examples of a writer sending several letters to different recipients. Because the recipients were close together or along the way, the same carrier took all the letters. Ignatius sent Burrhus to carry a letter to Philadelphia and two to Smyrna.[34] Cicero mentioned numerous times sending or receiving packets of letters. Tychicus carried Paul's letters

---

[34]See the discussion in Richards, "Silvanus," pp. 421-22.

to the church at Colossae (Col 4:7), and likely to Philemon and the church at Ephesus (Eph 6:22). If Ephesians was originally a circular letter, then Tychicus likely delivered copies to other towns along the way, such as Laodicea. Obviously, then, one carrier sometimes carried several letters intended for several destinations. We would not expect otherwise.

Sometimes the same letter was sent to multiple destinations. Sending a letter to more than one recipient usually occurred in three ways. One, the writer originally intended the one letter to be shown to more than one recipient. Two, the writer sent a letter to someone and then sent a copy of the letter to a second person. Third, the recipient of a letter shared the letter with another person, sometimes without the knowledge of the original writer. An example or two of each use will suffice.

Sometimes the author intended more than one original recipient. The most common examples are official letters from a leader to a community, and the letter was to be circulated throughout the community. The best example of a private letter doing this is 1 Peter. This letter was clearly intended to be circulated among the churches listed in the address. In fact, many scholars believe the address (1 Pet 1:1) lists the route the carrier was to take in circulating the letter.[35] Paul's letter to the churches of Galatia is another example. The letter carrier carried the original letter from one church to another.[36]

Perhaps the author shared a copy of a letter with a third person. For example, Pollio wrote a letter to Balbus and sent a copy to Cicero.[37] Cicero wrote a letter to Pompey and sent a copy to Atticus.[38]

Sometimes a letter might go to more than one recipient because the recipient shared a letter with another person. Quintus wrote a letter to Atticus, and Atticus sent a copy of the letter to Cicero.[39] Cicero wrote a letter to Octavius and sent a copy to Atticus, who in turn sent a copy to Brutus.[40] Sosipatros sent a letter to Antimenes, who sent a copy to Zenon, along with a cover letter.[41] In the first of these three scenarios, the same carrier probably was used for all the deliveries. In the other two scenarios it is impossible to say.

CONCLUSIONS FOR PAUL AS A LETTER WRITER

It is not possible to predict accurately the time that was needed for Paul's carriers to deliver the letters. Ancient travelers averaged 20 miles per day, but too many unpredictable factors (e.g., seasons, Sabbaths, swamps and stopovers) often lengthened the time needed for a journey. It is possible to assert that Paul most likely used happenstance carriers to deliver his early letters, Galatians and 1-2 Thessalonians.

---

[35]Originally proposed by F. J. A. Hort; see, e.g., J. R. Michaels, *1 Peter,* WBC 49 (Waco, Tex.: Word, 1988).
[36]Paul did not dispatch multiple copies; see the discussion in chapter three. I think it likely each church made a copy of the letter to retain before it was sent on.
[37]Cic. *Fam.* 10.32.5.
[38]Cic. *Att.* 3.9.
[39]Cic. *Att.* 1.17; see also *Fam.* 3.3.2; 10.12.2; 10.33.2.
[40]Cic. *Br.* 1.16.1.
[41]PMich. 1.10.

13

PAUL'S USE OF HIS LETTER CARRIERS

*A*ncient letter carriers in the Mediterranean world often also carried supplies or other materials to deliver. Carriers sometimes brought other things as well. Carriers were often rich sources of information (and gossip) about the letter writer. Paul's letter carriers were no exception.

ADDITIONAL TASKS OF A LETTER CARRIER

Bringing materials or supplies. It was not uncommon for a letter carrier to bring additional materials, such as a gift or supplies, from the sender along with the letter. Paul's letters do not specifically list any supplies brought by the letter carrier, but there are several related remarks. When the church of Philippi sent gifts to Paul while he was in prison in Rome (Phil 4:18), it is likely the gifts were accompanied by a letter, for Paul seems aware of some of the issues the Philippian church was currently facing (Phil 2:26; 3:2; 4:2). When Paul requested Timothy to come to him, he was not hesitant to expect Timothy to also bring some items with him (2 Tim 4:13).

Providing additional information. It was shown that when a letter carrier brought a letter, he or she often provided additional details about the sender. Paul's letters provide several excellent examples. Paul explicitly mentioned that Tychicus, who was carrying the letter to the Colossians, was going to fill them in on all the news of Paul.

However, the additional information divulged by the carrier may not have been at the request of the sender. The Corinthian church sent a letter to Paul requesting clarification on several topics. The letter was probably brought to Paul by some Chloe's slaves. Paul responded to the written questions of the Corinthian church, "Now concerning the matters about which you wrote . . ." (1 Cor 7:1). However, before he responded to their written questions, he first addressed what he had heard, "It has been reported to me by Chloe's people that there are quarrels among you" (1 Cor 1:11). It is possible the church did not necessarily wish Paul to know it was wracked with dissension and factions; Paul mentioned how he heard about it, in the unlikely event the news was wrong. Chloe's slaves, likely typical private letter carriers, told Paul additional details of the more unsavory kind (the news of the immoral church member [1 Cor 6] was also likely from Chloe's people). Because Paul made it clear when he began to deal with topics that came from the church's written letter (1 Cor 7:1ff.), it seems safe to conclude that the previous topics (1 Cor 1—

6) came from the news the carriers brought.

Corinth isn't the only example. Since additional information could have been without the sender's blessing, particularly if it was less than flattering, Paul wanted the Ephesians to know that the information Tychicus divulged was given, not only with Paul's blessing but at his instructions (Eph 6:21-22). Telling that Paul was in prison was the type of unflattering information one might not want told. The Ephesians might assume Paul did not wish it told. Yet Paul was not ashamed of his imprisonment. To demonstrate this, he explicitly called himself an "ambassador in chains" (Eph 6:20). Paul wanted it clear that Tychicus was not "spilling the beans."

Reading the letter. Often rhetorical studies speak of a letter's "performance" in a public reading to an assembly. Ancient authorities on rhetoric dating to Paul's time considered the reader's voice, gestures and even his face to be an essential part of effective communication.[1] Ancient letter writers gave thought to how their letters would be read, meaning read aloud before a congregation. To "read" never meant "read silently to oneself," as it commonly does today. Therefore, at the very least a serious ancient letter writer considered the role a reader would play in the performance of the letter. Thus, Botha asserts:

> In antiquity, the letter carrier was . . . the vital link between sender and recipients. . . . Presentation of the rhetorical act . . . is fundamentally the essence of rhetorical activity.[2]

Ancient people were trained to read aloud. Intonation, rhythm and cadence of syllables (elements now called "oral interpretation") were part of ancient education. Paul seemed to share this interest in the public performance of a letter. His request in 1 Thessalonians 5:27 seems to be a formal request for a public performance of the letter.[3] He fully expected his letters to be read publicly. It is even possible that he chose carriers who could read his letter effectively. An informed carrier provided additional information and perhaps also could comment and expound upon the letter. It was advantageous to both Paul and his recipients to have an informed carrier read the letter so as to provide the proper inflections and nuances.

The carrier as Paul's "envoy." Private carriers often provided additional information. Sometimes the carrier had a more exalted role; he read the letter, probably with commentary, elaboration and clarifications afterwards. Sometimes this role expanded further, so that carrier functioned as Paul's envoy. Thus Timothy or Titus was sent, not just because Tychicus or Epaphroditus was busy, but because they had an increased function. They were another form of Paul's apostolic presence (*parousia*).

---

[1]See the excellent discussion by Pieter J. J. Botha, "The Verbal Art of the Pauline Letters: Rhetoric, Performance and Presence," in *Rhetoric and the New Testament: Essays from the 1992 Heidelberg Conference,* eds. Stanley Porter and Thomas Olbricht, pp. 409-28, JSNTS 90 (Sheffield: JSOT Press, 1993), pp. 417-19.
[2]Botha, "Verbal Art," pp. 417-18.
[3]So W. Beilner, "*epistolē*," EDNT, 2:39.

Ever since the 1967 essay of Robert Funk, modern scholars speak of Paul's apostolic *parousia*; that is, how Paul made his presence felt, either by announcing a visit, by sending an envoy, or by writing a letter. Funk came to the conclusion that with churches Paul preferred to come personally. If it was not possible, he sent an envoy. If an envoy was not possible, then he sent a letter.[4] A letter then was an inferior substitute.

This hierarchy (with letters ranked last) remained unchallenged until Margaret Mitchell questioned if Paul himself indicated such a preference. Mitchell argued there is no evidence that Paul sent envoys and letters as only "inadequate substitutes" when his own schedule did not permit a personal visit.[5] It is more likely Paul sent envoys and/or letters when he thought these might be more effective than a personal visit. After a personal visit to Corinth resulted in disaster (2 Cor 2:1-3), Paul chose to send a letter (2 Cor 2:4) by an envoy, Titus (2 Cor 7:5-16). Mitchell grants that the church would feel disappointment, perhaps even offense that Paul had not come himself, but those feelings represent the expectations of the church (and culture) and not necessarily Paul's strategy. He soothed ruffled feelings and avoided offense by offering acceptable excuses for not coming in person (2 Cor 1:12—2:13). However, these excuses should not be misread as indicating Paul actually preferred to go in person. Mitchell rightly concludes that Paul had no order of preference for contacting his churches. He visited personally or sent envoys or wrote letters, depending upon which method he thought would be most effective in that particular situation.[6]

When Paul's ministry is reconstructed solely from his letters, a picture arises of hurt feelings, damaged relationships and strained relations. We must be wary of assuming this characterized Paul's entire ministry. In the East, the proper way to heal a breach in a relationship was through an intermediary. When Paul's relationship with a church became strained, the best Mediterranean course of action was to send an intermediary to heal the rift. Paul sent a letter to express his position and a carrier/envoy to act as his intermediary. Thus, it is not surprising that many of Paul's letters dealt with relational issues.

Paul's answers to the theological questions of the Corinthians (seen in 1 Cor 7ff.) were answered in a letter rather than by a visit. It was not because Paul was too busy to visit; as argued throughout this book, the writing of the letter actually might have taken more time than a visit, or at least not significantly less time. Rather, Paul answered the Corinthian questions by a letter because of the interpersonal problems seen in chapters 1—4. With the church divided, Paul's presence might have been more divisive. He chose to remain away, as Apollos also did (1 Cor 16:12), and sent answers by a letter. Paul's letters provide a glimpse into the ministry of Paul, but only a part of his ministry.

Eventually, as his team members matured, this increased role for the letter carrier as

---

[4]Funk, "Apostolic *Parousia*," pp. 249-69, esp. pp. 258-60.
[5]See the arguments of M. Mitchell, "New Testament Envoys," pp. 641-62, esp. p. 642.
[6]So ibid., p. 643.

Paul's "presence" developed to the point of where Timothy and Titus functioned as Paul's delegates. Thus 1 Timothy and Titus, as L. T. Johnson demonstrates, are examples of "letters to a delegate." Such letters were a reminder from the ruler (Paul) to his delegate (Timothy or Titus) to be read before the assembly. These letters contained a combination of personal and public commands. The personal commands outlined the delegate's authority as well as what should be the delegate's general attitude and behavior. The public commands outlined the delegate's job description as well as any mandates he was to implement. The purpose of the letter was for both the delegate *and* the assembly to hear, in the presence of the other, the tasks of the delegate while he was serving there as the ruler's representative.[7] While most letters to a delegate were official documents, commonly carried by a governmental appointee to his new place of service,[8] there were also a few private examples. When Cicero was appointed proconsul of Cilicia in 51 B.C., his friend Atticus wrote him a letter with many of the same elements. Atticus was not the commissioning authority. His letter was another example of an individual adopting a public letter form for personal use.[9] In a similar way Paul used a personal letter (1 Timothy) to place Timothy as his delegate in Ephesus.[10]

THE AVAILABILITY OF A CARRIER

As seen in chapter eleven, the availability of a carrier generated a letter in two ways: (1) the opportunity that came from having an available carrier often generated a letter; and (2) the delivery of a letter by a carrier who was returning home often prompted a response letter.

Precipitating a letter. When someone was headed on a journey, others often wrote a letter to be carried to that destination. In the third century a papyrus began: "As an opportunity was afforded me by someone going up to you I could not miss this chance of addressing you."[11] Earlier we read a similar line from a Greco-Roman letter with a fascinating addition: "Having chanced on someone going up to you, I have been moved to write and tell you of my plight."[12] It is noteworthy that it was not his plight that prompted the letter but rather the availability of a carrier. Many papyrus letters appear to have been written more from the opportunity provided by an available carrier than from any actual

---

[7]Johnson, *1-2 Timothy*, p. 141. This outstanding commentary completed what was begun by Quinn's volume on Titus. However, Johnson draws significantly different conclusions than Quinn. Although Johnson does not exegete the letter to Titus, he does note that he considers Titus also to be a letter to a delegate.

[8]See, e.g., Dio Cassius *Roman History* 53.15.4.

[9]See Johnson, *1-2 Timothy*, pp. 140-41. Johnson does not draw this inference.

[10]2 Timothy is a different type of letter. According to Johnson, 2 Timothy is not a farewell discourse but a personal paranetic letter—a letter of exhortation (*1-2 Timothy*, p. 322), with clear parallels to Greek discourses (pp. 323-26, 394) that commonly cite themes of memory, model and imitation, followed abruptly with maxims (thus the sudden maxim in 2 Tim 2:14).

[11]POxy. 123.

[12]Quoted in Epp, "Letter Carrying," p. 45.

need.[13] A Karanis papyrus from the second century illustrates this well: "From Cyrene, where I found a man who was journeying to you, I deemed it necessary to write to you about my welfare."[14]

In general Paul's letters did not fit into this category. Paul responded to a particular situation, his decision to write was not prompted by an available carrier. There may, however, be one exception, one letter that does not fit the normal Pauline pattern, and that is Romans. Scholars have long argued over whether Paul was responding to a particular situation in Rome (i.e., Romans was situational, like Paul's other letters) or introducing himself (i.e., Romans was an unprecipitated letter).[15]

Paul's letter to the Romans may be a mixture of both. The key is in the letter's composition. Romans has several unique elements:

1. Romans has more oratorical rhetoric than Paul's other letters, meaning more of the type of rhetoric used in speaking (such as the diatribe) than in writing.[16]

2. Romans seems to have fewer specific references to problems in Rome than Paul's other letters. Clearly there are issues Paul addresses; Romans is not merely a theological treatise. Nonetheless, it is not the same as, for instance, 1 Corinthians where Paul addresses questions raised by the church.

3. Tertius is identified as the secretary of the letter (Rom 16:22).[17] (A secretarial remark like Rom 16:22 was not uncommon.[18])

A secretary was likely to be so brash as to insert a personal comment into his client's letter only when he was known to the recipients and when his status with the author went beyond that of employer or slave-owner. Thus Alexis, a secretary for Atticus, felt confident enough to include a personal greeting to Cicero,[19] because he had a good relationship with both Atticus and Cicero. With some confidence then we may suggest several things about Tertius:

1. Tertius was a believer, for he greeted them "in the Lord."[20]

2. Tertius was known to Paul; he was not merely a secretary hired in the market. Even if Tertius were well known to the Roman church, he would not have felt the freedom to

---

[13]See the discussion in White, *Light*, p. 215.

[14]PMich. 8.490.

[15]See the earlier discussion in chapter four.

[16]See the extended discussion in Richards, *Secretary*, pp. 133-35, 141-44.

[17]See Richards, *Secretary*, p. 170.

[18]Cic. *Att.* 5.20; *Fam.* 7.29.2 (both referring to letters *to* Cicero); see the discussion in Richards, *Secretary*, p. 76.

[19]Cic. *Att.* 5.20 (*vid*).

[20]Gordon Bahr, "Letter Writing," p. 465, argued that "in the Lord" modifies "writing this letter" and should be translated "I, Tertius, who write this letter in the service of [my] master [Paul], greet you." This translation has too many problems to be an option; see my critique in Richards, *Secretary*, p. 172 n. 202. Clearly, this phrase is an indication that Tertius is a believer.

insert a greeting into Paul's letter unless he knew Paul well. If he did not know Paul, he would have merely sent a short letter of his own to be carried along with Paul's letter to the Romans.

3. Tertius was also known to the recipients in Rome, since he did not further identify himself. He assumed those in Rome knew who he was. Tertius does not appear elsewhere in Paul's letters (numerous other coworkers of Paul are mentioned only once in his letters but usually as recipients of greetings or in a particular context, for example, Syntyche and Euodia). The names of those more closely associated with Paul usually resurface in other letters of Paul. Tertius was not mentioned in Romans 16:22 because he was the secretary (for Paul identified his secretary in no other letter), but because he was known to the Roman church.

I can feel confident about the first three points. These last two points are more tenuous.

4. Why was Tertius used to record Romans? It may well be no other reason than he was an available secretary. It should be asked, however, is it merely coincidence that Romans is the longest letter of Paul, the letter that contains the strongest oral features, that contains the highest frequency of oratorical rhetoric? Ever since Deissmann, scholars have noticed rhetorical parallels between Epictetus and Paul. Epictetus's works claimed to be the recorded speeches of Epictetus, taken down by Arrian. The surface similarities between Epictetus and Romans may well be because both were accurate recordings of spoken preaching style.

5. Ever since the exhaustive study by Otto Roller, it has been unreasonable to imagine Romans being dictated syllable by syllable in laborious fashion.[21] Romans has a dramatic oral flair, with imaginary interlocutors, energy carried over sustained arguments, a careful cadence of syllables. If any of Paul's letters were dictated at the speed of speech, Romans is the most likely candidate.

Perhaps Tertius was not used because Romans was so long, but actually Romans was so long because Tertius was used. Perhaps Tertius was a professional secretary. He may well have been trained in Greek shorthand (tachygraphy), since Rome was most known for housing professional stenographers. I must point out that Paul's letter to the Romans had no coauthor, and yet Timothy was present during its composition (Rom 16:21). Romans is the only letter where Paul states that Timothy was present but does not also name him as a coauthor.

A scenario suggests itself. Paul's attention and focus was upon the collection and delivery of the offering for the church in Jerusalem. As seen from his letters, the offering dominated his attention. Nevertheless, the availability in Corinth of a professional secretary, who knew the situation in the Roman church, was too great an opportunity for Paul to miss. Although he had no direct affiliation with the church in Rome, he saw an oppor-

---

[21]Roller, *Formular,* pp. 8-14.

tunity to mend the division in the church.[22] Paul felt qualified to address this issue. He also saw an opportunity for the church to assist him in his larger goal of preaching in Spain. The opportunity provided by Tertius was too good to miss and may well have precipitated the letter to the Romans.

Generating a response. To illustrate the ancient practice of responding to letters I again revisit my experiences in Indonesia. Whenever I visited a village, playing the part of a happenstance letter carrier in the process, those who received a letter through me would ask when I planned to return home. The evening before my return they reappeared with a letter to send back. In these cases they wrote the letter not because there was pressing need but because I was available to carry a letter.

One ancient Egyptian writer, wearied by excuses, sent blank papyrus to his friend so that there would be no possible excuse for his friend not writing back.[23] The one who brought his letter (and the blank papyrus) was available to bring back the reply letter. The writer thus boxed in his friend. Ancients considered it rude for someone not to send a letter when a carrier was coming, but it was even more injurious to send a letter and not to receive a reply, if the person who carried the letter was planning to return and was available to carry back a letter. Thus, most writers felt obliged to send a reply back if the carrier was returning.

This may explain the occasion of a few of Paul's letters. According to Philippians 4:18, Epaphroditus brought a gift from the Philippian church (Lydia?) to Paul while he was in prison in Rome. The church expected Epaphroditus to return with a note of thanks from Paul. When he did not return immediately, an acceptable explanation was needed. Paul explained that Epaphroditus had fallen ill (Phil 2:25-27). Once he was well, Paul sent him back to Philippi. Presumably, he carried Paul's letter. It would have been particularly awkward for Epaphroditus to return empty-handed to Philippi.

PAUL'S DEVELOPING USE OF LETTER CARRIERS

Some of Paul's letters did not mention the name of the carrier (Galatians, 1-2 Thessalonians and 2 Timothy). Some letters mentioned the carrier and even endorsed the carrier as a reliable source of information about Paul (1-2 Corinthians, Romans, Ephesians, Philippians and Colossians/Philemon). Two letters seem to be "letters to a delegate" (1 Timothy, Titus); two are "personal" (Philemon, 2 Timothy). Paul's choice of a carrier may have been entirely haphazard; however, a pattern suggests itself.

Initially Paul did not consider any role for a letter carrier beyond that of transporting the letter. His early letters (Galatians, 1-2 Thessalonians) were sent by unnamed, presum-

---

[22]Jewish Christians were the original leaders in the church. When evicted by Claudius in A.D. 49 (Acts 18:2), Gentile Christians were forced to assume leadership. When Jewish Christians returned after the death of Claudius, conflict arose between the two leadership groups.

[23]PMich. 8.481: "I send you papyrus so that you might be able to write me concerning your health." The papyrus, probably a roll, was produced in that area.

ably trusted, individuals who were traveling that way. It was the most economic means to send a letter. This is not to imply that Paul was cheap, but to argue that he was not extravagant. Frugality was somewhat second nature for most people of the first century. Why pay to send a carrier if someone trustworthy was already going? Paul's first letter to Corinth, the so-called previous letter, was probably sent the same way, by a trustworthy, happenstance carrier. I suggest, however, that Paul learned from this experience. This previous letter to Corinth had been misunderstood: "I wrote to you in my letter not to associate with sexually immoral persons—not at all meaning the immoral of this world" (1 Cor 5:9-10).[24] This is the type of misunderstanding that an informed letter carrier should have been able to immediately clarify.[25] It should not have developed into such a problem that it needed to be readdressed in a subsequent letter. For this reason, I suggest that when Paul sent the next letter, 1 Corinthians, he used an informed carrier, Timothy.[26] Interestingly, Paul's first four letters (Galatians, 1-2 Thessalonians and the "previous letter") are commonly thought by scholars to have been misunderstood in some way by each receiving church.

From 1 Corinthians onward, Paul's letters were carried by named, private letter carriers, who bore Paul's endorsement and whom Paul said had authority to elaborate his meaning (Col 4:7-9).[27] Sending letters in the less expensive manner, by way of a trusted person already heading that way, had led to more trouble and expense for Paul, because the carrier was not able to explain a confusing part of the letter.

I am suggesting that Paul, from experience, learned to use his letter carriers more wisely. Progressing from unnamed and uninformed carriers early in his ministry to named, endorsed and informed carriers in his later ministry. Paul's later carriers were team members who could explain his meaning to avoid problems like that seen in his "previous letter" to Corinth. It is not frugal to send a letter by a happenstance carrier if misunderstandings were going to require a second letter. Near the conclusion of his ministry, Paul developed beyond letters with an informed carrier, who could explain the letter, to the point of sending delegates, who had authority themselves to deal with issues as they arose.

It has long been argued that Paul's letters, from 1 Corinthians onwards, became more

---

[24]In researching the problem of the "previous letter," I noticed Thiselton, in his magisterial commentary on 1 Corinthians (NIGTC), makes a brief mention of the problem of the "previous letter" (p. 72). He seems to imply that the problem arose because the Corinthians gave the letter a "hearing" but not a prolonged study. However, the problem, it seems to me, was not superficial reading in the sense of a shallow commitment, but rather failure to clarify an ambiguous expression in Paul's first letter.

[25]This was not Paul's view of the Law or some other deeply convoluted concept. A simple clarification, such as Paul gave in 1 Corinthians, was all that was needed. Thus Fee, *1 Corinthians,* p. 220, argues that Paul's opponents deliberately chose to misunderstand it. Fee may be correct, but this does not change my point. An informed carrier could have countered this deliberate misunderstanding.

[26]As customary, I am reading 1 Cor 4:17 "I sent" as an epistolary aorist (thus "I am sending"), because Timothy was still with him (1 Cor 16:10-11); see the note in the NRSV.

[27]Personal letters (Philemon, 2 Timothy) and letters to an envoy (1 Timothy, Titus) had more specialized purposes and did not require a carrier to read and elaborate the letter.

theologically complex and difficult. Did Paul's theology develop or did he begin to feel more comfortable writing complex letters as he developed team members capable of carrying and explaining the ideas? In other words, what developed, Paul's theology or his team? I suggest Paul's theology did not develop as dramatically as some imply. Paul did not grow more skilled at writing complex theology, but rather was able to write more complex theology as his carriers became more able to explain it.

CONCLUSIONS FOR PAUL AS A LETTER WRITER

Paul switched to using private carriers because of the standard benefit of a safe and expeditious delivery. His private carriers, since they were members of his team, also provided additional insight into his personal situation, and probably expounded upon parts of the letter.

It is fair to ask whether Paul used Tertius because Romans was so long or Romans was so long because Paul used Tertius. It is also fair to ask whether Paul's theology developed over time (and thus his letters to churches became longer and more complex) or his letters to churches became longer and more complex as he developed team members who could carry and explain them.

14

COLLECTING PAUL'S LETTERS

*H*aving looked at letter writing, we shall now attempt to outline briefly how a better understanding of Paul as a letter writer might impact the question of the collection of Paul's letters.

FORMATION OF THE PAULINE CORPUS

At some point in time, the individual letters of Paul, sent to a wide variety of destinations, were published as a single group, often called the "Pauline Corpus." Today in our New Testaments, we have a Pauline Corpus consisting of thirteen letters. When and how were these individual letters gathered into a single collection?

Old collection theories. In times past, the formation of the Pauline Corpus was viewed largely as stymied among several major theories. These theories may be broken down into two groups: (1) those advocating that the letters were collected through a gradual process, like a snowball growing and gaining momentum as it rolls, and (2) those contending there was a sudden move toward collection, like a big bang. Although grouped thematically, it is also a chronological presentation, since "snowball" theories have given way to "big bang" theories.

"Snowball" theories. Early in the twentieth century the collection of Paul's letters was often argued to be a gradual process. Since churches esteemed their own letter(s) of Paul, they also began to collect copies of his letters written to other churches.[1] Thus partial collections arose in various regions (e.g., Ephesus and Achaia), leading finally to a complete collection in the second century.[2] Harry Gamble calls this approach "the snowball theory."[3]

"Big Bang" theories. These older theories gave way to the reasoning of Edgar J. Goodspeed. His theory broached a new approach by arguing that a single individual took it upon himself to collect the letters of Paul from the various churches.[4] He argued Onesi-

---

[1]P. N. Harrison is a classic example, positing Colossians 4:16 as the first sign; *Polycarp's Two Epistles to the Philippians* (London: Cambridge University Press, 1936).

[2]E.g., G. Zuntz, *The Text of the Epistles: A Disquisition upon the Corpus Paulinum* (Oxford: Oxford University Press, 1963), pp. 278-79.

[3]Harry Gamble, *Canon*, p. 36. Jerome Murphy-O'Connor calls this "the evolutionary theory." He gives an insightful summary and analysis; *Paul the Letter-Writer*, pp. 114-20.

[4]E. J. Goodspeed, *New Solutions to New Testament Problems* (Chicago: University of Chicago Press, 1927), pp. 1-64.

mus began collecting Paul's letters after the publication of Acts renewed interest in Paul. Although Goodspeed's theory has fallen upon rough times, his basic premise remains in vogue. Günther Zuntz argued more persuasively for Alexandria as the home of the first collection. F. F. Bruce led to widespread adoption of this model, after he argued for someone collecting the letters in Alexandria about the year A.D. 100.[5] Even now, the various collection theories all seek to find the three keys: "an occasion, an agent and a motive."[6] The years that followed saw the suggestions of Walter Schmithals[7] and others. While having unique elements, all these theories share the commonality of positing an individual (or an individual school) that took the initiative to collect the dispatched letters of Paul. Arthur Patzia encapsulated this view in his conclusion: "It is difficult to imagine this early circulation and collection of Paul's letters without the guidance of some significant individual(s)."[8]

New "codex and collection" theories. Recently there has been a revival of interest in the formation of the Pauline Corpus. This is largely the result of a 1994 article by T. C. Skeat[9] and the 1995 book by Harry Gamble.[10] Scholars have long noticed that the ancients moved from using the scroll form of a book to using the codex form (our modern "book" form). Moreover, it is clear that initially it was Christians who adopted the codex. All manuscript copies of the New Testament came from codices.[11]

For our purposes the most interesting aspect of the work of Skeat and Gamble—and the tie that joins them—is that they both take a new approach to the collection issue. Both Skeat and Gamble tie the early Christian fondness for the codex to the issue of collection. That is, they both argue that Christians began to collect parts of the New Testament and they published these collections in the codex format. Skeat argues for the collection and formation of a four-fold Gospel, while Gamble argues for the collection of Paul's letters.

T. C. Skeat is well known for his works arguing that Christians preferred the codex to the

---

[5] See F. F. Bruce, "Origins of the New Testament Canon," in *New Dimensions in New Testament Study*, ed. Richard Longenecker and Merrill Tenney (Grand Rapids: Zondervan, 1974), pp. 9-10.

[6] To borrow Gamble's phraseology (*Canon*, p. 39).

[7] W. Schmithals, "On the Composition and Earliest Collection of the Major Epistles of Paul" in *Paul and the Gnostics* (Nashville: Abingdon, 1972), pp. 239-74. David Trobisch (*Paul's Letter Collection*, esp. pp. 50-54) adds a new twist by arguing that it was Paul himself who started this by collecting, selecting and editing an "authorized" collection of his letters (the *Hauptbriefe*), which was later expanded.

[8] Arthur Patzia, "Canon," in *Dictionary of Paul and His Letters*, ed. Gerald F. Hawthorne, Ralph P. Martin and Daniel G. Reid (Downers Grove, Ill.: InterVarsity Press, 1993), p. 87. His more recent work moves away from this position, finding some merit in the theory I am suggesting here; Patzia, *The Making of the New Testament: Origin, Collection, Text and Canon* (Downers Grove, Ill.: InterVarsity Press, 1995), esp. pp. 80-84.

[9] Skeat, "The Origin of the Christian Codex," *ZPE* 102 (1994): 263-68.

[10] Gamble, *Books and Readers*. In fact, the entire topic of the formation of the canon has received renewed interest as seen in the recent volume of essays, *The Canon Debate*, ed. L. M. McDonald and J. A. Sanders (Peabody, Mass.: Hendrickson, 2002).

[11] With a few very small fragments it is impossible to be certain, but even these seem to have come from codices.

roll because of practical considerations. His arguments (while well reasoned) and his evidence (while thorough) fail to explain adequately why it was Christians who noticed this practicality and not others. That is, why was the preference for the codex a Christian phenomenon? Recently, further research has led Skeat to retract some of his earlier assertions about the overwhelming practicality of the codex over the roll. For example, a codex was more frugal (technically using about 26% less papyrus) but not significantly, due to the customary wide margins in a codex. A codex did perhaps make it easier to locate a passage in the middle of a book; yet ancients were quite adept at scrolling a roll and were less familiar with the codex.[12]

In his 1994 article Skeat makes a shift, arguing for a Christian preference for the codex, yet not with his customary "practicality" argument, but with a "deliberate ecclesiastical" rationale. His thesis is built in four steps.

1. A codex was more practical than a scroll, but the difference was only a matter of degree:

    Hitherto, all the advantages claimed for the codex as opposed to the roll have been matters of degree—the codex is more comprehensive, more convenient in use, more suited for ready reference, more economical (because both sides of the writing material were used), and so on.

2. The problem, according to Skeat, is that practicality cannot explain why all copies of the Gospels used the codex format:

    But in the case of the Gospels, representation of the codex is not a matter of degree—it is total, 100%, and the motive for adopting it must have been infinitely more powerful than anything hitherto considered.

3. To explain why Christians had a wholesale adoption of the codex, Skeat contended, one must find something unique about the codex over the roll:

    What we need to do, in fact, is to look for something which the codex could easily do, but which the roll could not, in any circumstances, do. And if the question is posed in this way, we do not have to look very far, for a codex could contain the texts of all four Gospels. No roll could do this.

4. Early Christians then made universal use of the codex, because it was the format holding the sacred stories of the Lord.[13]

Harry Gamble rightly notes that Skeat is tacitly assuming that "nothing short of a Gospel-type document that evoked dominical authority could have predisposed Christians to the codex. Yet this is neither self-evident nor plausible."[14] Gamble then follows by building upon a part of the premise of Skeat's thesis:

---

[12]Skeat goes so far as to concede that an ancient might have preferred a single gospel roll to a single gospel codex for practical reasons; see Skeat, "Origin," p. 264.

[13]Ibid., p. 263.

[14]Gamble, *Books and Readers*, p. 58.

Though the theories of Roberts and Skeat are unconvincing, the basic assumption behind them is sound: there must have been a decisive, precedent-setting development in the publication and circulation of early Christian literature that rapidly established the codex in Christian use, and it is likely that this development had to do with the religious authority accorded to whatever Christian document(s) first came to be known in codex form.[15]

Gamble shares the first three steps of Skeat's argument and then switches from Gospels to letters. He argues that there was a drive to collect the ten letters of Paul, written to seven churches,[16] to emphasize Paul's catholicity. Paul's letters were published in this format to make a theological statement. Such a sevenfold theme works only if all ten letters were contained in one book, whether roll or codex. He then argues, correctly, that only a codex could hold all ten.[17]

While the conclusions of these two theories are different, I am struck that the framework of both theories is the same. Both Skeat and Gamble argue for a theological motivation to publish a specific body of literature: the publisher wanted to present one book, yet for the publication to make the necessary theological point, all the relevant writings (either the four gospels or the letters of Paul) needed to be in one book. The length of the resulting book necessitated the use of a codex rather than a roll. If the publisher had to divide the writings into two scrolls, the theological impact was lost. Since "one book" was the driving force behind the publication, the publisher switched to a codex to keep the writings as a single book. Both men argue this publishing concept set Christians irrevocably upon the path of the codex. Both contend that Christians then encountered authoritative Christian writings in codex form and this cemented the two together in Christian thinking. Form (codex) was wedded to substance (Christian Scripture).

Both theories give rise to the same two observations. First, both theories primarily address the process of publication. Neither theory specifically explains how the material originally was collected (whether for private use or for publication).[18] "Collection" need not be tied to "publication." Second, while there are no necessary objections to a theory

---

[15]Ibid.

[16]I.e., Philemon followed Colossians (to tie them together) and, of course, 1-2 Corinthians and 1-2 Thessalonians; see Gamble, *Books and Readers*, pp. 61-62.

[17]Epp, "Issues" p. 511, notes that a roll would need to be 80 feet long to hold these ten letters of Paul, a practical impossibility.

[18]Skeat does not address the issue of "collecting," nor did Gamble in earlier works. Although how Paul's initial collection arose is not germane to Gamble's theory regarding the publication of Paul's letters, he now suggests this reconstruction here as the preferred one (Gamble, *Books and Readers*, pp. 100-101), as does Witherington, *Paul Quest*, p. 102, Murphy-O'Connor, *Paul the Letter Writer*, and Everett Ferguson, "Factor's Leading to the Selection and Closure of the New Testament Canon," in *The Canon Debate*, ed. Lee Martin McDonald and James A. Sanders (Peabody, Mass.: Hendrickson, 2002), p. 301. Gamble now rightly argues that scholars must separate the discussion of how Paul's letters were collected from the (much more complex) issue of how published editions of Paul's letters arose. See Harry Gamble, "The New Testament Canon: Recent Research and the Status Quaestionis," *The Canon Debate*, ed. Lee Martin McDonald and James A. Sanders (Peabody, Mass.: Hendrickson, 2002), pp. 285-86.

that requires a deliberate, well-designed, well-orchestrated, theologically-motivated drive behind the adoption of the codex, another explanation may be more plausible.[19]

I am positing an unintentional adoption of the codex. Thus, the continued use of the codex was insured because: (1) it was more practical, (2) it enabled a unit to remain a unit rather than be divided into rolls, and (3) form and substance had been wed in the minds of Christians. Since this theory posits that the collection began as a codex, it does not require careful deliberation, an intentional choice, by someone to begin using a codex.

RETAINING PERSONAL COPIES

When letters were collected for publication, an ancient publisher had three sources from which he could collect copies of the letters. He could collect copies (1) from the various recipients, making copies of the dispatched letters, or (2) from various individuals who had partial copies or perhaps even a full set, or (3) from the copies retained by the author himself. It was routinely assumed in scholarly discussions that whoever published Paul's letters did so by first collecting the dispatched letters or partial collections from various churches. The other possibility merits examination.

In chapter ten we demonstrated that ancient letter writers retained copies of their letters.[20] Although this has long been the consensus of classical scholars, it is now being argued in New Testament circles. Thus, Harry Gamble concludes:

> Ancient writers often kept copies of their private letters even when no particular literary merit or topical importance was attached to them; and copies of instructional, administrative letters were all the more likely to be kept.[21]

As for Paul, he unfortunately did not mention retaining copies; yet he also did not refer to most other aspects of the epistolary process. Although there is no direct evidence, one may ask if there is any indirect evidence. Paul valued his letters and encouraged others to read copies (Col 4:16). Are there other clues? Are Romans 4 and Galatians 3 sufficiently similar to argue one was a modification of the other? No. The old theory of an Ephesian destination for Romans would, of course, be easier to argue if Paul had retained a copy of his original, fifteen-chapter letter to Rome.[22] One then argues that Paul took this shorter letter, cut off the generic closing to Rome, and added a stereotypical commendation letter and extended greetings

---

[19]Eldon Epp expressed a similar desire when he responded to the discussion of Gamble's book, arguing that we need a simpler approach than "the big bang theories of Skeat and Gamble" ("New Testament Textual Criticism Seminar," S206, Society of Biblical Literature, Annual Meeting, Nov. 25, 1996). Epp suggested that we consider that ancient teachers, who were on the move, preferred the portable and more durable codices to rolls or tablets.

[20]As another example, when Zenon, the manager of the large estate of Apollonius (the finance minister under Ptolemy II) moved permanently from Alexandria out to the estate, he took with him the entire collection of letters he had retained over the previous four years. See Edgar, *Zenon Papyri,* pp. 25-26.

[21]Gamble, *Books and Readers,* p. 101.

[22]The even shorter version of Romans that has some manuscript attestation can be explained as another dispatched edition.

when he sent a copy to Ephesus. Nevertheless, most scholars—myself included—are not persuaded there was an Ephesian destination for the longer version of Romans.

A stronger case may be made from the Ephesians-Colossians debate, which is the old circular letter hypothesis for Ephesians. As mentioned in chapter ten, often a copy of a letter was retained and a portion reused when a writer wanted to send a more lengthy recounting of information to more than one recipient. Any argument that maintains a literary relationship between Ephesians and Colossians lends support to the point that Paul retained copies of his letters.

The literary relationship of Ephesians and Colossians is still unsettled; yet for the purpose here, most reconstructions, no matter which direction they argue it, posit that Paul worked from his copy of one to prepare the other.[23] Furthermore, the parallel commendations of the letter carrier (Eph 6:21 and Col 4:7-8) are compelling since this was the very type of material secretaries often merely recopied from one letter to another. The letters of Ignatius show the same custom of repeating verbatim a commendation for the letter carrier (Ign. *Phld* 11:2 and *Smyrn* 12:1). This point, however, is not decisive, because Paul could have held the dispatched copy of one until the other was prepared. Both letters were then dispatched together.

The question of the relationship of 1 and 2 Thessalonians might also be helpful to this discussion. If 1 Thessalonians was indeed written first and was the source of some confusion in the Thessalonian church, then it is quite easy to see how Paul would refer back to his copy of 1 Thessalonians when writing his second letter to them. Many scholarly discussions of Paul's letters describe him using or referring to previously written material.

Despite some intriguing possibilities in Paul's letters, we must conclude that Paul gives no decisive evidence that he retained personal copies. Most ancient writers did not give such evidence. Often, it was discovered only by incidental remarks. Thus, we learn that Alexander kept copies of his letters only because of a story where a fire (which he set) destroyed his copies and he had to request new ones. It was very unusual for a writer to make a reference to making a copy of his letter to keep. Even Cicero's remarks to that effect were told in passing as he was making a different point. It is not surprising, then, that Paul made no explicit references to keeping copies of his letters (however, the skimpy evidence available always supports the practice of writer keeping copies[24]). There is no reason to posit Paul as the exception to the custom. I argue it is safe to assume that Paul retained copies of most if not all of his letters, as is beginning to be seen among Pauline scholars.[25]

---

[23]See the discussion in Richards, "Silvanus," pp. 421-22.

[24]When fate caused the personal effects of a Roman soldier in Britain to be preserved (socks, sandals, a piece of his horse's armor), archaeologists also uncovered the soldier's copies of letters he had sent. See the discussion in Alan Bowman, *Life and Letters on the Roman Frontier: Vindolanda and Its People* (New York: Routledge, 1994).

[25]See, among others, Witherington, *Paul Quest*, p. 102; Ellis, *Making*, p. 86; Patzia, *Making of the New Testament*, p. 83; Millard, *Reading and Writing*, p. 76; L. Hartman, "On Reading Others' Letters," p. 139; Gamble, *Books and Readers*, pp. 100-101; and idem, "Recent Research," p. 286.

COPIES AND THE CODEX

As seen in chapter three, there is abundant evidence for tablets being carried about and used for jotting down notes, writing rough drafts and dashing off informal letters. By the first century B.C., small codices of parchment were beginning to usurp the place of the traditional wax tablets,[26] since, like a tablet, a specially prepared parchment was easily washed off and reused. Yet unlike a tablet notebook, a parchment notebook was lighter, less easily smeared, more easily read,[27] more easily handled and more durable.[28] "Notebook" is an accurate description of the early codex. As Gamble notes: "a codex or leaf book was not recognized in antiquity as a proper book. It was regarded as a mere notebook, and its associations were strictly private and utilitarian."[29] Roberts and Skeat offer ample evidence that in the first century these parchment notebooks were used in much the same form and for much the same purpose as the wooden tablets.[30] When Pliny the Younger distinguished between his books and his tablets, Sherwin-White notes that he was referring to rolls and parchment notebooks.[31]

Significant for the discussion here, these parchment codices were also used to retain copies of letters. Cicero, in describing the events of an evening, remarked casually that he was writing a copy of a letter into his notebook while at the meal table.[32] This was not unusual since these notebooks were also used for preparing the rough drafts of letters,[33] later to be written on papyrus or parchment for dispatch.[34]

---

[26]Several hundred wooden leaves of writing material were found at the excavation in the fort of Vindolanda on Hadrian's Wall in Britain. These only survived because they remained waterlogged. They were cut wafer thin and hinged as a codex. Ink was written directly upon the wood. It has recently been suggested that codices of these wooden leaves were more common than either wax tablets or papyrus; see Millard, *Reading and Writing*, pp. 29-30. His assessment may be correct. Hezser, *Jewish Literacy*, pp. 127-30, maintains rabbis also used *pinax* (a Greek term for the Latin *codicilli*), which appear to have been of the same construction (only hinged concertina-style). According to Hezser, the rabbis considered these "a notebook" (p. 129). Whether wax tablet, washable parchment, papyrus, or even wooden leaves, it remains evident that the codex notebook was very popular.

[27]Quintilian 10.3.31 argued for writing directly on wooden tablets with ink rather than drawing in the wax because it was easier to read.

[28]It is still being debated as to whether parchment or papyrus was cheaper. In any case it is safe to assume that these parchment notebooks were not, at least, expensive.

[29]Gamble, *Books and Readers*, pp. 49-50.

[30]Roberts and Skeat, *Codex*, p. 30.

[31]Sherwin-White, *Letters of Pliny*, p. 225. See also Pliny *Epp.* 1.6.1 and 9.6.1. Sherwin-White (p. 100) defined *puguillares* as "either the usual waxed tablets or the recently introduced '*pugillares membranei.*'"

[32]Cic. *Fam.* 9.26.1: "I am jotting down a copy of this letter into my note-book."

[33]According to Roberts and Skeat, *Codex*, p. 11, these notebooks were used for "anything of an impermanent nature—letters, bills, accounts, school exercises, memoranda, *a writer's first draft.*" [Emphasis mine.]

[34]It is quite conceivable that an author might use the final copy of his rough draft as his copy. Thus the "copy" was actually the exemplar for the dispatched version. In the case of the Vindolanda tablets, the rough draft (with only the basic information) appears to have been kept by the soldier as his copy.

Obviously since there are no direct references to Paul retaining copies of his letters, then there would be no direct references to Paul retaining his copies in a codex form. Yet, is there any evidence that Paul used codex notebooks? Yes. According to Roberts and Skeat,[35] it is the familiar passage in 2 Timothy 4:13, where Paul was requesting that the "notebooks" be brought.

COLLECTIONS FROM RETAINED COPIES

There is also evidence that published collections of letters were made from an author's retained copies rather than from collecting the dispatched copies. Obviously, this is difficult to demonstrate. In most situations, how would one know that a published copy in a letter collection was made from the author's personal copy and not from the copy that was mailed? Again, Cicero's verbosity is helpful. Cicero wrote to his friend Atticus (2.12) and commented in the letter that he was not going to hold that particular letter for their usual carrier, a private carrier, to deliver. Rather, he was going to give the letter to the first available carrier, a happenstance carrier. This letter was lost in transit. This is known only because in the following letter to Atticus (2.13), Cicero lamented his decision to use an unfamiliar carrier once he found out from Atticus that the letter had been lost. Well, letters were often lost in transit. What is significant here is that this "lost" letter is part of Cicero's published collection of letters. Since the dispatched copy was lost, this published copy had to have come from Cicero's retained copy. In actuality, it is a well-accepted fact that the collections of Cicero's letters arose from his retained copies.[36]

There is another example to cite. A generation after John, the early church father Ignatius wrote multiple letters to churches in Asia Minor, while making a journey to Rome (where he was martyred). Later, the church at Philippi wished to publish a collection of Ignatius' letters, so they requested copies from Polycarp.[37] Why did Polycarp have copies? He was a contemporary of Ignatius but was not traveling with him at the time. It is possible that Polycarp decided later to gather up copies of the letters Ignatius wrote, but there is no other evidence that Polycarp had any particular interest in the letters of Ignatius. It was the Philippian church who had the interest.

There is another explanation for why Polycarp had copies of Ignatius' letters. At one point during the journey, Ignatius' plans were changed and he had to sail from Asia Minor sooner than expected. He was thus unable to finish writing to various churches in Asia Minor. He wrote to Polycarp, as a fellow church leader, and requested Polycarp to write to the other churches "on this side," meaning Asia Minor.[38]

---

[35]Roberts and Skeat, *Codex*, p. 30.

[36]Cic. *Att.* 13.6.3 indicates that Tiro, Cicero's trusted secretary, kept copies of the letters which were published after Cicero's death; so also Tyrrell and Purser, *Cicero,* 5:18 n. 3; 5:379 n. 5.

[37]Polycarp *Philippians* 13.

[38]Ign. *Polycarp* 8.1.

It would have been natural for Ignatius to send along copies of the letters he had already written to various churches in order to assist Polycarp.[39] In any event, at the very least it can be demonstrated that the Philippian church did not seek copies of the dispatched letters from each church. Rather, they looked for a personal set of copies, in this case Polycarp's, who probably got them from Ignatius. Although the evidence is less than desirable, all available evidence argues ancient publishers used an author's personal set of copies. Thus Harry Gamble cautiously concludes:

> In antiquity, collected editions of letters were nearly always produced by their author or at their author's behest, often from copies belonging to the author.[40]

THE COLLECTION OF PAUL'S LETTERS

The relevant data. Let me summarize the Pauline situation. Paul probably retained copies of his letters. It was customary practice to do so. There is some indication in his letters to this effect, and there is no evidence to suggest Paul did not follow custom. Paul probably retained his copies in a small codex notebook. Again, it was customary practice to do so. There is some indication in his letters to this effect as well. Since it was the most practical option, it was the most common method. Obviously, I am talking plausibilities. Yet all theories dealing with the collection of the Pauline Corpus, by virtue of the evidence, speak in terms of probabilities. The question is always which reconstruction best fits the historical situation.

A suggested historical reconstruction. It is argued here that Paul's letters were not collected by someone circulating among the churches after Paul's death and gathering up copies of dispatched letters. Rather the Pauline Corpus originated with Paul himself.[41] However, it was unintentional; that is, Paul was not seeking to publish his letters but merely retain personal copies, as was customary. Since published collections routinely arose from an author's personal set of copies rather than from re-collecting dispatched letters, there is no reason to posit otherwise for Paul.

Since it was customary to do so, Paul most likely retained the copies of his letters in a parchment codex notebook. The set of copies was likely one of the notebooks he requested Timothy to bring (2 Tim 4:13). Upon his death, this notebook along with other books as well as his personal effects fell into the hands of his disciples. It is even possible Luke was the one who inherited the notebooks, since he was present (2 Tim

---

[39]These letters would include all he had currently written, but not all that he would write before his martyrdom, perhaps helping to explain the existence of at least two recensions of his letters. Nevertheless, the collection of Ignatius' letters is complex, having three different recensions. The middle recension is widely accepted as authentic, but the shorter recension also contains only authentic letters. See Schoedel, *Ignatius*, pp. 3-7.

[40]Gamble, *Books and Readers*, p. 101, and "Recent Research," p. 286.

[41]David Trobisch also argues Paul himself began the process. He argues, however, that Paul himself published a collection.

4:11) and obviously had an interest in writing.[42]

Related issues. Which historical reconstruction best explains the available data? Any theory should be able to explain more than just the immediate situation. What of other historical data related to the formation of the Pauline Corpus? Three additional points may be brought to the discussion: the use of the codex, the "lost" letters, and early references to a Pauline Corpus.

The Christian adoption of the codex. As stated at the outset, most scholars concede that the practicality of a codex can explain why Christians continued to use the codex. Two items are missing: (1) What was the link or "trigger" that caused Christians, rather than others, to adopt the codex? (2) What caused the Christian adoption of the codex to be universal? Arguments from practicality are inadequate. Both Skeat and Gamble offer theories to explain what triggered the use of a codex. Their theories deal primarily with publication. While Gamble's reconstruction of how and why Paul's letters were published is compelling, it is not necessary, or even helpful, to include "collection" in the process.[43]

I do not attempt here to discuss how and why Paul's letters were published, only how they came to be collected. I argue the first collection was unintentional. It is not necessary to posit a theological force driving the formation of the Pauline Corpus (although there may well have been one behind the move to publish them). There is no need to argue for an early appreciation of Paul's letters. At the time of his death, it is possible no one but Paul valued his letters.[44] The set of copies fell into a disciple's hands, along with the more valued notebooks of Scripture excerpts, traditions, etc.

This set of personal copies was, quite unintentionally, in codex form since it was Paul's private notebook. Eventually, individuals or churches began to appreciate Paul's letters more (perhaps after the publication of Acts) and wanted copies. As seen with Ignatius, they sought an existing collection. When copies were ordered, the copyist retained the codex format, since it could hold all the letters in one volume. Even if the codex was not seen as immensely more practical—a recent contention by Skeat—it was just practical enough to keep someone from taking the initiative to alter the format of the exemplar. It is not necessary to have a trigger to explain why the codex form was

---

[42]Many scholars think Luke kept a travel diary. If so, it would almost certainly have been a notebook. The "we passages" include the details one expected of an eyewitness; see Martin Dibelius's critique in A. D. Nock, *Essays on Religion and the Ancient World* (Oxford: Clarendon Press, 1986), pp. 821-32. Furthermore, the types of details (e.g., ports of call, travel times and weather) are the types likely recorded in a travel diary, rather than merely recollected a decade later.

[43]Harry Gamble and David Trobisch have quite divergent opinions of how the published editions arose. Gamble's thesis is to be preferred. See his discussion and critique of Trobisch in Gamble, "Recent Research," p. 285.

[44]Luke's story of Paul (Acts) shows no appreciation for Paul's letters. I personally would argue the Spirit was driving the entire collection process, but that is a faith statement and not a necessary part of this historical reconstruction.

retained, while a trigger is necessary if the codex was a *new* format.[45] When someone
decided to publish Paul's letters, it was easier to retain the codex format, then to divide
the letters onto two or more rolls (which required deciding how to divide them) or to
edit them down to fit on one roll (which required deciding which letters to omit).[46]
Therefore the codex remained. Also, quite likely, form was becoming wed to content.
This reconstruction seems a more plausible explanation for the early Christian adoption
of the codex format.[47]

The "lost letters" of Paul. A second issue related to the formation of the Pauline Corpus
is the problem of the so-called lost letters of Paul. Collection discussions usually swirl
around how certain letters came to be a part of the collection or were excluded from the
collection. A more basic problem is the question of how some letters were "lost." An historical reconstruction needs to offer a reasonable explanation for the loss of the "previous
letter" and the "severe letter"[48] to the Corinthians. This is rarely explained. Were these two
letters not esteemed enough to be included in the collection, when the follower of Paul
came to Corinth to collect letters? Or perhaps the Corinthians themselves objected to the
contents and disposed of the letters? Both options are possible, though the second explanation is more plausible, since the first letter had a least one confusing part in it and the
other letter was painful to the Corinthians (2 Cor 2:4). Perhaps they were thrown away
when leadership was snatched from Paul. Yet, why was 1 Corinthians not lost? It is difficult to reconstruct an historical scenario in Corinth that would lead to the loss of the first
and third letters but the retention of the second (1 Cor).

It is easier to place the problem, not in Corinth, but with Paul. These letters are lost
because copies were not made of them before they were dispatched. Thus Paul's personal
set of copies did not have them. It is impossible to determine why he did not make copies
of these two letters before dispatch. Was it the temporary absence of a secretary perhaps,

---

[45]Gamble's thesis would explain why a *published* edition of Paul's letters retained their original codex
form.

[46]From the letter collections of other ancient writers, such as Cicero (Att. 16.5.5), we see that editors often
began with a truncated canon which was later expanded to include other authentic letters. The same process may well have occurred with Paul. I am at great risk of oversimplifying the complex history of the
Pauline canon. Epp, "Issues," pp. 487-508, demonstrates that manuscripts were quite fluid, including
which letters of Paul were included and even in what order. Since a complete collection of Paul's letters
would require a large codex, it is quite likely initial publications had select letters. Hundreds of years
later, as Paul's popularity grew, demand arose for a complete set. Nevertheless, Gamble's caution ("Recent
Research," p. 286) is well-placed: ". . . all hypotheses are tenuous. The evidence for the history of the
Pauline corpus is so complex and multifaceted that no single theory seems capable of accounting for it
all." I defer to Gamble's and Epp's wise counsel and limit this reconstruction only to the original collection of Paul's letters and not subsequent publications.

[47]In a private observation Larry Hurtado raised the insightful question that, since early notebooks are
parchments while early NT codex manuscripts are papyrus, can we make a connection? I would suggest
that once publication began, copies were made on papyrus because the two advantages of a parchment
notebook (washability and durability) were no longer needed.

[48]Mentioned in 1 Cor 5:9 and 2 Cor 2:3-4.

or the sudden departure of the carrier because of boat schedules?[49] Paul might wish a letter that he had written in urgency and anger, such as often posited for the "severe letter," to be sent immediately, not caring to delay. It is not ascertainable why, but it is quite plausible. Even though writers kept copies of their letters, they did not always make copies of every letter. Even as fastidious as Cicero was, he did not always keep a copy of every letter. Some were missing from his personal set. Again, we know this only because he happened to mention it.[50]

The problem of the "lost" letters was thus on the sending end not the receiving end. It is not necessary to find a reason for the Corinthians to have treasured 1 Corinthians and not the "previous letter." It is not necessary to posit a theological or ecclesiastical cause in Corinth that led to the loss or destruction of some letters but not others. All four letters dispatched to Corinth shared the same fate. The canonical collection of Paul's letters arose from his personal set of copies. This reconstruction seems a more plausible explanation for the loss of two of the four letters to the Corinthian church.

The Pauline Corpus in Rome. There are two early references that seem to indicate a very early collection of Paul's letters. An historical reconstruction needs to be able to explain 2 Peter 3:16 and allusions to multiple letters of Paul in 1 Clement. Typically, the 2 Peter passage is dismissed and the allusions in 1 Clement are minimized.

This troubling passage in 2 Peter has long been the mainstay for pseudonymous theories regarding the letter. Stylistic variations between 1 and 2 Peter, as well as vocabulary concerns, can all be explained by secretarial mediation (or the lack thereof) in one or both of the letters of Peter. Nevertheless, to posit a published collection of Paul's letters in the early 60s, as seemingly implied by 2 Peter 3:16, is often too much for even the most conservative scholar. In the opinion of most scholars, history does not give sufficient indication of an early veneration of Paul. It is difficult to point to someone in the early 60s who was sufficiently motivated to circulate among the churches, gathering up copies of Paul's letters. To argue Paul's letters were treasured early enough for a publication of Paul's letters to be available in the early 60s, early enough for Peter to own a copy, stretches the limits of most conservative scholars.[51]

---

[49]For those of us who see the New Testament as authoritative Scripture, the Spirit superintended the process that led to certain letters being retained in Paul's set and others being dispatched without first being copied.

[50]Cicero's corpus is a massive, 774 letter collection. Because Cicero's publisher, Atticus, wished to make as complete a collection as possible, he solicited copies of dispatched letters that were not in Cicero's personal collection. We see this from Cicero's response to Atticus's request: "So far there is no collection of my letters. But Tiro has about seventy now. And some more will have to be taken from you. But I still will have to go over them and correct them. Then they might be published" (Cic. *Att.* 16.5.5). A desire to publish an exhaustive collection led Atticus to seek letters beyond those retained by Cicero.

[51]E. E. Ellis argues Paul's letters were esteemed from the beginning and quickly elevated to an equal status with OT texts; cf. 2 Thess 2:15 with 1 Thess 2:13; also 1 Cor 14:37; Col 4:16; 1 Thess 5:27 (Ellis, "New Directions in the History of Early Christianity" in *Ancient History in a Modern University*, 2 vols., ed. A. Nobbs [Grand Rapids: Eerdmans, 1997], 2:1-22). Paul expected, even commanded, that his letters be read in church (Col 4:16; see, e.g., Christiaan Beker, *Paul the Apostle: The Triumph of God in Life and*

Yet if Paul retained personal copies, then in the early 60s there was possibly only one "collection" in existence, namely, his personal set of copies. If Peter was in Rome in the early 60s as early tradition states, then he was in the only place where he could have seen copies of Paul's letters. It is not unreasonable to suggest that Peter reviewed what had been written to churches in Asia Minor by Paul before he himself wrote to them, particularly if he was aware that some were confused by Paul's letters. In fact, some commentators on 2 Peter see allusions to specific letters of Paul.[52]

The second early reference is found in 1 Clement. Clement was the leader of the church in Rome during the last decades of the first century. He wrote a letter, 1 Clement, dated about A.D. 96.[53] It is not surprising that 1 Clement alluded to sections of Paul's letter to the Romans. It is more difficult that Clement was knowledgeable of at least one of Paul's letters to the Corinthians.[54] Customarily, it is suggested that Clement, in his travels, had opportunity to visit and hear the Corinthian letters. Yet the numerous allusions to Paul's Corinthian letters suggest more than a casual acquaintance. Certainly Clement could have secured copies for himself while traveling. What becomes more difficult is the way Clement referred to the letter:

> Take up the epistle of the blessed Paul the Apostle. What did he *first* write to you at the beginning of his preaching? With true inspiration he charged you concerning himself and Cephas and Apollos, because even then you had made yourselves partisans.[55]

It is undisputed that Clement was referring to 1 Corinthians. However, he called it Paul's "first" letter to Corinth. If Clement became familiar with the letter while in Corinth, then how did he not know this was actually Paul's second letter to them? In the standard reconstruction, it would be necessary to argue the church in Corinth had not only already lost the "previous letter" but also had already forgotten it.[56] If however Clement was using Paul's personal set of copies, which did not contain the "previous letter," then Clement

---

Thought [Philadelphia: Fortress, 1980], p. 23). According to Ellis: "In the light of this Jewish background in which only canonical Scripture could be read in the synagogue, the reading of New Testament gospels and letters in Christian synagogues implies that they had an inspired and normative, i.e., canonical, status for the congregations using them" ("Directions," p. 19). Nevertheless, I have never heard Ellis contend for a published edition of Paul's letters in the mid-60s.

[52]E.g., recently James Starr claims 2 Peter knew Philippians, 1 Corinthians, Colossians, 1 Thessalonians and Philemon; *Sharers in Divine Nature: 2 Peter 1:4 in Its Hellenistic Context* (Stockholm: Almqvist & Wiksell, 2000), chap. 8.

[53]So Kirsopp Lake, *The Apostolic Fathers*, LCL, 2 vols. (Cambridge, Mass.: Harvard University Press, 1977), 1:3-5.

[54]E.g., 1 Clem. 47. This is widely acknowledged. See e.g., F. F. Bruce, *Paul: Apostle of the Heart Set Free* (Grand Rapids: Eerdmans, 1977), p. 465: Clement "plainly had access to a copy of the letter which we know as 1 Corinthians, for he quotes it freely."

[55]1 Clem 47.1-3 (LCL). [Emphasis mine.]

[56]I read no one who drew this inference, but scholars seldom discuss the issue of how Clement acquired a copy of 1 Corinthians. See *pace*, Bruce, *Paul*, p. 465, who makes no attempt to explain how Clement gained access to a copy.

would mistakenly assume that 1 Corinthians was Paul's first letter to them.

We cannot prove this reconstruction any more than we can prove the assumption that Clement acquired a copy while in Corinth. Yet, it is noteworthy that the two earliest references, suggesting a Pauline Corpus, both originated in Rome. I suggest that Rome was the only place that had a collection of Paul's letters. This reconstruction seems a more plausible explanation for the seemingly very early references to a Pauline Corpus. Patzia summarizes well the question of the formation of the Pauline Corpus: "It is impossible to determine with certainty, . . . we are left to determine which theory best fits the evidence."[57]

CONCLUSIONS FOR PAUL AS A LETTER WRITER

Paul retained copies of most of his letters; it was the standard practice for those who regularly wrote letters because letters were sometimes lost. Also, since letter writers sometimes wanted to reuse parts of a letter in subsequent letters, retaining copies made it possible to refer back to what had been written already.[58]

Letter writers commonly kept their personal set of copies in fashionable "notebooks," parchment codices. Paul's personal copies were likely kept in notebooks, which probably explains his request in 2 Timothy 4:13 for one of the "parchments" (or notebooks). These letters, along with his other personal effects, fell into the hands of a disciple when Paul died. At a later point someone desired to publish his letters; that is, the published collection arose from Paul's personal set of copies. These published editions of Paul's letters retained the codex format, accounting for the early Christian preference for the codex over the scroll.

---

[57]Patzia, *Making of the New Testament,* p. 83.
[58]Gamble, "Recent Research," p. 286, comments, "A dossier of Paul's letters would surely have been useful both to Paul and to his coworkers."

15

INSPIRATION AND FIRST-CENTURY LETTER WRITING

I attempt here to outline how a better understanding of Paul as a letter writer impacts the issue of biblical authority, including inspiration and inerrancy. No attempt is made to be exhaustive, but rather to suggest a way to approach a theology of inspiration in light of what has been said about first-century letter writing.

LETTER WRITING AND INSPIRATION

While quite beyond the scope of this book, the conclusions of this study on Paul as a letter writer can raise questions about the related issues of inspiration and inerrancy. When we envision letter writing as far more than a solitary Paul huddled over a papyrus that was his first and final draft, we raise theological questions about inspiration. When a lone Paul produced a single draft (and this dispatched copy became the canonical copy), inspiration remained a fairly straightforward argument, whether one took a loose view of inspiration or one as tight as inerrancy (a view I personally hold). Nevertheless, the way in which we portray the writing of Paul's letters must impact how we view inspiration. The simplistic view I held as a youth had Paul falling into a trance, awakening to find a completed letter to a church. He merely had to mail the letter.

As Christians become better informed in biblical studies, they often adopt a less robotic view of inspiration, even allowing Paul to use a secretary (as long as he was dictating the letter verbatim). Nonetheless, most Christians do not envision a process that includes coauthors, notes, rough drafts and editing. Since I argue Paul's letters underwent these processes, it is appropriate for me also to address briefly how this impacts the doctrine of inspiration.

Paul as inspired. Older views of inspiration centered upon Paul as the solitary author. Paul was inspired, whether by right of his apostolic authority or some divine anointing. Paul was divinely inspired and thus whatever he preached and wrote was divinely inspired. This view has the advantage of limiting inspiration to a single individual. When Paul died, so did this source of inspired writings. This view helps to bring the canon neatly to a close.

There are, however, two distinct disadvantages to this view. First, anyone or anything that stands between the "inspired author" and his text was a hindrance or an obstacle to inspiration. Thus if Paul used a secretary, the secretary stood between the inspired author and the text. Therefore a priori the influence of the secretary was negative and needed to be reduced as close to zero as possible. Any secretary or coauthor was actually a corrupting influence. Since inspiration started and ended with Paul, the more steps between Paul and the letter, the greater the risk of contamination. In such a view, a video of Paul would have been ideal. We must settle for a letter, but those who subscribe to this view must work to minimize any input other than Paul.

The second disadvantage is that Paul was the source of inspired material. Was his "inspiration faucet" turned on and off? Was anything he wrote a potentially inspired document? Are the "lost letters" lost inspired documents? (In such a case, if Paul's missing letter to the Laodiceans were found under some rock in Asia Minor, it would require reopening the canon since, by definition, it is a priori inspired.) What of a letter Paul wrote to his mother? These questions are not meant to ridicule a particular theological position, but to ask the genuine question of how we differentiate between all of Paul's writings. Some suggest the Spirit has done that for us by only allowing select documents to survive.

Letters as inspired. Early Christians tied "inspiration" to writings and not to individuals. Second Timothy 3:16 claimed that every *writing* rather than every prophet/apostle was inspired by God. In the minds of first-century Christians, inspiration resided in a writing, a scripture. In such a view, Paul was not inspired, but 1 Corinthians, for example, was inspired. Inspiration was placed on the final product not the initial source. While this view resolves the problems of the previous view, it does create questions of its own. In this book I have described a writing process for 1 Corinthians that may be visualized as in figure 15.1.

The question becomes, "Where did inspiration occur?" Or perhaps more specifically, "Where did inspiration end?" Was Sosthenes inspired? Did inspiration include the secretary? Did it include the editing process? Did inspiration include how the reader read aloud the letter? Did it include his explanations or his answers to the Corinthians' questions? When I read 1 Corinthians today and grasp meaning from it, is that also inspired? Where do we draw the ending line in our definition of *inspiration*? To use terms from systematic theology, when does *inspiration* end and *illumination* begin?

A suggested model of inspiration. Theology should arise from the data and not dictate historical reconstructions. Since Paul's letters were written in this way, our theology of inspiration also should address the situation. When looking at the writing process for Paul's letters, where did inspiration occur? Let us ask some questions using the model shown in figure 15.2.

This has additional implications for Christians who adopt a theological position called *inerrancy.* Inerrancy is usually maintained for the immediate product of inspiration; that is, inerrancy is usually argued only as far as the process of inspiration and no further. We can ask further questions of our model, as shown in figure 15.3.

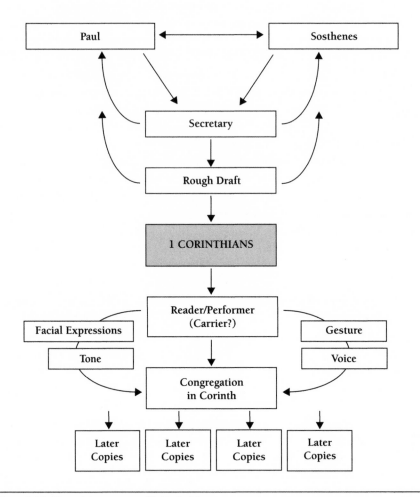

Figure 15.1. The writing process of 1 Corinthians

Obviously, the issue of inspiration (as well as inerrancy) is simpler when a solitary author produced a single draft. Unfortunately, first-century letter writers did not compose letters in this way, so our understanding of inspiration needs to incorporate letter-writing techniques of the first century.

Perhaps a better approach is not to argue that Paul was inspired, but that Paul and his other team members were "divinely prepared." Their background, education, experiences, even their genetic makeup was part of God's divine plan. Paul was not an "inspiration canon" walking around the first-century world, so that whenever he picked up a pen, an inspired document ensued. Rather, Paul was divinely prepared, as were his coauthors and secretary.

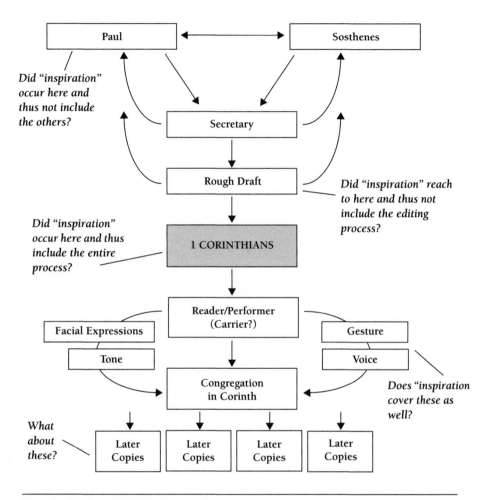

Figure 15.2. Where did inspiration occur?

The local situation was also divinely prepared. Problems, for example, arose in Corinth (as they do in any church); however, the problems in Corinth were divinely selected so that the responses of Paul's team would be appropriate for Christians in all places at all times. On most Sundays, a minister delivers a "word from the Lord" to that particular church at that particular time. Paul did the same in Corinth. Nevertheless, the situation in Corinth and the responses of Paul's team were divinely selected to result in a letter (a word from the Lord) that was also relevant to all Christians in all places at all times.[1] Paul

---

[1]The message is still culturally conditioned and must be understood in its original context. Nevertheless, with "inspired documents" there are applications that are relevant for all generations. See the methodology described in Duvall and Hays, *Grasping God's Word*.

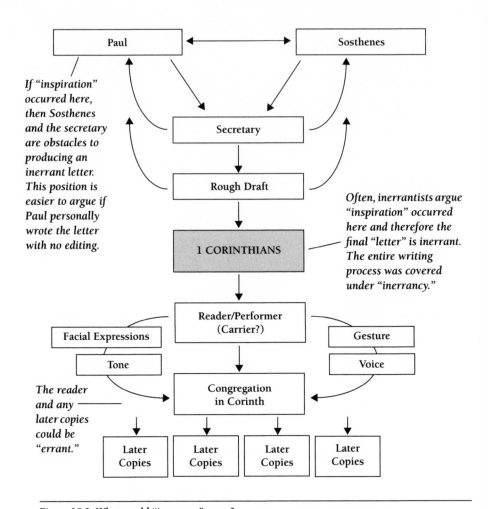

Figure 15.3. What would "inerrancy" cover?

and his team were prepared with background, education, temperament, etc., so that when they heard what was happening in the churches in Galatia, they—especially Paul—responded with a fiery letter, blasting the Judaizers who were confusing those churches, resulting in Galatians, a divinely inspired letter (see figure 15.4).

A divinely prepared person(s), responding to a divinely prepared situation, produced an inspired letter. Thus, not everything Paul ever wrote was inspired. Not everything ever written to Corinth was inspired; only 1-2 Corinthians were inspired. If either the divinely prepared person(s) or the divinely prepared situation was missing, an inspired document did not result. Other letters Paul wrote to Corinth addressed a situation that was not divinely prepared to create an inspired document. Only when the right persons encoun-

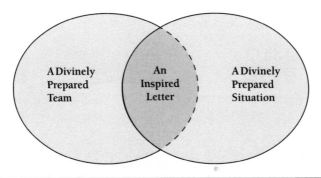

Figure 15.4. Two necessary ingredients for an inspired letter

tered the right situation, did we receive an inspired document. Finding another letter of Paul would be a wonderful historical discovery, but would not by definition require reopening the canon.

In the end, a more complete understanding of the way first-century writers composed letters does not pose new difficulties to understanding inspiration or inerrancy. Theologians who maintain inspiration or inerrancy for Paul's letters can continue to argue these positions even though the letter-writing process was more complex than perhaps previously thought.

CONCLUSIONS FOR PAUL AS A LETTER WRITER

The entire letter-writing process can be considered "inspired." Inspiration does not require that a single writer produce a single draft of a letter. A team, led by Paul, using a secretary, making multiple drafts can all be part of the divinely supervised process which resulted in an inspired letter. We need only consider 1 Corinthians (regarded as inspired by most Christians), which tells us that it was written by Paul and Sosthenes (1 Cor 1:1) with the aid of a secretary (1 Cor 16:21).

CONCLUSION

Understanding how Paul wrote his letters helps remove Paul from the pedestal that lifts him out of the real world. The Paul who wrote "Imitate me" is often described in terms that place him well beyond the reach of us mortals. For many Christians today, it seems impossible to imitate Paul. Yet, the more we can see a flesh-and-blood Paul scribbling notes under a shade tree during an afternoon rest stop or huddled with a colleague and a secretary in the living room of a third-story apartment on a cold, blustery winter's day, the more we have a real person whose life we can strive to emulate. A Paul who argued with colleagues over how something should be worded, who modified material from sermons to use in other presentations, who juggled writing with preaching and ministry, is a Paul that many Christians can easily identify with, and even follow.

First-century letter writing is now gaining new scholarly attention. Data from related fields are finding their way into these studies, and allowing us to paint a more accurate picture of Paul as a letter writer. In this work, I hoped to have achieved four results.

First, I wanted to highlight some aspects of first-century letter writing that I think have been underemphasized in modern studies of Paul:

a. Many of us unconsciously imagine Paul writing his letters in a way that mimics how we modern Westerners write letters. Such an anachronism leads to several misconceptions about Paul. He is often pictured as writing in solitude, producing a single, unedited draft. If our picture grants Paul a secretary, we imagine Paul dictating word for word. After he finished his dictation, he signed that original draft and sent it off.

b. I argued that the named cosenders of Paul's letters were contributors to the letter's content; that is, they were coauthors. Material from a coauthor was non-Pauline but not un-Pauline.

c. Paul used a secretary to write his letters. This secretary was likely contracted, rather than being a conscripted team member. Secretaries had specialized skills. Paul's various secretaries had minor influences on the text, such as in some grammar and vocabulary.

d. Paul's letters contained preformed material such as Old Testament quotations, excerpts from early Christian hymns and traditions, and material Paul or another had composed previously.

e. As the leader of the team, Paul accepted full responsibility for the content of his letters. He checked it carefully because it had his authorization.

Second, I suggested that procedures and customs of first-century letter writing allow some possibilities that have not been considered in many analyses of Paul's letters:

a. Paul's letters likely went through multiple drafts involving editing material and even inserting preformed material.

b. Paul and his team were constantly preparing and polishing material.

c. Without external evidence (manuscript attestation), material injected by a coauthor into a letter would be indistinguishable from a post-Pauline interpolation.

d. Paul likely retained copies of his letters. These copies were usually kept in notebooks. The first collection of Paul's letters was probably his personal set, which he had with him when he died. I suggested that published collections of Paul's letters arose from this set and retained the notebook format (codex) of the original, thus explaining the early Christian preference for the codex.

Third, I presented some rough estimates concerning some mechanics and expenses involved in Paul writing a letter. I attempted to express those estimates in today's dollars, in order to be more meaningful to the modern reader:

a. Paul's letters were much longer than the typical letter of his day, including the letters of the literary elite, such as Seneca or Cicero. Initially, the church at Rome probably was more stunned by the length of Paul's letter than by its contents.

b. Writing out a copy of a letter took time. To use an example, Paul's letter to the Corinthians (1 Cor) probably took a secretary about two days to write out a single copy.

c. If 1 Corinthians was prepared with a minimum of editing, it still cost (in today's dollars) about $2,000 to write. This estimate does not include the expense of sending someone like Titus on an extended journey to deliver it.

Fourth and lastly, I raised what I think are some intriguing questions in the hope of stimulating some new discussions or directions of study:

a. Paul identifies himself in the letter address in a manner that indicates he considers himself a member of a new household, the household of Christ. Paul often argues there are no longer differences such as Jew and Greek, slave and free. Since all Christians have been purchased into this new household, old allegiances or hostilities have passed away. Is Paul contending that we are all one in Christ, because we are all slaves of the same master and thus members of the same household? Should that be how we identify ourselves?

b. Did Paul use Tertius (a secretary) because Romans was so long, or was Romans so long because Paul used Tertius?

c. Did Paul's theology develop over time and thus his letters to churches became gradually longer and more complex, or did his letters to churches become gradually longer and more complex as he developed team members who could carry and explain his letters?

d. 1 Corinthians, for instance, describes itself as sent by Paul and Sosthenes (1:1) and written down by a secretary (16:21). How is one's view of inspiration (or inerrancy) impacted by a better understanding of coauthors, secretaries and other aspects of first-century letter writing? Are coauthors and secretaries obstacles to be overcome by the Spirit or were they also vital elements of the divine process?

e. If Paul's letter-writing practices included rough drafts, editing, dispatched copies and retained copies, what do we mean when we speak of an "original"?

In this book we examine the actual mechanics of how Paul wrote his letters. The findings influence how we view Paul. It may complicate some exegetical discussions and even require some revision of other related topics. Debate over Pauline authorship or arguments for interpolations (or dislocations), discussions of rhetoric, all need to be informed by a realistic appraisal of first-century letter writing. Whether considered or unconscious, the image we hold of Paul as a letter writer carries with it certain assumptions that do affect how we interpret Paul's letters.[1]

---

[1]For example, the ideas in this book contribute one more straw on the back of an apparently collapsing camel carrying the theories that some of Paul's letters were written by disciples after Paul's death. We have seen that many of the arguments used to support this view (pseudonymous authorship) can be explained by common procedures in first-century letter writing. Any discussion must seriously consider the role of coauthors and secretaries, as well as the heavy use of preformed traditional material in the Pastorals. Scholars seem reluctant to acknowledge even secretarial influences, a complaint made nearly 70 years ago by H. St.-J. Thackeray (*Josephus the Man and the Historian* [New York: Ktav, 1929], pp. 100, 105, 144), and echoed currently (2001) in Johnson's Anchor Bible commentary on 1-2 Timothy. See also the arguments of E. E. Ellis, *Pauline Theology: Ministry and Society* (Grand Rapids: Eerdmans, 1989), pp. 104-7. I further question the usual assertions that pseudonymous letters were (a) common, (b) written as a compliment to the author and (c) usually composed by his friends/followers. I see no evidence to support this. These assumptions about pseudonymity have led to a myth of innocent apostolic Pseudepigrapha; see E. E. Ellis, "Traditions," pp. 237-53. A letter should be termed "Pauline" or "Pseudo-Pauline." The euphemistic or conciliatory "Deutero-Pauline" label seems unsubstantiated. In fact, the term "pseudonymity" needs more clarification as demonstrated by Kent Clarke, "The Problem of Pseudonymity in Biblical Literature and Its Implications for Canon Formation," *The Canon Debate*, pp. 440-68; and Terry Wilder, *Pseudonymity*.

BIBLIOGRAPHY

Achtemeier, Paul. "*Omne verbum sonat:* The New Testament and the Oral Environment of Late Western Antiquity." *Journal of Biblical Literature* 109 (1990): 3-27.

Andrews, Mary E. "Paul, Philo, and the Intellectuals." *Journal of Biblical Literature* 53 (1934): 150-66.

Bagnall, Roger S., and Peter Derow, eds. *Greek Historical Documents: The Hellenistic Period.* Society of Biblical Literature Sources for Biblical Studies, no. 16. Chico, Calif.: Scholars, 1981.

Bahr, Gordon J. "Paul and Letter Writing in the First Century." *Catholic Biblical Quarterly* 28 (1966): 465-77.

———. "The Subscriptions in the Pauline Letters." *Journal of Biblical Literature* 87 (1968): 27-41.

Banks, Robert J. *Paul's Idea of Community.* Rev. ed. Peabody, Mass.: Hendrickson, 1994.

Barnett, Paul. *Jesus and the Rise of Early Christianity: A History of New Testament Times.* Downers Grove, Ill.: InterVarsity Press, 2002.

———. *The Second Epistle to the Corinthians.* New International Commentary on the New Testament. Grand Rapids: Eerdmans, 1997.

Barrett, Charles Kingsley. *A Commentary on the First Epistle to the Corinthians.* Black's New Testament Commentaries. London: A. & C. Black, 1968. Reprint, Peabody, Mass.: Hendrickson, 1993.

———. *Freedom and Obligation: A Study of the Epistle to the Galatians.* Philadelphia: Westminster Press, 1985.

Barth, Markus. "Traditions in Ephesians." *New Testament Studies* 30 (1984): 3-25.

Beilner, Wolfgang. "*epistolē.*" *Exegetical Dictionary of the New Testament.* 3 vols. Edited by Horst Balz and Gerhard Schneider. Translated by James Thompson and John Medendorp, 2:38-39. Grand Rapids: Eerdmans, 1991.

Beker, Christiaan. *Paul the Apostle: The Triumph of God in Life and Thought.* Philadelphia: Fortress, 1980.

Bell, Harold Idris. "Some Private Letters of the Roman Period from the London Collection." *Revue Egyptologique,* new series 1 (1919): 203-6.

Benoit, P., Joseph Tandeusz, J. T. Milik and Roland de Vaux. *Les grottes de Murabbaʿat.* Discoveries in the Judean Desert Series 2. Oxford: Oxford University Press, 1961.

Berry, Paul. *Roman Handwriting at the Time of Christ.* Studies in Classics 15. Lewiston, N.Y.: Edwin Mellen Press, 2001.

Betz, Hans Dieter. "2 Cor 6:14—7:1: An Anti-Pauline Fragment?" *Journal of Biblical Literature* 92 (1973): 88-108.

———. *Galatians: A Commentary on Paul's Letter to the Churches in Galatia.* Hermeneia Series. Minneapolis: Fortress, 1979.

Bligh, John. *Galatians: A Discussion of St. Paul's Epistle.* Householder Commentary Series. London: T & T Clark, 1969.

Boge, Herbert. *Griechische Tachygraphie und Tironische Noten: Ein Handbuch der antiken und Mittelalterlichen Schnellschrift.* Berlin: Akademie Verlag, 1973.

Bornkamm, Günther. "The Letter to the Romans as Paul's Last Will and Testament." In *The Romans Debate,* edited by Karl Paul Donfried, pp. 17-31. Minneapolis: Augsburg, 1977; 3rd ed., Peabody, Mass.: Hendrickson, 2001.

Botha, Pieter J. J. "The Verbal Art of the Pauline Letters: Rhetoric, Performance and Presence." In *Rhetoric and the New Testament: Essays from the 1992 Heidelberg Conference*, edited by Stanley Porter and Thomas Olbricht, pp. 409-28. Journal for the Study of the New Testament Supplement Series 90. Sheffield: JSOT Press, 1993.

Bowman, Alan. *Life and Letters on the Roman Frontier: Vindolanda and Its People.* New York: Routledge, 1994.

Bowman, Alan, and J. David Thomas. *The Vindolanda Writing Tablets.* London: British Museum Publication, 1995.

Bradley, David. "The *Topos* as a Form in the Pauline *Paraenesis.*" *Journal of Biblical Literature* 72 (1953): 238-46.

Bruce, Frederick Fyvie. "Origins of the New Testament Canon." *New Dimensions in New Testament Study.* Edited by Richard Longenecker and Merrill Tenney. Grand Rapids: Zondervan, 1974.

———. *Paul: Apostle of the Heart Set Free.* Grand Rapids: Eerdmans, 1977.

Carrez, Maurice. "Le 'nous' en 2 Corinthiens: Contribution à l'étude de l'apostolocité dans 2 Corinthiens." *New Testament Studies* 26 (1980): 474-86.

Carson, D. A., Douglas J. Moo and Leon Morris. *An Introduction to the New Testament.* Grand Rapids: Zondervan, 1992.

Casson, Lionel. *Ships and Seamanship in the Ancient World.* Princeton, N.J.: Princeton University Press, 1971.

———. *Travel in the Ancient World.* Baltimore: Johns Hopkins University Press, 1994.

Catchpole, David R. "Tradition History." *New Testament Interpretation: Essays on Principles and Methods,* ed. I. Howard Marshall, pp. 165-80. Grand Rapids: Eerdmans, 1972.

Charlesworth, James H. *The Pesharim and Qumran History: Chaos or Consensus?* Grand Rapids: Eerdmans, 2002.

Cicero, Marcus Tullius. *Letters to Atticus [Epistulae ad Atticum].* Edited and translated by Eric Otto Winsteadt. 3 vols. The Loeb Classical Library Latin Series. Cambridge, Mass.: Harvard University Press, 1966-1970.

———. *Letters to His Friends [Epistulae ad Familiares].* Edited and translated by W. Glynn Williams. 3 vols. The Loeb Classical Library Latin Series. Cambridge, Mass.: Harvard University Press, 1965-1972.

———. *Letters to Quintus [Epistulae ad Quintum Fratrem], Brutus [ad Brutum]; Comment. Petit.; Ep. ad Octav.* Edited and translated by William Armistead Falconer. Enlarged ed. The Loeb Classical Library Latin Series. Cambridge, Mass.: Harvard University Press, 1972.

Clarke, Kent D. "The Problems of Pseudonymity in Biblical Literature and Its Implications for Canon Formation." *The Canon Debate,* edited by Lee Martin McDonald and James A. Sanders, pp. 440-68. Peabody, Mass.: Hendrickson, 2002.

Conzelmann, Hans. *1 Corinthians*. Translated by James W. Leitch. Hermeneia Series. Philadelphia: Fortress, 1975.

Cope, Lamar. *First Corinthians 8—10: Continuity or Contradiction*. Anglican Theological Review Supplement Series 11. Evanston, Ill.: Anglican Theological Review, 1990.

Corpus Inscriptionum Graecarum [CIG]. 4 vols. Edited by Augustus Boeckhius (vols. 1-2), Ioannes Franzius (vol. 3), and Ernestus Curtius and Adolphus Kirchoff (vol. 4). Studia Epigraphica: Auellen und Abhandlungen zur griechischen Epigraphik. New York: Georg Olms, 1977.

Corpus Inscriptionum Latinarum [CIL]. Edited by Attilio Degrassi. Berolini: De Gruyter, 1965.

Costa, C. D. N. *Greek Fictional Letters: A Selection with Introduction, Translation and Commentary*. Oxford: Oxford University Press, 2001.

Cribiore, Raffaella. *Gymnastics of the Greek Mind: Greek Education in Hellenistic and Roman Egypt*. Princeton, N.J.: Princeton University Press, 2001.

Davies, William David. *Paul and Rabbinic Judaism*. 4th ed. Philadelphia: Fortress, 1980.

Deissmann, Adolf. *Bible Studies*. 2nd ed. Translated by Alexander Grieve. Edinburgh: T & T Clark, 1909.

————. *Light from the Ancient East: The New Testament Illustrated by Recently Discovered Texts of the Graeco-Roman World*. Translated by Lionel R. M. Strachan. London: Hodder & Stoughton, 1912. Reprint, Grand Rapids: Baker, 1978.

————. *St. Paul: A Study in Social and Religious History*. Translated by Lionel R. M. Strachan. London: Hodder & Stoughton, 1912.

Dibelius, Martin. *An Philemon*. 3rd ed. Edited by Heinrich Greeven. Handbuch zum Neuen Testament Series. Tübingen: Mohr, 1953.

Dio Cassius Cocceianus. *Roman History*. 9 vols. Edited and translated by Earnest Cary. The Loeb Classical Library Greek Series. Vols. 1-6, New York: Putnam's Sons; vols. 7-9, Cambridge, Mass.: Harvard University Press, 1914-1955.

Diogenes Laertius. *Lives of Eminent Philosophers*. Edited and translated by Robert Drew Hicks. The Loeb Classical Library Greek Series. Cambridge, Mass.: Harvard University Press, 1925.

Donfried, Karl Paul. "False Presuppositions in the Study of Romans." In *The Romans Debate*, edited by Karl Paul Donfried, pp. 120-48. Minneapolis: Augsburg, 1977; 3rd ed., Peabody, Mass.: Hendrickson, 2001.

Doty, William. *Letters in Primitive Christianity*. Guides to Biblical Scholarship, New Testament Series. Philadelphia: Fortress, 1973.

————. "The Epistle in Late Hellenism and Early Christianity: Developments, Influences, and Literary Form." Ph.D. diss., Drew University, 1966.

Duvall, J. Scott, and J. Daniel Hays. *Grasping God's Word: A Hands-on Approach to Reading, Interpreting, and Applying the Bible*. Grand Rapids: Zondervan, 2001.

Edwards, Gene. *The Gaius Diary*. First-Century Diaries Series 5. Wheaton, Ill.: Tyndale House, 2002.

————. *The Priscilla Diary*. First-Century Diaries Series 4. Wheaton, Ill.: Tyndale House, 2001.

————. *The Silas Diary*. First-Century Diaries Series 1. Wheaton, Ill.: Tyndale House, 1998.

————. *The Timothy Diary*. First-Century Diaries Series 3. Wheaton, Ill.: Tyndale House, 2000.

————. *The Titus Diary*. First-Century Diaries Series 2. Wheaton, Ill.: Tyndale House, 1999.

Ellingworth, Paul. *The Epistle to the Hebrews*. New International Greek Testament Commentary Series. Grand Rapids: Eerdmans, 1993.

Ellis, E. Earle. "The Authorship of the Pastorals: A Resume and Assessment of Recent Trends." In *Paul and His Recent Interpreters*. Grand Rapids: Eerdmans, 1961. Reprint, Eugene, Ore.: Wipf & Stock, 2004.

———. *The Making of the New Testament Documents*. Leiden: Brill, 2002.

———. "Midrash *Pesher* in Pauline Hermeneutics." *Prophecy and Hermeneutic in Early Christianity: New Testament Essays*, pp. 3-22. Wissenschaftliche Untersuchungen zum Neuen Testament 18. Tübingen: Mohr, 1978; reprint, Grand Rapids: Eerdmans, 1980. Reprint, Eugene, Ore.: Wipf & Stock, 2003.

———. "New Directions in the History of Early Christianity." In *Ancient History in a Modern University*. 2 vols. Edited by A. Nobbs, 2:1-22. Grand Rapids: Eerdmans, 1997.

———. "Pastoral Letters" In *Dictionary of Paul and His Letters*, edited by Gerald F. Hawthorne, Ralph P. Martin and Daniel G. Reid, pp. 658-66. Downers Grove, Ill.: InterVarsity Press, 1993.

———. *Pauline Theology: Ministry and Society*. Grand Rapids: Eerdmans, 1989. Reprint, Lanham, Md.: University Press of America, 1998.

———. *Paul's Use of the Old Testament*. Edinburgh: Oliver & Boyd, 1957; Grand Rapids: Baker, 1957, 1981. Reprint, Eugene, Ore.: Wipf & Stock, 2003.

———. "The Silenced Wives of Corinth (1 Cor 14:34-35)." *New Testament Textual Criticism and Its Significance for Exegesis* (Festschrift, Bruce M. Metzger), eds. Eldon Jay Epps and Gordon D. Fee. Oxford: Clarendon Press, 1981.

———. "Traditions in 1 Corinthians." *New Testament Studies* 32 (1986): 481-502.

———. "Traditions in the Pastoral Epistles." In *Early Jewish and Christian Exegesis* (Festschrift, William Hugh Brownlee), edited by Craig A. Evans and William F. Stinespring. Atlanta: Scholars Press, 1987.

Epictetus. *The Discourses as Reported by Arrian [Epicteti Dissertationes], the Manual, and Fragments*. Edited and translated by William Abbott Oldfather, 2 vols. The Loeb Classical Library: Greek Series. Cambridge, Mass.: Harvard University Press, 1925-1928.

Epp, Eldon. "New Testament Papyrus Manuscripts and Letter Carrying in Greco-Roman Times." In *The Future of Early Christianity*, edited by Birger A. Pearson, pp. 35-56. Minneapolis: Fortress, 1991.

———. "Issues in the Interrelation of New Testament Textual Criticism and Canon."In *The Canon Debate*, edited by Lee Martin McDonald and James A. Sanders, pp. 485-515. Peabody, Mass.: Hendrickson, 2002.

Erman, Adolf. *Die Literatur der Aegypter.* Leipzig: Teubner, 1923.

Eschlimann, Jean-Paul A. "La rédaction des epîtres pauliniennes: d'après une comparison avec les letters profanes de son temps." *Revue Biblique* 53 (1946): 185-96.

Eusebius. *The Ecclesiastical History [Historia ecclesiastica]*. 2 vols. Edited and translated by Kirsopp Lake (vol. 1) and John Ernest Leonard Oulton (vol. 2). The Loeb Classical Library Greek Series. Cambridge, Mass.: Harvard University Press, 1980.

Exler, Francis X. J. *The Form of the Ancient Greek Letter: A Study in Greek Epistolography.* Washington, D.C.: Catholic University of America Press, 1922.

Fee, Gordon D. *The First Epistle to the Corinthians*. New International Commentary on the New Testament. Grand Rapids: Eerdmans, 1987.

———. *Philippians*. New International Commentary on the New Testament. Grand Rapids: Eerdmans, 1995.

Ferguson, Everett. "Factors Leading to the Selection and Closure of the New Testament Canon: A Survey of Some Recent Studies." In *The Canon Debate*, edited by Lee Martin McDonald and James A. Sanders, pp. 295-320. Peabody, Mass.: Hendrickson, 2002.

Fitzmyer, Joseph A. *Pauline Theology: A Brief Sketch.* Englewood Cliffs, N.J.: Prentice-Hall, 1967.

———. "Qumran and the Interpolated Paragraph in 2 Cor 6, 14—7, 1." *Catholic Biblical Quarterly* 23 (1961): 271-80.

French, David. "Acts and the Roman Roads of Asia Minor." In *The Book of Acts in Its Greco-Roman Setting*, edited by David Gill and Conrad Gempf, pp. 49-58. Vol. 2 in The Book of Acts in Its First Century Setting Series. Grand Rapids: Eerdmans, 1994.

Funk, Robert. "The Apostolic *Parousia*: Form and Significance." In *Christian History and Interpretation: Studies Presented to John Knox*, edited by William Reuben Farmer, Charles Francis Digby Moule and Richard R. Niebuhr, pp. 249-69. Cambridge: University Press, 1967.

Furnish, Victor. "Pauline Studies." *The New Testament and Its Modern Interpreters,* edited by Eldon Jay Epp and George MacRae, pp. 321-50. Philadelphia: Fortress, 1989.

Gamble, Harry. *Books and Readers in the Early Church: A History of Early Christian Texts.* New Haven, Conn.: Yale University Press, 1995.

———. *New Testament Canon: Its Making and Meaning.* Guides to Biblical Scholarship, New Testament Series. Philadelphia: Fortress, 1985. Reprint, 2002.

———. "New Testament Canon: Recent Research and the Status Quaestionis." In *The Canon Debate*, edited by L. M. McDonald and J. A. Sanders, pp. 267-94. Peabody, Mass.: Hendrickson, 2002.

Gardthausen, Viktor Emil. "Zur Tachygraphie der Griechen." *Hermes* 2 (1876): 444-45.

Gerhard, Gustav Adolf. "Untersuchungen zur Geschichte des griechischen Briefes, I. Die Anfangsformel." *Philologus* 64 (1905): 27-65.

Goodspeed, Edgar J. *New Solutions to New Testament Problems.* Chicago: University of Chicago Press, 1927.

Gorman, Michael. *Apostle of the Crucified Lord: A Theological Introduction to Paul and His Letters.* Grand Rapids: Eerdmans, 2004.

Güting, Eberhard W., and David L. Mealand. *Asyndeton in Paul: A Text-Critical and Statistical Enquiry into Pauline Style.* Studies in the Bible and Early Christianity 39. Lewiston, N.Y.: Mellen Press, 1998.

Haenchen, Ernst. *Acts of the Apostle.* Translated by Bernard Noble and Gerald Shinn. Oxford: Basil Blackwell, 1971.

Haran, Menahem. "Book-Scrolls in Israel in Pre-Exilic Times." *Journal of Jewish Studies* 33 (1982): 161-73.

Harris, William V. *Ancient Literacy.* Cambridge, Mass.: Harvard University Press, 1989.

Harrison, Percy Neal. *Polycarp's Two Epistles to the Philippians.* London: Cambridge University Press, 1936.

———. *The Problem of the Pastorals.* London: Oxford University Press, 1921.

Hartman, L. "On Reading Others' Letters." *Harvard Theological Review* 79 (1986): 137-46.

Hartmann, Karl. "Arrian und Epiktet." *Neue Jahrbücher für das klassische Altertum, Geschichte und deutsche Literatur und für Pädogogik* 8 (1905): 248-75.

Havelock, Eric. *The Literate Revolution in Greece and Its Cultural Consequences.* Princeton, N.J.: Princeton University Press, 1982.

Hays, Richard B. *First Corinthians.* Interpretation Series. Louisville, Ky.: Westminster John Knox, 1997.

Hemer, Colin J. "The Address of 1 Peter." *Expository Times* 89 (1978): 239-43.

Hermansen, Gustav. *Ostia: Aspects of Roman City Life.* Edmonton: University of Alberta Press, 1981.

Henshaw, Thomas. *New Testament Literature.* London: Hodder and Stoughton, 1963.

Hezser, Catherine. *Jewish Literacy in Roman Palestine.* Texts and Studies in Ancient Judaism 81, edited by Martin Hengel and Peter Shäfer. Tübingen: Mohr/Siebeck, 2001.

Hitchcock, F. R. Montgomery. "The Use of *graphein*." *Journal of Theological Studies,* old series, 31 (1930): 271-75.

Hock, Ronald. "Writing in the Greco-Roman World." Society of Biblical Literature forum (May 10, 2004). Online: http://www.sbl-site.org/Article.aspx?ArticleId=264.

Hodgson, Robert. "Paul the Apostle and First Century Tribulation Lists." *Zeitschrift für die neutestamentliche Wissenschaft* 74 (1983): 1-2, 59-80.

Horsley, Richard A. "*Gnosis* in Corinth: 1 Corinthians 8.1-6." *New Testament Studies* 27 (1980): 32-51.

Hunt, Arthur S. and Campbell Cowan Edgar. *Select Non-Literary Papyri [PSel.].* 2 vols. The Loeb Classical Library Greek Series. Cambridge, Mass.: Harvard University Press, 1932-1934.

Hunter, Archibald M. *Paul and His Predecessors.* 2nd ed. London: SCM, 1961.

Ignatius of Antioch. *The Letters of Ignatius.* In *The Apostolic Fathers.* 2 vols. Translated by Kirsopp Lake. The Loeb Classical Library Greek Series. Cambridge, Mass.: Harvard University Press, 1977.

Jeremias, Joachim. "Chiasmus in den Paulusbriefen." *Zeitschrift für die neutestamentliche Wissenschaft* 49 (1958): 139-56.

Jewett, Robert. "The Redaction and Use of an Early Christian Confession in Romans 1:3-4." In *The Living Text,* edited by Dennis E. Groh. Lanham, Md.: University Press of America, 1985.

———. *A Chronology of Paul's Life.* Philadelphia: Fortress, 1979.

Johnson, Luke Timothy. *The First and Second Letters to Timothy.* Anchor Bible Commentary Series 35A. New York: Doubleday, 2001.

Johnson, R. R. "The Role of Parchment in Graeco-Roman Antiquity." Ph.D. dissertation, University of California, 1968.

Judge, Edwin A. *Rank and Status in the World of the Caesars and St. Paul.* University of Cantebury Series 29. Christchurch: University of Cantebury, 1982.

Keck, Leander. *Paul and His Letters.* Proclamation Commentaries. 2nd ed. Minneapolis: Fortress, 1988.

Kelber, Werner. *The Oral and the Written Gospel: The Hermeneutics of Speaking and Writing in the Synoptic Tradition, Mark, Paul, and Q.* Philadelphia: Fortress, 1983.

Kennedy, George. *Progymnasmata: Greek Textbooks of Prose Composition and Rhetoric.* Writings from the Greco-Roman World Series. Atlanta: Society of Biblical Literature, 2003.

Kenny, Anthony. *A Stylometric Study of the New Testament.* Oxford: Clarendon, 1986.

Kim, C. -H. "Index of Greek Papyrus Letters." *Semeia* 22 (1981): 107-12.

Kim, Seyoon. "Imitatio Christi (1 Cor 11:1): How Paul Imitates Jesus Christ in Dealing with Idol Food." *Bulletin for Biblical Research* 13 (2003): 193-226.

Koskenniemi, Heikki. *Studien zur Idee und Phraseologie des griechischen Briefes bis 400 n. Chr.* Helsinki:

Suomalainen Tiedeakatemia, 1956.

Kümmel, Werner. *Introduction to the New Testament*. Rev. ed. Translated by H. C. Kee. Nashville: Abingdon, 1975.

Lake, Kirsopp. *The Apostolic Fathers*. Vol 1. The Loeb Classical Library Greek Series. Cambridge, Mass.: Harvard University Press, 1977.

Lewis, Naphtali. *Papyrus in Classical Antiquity*. Oxford: Clarendon, 1974.

Lohse, Eduard. *Colossians and Philemon*. Hermeneia Series. Philadelphia: Fortress, 1971.

Longenecker, Bruce. *The Lost Letters of Pergamum: A Story from the New Testament World*. Grand Rapids: Baker, 2002.

Malherbe, Abraham, ed. *The Cynic Epistles: A Study Edition*. Society of Biblical Literature Sources for Biblical Studies 12. Missoula, Mont.: Scholars, 1977.

———. "Ancient Epistolary Theorists." *Ohio Journal of Religious Studies* 5 (1977): 3-77.

Malina, Bruce, and Jerome Neyrey. *Portraits of Paul: An Archaeology of Ancient Personality*. Louisville: Westminster John Knox, 1996.

Marrou, Henri Irénée. *A History of Education in Antiquity*. Translated by George Lamb. New York: Sheed & Ward, 1956. Reprint, Madison: University of Wisconsin Press, 1981.

Marshall, I. Howard. *The Pastoral Epistles*. International Critical Commentary Series. Edinburgh: T & T Clark, 1999.

Martin, Ralph. *Carmen Christi: Philippians 2:5-11 in Recent Interpretation and in the Setting of Early Christian Worship*. Society for New Testament Studies Monograph Series 4. Rev. ed. Grand Rapids: Eerdmans, 1983.

McKenzie, John. *Light on the Epistles: A Reader's Guide*. Chicago: Thomas Moore, 1975.

McRay, John. *Paul, His Life and Teaching*. Grand Rapids: Baker, 2003.

Meecham, Henry G. *Light from Ancient Letters*. New York: Macmillan, 1923.

Meeks, Wayne. *First Urban Christians: The Social World of the Apostle Paul*. New Haven, Conn.: Yale University Press, 1983.

Mentz, Arthur. *Die Geschichte der Kurzschrift*. Wolfenbüttel: Heckners, 1949.

———. "Die Grabschrift eines griechischen Tachygraphen." *Archiv für Stenographie* 54 (1902): 49-53.

———. *Die Tironischen Noten: Eine Geschichte der römischen Kurzschrift*. Berlin: de Gruyter, 1944.

Metzger, Bruce. "The Furniture of the Scriptorium at Qumran." *Revue de Qumran* 1 (1958-1959): 509-15.

———. *Manuscripts of the Greek Bible: An Introduction to Paleography*. Oxford: Oxford University Press, 1981.

———. *A Textual Commentary on the Greek New Testament*. Corrected ed. New York: United Bible Societies, 1975.

———. "When Did Scribes Begin to Use Writing Desks?" *Historical and Literary Studies: Pagan, Jewish, and Christian*, pp. 123-37. Grand Rapids: Eerdmans, 1968.

The Michigan Papyri [PMich.]. Vol. 8: *Papyri and Ostraca from Karanis*. 2nd series. Edited and translated by Herbert Chayyim Youtie and John Garrett Winter. Ann Arbor: University of Michigan Press, 1951.

Millard, Alan. *Reading and Writing in the Time of Jesus*. Biblical Seminar 69. Sheffield: Sheffield Academic Press, 2000.

Milligan, George. *New Testament Documents: Their Origin and Early History.* London: Macmillan, 1913.

Milne, Herbert John Mansfield. *Greek Shorthand Manuals: Syllabary and Commentary.* London: Oxford University Press, 1934.

Mitchell, Margaret. "New Testament Envoys in the Context of Greco-Roman Diplomatic and Epistolary Conventions: The Example of Timothy and Titus." *Journal of Biblical Literature* 111 (1992): 641-62.

Montagnini, Felice. "Christological Features in Eph 1:3-14." In *Paul de Tarse: Apôtre du notre temps*, edited by Lorenzo De Lorenzi. Rome: Abbey of St. Paul, 1979.

Moo, Douglas J. *The Epistle to the Romans.* New International Commentary on the New Testament. Grand Rapids: Eerdmans, 1996.

Morris, Leon. *The First Epistle of Paul to the Corinthians: An Introduction and Commentary.* Tyndale New Testament Commentaries 7. Rev. ed. Grand Rapids: Eerdmans, 1988.

———. *The First and Second Epistles to the Thessalonians.* New International Commentary on the New Testament. Grand Rapids: Eerdmans, 1959.

Morton, Andrew Queen, and James McLeman. *Paul, the Man and the Myth: A Study in the Authorship of Greek Prose.* London: Hodder and Stoughton, 1966.

Mullins, Terrance Y. "Disclosure: A Literary Form in the New Testament." *Novum Testamentum* 7 (1972): 44-50.

———. "Formulas in New Testament Epistles." *Journal of Biblical Literature* 91 (1972): 380-90.

———. "*Topos* as a NT Form." *Journal of Biblical Literature* 99 (1980): 541-47.

Murphy-O'Connor, Jerome. "Co-Authorship in the Corinthian Correspondence." *Revue Biblique* 100 (1993): 562-79.

———. *Paul the Letter-Writer: His World, His Options, His Skills.* Good News Studies 41. Collegeville, Minn.: Liturgical Press, 1995.

———. "Traveling Conditions in the First Century: On the Road and on the Sea with St. Paul." *Bible Review* 1 (1985): 38-47.

Neufeld, Vernon H. *The Earliest Christian Confessions.* New Testament Tools and Studies Series 5. Grand Rapids: Eerdmans, 1963.

Neumann, Kenneth. *The Authenticity of the Pauline Epistles in the Light of Stylostatistical Analysis.* Society of Biblical Literature Dissertation Series 120. Atlanta: Scholars, 1990.

Neyrey, Jerome. "Dyadism." In *Biblical Social Values and Their Meanings: A Handbook,* edited by John Pilch and Bruce Malina, pp. 49-52. Peabody, Mass.: Hendrickson, 1993.

Nock, Arthur Darby. *Essays on Religion and the Ancient World.* Edited by Zeph Steward. Oxford: Clarendon, 1986.

Norden, Eduard. *Die antike Kunstprosa.* 2 vols. Leipzig: Weidmann, 1898. Reprint, 1958.

Oates, Whitney J., ed. and trans. *The Stoic and Epicurean Philosophers: The Complete Extant Writings of Epicurus, Epictetus, Lucretius, Marcus Aurelis.* New York: Random House, 1940.

O'Brien, Peter. *Ephesians.* Pillar Series. Grand Rapids: Eerdmans, 1999.

Ohly, Kurt. *Stichometrische Untersuchungen.* Beiheft zum Zentralblatt für Bibliothekswesen 61. Leipzig: Otto Harassawitz, 1928.

The Oxyrhynchus Papyri. Edited by Bernard P. Grenfell and Arthur S. Hunt. 51 vols. London: Oxford University Press, 1898-1951.

Palmer, Darryl. "Acts and the Ancient Historical Monograph." In *The Book of Acts in Its Ancient Literary Setting*, edited by Bruce Winter and Andrew Clark, pp. 1-29. The Book of Acts in Its First Century Setting Series 1. Grand Rapids: Eerdmans, 1993.

Palmer, L. "The Use of Traditional Materials in Hebrews, James, and 1 Peter." Ph.D. dissertation. Southwestern Baptist Theological Seminary, 1985.

Pate, C. Marvin. *The End of the Ages Has Come: The Theology of Paul*. Grand Rapids: Zondervan, 1995.

————. *The Reverse of the Curse: Paul, Wisdom and the Law*. Wissenschaftliche Untersuchungen zum Neuen Testament Series 2/114. Tübingen: Mohr/Siebeck, 2000.

Pate, C. Marvin, and J. Daniel Hays. *The Apocalypse: A Stirring Tale of Mystery, Intrigue, Romance, and Persecution*. Grand Rapids: Zondervan, 2004.

Patzia, Arthur. "Canon." In *Dictionary of Paul and His Letters*, edited by Gerald F. Hawthorne, Ralph P. Martin and Daniel G. Reid, pp. 85-92. Downers Grove, Ill.: InterVarsity Press, 1993.

————. *The Making of the New Testament: Origin, Collection, Text and Canon*. Downers Grove, Ill.: InterVarsity Press, 1995.

Peter, Hermann W. G. *Die Quellen Plutarchs in den Biographien der Römer*. Halle: Waisenhaus, 1865.

————. *Der Brief in der römischen Literatur*. Leipzig: Teubner, 1901.

Pliny the Elder. *Natural History [Naturalis Historia]*. Edited and translated by Harris Rackham. 10 vols. The Loeb Classical Library Latin Series. Cambridge, Mass.: Harvard University Press, 1960-1968.

Pliny the Younger. *Letters [Epistulae] and Panegyricus*. Edited and translated by Betty Radice. 2 vols. The Loeb Classical Library Latin Series. Cambridge, Mass.: Harvard University Press, 1972-1975.

Plutarch. *The Parallel Lives*. Edited and translated by Bernadotte Perrin. The Loeb Classical Library Greek Series. Cambridge, Mass.: Harvard University Press, 1967-1970.

Porten, Bezadel. "Address Formulae in Aramaic Letters: A New Collection of Cowley 17." *Revue Biblique* 90 (1980): 398-413.

Prior, M. *Paul the Letter-Writer and the Second Letter to Timothy*. Journal for the Study of the New Testament, Supplement Series 23. Sheffield: JSOT, 1989.

Pseudo-Socrates and the Socratics. *Epistles*. Edited and translated by Stanley Stowers. In *The Cynic Epistles*, edited by Abraham Malherbe, pp. 217-308. Missoula, Mont.: Scholars, 1977.

Quintilianus, Marcus Fabius. *Institutio oratoria*. 4 vols. Edited and translated by J. S. Watson. The Loeb Classical Library Latin Series. New York: Putnam's Sons, 1921-22.

Rapske, Brian M. "Acts, Travel and Shipwreck." In *The Book of Acts in Its Greco-Roman Setting*, edited by David Gill and Conrad Gempf, pp. 1-47. The Book of Acts in Its First-Century Setting Series. Grand Rapids: Eerdmans, 1994.

Richards, E. Randolph. *The Secretary in the Letters of Paul*. Wissenschaftliche Untersuchungen zum Neuen Testament 2/42. Tübingen: Mohr/Siebeck, 1991.

————. "Silvanus Was Not Peter's Secretary: Theological Bias in Reading 1 Pet 5:12." *Journal of the Evangelical Theological Society* 43/3 (2000): 417-32.

————. "Stop Lying." *Biblical Illustrator* (Spring 1999): 77-80.

Rigaux, Beda. *The Letters of St. Paul: Modern Studies*. Edited and translated by S. Yonick. Chicago: Franciscan Herald, 1968.

Roberts, Colin Henderson, and Theodore Cressy Skeat. *The Birth of the Codex*. 2nd ed. London: Oxford University Press, 1983.

Robertson, A. T. *A Grammar of the Greek New Testament in the Light of Historical Research.* 3rd ed. New York: Hodder & Stoughton, 1919.

Robinson, Cyril Edward. *Everyday Life in Ancient Greece.* Oxford: Clarendon, 1933.

Robson, E. Iliff. "Composition and Dictation in New Testament Books." *Journal of Theological Studies,* old series, 18 (1917): 288-301.

Rohrbaugh, Richard L. "Introduction." In *The Social Sciences and New Testament Interpretation,* edited by Richard L. Rohrbaugh, pp. 1-15. Peabody, Mass.: Hendrickson, 1996.

Roller, Otto. *Das Formular der paulinischen Briefe: Ein Beitrag zur Lehre vom antiken Briefe.* Stuttgart: W. Kohlhammer, 1933.

Salles, Catherine. "Le genre littéraire de la letter dan l'antiquité." *Foi et Vie* 84/5 (1985): 41-47.

Sanders, Jack. *The New Testament Christological Hymns.* Society for New Testament Studies Monograph Series 15. Cambridge: University Press, 1971.

———. "The Transition from Opening Epistolary Thanksgiving to Body in the Pauline Corpus." *Journal of Biblical Literature* 81 (1962): 352-62.

Schiffman, Lawrence. *Reclaiming the Dead Sea Scrolls: The History of Judaism, the Background of Christianity, the Lost Library of Qumran.* New York: Doubleday, 1995.

Schmeller, Thomas. *Paulus und die "Diatribe": Eine vergleichende Stilinterpretation.* Neuetestamentliche Abhandlungen, n.s. 19. Munich: Aschendorffsche, 1987.

Schmithals, Walter. "On the Composition and Earliest Collection of the Major Epistles of Paul." In *Paul and the Gnostics,* translated by John E. Steely, pp. 239-74. Nashville: Abingdon, 1972.

Schoedel, William R. *Ignatius of Antioch.* Hermeneia Series. Philadelphia: Fortress, 1985.

Schubert, Paul. *The Form and Function of the Pauline Thanksgiving.* Berlin: Alfred Topelmann, 1939.

Selby, Donald Joseph. *Toward the Understanding of St. Paul.* Englewood Cliffs, N.J.: Prentice-Hall, 1962.

Seneca. Lucius Annaeus. *Ad Lucilium epistulae morales.* Edited and translated by Richard M. Bummere. 3 vols. The Loeb Classical Library Latin Series. New York: Putnam's Sons, 1920-1925. Rev. ed., John W. Basore. 3 vols. Cambridge, Mass.: Harvard University Press, 1970.

Sherwin-White, Adrian Nicholas. *Letters of Pliny: A Historical and Social Commentary.* Oxford: Oxford University Press, 1966. Reprint, with corrections, 1985.

Skeat, Theodore Cressy. "Especially the Parchments: A Note on 2 Timothy IV.13." *Journal of Theological Studies,* new series 30 (1979): 172-77.

———. "The Origin of the Christian Codex." *Zeitschrift für die Papyrologie und Epigraphik* 102 (1994): 263-68.

Soden, Hermann von. *Griechisches Neues Testament.* Göttingen: Vandenhoeck & Ruprecht, 1913.

Starr, James. *Sharers in Divine Nature: 2 Peter 1:4 in Its Hellenistic Context.* Coniectanea Biblica 33. Stockholm: Almquist & Wiksell, 2000.

Steele, Robert Brown. "Anaphora and Chiasmus in Livy." *Transactions of the American Philological Association* 32 (1901): 166ff.

———. "Chiasmus in the Epistles of Cicero, Seneca, Pliny and Fronto." *Studies in Honor of B. L. Gildersleeve,* edited by C. A. Briggs, pp. 339-52. Baltimore: Johns Hopkins University Press, 1902.

———. *Chiasmus in Sallust, Caesar, Tacitus and Justinus.* Northfield, Minn,: Independent Publishing, 1891.

Stein, Arthur. "Die Stenographie im romischen Senat." *Archiv für Stenographie* 56 (1905): 177-86.

Stirewalt, Luther. *Paul, the Letter Writer*. Grand Rapids: Eerdmans, 2003.

Stowers, Stanley K. *Letter Writing in Greco-Roman Antiquity*. Library of Early Christianity Series. Philadelphia: Westminster Press, 1986.

———. *The Diatribe and Paul's Letter to the Romans*. Society of Biblical Literature Dissertation Series 57. Chico, Calif.: Scholars, 1981.

Strange, Eduard. "Diktierpausen in den Paulusbriefen." *Zeitschrift für die neutestamentliche Wissenschaft* 18 (1918): 109-117.

Suetonius Tranquillus, C. *Lives of the Caesars*. 2 vols. Edited and translated by J. C. Rolfe. The Loeb Classical Library Latin Series. Cambridge, Mass.: Harvard University Press, 1935.

Tarn. William Woodthorpe. *Alexander the Great. II: Sources and Studies*. Cambridge: Cambridge University Press, 1948.

The Tebtunis Papyri. Edited by Bernard P. Grenfell, Arthur S. Hunt and Josiah Gilbert Smyly. 3 vols. in 4. University of California Graeco-Roman Archaeological Series. London: Oxford University Press, 1902-1938.

Thackeray, Henry St. John. "Introduction." In *The Life, Against Apion, and the Jewish War [Bellum Judaicum]*. 3 vols. Loeb Classical Library, Greek Series. Cambridge, Mass.: Harvard University Press, 1976.

Theissen, Gerd. *Social Setting of Pauline Christianity*. Philadelphia: Fortress, 1982.

Thiselton, Anthony. *1 Corinthians*. New International Greek Testament Commentary Series. Grand Rapids: Eerdmans, 2000.

Triandis, Harry. "Cross-Cultural Studies of Individualism and Collectivism." In *Nebraska Symposium on Motivation, 1989*, edited by J. J. Berman, pp. 41-133. Lincoln: University of Nebraska Press, 1990.

Trobisch, David. *Paul's Letter Collection: Tracing the Origins*. Minneapolis: Fortress, 1994.

Trudinger, Peter. "Computers and the Authorship of the Pauline Epistles." *Faith and Freedom* 39 (1986): 24-27.

Turner, Eric Gardiner. *Greek Papyri: An Introduction*. Oxford: Clarendon, 1968. Reprint, 1980.

Turner, Nigel. *Style*. Vol. 4 in *A Grammar of New Testament Greek,* edited by J. H. Moulton. Edinburgh: T & T Clark, 1976.

Tyrrell, Robert Yelverton, and Louis Claude Purser. *The Correspondence of M. Tullius Cicero*. 7 vols. 3rd ed. London: Longmans, Green, 1901-1933.

Unnik, Willem Cornelis van. *Tarsus or Jerusalem: The City of Paul's Youth*. Translated by George Ogg. London: Epworth, 1962.

Vinson, Steve. "Ships in the Ancient Mediterranean." *Biblical Archaeologist* 53 (March 1990): 13-18.

Wake, W. C. "Numbers, Paul and Rational Dissent." *Faith and Freedom* 37 (1984): 59-72.

Walker, William. "The Burden of Proof in Identifying Interpolations in the Pauline Letters." *New Testament Studies* 33 (1987): 610-18.

———. *Interpolations in the Pauline Letters*. Journal for the Study of the New Testament, Supplement Series 213. New York: Sheffield Academic Press, 2001.

Wardman, Alan. *Rome's Debt to Greece*. New York: St. Martin's, 1976.

Weima, Jeffrey A. D. *Neglected Endings: The Significance of the Pauline Letter Closings*. Journal for the Study of the New Testament, Supplement Series 101. Sheffield: JSOT, 1994.

Welch, John W. "Chiasmus in the New Testament." In *Chiasmus in Antiquity: Structure, Analyses, and Exegesis*, edited by John W. Welch, pp. 250-68. Hildesheim: Gerstenberg, 1981.

Wendland, Paul. *Die hellenistische-römische Kultur in ihren Beziehungen zu Judentum und Christentum*. 2nd ed. Tübingen: Mohr, 1912.

―――. *Neutestamentliche Grammatik: Das Griechisch der neuen Testaments im Zusammenhang mit der Volkssprache dargestellt*. Vol. 2, *Der urchristliche Literaturformen*. Tübingen: Mohr, 1912.

White, John Lee. "The Ancient Epistolography Group in Retrospect." *Semeia* 22 (1981): 1-14.

―――. "The Greek Documentary Letter Tradition, Third Century B.C.E. to Third Century C.E." *Semeia* 22 (1981): 89-106.

―――. *Light from Ancient Letters*. Foundations and Facets Series. Philadelphia: Fortress, 1986.

Wikenhauser, Alfred, and Josef Schmid. *Einleitung in das Neue Testament*. Freiburg: Herder, 1973.

Wilamowitz-Moellendorff, Ulrich von. *Antigonos von Karystos*. Philologische Untersuchungen 4. Berlin: Weidmann, 1881.

Wilder, Amos. *Early Christian Rhetoric: The Language of the Gospel*. 2nd ed. Cambridge, Mass.: Harvard University Press, 1971.

Wilder, Terry. *Pseudonymity, the New Testament, and Deception: An Inquiry into Intention and Reception*. Lanham, Md.: University Press of America, 2004.

Winter, Bruce. *After Paul Left Corinth: The Influence of Secular Ethics and Social Change*. Grand Rapids: Eerdmans, 2001.

Winter, John G. *Life and Letters in the Papyri*. Ann Arbor: University of Michigan Press, 1933.

Wire, Antoinette Clark. *The Corinthian Women Prophets*. Minneapolis: Fortress, 1990.

Witherington, Ben. *The Acts of the Apostles: A Socio-Rhetorical Commentary*. Grand Rapids: Eerdmans, 1998.

―――. *Conflict and Community in Corinth*. Grand Rapids: Eerdmans, 1995.

―――. *Grace in Galatia: A Commentary on Paul's Letter to the Galatians*. Grand Rapids: Eerdmans, 1998.

―――. *New Testament History: A Narrative Account*. Grand Rapids: Baker, 2001.

―――. *The Paul Quest: The Renewed Search for the Jew of Tarsus*. Downers Grove, Ill.: InterVarsity Press, 1998.

―――. *Women in the Earliest Churches*. Society for New Testament Studies Monograph Series 59. Cambridge: Cambridge University Press, 1988.

Yaghjian, Lucretia. "Ancient Reading." In *The Social Sciences and New Testament Interpretation*, edited by Richard L. Rohrbaugh, pp. 206-30. Peabody, Mass.: Hendrickson, 1996.

Yale, George Udny. *The Statistical Study of Literary Vocabulary*. Cambridge: Cambridge University Press, 1944.

Youtie, Herbert Chayyim. "P.Mich.Inv. 855: Letter from Herakleides to Nemesion." *Zeitschrift für Papyrologie und Epigraphik* 27 (1977):147-50.

Zenon Papyri [PZen.] in the University of Michigan Collection. Edited and translated by Campbell Cowan Edgar. Ann Arbor: University of Michigan Press, 1931.

Zieliński, Tadeusz. *Das Clauselgesetz in Ciceros Reden: Grundzüge einer oratorischen Rhythmik*. Philologus Supplementband XIII, 1a. Leipzig: Dieterich, 1904.

Ziesler, J. A. *The Epistle to the Galatians*. London: Epworth, 1992.

Zuntz, Günther. *The Text of the Epistles: A Disquisition upon the* Corpus Paulinum. Oxford: Oxford University Press, 1963.

Modern Authors Index

Subject Index

Scripture Index